WITHDRAWN

# African American American History

# African American History

## Volume 3

*Scott v. Sandford — Yarbrough, Ex parte*
Appendices
Indexes

*Edited by*
**Carl L. Bankston III**
*Tulane University*

SALEM PRESS INC.
Pasadena, California    Hackensack, New Jersey

*Frontispiece: World War II recruiting poster using a Tuskegee airman to appeal to African Americans.* (National Archives)

Some essays originally appeared in *American Justice* (1996), *Encyclopedia of the U.S. Supreme Court* (2000), *Great Events from History II: Arts and Culture* (1993), *Great Events from History II: Human Rights* (1992), *Great Events from History: North American Series*, Revised Edition (1997), *Great Events of the 20th Century* (2002), *Racial and Ethnic Relations in America* (2000), *The Fifties in America* (2005), *The Sixties in America* (1999), and *Women's Issues* (1997). New material has been added.

**Library of Congress Cataloging-in-Publication Data**
African American history / edited by Carl L. Bankston, III.
    p. cm. -- (Magill's choice)
    Includes bibliographical references and index.
    ISBN-13: 978-1-58765-239-4 (set : alk. paper)
    ISBN-10: 1-58765-239-0 (set : alk. paper)
    ISBN-13: 978-1-58765-242-4 (v. 3 : alk. paper)
    ISBN-10: 1-58765-242-0 (v. 3 : alk. paper)
    [etc.]
    1. African Americans--History. I. Bankston, Carl L. (Carl Leon),
1952- II. Series.
    E185.A25355 2005
    973'.0496073--dc22

                                            2005015348

8/05
Salem Press
69.00

973.0496
A
V3

First Printing

# Contents

Complete List of Contents . . . . . . . . . . . . . . . . . . . . . . lvii

*Scott v. Sandford* . . . . . . . . . . . . . . . . . . . . . . . . . . 783
Scottsboro trials . . . . . . . . . . . . . . . . . . . . . . . . . . . 786
Segregation . . . . . . . . . . . . . . . . . . . . . . . . . . . . . 790
Segregation on the frontier . . . . . . . . . . . . . . . . . . . . . 793
Selma-Montgomery march . . . . . . . . . . . . . . . . . . . . . 797
Separate but equal doctrine . . . . . . . . . . . . . . . . . . . . . 805
Sharecropping . . . . . . . . . . . . . . . . . . . . . . . . . . . . 806
*Shaw v. Hunt* . . . . . . . . . . . . . . . . . . . . . . . . . . . . 808
*Shaw v. Reno* . . . . . . . . . . . . . . . . . . . . . . . . . . . . 810
*Shelley v. Kraemer* . . . . . . . . . . . . . . . . . . . . . . . . . 812
Simpson murder trial . . . . . . . . . . . . . . . . . . . . . . . . 813
Sit-ins . . . . . . . . . . . . . . . . . . . . . . . . . . . . . . . . 818
*Slaughterhouse Cases* . . . . . . . . . . . . . . . . . . . . . . . . 819
Slave codes . . . . . . . . . . . . . . . . . . . . . . . . . . . . . . 821
Slavery . . . . . . . . . . . . . . . . . . . . . . . . . . . . . . . . 826
Slavery and families . . . . . . . . . . . . . . . . . . . . . . . . . 835
Slavery and race relations . . . . . . . . . . . . . . . . . . . . . . 843
Slavery and the justice system . . . . . . . . . . . . . . . . . . . 850
Slavery and women . . . . . . . . . . . . . . . . . . . . . . . . . 858
Slavery in Massachusetts . . . . . . . . . . . . . . . . . . . . . . 865
Slavery in Virginia . . . . . . . . . . . . . . . . . . . . . . . . . . 870
*Smith v. Allwright* . . . . . . . . . . . . . . . . . . . . . . . . . . 875
Southern Christian Leadership Conference . . . . . . . . . . . . 879
Southern Manifesto . . . . . . . . . . . . . . . . . . . . . . . . . 887
Sports . . . . . . . . . . . . . . . . . . . . . . . . . . . . . . . . . 889
Stereotypes . . . . . . . . . . . . . . . . . . . . . . . . . . . . . . 898
Stono Rebellion . . . . . . . . . . . . . . . . . . . . . . . . . . . . 902
*Strauder v. West Virginia* . . . . . . . . . . . . . . . . . . . . . . 907
Student Nonviolent Coordinating Committee . . . . . . . . . . 908
Summit Meeting of National Negro Leaders . . . . . . . . . . . 912
*Swann v. Charlotte-Mecklenberg Board of Education* . . . . . . . . 913
*Sweatt v. Painter* . . . . . . . . . . . . . . . . . . . . . . . . . . . 917

Talented Tenth . . . . . . . . . . . . . . . . . . . . . . . . . . . . 919
*Terry v. Adams* . . . . . . . . . . . . . . . . . . . . . . . . . . . . 921
Thirteenth Amendment . . . . . . . . . . . . . . . . . . . . . . . 922
Thomas-Hill hearings . . . . . . . . . . . . . . . . . . . . . . . . 928
Three-fifths compromise . . . . . . . . . . . . . . . . . . . . . . . 930
Till lynching . . . . . . . . . . . . . . . . . . . . . . . . . . . . . . 931

Turner's slave insurrection . . . . . . . . . . . . . . . . . . . . . . . . 933
Tuskegee Airmen. . . . . . . . . . . . . . . . . . . . . . . . . . . . . . 937
Tuskegee experiment. . . . . . . . . . . . . . . . . . . . . . . . . . . . 939
Twenty-fourth Amendment. . . . . . . . . . . . . . . . . . . . . . . . 941

Underground Railroad. . . . . . . . . . . . . . . . . . . . . . . . . . . 947
Understanding tests . . . . . . . . . . . . . . . . . . . . . . . . . . . . 952
United Negro College Fund. . . . . . . . . . . . . . . . . . . . . . . . 953
United States Commission on Civil Rights . . . . . . . . . . . . . 954
*United States v. Classic* . . . . . . . . . . . . . . . . . . . . . . . . . . 958
*United States v. Cruikshank* . . . . . . . . . . . . . . . . . . . . . . . 959
*United States v. Reese* . . . . . . . . . . . . . . . . . . . . . . . . . . . 961
*United Steelworkers of America v. Weber* . . . . . . . . . . . . . . . 962
Universal Negro Improvement Association. . . . . . . . . . . . . . 969
University of Mississippi desegregation. . . . . . . . . . . . . . . . 974

Vietnam War . . . . . . . . . . . . . . . . . . . . . . . . . . . . . . . . . 979
Voting Rights Act of 1965 . . . . . . . . . . . . . . . . . . . . . . . . . 983
Voting Rights Act of 1975 . . . . . . . . . . . . . . . . . . . . . . . . . 990

*Washington v. Davis*. . . . . . . . . . . . . . . . . . . . . . . . . . . . . 996
Washington, D.C., riots . . . . . . . . . . . . . . . . . . . . . . . . . . 997
Watts riot . . . . . . . . . . . . . . . . . . . . . . . . . . . . . . . . . . . 999
West Indians. . . . . . . . . . . . . . . . . . . . . . . . . . . . . . . . . 1002
White Citizens' Councils . . . . . . . . . . . . . . . . . . . . . . . . . 1007
White primaries. . . . . . . . . . . . . . . . . . . . . . . . . . . . . . . 1009
Wilder's election to Virginia governorship. . . . . . . . . . . . . . 1010
*Williams v. Mississippi* . . . . . . . . . . . . . . . . . . . . . . . . . . 1017
*Wisconsin v. Mitchell*. . . . . . . . . . . . . . . . . . . . . . . . . . . . 1018
World War II. . . . . . . . . . . . . . . . . . . . . . . . . . . . . . . . . 1020

*Yarbrough, Ex parte*. . . . . . . . . . . . . . . . . . . . . . . . . . . . . 1025

Bibliography. . . . . . . . . . . . . . . . . . . . . . . . . . . . . . . . . 1027
Time Line of African American History . . . . . . . . . . . . . . . 1076
Notable Figures in African American History. . . . . . . . . . . . 1096

Category Index . . . . . . . . . . . . . . . . . . . . . . . . . . . . . . . 1127
Personages Index . . . . . . . . . . . . . . . . . . . . . . . . . . . . . . 1143
Subject Index. . . . . . . . . . . . . . . . . . . . . . . . . . . . . . . . . 1153

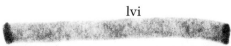

# Complete List of Contents

## Volume 1

Abolition , 1

Abolitionist movement and women, 5

*Adarand Constructors v. Peña*, 13

Affirmative action, 15

African Liberation Day, 25

African Methodist Episcopal Church, 26

African Methodist Episcopal Zion Churches, 30

Afrocentrism, 31

Agriculture, 32

*Albemarle Paper Company v. Moody*, 39

*Alexander v. Holmes County Board of Education*, 40

American Anti-Slavery Society, 42

American Colonization Society, 46

*Amistad* slave revolt, 47

Anderson's Lincoln Memorial concert, 51

Antislavery laws of 1777 and 1807, 58

Ashmun Institute, 62

Atlanta Compromise, 67

*Bakke* case, 71

Baptist Church, 78

Baseball's racial integration, 82

*Batson v. Kentucky*, 90

Birmingham March, 91

Black cabinet, 94

Black Christian Nationalist Movement, 95

Black church, 97

Black codes, 103

Black colleges and universities, 107

Black flight, 112

Black Is Beautiful movement, 114

Black Jews, 115

"Black Manifesto," 117

Black nationalism, 118

Black Panther Party, 123

Black Power movement, 129

Black United Students, 132

Bleeding Kansas, 134

*Bolling v. Sharpe*, 137

Brotherhood of Sleeping Car Porters, 138

*Brown v. Board of Education*, 140

*Brown v. Mississippi*, 144

Brownsville incident, 145

*Buchanan v. Warley*, 147

Buffalo soldiers, 147

*Burton v. Wilmington Parking Authority*, 150

Charleston race riots, 151

Chicago riots, 152

Chicago sit-ins, 154

Chisholm's election to Congress, 161

Church bombings, 169

Church burnings, 174

Civil Rights Act of 1866, 177

Civil Rights Act of 1957, 182

Civil Rights Act of 1960, 183

Civil Rights Act of 1964, 188

Civil Rights Act of 1968, 195

Civil Rights Act of 1991, 198

Civil Rights Acts of 1866-1875, 199

*Civil Rights* cases, 202

Civil Rights movement, 204

Civil Rights movement and children, 214

Civil Rights Restoration Act, 215
Civil rights worker murders, 219
Civil War, 226
Clinton massacre, 233
*Clotilde* capture, 234
Colfax massacre, 239
Colored Women's League, 240
Combahee River Collective, 241
Compromise of 1850, 243
Compromise of 1877, 248
Confiscation Acts of 1861 and
    1862, 249
Congress of Racial Equality, 250
Congressional Black Caucus, 256
*Cooper v. Aaron*, 258
Council of Federated
    Organizations, 260
Cowboys, 267
Crown Heights conflicts, 268
Cubans and African Americans,
    270
*Cumming v. Richmond County
    Board of Education*, 276
Defense industry desegregation,
    277
Demographic trends, 283
Disfranchisement laws in
    Mississippi, 294

Draft riots, 298
Dyer antilynching bill, 302
Economic trends, 304
*Edmonson v. Leesville Concrete
    Company*, 314
Education, 315
*Edwards v. South Carolina*, 322
Emancipation Proclamation,
    323
Employment, 327
Equal Employment Opportunity
    Act of 1972, 331
Equal Employment Opportunity
    Commission, 338
*Evans v. Abney*, 340
Fair Employment Practices
    Committee, 340
Fair Housing Act, 342
Fifteenth Amendment, 347
Film history, 352
Fourteenth Amendment, 357
Free African Society, 362
Free blacks, 366
Freedmen's Bureau, 367
Freedom Rides, 372
Freedom Summer, 374
Freemasons in Boston, 377
Fugitive Slave Law of 1793, 382

## Volume 2

Fugitive Slave Law of 1850, 387
*Fullilove v. Klutznick*, 391
Gerrymandering, 393
*Gomillion v. Lightfoot*, 397
Grandfather clauses, 398
Great Migration, 399
*Green v. County School Board of
    New Kent County*, 404
Greensboro sit-ins, 406
*Griffin v. Breckenridge*, 413
*Griggs v. Duke Power Company*, 415
*Groves v. Slaughter*, 417

*Grovey v. Townsend*, 418
*Guinn v. United States*, 419
Haitians, 421
Hampton-Clark deaths, 424
Harlem Renaissance, 426
Harlins murder, 434
*Harper v. Virginia Board of
    Elections*, 435
Harpers Ferry raid, 436
Hawkins murder, 441
*Heart of Atlanta Motel v. United
    States*, 442

"I Have a Dream" speech, 449
Integration, 454
Irish and African Americans,
    460
Jackson's run for the presidency,
    461
Jamaicans, 466
Jews and African Americans, 470
Jim Crow laws, 476
*Jones v. Alfred H. Mayer Company*,
    479
Journey of Reconciliation, 481
Kansas-Nebraska Act, 490
*Katzenbach v. McClung*, 496
Kerner Commission, 499
*Keyes v. Denver School District
    No. 1*, 506
King assassination, 507
King beating case, 515
Koreans and African Americans,
    520
Ku Klux Klan, 523
Ku Klux Klan Acts, 529
*Lassiter v. Northampton County
    Board of Elections*, 530
League of Revolutionary Black
    Workers, 530
*The Liberator*, 532
Literature, 537
Little Rock school desegregation
    crisis, 544
Los Angeles riots, 548
*Louisville, New Orleans, and Texas
    Railway
    Company v. Mississippi*, 552
Lynching, 553
*McCleskey v. Kemp*, 557
*McLaurin v. Oklahoma State
    Regents for Higher Education*,
    558
Malcolm X assassination, 559
Marshall's appointment to the
    Supreme Court, 564
*Martin v. Wilks*, 568

The Media, 569
Miami riots, 576
Military, 579
Military desegregation, 583
*Milliken v. Bradley*, 592
Million Man March, 593
Million Woman March, 597
Miscegenation laws, 600
Mississippi Freedom Democratic
    Party, 603
Missouri Compromise, 606
*Missouri ex rel. Gaines v. Canada*,
    612
*Mobile v. Bolden*, 613
Montgomery bus boycott, 614
*Moore v. Dempsey*, 619
*Moose Lodge v. Irvis*, 620
MOVE bombing, 621
Moynihan Report, 623
Music, 624
Nation of Islam, 631
National Advisory Commission
    on Civil Disorders, 635
National Association for the
    Advancement of
    Colored People, 636
National Association for the
    Advancement of Colored
    People Legal Defense and
    Educational Fund, 643
*National Association for the
    Advancement of
    Colored People v. Alabama*, 650
National Association of Colored
    Women, 651
National Black Women's Political
    Leadership Caucus, 652
National Coalition of Blacks for
    Reparations in America, 653
National Council of Colored
    People, 654
National Council of Negro
    Women, 658
National Urban League, 659

Native Americans and African Americans, 661
Negro Conventions, 667
New York City slave revolt, 669
New York riots, 674
Newark riot, 677
*Newberry v. United States*, 679
Niagara Movement, 681
*Nixon v. Condon*, 685
*Nixon v. Herndon*, 686
*Norris v. Alabama*, 687
*The North Star*, 689
Northwest Ordinance, 694
One-drop rule, 698
Orangeburg massacre, 699
*Palmer v. Thompson*, 700
Pan-Africanism, 701
*Patterson v. McLean Credit Union*, 702
Pennsylvania Society for the Abolition of Slavery, 703
*Plessy v. Ferguson*, 708
Politics and government, 713

Poll taxes, 723
Poor People's March on Washington, 725
*Powell v. Alabama*, 727
*Powers v. Ohio*, 728
President's Committee on Civil Rights, 729
Proslavery argument, 731
*R.A.V. v. City of St. Paul*, 735
Race riots of 1866, 737
Race riots of 1943, 741
Race riots of 1967, 745
Race riots of the twentieth century, 750
Rainbow Coalition, 753
Reconstruction, 755
*Reitman v. Mulkey*, 763
Republic of New Africa, 765
Restrictive covenants, 766
*Roots*, 767
*Runyon v. McCrary*, 768
School desegregation, 770
Science and technology, 776

# Volume 3

*Scott v. Sandford*, 783
Scottsboro trials, 786
Segregation, 790
Segregation on the frontier, 793
Selma-Montgomery march, 797
Separate but equal doctrine, 805
Sharecropping, 806
*Shaw v. Hunt*, 808
*Shaw v. Reno*, 810
*Shelley v. Kraemer*, 812
Simpson murder trial, 813
Sit-ins, 818
*Slaughterhouse Cases*, 819
Slave codes, 821
Slavery, 826
Slavery and families, 835
Slavery and race relations, 843

Slavery and the justice system, 850
Slavery and women, 858
Slavery in Massachusetts, 865
Slavery in Virginia, 870
*Smith v. Allwright*, 875
Southern Christian Leadership Conference, 879
Southern Manifesto, 887
Sports, 889
Stereotypes, 898
Stono Rebellion, 902
*Strauder v. West Virginia*, 907
Student Nonviolent Coordinating Committee, 908
Summit Meeting of National Negro Leaders, 912

Complete List of Contents

*Swann v. Charlotte-Mecklenberg Board of Education*, 913
*Sweatt v. Painter*, 917
Talented Tenth, 919
*Terry v. Adams*, 921
Thirteenth Amendment, 922
Thomas-Hill hearings, 928
Three-fifths compromise, 930
Till lynching, 931
Turner's slave insurrection, 933
Tuskegee Airmen, 937
Tuskegee experiment, 939
Twenty-fourth Amendment, 941
Underground Railroad, 947
Understanding tests, 952
United Negro College Fund, 953
United States Commission on Civil Rights, 954
*United States v. Classic*, 958
*United States v. Cruikshank*, 959
*United States v. Reese*, 961
*United Steelworkers of America v. Weber*, 962
Universal Negro Improvement Association, 969

University of Mississippi desegregation, 974
Vietnam War, 979
Voting Rights Act of 1965, 983
Voting Rights Act of 1975, 990
*Washington v. Davis*, 996
Washington, D.C., riots, 997
Watts riot, 999
West Indians, 1002
White Citizens' Councils, 1007
White primaries, 1009
Wilder's election to Virginia governorship, 1010
*Williams v. Mississippi*, 1017
*Wisconsin v. Mitchell*, 1018
World War II, 1020
*Yarbrough, Ex parte*, 1025

Bibliography, 1027
Time Line of African American History, 1076
Notable Figures in African American History, 1096

Category Index, 1127
Personages Index, 1143
Subject Index, 1153

# African American History

# Scott v. Sandford

**The Case:** U.S. Supreme Court ruling on slavery and citizenship
**Date:** March 6-7, 1857
*The U.S. Supreme Court ruled that Congress could not limit slavery in the territories, nullifying the Missouri Compromise.*

In 1834, Dred Scott, a slave of African descent, was taken by his owner, John Emerson, an army surgeon, to the free state of Illinois and then to Wisconsin Territory, which was free by the provisions of the Missouri Compromise of 1820. Emerson returned to Missouri with Scott in 1838. After Emerson's death in 1846, Scott sued Mrs. Emerson in the Missouri courts for his freedom, on the grounds of his residence in a free state and later in a free territory. Although he won in the lower court, the state supreme court reversed the decision in 1852 and declared that Scott was still a slave because of his voluntary return to Missouri. During this litigation, Mrs. Emerson remarried and, under Missouri law, the administration of her first husband's estate passed to her brother, John F. A. Sanford. (Sanford's name was misspelled when the suit was filed.) Because Sanford was a citizen of New York, Scott's lawyer, acting on the grounds that the litigants were residents of different states, sued for Scott's freedom in the U.S. circuit court in Missouri. The verdict there also went against Scott.

## The Supreme Court's Ruling

The case was appealed to the U.S. Supreme Court, where it was argued in February, 1856, and reargued in January, 1857. For a variety of reasons, the Supreme Court justices determined to deal with the controversial questions of African American citizenship and congressional power over slavery in the territories. The Supreme Court announced its decision on March 6, 1857.

Although each of the nine justices issued a separate opinion, a majority of the Supreme Court held that African Americans who were descendants of slaves could not belong to the political community created by the Constitution and enjoy the right of federal citizenship; and that the Missouri Compromise of 1820, forbidding slavery in the part of the Louisiana Purchase territory north of 36° north latitude, was unconstitutional. According to the opinion of Chief Justice Roger B. Taney, African Americans were "beings of an inferior order" who "had no rights which the white man was bound to respect." Taney's comments established a perception of African Americans that transcended their status as slaves. In considering the issue of equality, Justice Taney did not limit his assessment of African Americans to those who were slaves, but also included African Americans who were free. Taney's opinion raises questions about the extent to which this precept of the inferiority of African Americans helped to establish conditions for the future of race relations in the United States.

Although individual states might grant citizenship to African Americans, state action did not give African Americans citizenship under the federal Constitution. Therefore, concluded Taney, "Dred Scott was not a citizen of Missouri within the meaning of the Constitution of the United States, and not entitled as such to sue in its courts."

Taney also declared that, since slaves were property, under the Fifth Amendment to the Constitution—which prohibited Congress from taking property without due process of law— Congress had only the power and duty to protect the slaveholders' rights. Therefore, the Missouri Compromise law was unconstitutional. This part of Taney's opinion was unnecessary, an *obiter dictum*, for, having decided that no African American could become a citizen within the meaning of the Constitution, there was no need for the Supreme Court to consider the question of whether Congress could exclude slavery from the territories of the United States.

### Reaction

The nation reacted strongly to the Supreme Court's decision. The South was delighted, for a majority of the justices had supported the extreme southern position. All federal territories were now legally opened to slavery, and Congress was obliged to protect the slaveholders' possession of their chattel. The free-soil platform of the Republicans was unconstitutional. The Republicans denounced the decision in the most violent terms, as the product of an incompetent and partisan body. They declared that when they obtained control of the national government, they would change the membership of the Supreme Court and secure reversal of the decision. Northern Democrats, while not attacking the Supreme Court, were discouraged by the decision, for if Congress could not prohibit slavery in any territory, neither could a territorial legislature, a mere creation of Congress. Therefore, popular sovereignty also would cease to be a valid way of deciding whether a federal territory should be slave or free.

*John G. Clark*
*Updated by K. Sue Jewell*

## Further Reading

Paul Finkelman's *Dred Scott v. Sandford: A Brief History with Documents* (Boston: Bedford Books, 1997), Don Edward Fehrenbacher's *The Dred Scott Case: Its Significance in American Law and Politics* (New York: Oxford University Press, 1978), and Walter Ehrlich's *They Have No Rights: Dred Scott's Struggle for Freedom* (Westport, Conn.: Greenwood Press, 1979) take a closer look at the famous case. Charles Morrow Wilson's *The Dred Scott Decision* (Philadelphia: Auerbach, 1973) combines a biography of Dred Scott with descriptions of the court cases and appeals. Derrick Bell's *Faces at the Bottom of the Well: The Permanence of Racism* (New York: Basic Books, 1992) employs literary models in addressing the issue of how African Americans experience racial injustice in the judicial system in the United States. Bell's *Race, Racism, and American Law* (2d ed., Boston: Little, Brown, 1980), presents a comprehensive analysis of U.S. law that asserts that racial inequality is integrated into the legislative and judicial system in the United States. K. Sue Jewell's *From Mammy to Miss America and Beyond: Cultural Images and the Shaping of U.S. Social Policy* (New York: Routledge, 1993) discusses how institutional policies and practices in the United States contribute to social inequality for African Americans in general, and African American women in particular. *Black Americans and the Supreme Court Since Emancipation: Betrayal or Protection?* (New York: Holt, Rinehart and Winston, 1972), edited by Arnold Paul, explores precedent-setting Supreme Court cases that reveal the Court's failure to ensure equal rights for African Americans.

**See also** Civil Rights Acts of 1866-1875; Civil War; Fugitive Slave Law of 1850; Kansas-Nebraska Act; Missouri Compromise; Proslavery argument; Slavery; Slavery and the justice system; Thirteenth Amendment

# Scottsboro trials

**The Event:** Trials of nine young American American men on trumped-up charges of rape
**Date:** 1931-1937
**Place:** Scottsboro, Alabama
*The 1930's trials of nine young African Americans for rape mirrored both entrenched southern bigotry and antiliberal sentiments.*

On March 25, 1931, nine young African Americans were pulled off a freight train in Scottsboro, Alabama, after an alleged fight with a group of white youths. As the African Americans were being rounded up by sheriff's deputies, two women riders told onlookers that they had been raped by the entire group. Within a month, the boys were tried in Scottsboro, and eight of them were convicted and sentenced to death; the case of the youngest boy, only thirteen years of age, was declared a mistrial. Because of the speed of the convictions, the questionable nature of much of the testimony, and the hostile atmosphere in which the trial had been held, the case soon attracted widespread attention. Both the International Labor Defense (ILD), an arm of the Communist Party, and the National Association for the Advancement of Colored People (NAACP) expressed concern about the possibility of injustice and launched an appeal for a new trial. The boys and their parents chose the ILD to manage their defense.

### The Retrials

In *Powell v. Alabama* (1932), the U.S. Supreme Court overruled the convictions and sent the cases back to a lower court. There followed another series of trials in Decatur, Alabama, beginning in March, 1933, and lasting until December. This time, only three of the boys were tried, all of whom received convictions and death sentences, but the Supreme Court sustained an appeal that irregularities in the selection of jurors invalidated the verdicts. The specific irregularity was that the voting rolls showed no African Americans registered to vote in that county, in spite of a large population of qualified African Americans.

In January, 1936, a third group of trials, held in Decatur, resulted in the conviction of Haywood Patterson, who was sentenced to seventy-five years' imprisonment. After more than a year of delay and behind-the-scenes negotiations between Alabama officials and a group of the defendants' supporters, the remaining eight were tried in the summer of 1937. One received the death penalty, three were sentenced to long prison terms, and the four others were released without charges. Although the one death sentence was later commuted to life imprisonment, the five convicted Scottsboro boys were unable to obtain a reversal. One was paroled in 1943, two more in 1946, and a fourth in 1950. The final prisoner escaped from a work gang in 1948 and managed to

*African Americans demonstrating outside the White House in 1933 to protest the unfair treatment accorded to the Scottsboro defendants by the justice system.* (National Archives)

reach Michigan, from where the governor refused to extradite him. The former defendant quickly found himself in trouble, committing a murder and being sentenced to Michigan's worst prison.

Most observers outside Alabama and an increasingly large number of people within the state came to believe that the defendants were innocent and were, therefore, the victims of southern racial injustice. One of the two women accusers, Ruby Bates, had retracted her testimony by 1934 and admitted that she had lied in her original accusations. The other, a prostitute named Victoria Price, presented testimony so full of contradictions that one of the judges in the 1933 trials, Alabamian James E. Horton, overruled the jury's guilty verdict and declared a mistrial. At least one of the defendants was ruled physically incapable of rape, and a physician testified that a medical examination of Bates and Price, performed shortly after the presumed attack, did not support their claims. Although both women were found to have had recent sexual intercourse, there were no contusions or other injuries that would have matched their stories about brutality at the hands of the nine men. None of this had any appreciable effect on the juries, the prosecutors, or Judge William W. Callahan, who presided after Horton was removed from the case. Even the milder sentences meted out in 1937 resulted as much from a desire to end the unfavorable publicity surrounding the trials as from any reevaluation of the evidence.

## Repercussions

Besides serving as a symbol of southern bigotry, the Scottsboro trials attracted attention because of the efforts of the Communist Party to identify the cause of the defendants with their own. Working through the ILD, the Communist Party was one of the first groups to protest the verdicts in the 1931 trials, and it was the only group to offer direct aid at that time. For several years, it engaged in a running battle with the NAACP and an "American Scottsboro Committee" over the right to manage the boys' defense. The effect of these struggles was to unite many Alabamians against all "reds and foreigners" and make it more difficult to revise the verdicts.

The chief defense counsel after 1931 was Samuel Leibowitz, a Jewish attorney from New York who became the target of attacks from the prosecutors. Even he, along with Judge Callahan and part of the Alabama press, came to regard the communist support as a liability and sought to dissociate the ILD from the case. In 1935, the NAACP, the American Civil Liberties Union, and the ILD joined to form the Scottsboro Defense Committee (SDC), designed to coordinate support for the defendants and to seek cooperation from moderate Alabamians. Although the ILD played a much smaller role in the case from that point on, there remained enough hostility toward outside interference in Alabama to frustrate the SDC's efforts.

The Scottsboro case mirrored many of the important social currents of the 1930's. While illustrating the extent to which white southerners would go to defend a system of white supremacy, it also marked a change from the not too distant era when the defendants might well have been summarily lynched. The hysterical attitude with which many Alabamians reacted to outside interest in the case underlined a regional insecurity that had been intensified by the unsettled conditions of the Depression. It was common for both men and women to hop onto freight trains, which the nine men had done, as had the two alleged victims. The Scottsboro boys had gotten into a fight with several white men. In Scottsboro and Decatur, race was on trial, not nine boys and men, much to the lasting chagrin of the state of Alabama. In 1976, the Alabama Board of Pardons and Paroles granted Clarence Norris a full pardon.

*Courtney B. Ross*
*Updated by John Jacob*

**Further Reading**

Dan T. Carter's *Scottsboro: A Tragedy of the American South* (Rev. ed., Baton Rouge: Louisiana State University Press, 1979) analyzes the trials and treatment of the nine African Americans and discusses the impact of the events on the South. Allan Knight Chalmers's *They Shall Be Free* (Garden City, N.Y.: Doubleday, 1951) is an account of the Scottsboro trials from the perspective of one of the defense attorneys who also argued before the Supreme

Court. In Clarence Norris and Sybil D. Washington's *The Last of the Scottsboro Boys* (New York: Putnam, 1979), the last and most literate of the defendants presents his case. Haywood Patterson and Earl Conrad's *Scottsboro Boy* (Garden City, N.Y.: Doubleday, 1950) is the first book to shed personal light on the plight of the nine.

**See also** Lynching

# Segregation

**Definition:** Physical separation of people based on their race or ethnic identity

*Segregation of members of minorities in the United States was a negative social and economic practice that kept the country from achieving "liberty, freedom, and equality," promises upon which the nation was founded; the practice consigned millions of people to second-class citizenship.*

American segregation was born in the colonial era, when the "majority" practiced de facto segregation. When most African Americans were slaves, free blacks suffered de facto segregation in housing and social segregation based on custom and folkways. As the northern colonies abolished slavery, de facto segregation sometimes became de jure separation supported by local ordinances and/or state law.

As long as the South maintained slavery, that institution regulated race relations, and de jure segregation was not needed. In 1865, however, the southern slaves were set free and legal segregation made its appearance. After the Civil War, most southern states passed legislation known as black codes, which resembled the old slave codes. Under the new codes, social segregation was often spelled out. For example, most states moved immediately to segregate public transportation lines. By the end of Reconstruction (1866-1877), race lines had hardened, and social segregation was the rule rather than the exception.

**Unsuccessful Challenges**

Some African Americans challenged segregationist laws. In 1896, blacks from Louisiana sued a public transportation company (railroad) that operated segregated passenger cars, as stipulated by Louisiana's state laws. Black leaders argued that the state laws and the railroad's actions violated the Thirteenth and Fourteenth Amendments to the Constitution. The case, *Plessy v. Ferguson*, reached the U.S. Supreme Court, which ruled that segregation was legal as long as "separate but equal" facilities were made available for members of minorities. A lone dissenter, Justice John M. Harlan, who happened to be a white southerner, rejected the majority opinion, saying that the Constitution should be "colorblind" and that it should not tolerate "classes" among the citizens, who were all equal.

Despite Harlan's dissent, the *Plessy* decision gave absolute legal sanction to a practice that many states, including some in the North, were already practicing by custom and tradition—*Plessy* froze segregation into the highest law of the land. Thereafter, segregationists, especially those in the South, used their legislatures to pass a host of new laws that extended the supposed "separate but equal" doctrine to all areas of life. For example, restaurants, hotels, and theaters became segregated by law, not only by custom. Railroad cars and railroad stations divided the races; hospitals, doctors' offices, and even cemeteries became segregated. Some southern state laws called for segregated prisons, while prisons in other states took criminals from both races but separated them within the facility. At least one state passed a law that forbade a white and a black prisoner to look out the same prison window at the same time. If the prisoners were physically close enough to look out at the same time, they were too close to please segregationists.

As the United States matured during the twentieth century, segregation was extended to whenever technology made it seem necessary. For example, in 1915, Oklahoma became the first state in the Union to require segregated public pay telephone booths. When motor cars were first used as a taxi service, taxi companies were segregated—a "white" taxi serving whites only and a "black" taxi serving African Americans only.

Public water fountains became segregated, as did public restroom facilities.

Another problem became associated with segregation. Often, there was no separate facility for blacks, who were denied service altogether. For example, as late as the 1960's, President Lyndon B. Johnson's personal maid and butler-handyman experienced difficulty traveling by car from Washington, D.C., back to Johnson's Texas home. There were few if any motels along the way that would rent rooms to African Americans.

### Successful Challenges

Eventually, the National Association for the Advancement of Colored People (NAACP) launched new attacks against segregationist laws—especially in circumstances in which no separate facilities existed for African Americans.

For example, in *Gaines v. Missouri* (1938) and *Sweatt v. Painter* (1949; a Texas case), the Supreme Court ruled that blacks could attend white law schools because no separate school was available in state for African Americans. In 1950, in *McLaurin v. Oklahoma*, the NAACP tested the same concept and won another court battle. As *McLaurin* showed, the University of Oklahoma had admitted a black student to its graduate program but then had segregated him on campus. After the Supreme Court ruled that such segregation was unfair and illegal because it denied equal education, Thurgood Marshall of the NAACP became even more determined to challenge segregation. He did so successfully when, in *Brown v. Board of Education* (1954), the Court declared segregated public education illegal.

If segregation was unjust and unconstitutional in education, it seemed clear that it was also unjust in other areas of life. In 1955, under the leadership of Martin Luther King, Jr., and others, a nonviolent protest movement took to the streets and eventually won victories that included new laws such as the Civil Rights Act of 1964 and the Voter Registration Act of 1965. Ultimately, a limited social and economic revolution occurred that condemned segregation and, in part, created a new American society.

*James Smallwood*

**Further Reading**

Segregation and its consequences are discussed in Bob Blauner's *Racial Oppression in America* (New York: Harper & Row, 1972); Taylor Branch's *Parting the Waters: America in the King Years, 1954-1963* (New York: Simon & Schuster, 1988); Joe R. Feagin and Clairece B. Feagin's *Racial and Ethnic Relations* (5th ed., Englewood Cliffs, N.J.: Prentice-Hall, 1996); James Forman's *The Making of Black Revolutionaries* (2d ed., Washington, D.C.: Open Hand, 1985); Fred Powledge's *Free at Last? The Civil Rights Movement and the People Who Made It* (Boston: Little, Brown, 1991); and Harvard Sitkoff's *The Struggle for Black Equality, 1954-1992* (New York: Hill & Wang, 1993).

**See also** *Alexander v. Holmes County Board of Education*; Baseball's integration; Black codes; *Bolling v. Sharpe*; *Brown v. Board of Education*; Civil Rights movement and children; *Cooper v. Aaron*; *Evans v. Abney*; *Green v. County School Board of New Kent County*; *Heart of Atlanta Motel v. United States*; Integration; Jim Crow laws; *Jones v. Alfred H. Mayer Company*; *Keyes v. Denver School District No. 1*; *McLaurin v. Oklahoma State Regents for Higher Education*; *Milliken v. Bradley*; *Missouri ex rel. Gaines v. Canada*; Orangeburg massacre; *Palmer v. Thompson*; *Plessy v. Ferguson*; Restrictive covenants; Segregation; Segregation on the frontier; Separate but equal doctrine; *Shelley v. Kraemer*; Slavery; Sports; *Sweatt v. Painter*

# Segregation on the frontier

**Definition:** Several thousand African Americans moved to the American West in the late nineteenth and early twentieth centuries in an effort to escape the racism that existed in the eastern United States

*Once on the frontier, African Americans established segregated communities that allowed them to live apart from whites who would discriminate against them.*

Most people who have studied the western frontier have found that racial discrimination existed there, but that it was different from that found in the former slave states in the southeastern United States. For example, some western territories and states passed statutes requiring segregation of the races in schools and other public facilities, but these laws were not enforced as vigorously as in the South. Incidents of racial violence (such as white mobs lynching African Americans) were less numerous on the frontier than they were east of the Mississippi River.

Still, racism did exist on the frontier, and African Americans sought to avoid it. Even before the Civil War (1861-1865), free blacks established segregated communities in isolated areas of Arkansas, Louisiana, and Texas. After the war, African Americans who had been slaves to Native Americans created several all-black towns and agricultural colonies in Indian Territory. Other African Americans availed themselves of the provisions of the Homestead Act (1862), which allowed them to claim 160-acre parcels of public land on the frontier. Many of these black homesteaders created segregated communities where they could live by their own rules rather than those imposed upon them by white Americans.

**All-Black Communities**

Several of the all-black settlements were towns in which all of the businesses were owned by African Americans. Others were

*Migrants on their way from Mississippi to Kansas in 1897.* (Library of Congress)

agricultural colonies whose residents expected to earn their living primarily by farming. In reality, however, the distinction between the two types of communities often became blurred. The farmers needed businesses to supply some of their needs, and the business owners often farmed to make extra money. Consequently, many of the segregated frontier communities were small urban areas surrounded by farms.

Perhaps the most famous all-black frontier settlement was Nicodemus, Kansas. A few promoters of an all-black settlement chose a spot on the western Kansas prairie to establish Nicodemus. They filed homestead claims and mapped out town lots on part of their land. They then went back east to make speeches and distribute brochures encouraging people to move to the proposed town. The promoters then charged the recruits fees for helping them move to Kansas and for filing their homestead papers.

The Nicodemus settlers established churches, schools, and various social organizations to improve their quality of life. This attempt to create a sense of community was essential in making the colonists feel content in strange surroundings. As the people became friends with their neighbors and worked to help one another succeed, the sense of community began to grow and to become stronger. This sense of community was one of the main reasons that African Americans chose to live in segregated settlements on the frontier. However, while the sense of community was strong in Nicodemus and other all-black frontier colonies, other factors caused most of them to fail.

The frontier environment was such that droughts often led to crop failures, which sometimes caused residents to grow disillusioned and move elsewhere to farm. A second problem was that many of the settlers lacked the capital to obtain enough animals, supplies, and equipment to make farming successful. This, of course, had an adverse effect on the businesses that relied on the farmers' patronage. Many businesses went broke, and African American farmers often had to work for nearby whites in order to eke out a living from the harsh frontier land. Eventually, many inhabitants of all-black communities abandoned their claims and moved into or near towns where whites also lived.

*Members of the Shores family, who became famous as musicians in Nebraska in the late nineteenth century.* (Nebraska State Historical Society)

## Black Neighborhoods in White Communities

Even in these larger, predominantly white settlements, African Americans usually segregated themselves. Many frontier towns had a neighborhood where African Americans lived and socialized, creating a black community within the larger, white-controlled community. In these situations, African Americans experienced social segregation while participating in an integrated business environment that allowed them to benefit from their more prosperous white neighbors. Some African Americans worked as hired hands and domestic servants for white families, and others ran restaurants, hotels, barbershops, laundries, repair shops, and other businesses that catered to customers of all races.

Laws and customs of the late nineteenth and early twentieth centuries dictated that the social contact between black and white people be limited. This was true in the American West just as it was in the older eastern sections of the country. However, a relatively low level of prejudice on the western frontier allowed for much business activity between the races. Thus, although African Americans on the western frontier usually lived in segregated communities, their lives were more prosperous and successful when they engaged in commerce with their white neighbors.

*Roger D. Hardaway*

**Further Reading**
Norman L. Crockett discusses four all-black frontier towns (Nicodemus, Kansas, and Boley, Clearview, and Langston, Oklahoma) in *The Black Towns* (Lawrence: Regents Press of Kansas, 1979). Kenneth Marvin Hamilton examines Nicodemus, Boley, Langston, and Allensworth, California, in *Black Towns and Profit: Promotion and Development in the Trans-Appalachian West, 1877-1915* (Urbana: University of Illinois Press, 1991). Black communities in predominantly white towns are the subject of Thomas C. Cox's *Blacks in Topeka, Kansas, 1865-1915: A Social History* (Baton Rouge: Louisiana State University Press, 1982) and of William L. Lang's "The Nearly Forgotten Blacks on Last Chance Gulch, 1900-1912," in *Pacific Northwest Quarterly* (70, 1979). A general survey of the various types of western black settlements is Roger D. Hardaway's "African American Communities on the Western Frontier," in *Communities in the American West*, edited by Stephen Tchudi (Reno: Nevada Humanities Committee and University of Nevada Press, 1999).

**See also** Cowboys; Segregation

# Selma-Montgomery march

**The Event:** Demonstration to protest the lack of voting rights for African Americans in the South
**Date:** March, 1965
**Place:** Selma to Montgomery, Alabama
*The march from Selma to Montgomery had a significant impact on passage of the 1965 Voting Rights Act and marked an increased emphasis in civil rights reform upon political and economic issues.*

The Selma to Montgomery March of 1965 is often viewed as one of the most decisive events in the history of the American Civil

Rights movement. It was marked by considerable violent resistance, a high degree of emotional intensity for those who participated, and political impact not often matched. Its basic purpose was to extend voting rights to black Americans in a period when many southern white leaders adamantly resisted broadening the franchise. The Civil Rights Act signed by President Lyndon B. Johnson on July 2, 1964, did contain provisions for minority voting rights.

The Civil Rights Act's eleven titles spanned the spectrum of basic rights, including equal access to public accommodations, schools, and employment. Title VI gave the federal government the power to cut off funds to state or local authorities that discriminated, but there was little increased authority in the voting rights provisions of Title I. Nor was it certain that any of the desegregation mandates would be respected in the Deep South.

## SNCC and SCLC Involvement

Although Selma was a small city in an essentially rural part of Alabama, it was in the highly segregated Dallas County region that some civil rights leaders believed would be a good place to launch a concerted voter registration drive. In February, 1963, well before the 1964 Civil Rights Act, Student Nonviolent Coordinating Committee (SNCC) field workers such as Bernard and Colia Lafayette, John Love, Worth Long, and others began to work with local black leaders. The results were meager because of intense resistance by the forces of Sheriff James G. Clark and the entrenched white power structure. On the other hand, Clark's roughness provided the kind of focus needed to stir a grassroots movement.

Throughout 1963 and 1964, SNCC and the Dallas County Voters' League held monthly voter registration clinics and occasional mass rallies. Southern Christian Leadership Conference (SCLC) organizers such as James Bevel, C. T. Vivian, Harry Boyte, and Eric Kindberg participated in some of these activities and began to consider the Dallas County area as a possible target for the SCLC's heightened voter registration drive begun in earnest after the Civil Rights Act.

If voter registration was the chief focus of Dallas County black leaders such as Albert Turner, Amelia Boynton, and Voters' League president Frederick D. Reese, it was by no means the only issue. There was widespread concern among African Americans about police roughness, barriers to school integration, and widespread poverty because of job discrimination. They believed that gaining the vote would open the door to other reforms in the local communities. The Johnson administration had already introduced a voting rights act in Congress by late 1964, but passage was uncertain and some of its terms were considered weak by the SCLC, SNCC, the National Association for the Advancement of Colored People (NAACP), and other advocacy groups. Martin Luther King, Jr., the SCLC's president, shared these concerns and came into Selma in January, 1965, to spur the voter registration effort.

King met forceful resistance, as did several others. He was slightly injured when a white detractor attacked him as he tried to integrate Hotel Albert. On January 19, 1965, Sheriff Clark roughly shoved Mrs. Amelia Boynton as she participated in a march to the courthouse on behalf of black voter registration. That incident was pictured in the national and international media and drew the world's attention to Selma, a city in south central Alabama with fewer than thirty thousand residents. It became obvious that voting rights were tied to other basic American constitutional rights. When King, by then a Nobel Peace Prize recipient, was jailed in early February, a new wave of activists poured into Selma to give aid to the effort. Many of them were students, but ministers, workers, and others were also attracted to the increasingly dramatic Selma campaign. Even Malcolm X, just days before his assassination on February 21 in Harlem, went to Selma to support King.

The fatal shooting of young Jimmie Lee Jackson by police in nearby Marion added to the determination to continue the voting rights drive and the effort to deal with the various violations of rights that African Americans faced. The original plan for a motorcade from Selma to Montgomery was abandoned in favor of a walking demonstration along the rural highway leading to the state's capital. This brought to light a complex pattern of racial segregation that reached all the way to the governor's office and state laws.

### The First March Begins

The first effort to march from Selma to Montgomery was made on Sunday, March 7, 1965. King and Ralph Abernathy were at their churches preaching. The SCLC's Hosea Williams and SNCC chairman John Lewis led a crowd of more than five hundred people out of Brown Chapel to the Edmund Pettus Bridge and toward Montgomery, along Highway 80. Governor George Wallace had banned the march the previous day, and Clark was expected to try to stop it, but no one anticipated the military-like force that waited to confront the marchers. Across the bridge, a large volunteer posse put together by Sheriff Clark waited, along with well-equipped state troopers under Colonel Albert Lingo. As the marchers approached the bridge, they were ordered to stop and told to disband within two minutes.

Before the short warning period had ended, the police began to attack. Some were on horseback, swinging billy clubs and whips that lashed into the marchers' bodies. Tear gas canisters were fired as the crowd began to scatter. Some troopers pursued the fleeing demonstrators as they tried to find refuge. The Selma march had suddenly become a rout that would be remembered as "Bloody Sunday" by many people. About eighty injured people were treated at the Good Samaritan Hospital, seventeen of whom were admitted for more treatment and observation. The "Bloody Sunday" attack was publicized widely, both in the United States and abroad.

King rushed back to the city and prepared for another attempt on Tuesday. March 9, appealing for help from around the nation. Public concern deepened, and within two days about 450 white members of the clergy and a wave of other supporters poured into Selma. This time, a federal injunction prohibited the march, and President Johnson requested a postponement. Local Selma and Dallas County officials disagreed on how to approach any renewed effort to march to Montgomery. Public Safety Director Wilson Baker had opposed the use of force against the first attempted march, and now he urged compromise to avoid a repetition of its violence. Behind the scenes, federal and local officials worked with King and other leaders to arrange a symbolic march across the Edmund Pettus Bridge, with promises that police would let marchers pass. The march would then halt without continuing to Montgomery.

Few people knew of these arrangements, however, so that the March 9 trek caused confusion and some disillusionment. A crowd of about nine hundred people left Brown Chapel once again. The number swelled to more than fifteen hundred as they neared the bridge. King told them, "We must let them know that nothing can stop us, not even death itself." Most assumed that they were on their way to the capital. As the marchers crossed the bridge, the police lines widened to let them pass. The marchers paused to sing "We Shall Overcome," and then the march leaders turned the group around and headed back into town.

## Aftermath

Despite this ostensible retreat, the events in Selma were important in the history of civil rights activism in the United States. The week following the second attempted march was filled with significant legal and political moves. A federal court declared the Alabama bans on demonstrations invalid, and President Johnson spoke out forcefully to Congress and the nation on March 15 in support of the effort in Selma. He declared what had happened on March 7 to be "an American tragedy," and said that the Selma campaign was important to all Americans. In Johnson's words, "Their cause must be our cause, too." No president had ever taken this bold a public stand on civil rights. The fact that Johnson ended his address by saying, "And we shall overcome!" won wide applause from black activists.

On March 17, 1965, Judge Frank M. Johnson authorized the march to Montgomery and ordered Governor Wallace not to interfere. The same day, President Johnson sent his completed voting rights bill to Congress. Certain restrictions were placed on the march, such as a limit of three hundred on the number of marchers on two-lane sections of the road, but it would proceed with police protection to its destination. About eight thousand people started out of Selma on Sunday, March 21. It took five days to complete the trip. Along the way, a number of prominent entertainers and political figures participated, among them Harry Belafonte and Leonard Bernstein. King left on Wednesday, March 24, to fly to Cleveland for a speech, but rejoined the march as it entered Montgomery on Thursday. About thirty thousand people had taken part in the march.

There were some violent eruptions in places, but the march proceeded in an orderly way without major incident. After the march, however, a white Michigan housewife and mother, Mrs. Viola Liuzzo, was shot to death in her car as she drove black marchers back home from Montgomery. When the SCLC board of directors met in Baltimore in early April, 1965, they considered a boycott campaign against the state of Alabama in response to that and other violence.

**Impact**

The Selma march has a significant place in civil rights history. It helped to convince Congress that a voting rights act was necessary. Such a bill was passed by Congress in May, 1965, and signed into law by President Johnson on August 6. It covered all states where screening devices such as literacy tests were used to restrict voting and states in which either fewer than half of the voting-age citizens were registered as of November 1, 1964, or fewer than 50 percent voted in the 1964 presidential election.

In another major sense, this march was historically significant. After Selma, the Civil Rights movement gave more attention to the socioeconomic conditions of members of racial minorities and poor people in the United States. It seemed imperative after 1965 to exercise the right to vote and thereby seek to bring about some of the reforms that were impossible when black Americans were systematically prohibited from voting. The Selma march was also psychologically important. It boosted confidence and energized new enthusiasm for future changes.

King biographer Stephen B. Oates concluded that, "In truth, Selma was the movement's finest hour, was King's finest hour." There is much truth in this estimation. The Selma experience not only effected political changes but also infused the movement with a new confidence. Some scholars see in it the culmination of the trend from nonviolent persuasion to nonviolent coercion, that is, the transition from using marches and other demonstrations to win support to using them to bring higher legal and political authority to bear on local opposition. This distinction is not absolute since, from the beginning, both elements were present.

At the personal level, Selma is remembered as an inspirational experience. Marchers were resisted violently, yet they persisted. Many children and young people who witnessed the March 7 confrontation recalled years later being helped to safety by the adults. Voter registration efforts, furthermore, were thereafter regarded by increasing numbers of individuals as important direct action contributions to social reform in the United States. After Selma, the nonviolent Civil Rights movement in the United States began to venture out of the South into places such as Chicago, Cleveland, and Louisville.

*Thomas R. Peake*

### Further Reading

Fager, Charles E. *Selma, 1965*. New York: Scribner's, 1974. Written by a white participant who knew the black leaders involved in the Selma march, this account provides useful insight into the dynamics of the surrounding politics. Fager discusses the tensions between Sheriff James Clark and Police Chief Wilson Baker as well as the differences among Voters' League president Frederick D. Reese and various other voter registration campaign leaders. The book also provides valuable information on the alleged sexual misconduct of participants and shows that this was mostly a myth. Fager also traces the background of the march, its details, and its immediate results. Contains illustrations and an index, as well as some guides to sources.

Garrow, David J. *Protest at Selma: Martin Luther King, Jr., and the Voting Rights Act of 1965*. New Haven, Conn.: Yale University Press, 1978. The most thorough account of the background and development of the Selma campaign. Garrow draws upon a rich array of sources to trace methodically the work of SNCC, the Dallas County Voters' League, and local politics to show the importance of the Selma experience in forcing Congress to act on the Johnson administration's voting rights proposals. Garrow's account is a solid, basic study of the campaign and its effects. Contains elaborate notes and index.

Lewis, John with Michael D'Orso. *Walking with the Wind: A Memoir of the Movement.* New York: Simon & Schuster, 1998.

Oates, Stephen B. *Let the Trumpet Sound: The Life of Martin Luther King, Jr.* New York: Harper & Row, 1982. The first of the critical analyses of King's life. Oates presents little that is new, but he does take more seriously the charge of King's personal misconduct with women. His treatment of Selma is among the best parts of the book in the sense of capturing both the drama and the significance of the anti-integrationist violence that produced "Bloody Sunday" on March 7, 1965. Contains notes, bibliographical references, and index.

Webb, Sheyann, and Rachel West Nelson. *Selma, Lord, Selma: Girlhood Memories of the Civil Rights Days.* University: University of Alabama Press, 1980. A moving personal account by two women who were small children during the Selma campaign. Part of a growing genre of personal literature that is enriching civil rights studies, this work is warmly presented, very readable, and highly informative on the experience of young blacks during the intense period of civil rights activism. Fears, expectations, and personal views are presented in a refreshing way.

Wolk, Allan. *The Presidency and Black Civil Rights: Eisenhower to Nixon.* Madison, N.J.: Fairleigh Dickinson University Press, 1971. Although not specifically about the Selma campaign, Wolk's study puts the Johnson Administration in perspective, showing the evolution of the relationship between presidential politics and civil rights issues from the 1950's to the early 1970's. Its chief value in this connection is its information on Johnson's much higher level of involvement in civil rights than any other president of the period covered. Contains a chronological chart of civil rights policies, a selected bibliography, and an index.

**See also** Birmingham March; Million Man March; Million Woman March; Poor People's March on Washington

# Separate but equal doctrine

**Definition:** Proposition that equal protection of all citizens under the law as guaranteed by the Fourteenth Amendment is not threatened by social segregation of the races, so long as members of all groups are treated equally

*A concept that originated in a U.S. Supreme Court ruling in an 1896 case, the separate but equal doctrine legalized the practice of segregating public and private facilities and services by race, which was particularly common in the southern states.*

In *Plessy v. Ferguson* (1896), the Supreme Court made a distinction between political rights, which are protected under the Constitution, and social conditions, which are not legally protected. It held that social conditions related to race, such as segregation, were natural, inevitable, and not necessarily an indication of the inferiority or superiority of one race over another. This ruling reflected the federal government's growing willingness during the late nineteenth century to strike a compromise with the South on the issue of freed slaves' rights as citizens. The federal government's desire to gain the full participation of the former Confederate states in the Union affected its attitude toward segregation and other racial issues.

The separate but equal doctrine negatively affected the legal gains made by African Americans during the early Reconstruction period after the Civil War. The Court's ruling in *Plessy* legitimized the state laws establishing and enforcing racial segregation, known as Jim Crow laws, that proliferated throughout the South beginning in the 1880's. Whites-only and blacks-only neighborhoods were upheld as socially and legally correct. Transportation in all its forms—railroad cars, steamships, and buses—was likewise segregated. Separate facilities or entrances for whites and African Americans to such public and private places as schools, churches, restaurants, libraries, hotels, public parks, healthcare centers, and theaters became commonplace. Even water fountains, public restrooms, waiting areas, and public telephones became designated as either for whites or African Americans.

The social segregation of the races led to the firm entrench-ment of a separate but unequal social system. Consequently, the social distance between whites and African Americans that had existed during slavery was maintained, although with new norms and practices. This system had a tremendous impact on generations to follow, both in terms of people's attitudes toward members of minorities and in the opportunities African Ameri-cans were able to pursue. The separate but equal doctrine was not reversed until 1954 in *Brown v. Board of Education*.

*Pamela D. Haldeman*

**Further Reading**

Kromkowski, John A., ed. *Race and Ethnic Relations*. Guilford, Conn.: Dushkin/Brown & Benchmark, 1996.

Schuman, Howard, Charlotte Steeh, Lawrence Bobo, and Maria Krysan. *Racial Attitudes in America: Trends and Interpretations*. Cambridge, Mass.: Harvard University Press, 1997.

Weinstein, Allen, and Frank Otto Gatell. *The Segregation Era, 1863-1954: A Modern Reader*. New York: Oxford University Press, 1970.

**See also** *Brown v. Board of Education; Louisville, New Orleans, and Texas Railway Company v. Mississippi; McLaurin v. Oklahoma State Regents for Higher Education; Missouri ex rel. Gaines v. Canada; Plessy v. Ferguson;* Reconstruction; Segregation

# Sharecropping

**Definition:** System in which African Americans farmed on white-owned land, paying for the privilege with shares of their crops

*During the half century following the abolition of slavery in the South, sharecropping provided landless former slaves with meager incomes, while helping to keep the South's ruined economy going.*

In the aftermath of the American Civil War (1861-1865), the South faced many difficulties. Its cities, factories, and railroads had been shattered, and its valuable agricultural industry had been turned upside down. Many large planters lost their entire workforce when the Thirteenth Amendment to the U.S. Constitution freed southern slaves. Newly freed slaves, most of whom were farmworkers, had no land to cultivate. Landowners, former slaves, and small farmers negotiated a compromise: sharecropping. The system they created would eventually lead to a steady decline in southern agriculture during the twentieth century.

Deeply in debt after the war, many southern landowners were forced to give up all or fragments of their property to local merchants, banks, and corporations. By the end of Reconstruction (1863-1877), large portions of southern farmland were controlled by absentee landlords who neither lived on nor worked their land but managed it from afar. Southern landowners had a large number of acres to be planted and not enough money to hire farm laborers. At the same time, thousands of African Americans were free from slavery but without the homes, land, or tools they needed to support themselves.

To earn a living, agricultural laborers agreed to become tenants on farmland. Landlords provided tenants with land, a small house, and tools to grow a crop. Tenants worked the land and

*A sharecropping family returning home after spending their morning working on a North Carolina tobacco farm in 1939. (Library of Congress)*

promised a percentage of their annual crop yield, usually between 20 percent and 50 percent, to the landlord. Landlords frequently arranged credit for tenants with local merchants to help them establish a household and buy seed. Storekeepers and landowners, who sometimes were the same person, placed liens on the farmers' crops to protect their interests. Tenants hoped to yield enough profit from their labor not only to pay off their liens but also to eventually purchase the land they worked.

A bad year or depressed cotton prices could easily leave many farmers in debt at the end of the season. Sharecroppers frequently promised an additional percentage of their crop to local merchants to purchase the next year's seed and feed their families through the winter. Year after year, sharecroppers became more indebted. Forced to work until liens were paid, tenants became bound to their land, continually impoverished and with little hope of becoming property owners.

Sharecropping in the South increased steadily in the latter half of the nineteenth century until approximately 75 percent of all southern farmers were sharecroppers. Cotton prices began to drop after the turn of the century and then fell drastically during the Great Depression of the 1930's. These conditions forced thousands of tenants to leave the land and move to northern cities in search of employment. Others were forced to leave when landlords decided farming was no longer profitable. As a result of this loss of labor and increases in technology, sharecropping represented only a small percentage of farming in the South by the end of the twentieth century.

*Leslie Stricker*

**See also** Agriculture; Employment; Great Migration; Reconstruction

# Shaw v. Hunt

**The Case:** U.S. Supreme Court ruling on gerrymandering to create "majority-minority" districts
**Date:** June 13, 1996

*In this decision, the Supreme Court held that the equal protection clause of the Fourteenth Amendment prohibits the drawing of irregularly shaped congressional districts designed to produce electoral majorities of racial and ethnic minorities.*

One of the purposes of the Voting Rights Act of 1982 was to protect members of racial and ethnic minorities from vote dilution. After the census of 1990, the Department of Justice interpreted the act to mean that legislatures must adopt reapportionment plans that included, whenever possible, congressional districts with heavy concentrations of racial and ethnic minorities. Some of the resulting race-conscious districts were spread out and highly irregular in shape. In the election of 1992, these new districts helped elect an unprecedented number of African Americans to Congress.

In North Carolina, there were two race-based districts, with one following a narrow strip of land for 160 miles. Ruth Shaw and other white voters of North Carolina filed suit, claiming that these two voting districts violated their rights under the equal protection clause. In *Shaw v. Reno* (1993), the Supreme Court directed the federal district court to reconsider the reapportionment plan according to the strict scrutiny standard. This decision, often called *Shaw I*, clearly indicated that a majority of the justices did not approve of racial gerrymandering. The lower court, nevertheless, approved the districts.

In *Shaw v. Hunt* (also known as *Shaw II*), the Supreme Court reversed the lower court's judgment. Speaking for a majority of five, Chief Justice William H. Rehnquist noted that any law that classifies citizens on the basis of race is constitutionally suspect and concluded that the drawing of the two contested districts had not been narrowly tailored to further a compelling state interest. He insisted that the state's interest in remedying the effects of past or present racial discrimination must be justified by an "identified past discrimination" rather than simply a generalized assertion of such discrimination. Also, he argued that the Justice Department's policy of maximizing majority-black districts was not authorized by the Voting Rights Act, which said nothing about subordinating the traditional districting factors of compactness, contiguity, and respect for political subdivisions. Justice John Paul Stevens wrote a strong dissent, arguing that the white plaintiffs' claims of harm were "rooted in speculative and stereotypical assumptions."

In two closely related decisions, *Bush v. Vera* (1996) and *Abrams v. Johnson* (1997), the Court struck down race-based congressional districts in Texas and Georgia respectively. Each of these decisions was decided by a 5-4 vote, which meant that a future change in Court personnel could result in a different judgment about the controversial issue of racial gerrymandering.

*Thomas Tandy Lewis*

**See also** Gerrymandering; *Shaw v. Reno*; Voting Rights Act of 1975

# Shaw v. Reno

**The Case:** U.S. Supreme Court ruling on gerrymandering
**Date:** June 28, 1993

*By calling for close scrutiny of a predominantly black congressional district whose shape it considered "bizarre," the Supreme Court in* Shaw v. Reno *struck a blow against the practice of drawing district boundaries to create "majority-minority" electoral districts.*

After the 1990 census, the state legislature of North Carolina began the task of "reapportionment," or redrawing its electoral districts. Although about 22 percent of the state's population was African American, no African Americans had been elected to Congress for almost a century. To remedy this, and ostensibly to meet provisions of the Voting Rights Act, the legislature created two majority-nonwhite districts. In order to avoid disturbing incumbents' districts, the legislature drew one of the two districts largely along an interstate highway, snaking 160 miles through the north-central part of the state. The resulting district was 53 percent black.

Five voters filed suit against the reapportionment plan, objecting that the race-based district violated their right to participate in a nonracial electoral process. The case reached the

Supreme Court, whose 5-4 majority instructed the lower courts to reconsider the constitutionality of such a district in the light of its "bizarre" shape and its "uncomfortable resemblance to political apartheid." In essence, the majority expressed its concern about the practice of creating districts on the basis of race and of establishing contorted geographical boundaries. The coupling of the two practices presumably could result in districts that patently violated the Constitution's equal protection clause, unless a compelling state interest could be demonstrated.

When the *Shaw* case was subsequently returned to North Carolina, a federal panel upheld the reapportionment plan after finding that the state did indeed have a compelling interest in complying with the Voting Rights Act. Nevertheless, the Supreme Court's *Shaw* decision has been the basis for other important decisions concerning racially defined districts. In 1994, for example, a majority-black district in Louisiana was rejected by a federal district court invoking *Shaw*. The court expressed particular concern that the district was intentionally created on the basis of the voters' race. More significant, in 1995 the U.S. Supreme Court extended *Shaw*'s admonitions about racial reapportionment to argue that voters' rights are violated whenever "race was the predominant factor motivating the legislature's decision to place a significant number of voters within or without a particular district," irrespective of shape.

*Shaw* served as a watershed in the contest between advocates of racial representation and those who champion a "color-blind" electoral system. It came at a time when various racial issues that had for years remained largely outside sharp political debate— affirmative action, welfare reform, and so forth—had been thrust into the center stage of American political discourse. Although *Shaw* by no means resolved these debates, it helped to delineate the battle lines.

*Steve D. Boilard*

**See also** *Shaw v. Hunt*; Voting Rights Act of 1965

# Shelley v. Kraemer

**The Case:** U.S. Supreme Court ruling on restrictive covenants in
housing
**Date:** May 3, 1948

*Although it allowed private individuals to make racially restrictive covenants, this ruling meant that such covenants were worthless because they could not be legally enforced.*

After J. D. Shelley, an African American, purchased a house in a predominantly white neighborhood of St. Louis, Missouri, one of the neighbors, Louis Kraemer, sought and obtained an injunction preventing Shelley from taking possession of the property. Unknown to Shelley, the neighboring landowners had signed a contractual agreement barring owners from selling their property to members of "the Negro or Mongolian race."

Supported by the National Association for the Advancement of Colored People (NAACP), Shelley challenged the constitutionality of the contract in state court, but the Missouri Supreme Court upheld its legality. Appealing to the U.S. Supreme Court, Shelley's case was argued by the NAACP's leading counsels, Charles Houston and Thurgood Marshall. President Harry S. Truman put the weight of the executive branch in favor of the NAACP's position.

This was not the first time that the issue of residential segregation had appeared before the Court. In *Buchanan v. Warley* (1917), the Court had struck down state statutes that limited the right of property owners to sell property to a person of another race, but in *Corrigan v. Buckley* (1926) the Court upheld the right of individuals to make "private" contracts to maintain segregation. *Corrigan* was based on the establishment principle that the first section of the Fourteenth Amendment inhibited the actions of state governments, not those of individuals.

The Court refused to declare restrictive contracts unconstitutional, but it held 6-0 that the Fourteenth Amendment's equal protection clause prohibited state courts from enforcing the contracts, meaning that the contracts were not enforceable. The decision, written by Chief Justice Fred Vinson, emphasized that one of the basic objectives of the Fourteenth Amendment was to prohibit the states from using race to discriminate "in the enjoyment of property rights." The decision did not directly overturn *Corrigan*, but it interpreted the precedent as involving only the validity of private contracts, not their legal enforcement. In a companion case five years later, *Barrows v. Jackson* (1953), Chief Justice Vinson dissented when the majority used the *Shelley* rationale to block enforcement of restrictive covenants through private damage suits against covenant violators.

Eliminating the last direct method for legally barring African Americans from neighborhoods, *Shelley* was an important early victory in the struggle against state-supported segregation. Civil rights proponents hoped that a logical extension of the case would lead to an abolition of the distinction between private and state action in matters of equal protection, but in later decisions such as *Moose Lodge v. Irvis* (1972), the majority of judges were not ready to rule against private conduct that was simply tolerated by the state.

*Thomas Tandy Lewis*

**See also** *Buchanan v. Warley*; *Burton v. Wilmington Parking Authority*; Civil Rights Act of 1968; Civil Rights movement; Fair Housing Act; *Heart of Atlanta Motel v. United States*; *Jones v. Alfred H. Mayer Company*; *Moose Lodge v. Irvis*; *Patterson v. McLean Credit Union*; Restrictive covenants; Segregation

# Simpson murder trial

**The Event:** Criminal trial of former foootball star and media personality O. J. Simpson, who was charged with the murder of his former wife and another person

**Date:** 1994-1995

*The criminal murder trial and acquittal of former football star O. J. Simpson polarized racial attitudes about American criminal justice and police racism. Both before and after the trial, most whites thought Simpson was guilty, and most African Americans thought he was innocent.*

On the night of June 12-13, 1994, the slashed and stabbed bodies of Nicole Brown Simpson and her friend Ronald Goldman, both white, were discovered outside the Los Angeles condominium of Nicole Simpson. After making a preliminary investigation, police left the crime scene and went to the nearby Brentwood estate of Nicole Simpson's former husband, O. J. Simpson, the African American former football star. Finding blood on the door of a white Ford Bronco parked askew on the street in front of the house, Los Angeles Police Department detective Mark Fuhrman climbed the fence without a warrant, allegedly to protect Simpson from any possible danger, and admitted other detectives to the premises.

Simpson was not at home, but Fuhrman, who had been at the Simpson residence five years earlier to answer a domestic violence complaint, used the opportunity to search for evidence linking Simpson to the murder. A bloody glove he allegedly found behind the guest quarters later became a key factor in the trial.

When Simpson returned from Chicago, where he had flown the evening of the murder, he quickly became the only suspect in the case. After a bizarre low-speed vehicle chase watched by millions on live television, Simpson surrendered to police on June 17. Denied bail, he remained in jail during the lengthy trial. He used his wealth to hire a "dream team" of famous attorneys. Jury selection began in September, 1994, and took most of the fall.

**The Trial**

What the media dubbed the "trial of the century" began in late January, 1995, under Judge Lance Ito with a heavily sequestered jury of mostly African Americans. Shortly afterward, O. J. Simpson's self-exonerating book *I Want to Tell You* was published, the first of dozens of books about the case. Gavel-to-gavel coverage on Cable News Network (CNN) guaranteed continuous public attention, and the rest of the electronic and print media rapidly followed suit.

Prosecutors Marcia Clark and Christopher Darden began with a case emphasizing the history of domestic violence in the Simpsons' stormy marriage, but they soon shifted to an emphasis on

DNA (deoxyribonucleic acid) evidence linking the blood of O. J. Simpson and both victims to physical evidence found at the crime scene and the Brentwood estate. This made Detective Fuhrman a key witness, along with his partner Detective Philip Vannatter. Another key witness from the Los Angeles Police Department was Dennis Fung from the crime lab, who admitted under cross-examination that some of the blood evidence had been processed by a trainee, Andrea Mazzola.

The most damaging cross-examination was that of Fuhrman by defense attorney F. Lee Bailey, who scathingly portrayed Fuhrman as a bigoted racist and perjurer who denied his own racist statements and actions despite several witnesses to the contrary. Vannatter was also portrayed as a racist because of his association with Fuhrman and was accused of mishandling blood samples before turning them over to the crime lab.

These and various other defense accusations of police misconduct and conspiracy left sufficient doubts in the minds of jurors, and they acquitted Simpson of both murders after only a brief deliberation on October 3, 1995. The passionate summation by defense attorney Johnnie Cochran made it quite clear to both the jury and the general public that the alleged racism and misbehavior of Fuhrman and the rest of the Los Angeles Police Department were more important elements in the case than either DNA evidence or domestic violence, thus alienating Cochran from Simpson's other principal attorney, Robert Shapiro.

The cast of characters made race an obvious factor in the trial from the very beginning. Simpson, Darden, and Cochran were African Americans, as were nine of the jurors. The detectives, the other attorneys, and both victims were white. Judge Ito was a Japanese American married to a white police captain.

Near the end of the trial, surveys conducted by CBS News found that 64 percent of whites surveyed thought that Simpson was guilty, while 59 percent of African Americans thought that he was not guilty. Only 11 percent of whites surveyed thought Simpson was not guilty, and only 12 percent of African Americans thought he was guilty. Only about one-fourth of each group was undecided, and the disparity of perceptions between the races had actually increased during the trial.

## Reactions to the Trial

After the verdict was announced, many African Americans rejoiced and treated the outcome as if it were a conviction of the Los Angeles Police Department on charges of racism and conspiracy to frame Simpson. This response should be viewed in the light of the highly publicized 1991 Los Angeles beating of African American motorist Rodney King by white police officers, four of whom were acquitted of state criminal charges, leading to massive racially motivated rioting in Los Angeles, but two of whom were later convicted of federal criminal charges.

Meanwhile many white people expressed their dismay at the Simpson acquittal and asserted that a combination of Simpson's money and reverse jury bias had led to a serious miscarriage of justice. These feelings were not greatly diminished sixteen months later when Simpson was held liable for the deaths of the two victims in a civil lawsuit and assessed punitive damages of $25 million, which compares interestingly with the nearly $20 million that the criminal trial cost both sides.

## Explanations of the Verdict

Various explanations have been put forward to account for Simpson's acquittal in the criminal trial. They include reasonable doubt, the lack of a specific theory of the crime, jury nullification, and "evidence" of a police conspiracy.

The simplest explanation is that the jurors did not find persuasive evidence of Simpson's guilt and followed the judge's instructions to acquit the defendant if there was not proof beyond a reasonable doubt. Many African Americans hold this view and give the jury credit for a job well done despite the brevity of their deliberations.

A somewhat more complex version of this explanation is that the prosecution never advanced a specific theory of the crime. For example, they asserted throughout the trial that Simpson committed the entire crime by himself despite circumstantial evidence that an unknown accomplice may have been involved before, after, or during the murders. Some African Americans may have felt that this was condescending or patronizing to the jury and therefore have given jury members credit for realizing that a more complex theory might make better sense of the known facts. Simpson's DNA fairly clearly placed him at the crime scene on the night in question, but to this day, there is no specific scenario for the crime.

Many whites feel that some jury nullification of crucial evidence must have occurred to produce such a speedy acquittal. Very little of the evidence handled by Fuhrman and Vannatter was formally excluded by Judge Ito, and it was left up to the jurors to decide what weight to give each item of evidence. In the belief that evidence obtained through biased procedures by racist police officers ought not to count against the African American defendant, it would be quite conceivable for nullificationist jurors to neglect the entirety of the evidence found at the Brentwood estate and some of the evidence found at the crime scene. Many whites clearly felt that this was exactly what happened, so the jury may have neglected part of its job.

A further twist on this argument is that a police conspiracy was involved and that key pieces of evidence such as a bloody glove and a bloody sock found in the bedroom were planted by overzealous officers to incriminate Simpson. Cochran's very controversial summation encouraged this viewpoint, and many African Americans, including some of the jurors, may have agreed. However, most whites did not agree even if they thought Simpson was not guilty. This was probably the most divisive outcome of the trial, because despite Simpson's acquittal, it tended to reaffirm racially polarized opinions about the extent of previously alleged inequities toward members of minorities in the U.S. criminal justice system.

*Tom Cook*

**Further Reading**

Tapes from the Cable News Network (CNN) are crucial to a thorough study of the trial. However, more succinct analyses can be found in Vincent Bugliosi's *Outrage: The Five Reasons Why O. J. Simpson Got Away with Murder* (New York: W. W. Norton, 1996), Alan M. Dershowitz's *Reasonable Doubts: The O. J. Simpson Case and the Criminal Justice System* (New York: Simon & Schuster,

1996), and Frank Schmalleger's *The Trial of the Century: The People of the State of California vs. Orenthal James Simpson* (Englewood Cliffs, N.J.: Prentice-Hall, 1996).

**See also** King beating case; Los Angeles riots

# Sit-ins

**Definition:** Nonviolent civil rights protest tactic in which African Americans occupied seats in "white-only" restaurants and lunch counters while politely requesting service

*An important part of the fight against racial segregation in the South, sit-ins were an effective form of protest that helped to dramatize the Civil Rights movement.*

On February 1, 1960, four African American college students entered a Greensboro, North Carolina, Woolworth's and sat at the lunch counter. They were refused service because they were not white, but they remained seated until closing as an act of protest. In the following weeks, others who opposed "whites only" food service policies sat at Greensboro lunch counters for hours at a time. Six months later, the city's lunch counters were open to both African American and white patrons. This form of nonviolent protest came to be known as a "sit-in."

Sit-ins were an important part of the Civil Rights movement. Early in 1960, the technique quickly spread from Greensboro to other areas of the South. Typically, well-dressed African Americans, occasionally accompanied by white people, sat at segregated lunch counters from opening until closing. Despite their own peacefulness, protesters were sometimes physically abused or arrested. Eventually, stores lost money because of the disturbances and were forced to comply with protesters' demands. Sit-ins became the most effective tool for lunch counter desegregation across the South. In a broader sense, sit-in victories brought African Americans one step closer to equality.

*Robert D. Lukens*

**Further Reading**

For more information on the development and impact of sit-ins, consult Miles Wolf's *Lunch at the 5 & 10* (1990) and Martin Oppenheimer's *The Sit-in Movement of 1960* (1989).

**See also** Chicago sit-ins; Civil Rights movement; Greensboro sit-ins

# Slaughterhouse Cases

**The Case:** U.S. Supreme Court ruling on the Civil War amendments

**Date:** April 14, 1873

*In these cases, the U.S. Supreme Court for the first time interpreted the Thirteenth, Fourteenth, and Fifteenth Amendments and upheld a state statute granting monopoly status to a corporation. Although the case had no direct bearing on African Americans, its interpretation of the Civil War amendments would have important ramifications for later Supreme Court decisions regarding African American civil rights.*

In 1869, the state of Louisiana created a corporation and gave it monopoly status to operate a meat-slaughtering facility south of the city of New Orleans. It prohibited all other slaughterhouse operations in the three parishes surrounding the city. The goal of the law was to remove slaughterhouse operations from areas that polluted Mississippi River water traveling through the city and consolidate them at one central location downstream from the city. The law also regulated the prices charged for use of the facility by butchers. Butchers not included in the monopoly claimed the law was unconstitutional under the recently adopted Thirteenth and Fourteenth Amendments to the U.S. Constitution. The Louisiana Supreme Court affirmed the law, and the case was appealed to the U.S. Supreme Court.

Justice Samuel F. Miller, writing for the five-member majority of the Court, upheld the law. He used the case to reflect on the purpose of the three Reconstruction-era amendments to the

U.S. Constitution, the Thirteenth, Fourteenth, and Fifteenth Amendments which had been ratified between 1865 and 1870. He wrote that the three taken together were intended to end slavery and the effects of slavery on African Americans. This portion of the opinion is important, as it reflects contemporaneous thinking on the rationale for the ratification of the three amendments.

Justice Miller rejected the claim that granting a monopoly to the corporation created an "involuntary servitude" in violation of the Thirteenth Amendment, noting that the amendment intended to apply narrowly to the incidents of slavery. He also refused to find that the state of Louisiana had violated the Fourteenth Amendment protection of the "privileges and immunities of citizens of the United States" by awarding the monopoly. He refused to give the Fourteenth Amendment a broad interpretation or permit the concept of due process to be used to challenge state law through the U.S. Constitution.

The four-member minority opinion authored by Justice Stephen J. Field sharply disagreed with the majority. Justice Field wrote that the Fourteenth Amendment protects a broad array of privileges and immunities from state interference. Justice Joseph P. Bradley wrote a second dissenting opinion asserting that the Fourteenth Amendment due process clause requires that persons be protected from state actions and that the clause should be given a broad interpretation. This minority view later gained support by the Court majority in the use of substantive due process to limit state regulation of economic activities. It also has been used as a source to protect fundamental rights such as the right to privacy and in criminal law.

**Further Reading**

Labb, Ronald M., and Jonathan Lurie. *The Slaughterhouse Cases: Regulation, Reconstruction, and the Fourteenth Amendment.* Lawrence: University Press of Kansas, 2003.

**See also** Civil War; Compromise of 1877; Reconstruction

# Slave codes

**Definition:** Colonial and state laws dealing with slavery

*In slave-holding states, slave codes were used to make slavery an institution; in free states, such as Ohio, they were used to discourage African Americans from moving to the free states.*

The first colonial laws recognizing and institutionalizing slavery were enacted in Virginia in the mid-seventeenth century. A similar series of Ohio laws denying civil rights to African Americans were enacted to discourage black immigration to that state in the early nineteenth century.

### Virginia

In March, 1661, the Virginia General Assembly declared that "all children borne in this country shalbe held bond or free only according to the condition of the mother." Enacted to alleviate confusion about the status of children with English fathers and African mothers, this law was the first in a series recognizing perpetual slavery in Virginia and equating "freedom" with "white" and "enslaved" with "black." This law is especially indicative of the hardening of race relations in mid-seventeenth century Virginia society, as status in the patriarchal society of England traditionally was inherited from the father. By reversing this legal concept, perpetuation of enslavement for African Americans was ensured for their children, whether of black or white ancestry.

Despite the extent to which the 1661 law narrowed the options for defining Africans' status, this act did not in itself establish slavery. Africans had two available windows through which they could obtain freedom—conversion to Christianity and manumission (formal emancipation). In 1655, mulatto Elizabeth Key brought a successful suit for her freedom, using as her main argument the fact that she had been baptized. In 1667, a slave named Fernando contended that he ought to be freed because he was a Christian and had lived in England for several years. Not only did the court deny Fernando's appeal, but also that same year the General Assembly took another step toward more clearly defining the status of African Americans, by declaring "that the conferring of baptisme doth not alter the condition of the person as to his bondage or freedome." Planters felt that if baptism led to freedom, they would be without any assurance that they could retain their slave property. The 1667 law thereby built on the earlier one to define who would be a slave, and was clarified in 1670 and again in 1682, when the Assembly declared that any non-Christian brought into the colony, either by land or by sea, would be a slave for life, even if he or she later converted.

In 1691, colonial leaders provided a negative incentive to masters wishing to free their slaves by declaring that anyone who set free any "negro or mulatto" would be required to pay the costs of transporting the freedmen out of the colony within six months. Although manumissions still occurred and some free blacks managed to remain in the colony, the primary status for African Americans in Virginia was that of chattel.

Although who was to be a slave in Virginia had now been defined, it had yet to be determined precisely what being a slave meant on a daily basis for Africans and their descendants. Between 1661 and 1705, nearly twenty separate laws were passed limiting, defining, and prescribing the rights, status, and treatment of African Americans. In general, these laws were designed to protect planters' slave property and to protect the order and stability of white society from an "alien and savage race."

The piecemeal establishment of slavery in these separate laws culminated in 1705 in a comprehensive slave code in Virginia. This code reenacted and strengthened a number of earlier slave laws, added further restrictions and harsher punishments, and permanently drew the color line that placed African Americans at the bottom of Virginia society. Whites were prohibited from trading with, having sexual relations with, and marrying African Americans. African Americans were forbidden to own Christian servants "except of their own complexion," leave their home plantation without a pass, own a gun or other weapon, or resist whites in any way.

Many of the harsher penalties for slave crimes, for example, the death penalty and maiming, were not carried out nearly as frequently as the laws suggest, because doing so would harm or destroy the master's property. Laws prohibiting slaves from trad-

*Slaves chained together while being relocated.* (Library of Congress)

ing or hiring themselves out were disregarded almost routinely. The disadvantage for slaves of this lack of enforcement was that laws prohibiting cruel treatment or defining acceptable levels of correction often were ignored as well. Where abuse was blatant, action against white offenders was taken only reluctantly, and punishments were insignificant and rare. Generally, laws in the economic and political interest of the white planter elite were enforced and respected; laws that restrained planters' pursuits were not.

### Ohio and the Northwest Territory

The Northwest Territory was established in 1787 and ultimately became the states of Ohio, Indiana, Michigan, Illinois, and Wisconsin. In 1800, what was to become the state of Ohio separated from the rest of the territory. Two years later, Ohio elected delegates to a constitutional convention in preparation for a statehood petition, which was approved in 1803.

Although the Northwest Ordinance prohibited slavery in that territory, Ohio's constitutional convention debated the issue during its sessions. With the slaveholding states of Virginia on Ohio's eastern boundary and Kentucky on its southern boundary, there was considerable pressure for Ohio to recognize slavery. Many of the immigrants to Ohio came from slave states and saw nothing evil in the system. While many southern Ohioans did not object to slavery, persons in the northern part of the state were more likely to oppose it.

Delegates at the 1802 constitutional convention debated several questions that focused on African Americans. There was no strong feeling for instituting slavery in Ohio; there was, however, strong opinion in favor of limited rights for African Americans. After a major debate over allowing African Americans to vote, it was decided not to delete the word "white" from the qualifications for the franchise. Nevertheless, the African American population grew from five hundred in 1800 to nearly two thousand by 1810. In 1804, the legislature debated and passed the first of the "Black Laws," statutes intended to discourage African Americans from moving into Ohio and to encourage those already there to leave.

A few years later, an even stronger bill to restrict African Americans was presented in the Senate. In its final version, it forbade African Americans from settling in Ohio unless they could present a five-hundred-dollar bond and an affidavit signed by two white men that attested to their good character. Fines for helping a fugitive slave were doubled. Finally, no African American could testify against a white in court.

However restrictive the original Black Laws were, the new law was far worse. African Americans were stripped of legal protection and placed at the mercy of whites. Whites did not need to fear being tried for offenses against African Americans unless there was a white witness who would testify. There is evidence of at least one African American being murdered by whites, with only African American witnesses to the crime. African American witnesses could not provide evidence against a white assailant.

Even if a case went to court, it would be heard by an all-white jury before a white judge. African American victims could not testify on their own behalf, because of the restrictions against providing testimony against whites. Because they could not vote, African Americans could neither change nor protest these laws.

While the black codes of 1804 and 1807 were enforced only infrequently, they still were the law and were a constant reminder that African Americans in Ohio had only the barest minimum of human and civil rights—and those rights existed only at the whim of white society. The laws fell into disuse and finally were repealed in 1849, long after the abolitionist movement, with its western center located in Oberlin, Ohio, was well under way, and long after the Underground Railroad had opened several stations in Ohio.

*Laura A. Croghan*
*Duncan R. Jamieson*

**Further Reading**

Joseph Boskin's *Into Slavery: Racial Decisions in the Virginia Colony* (Philadelphia: J. B. Lippincott, 1976) provides an account of the evolution of perpetual slavery and a representative selection of relevant primary documents. *In the Matter of Color: Race and the American Legal Process, the Colonial Period* (New York: Oxford University Press, 1978), by A. Leon Higginbotham, Jr., recounts the events culminating in the legal recognition of slavery in the British mainland colonies. Philip J. Schwartz's *Twice Condemned: Slaves and the Criminal Laws of Virginia, 1705-1865* (Baton Rouge: Louisiana State University Press, 1988) uses criminal trial records to examine slave resistance and whites' efforts to control threatening slave behavior. Robert B. Shaw's *A Legal History of Slavery in the United States* (Potsdam, N.Y.: Northern Press, 1991) illustrates the history of slavery in terms of its legislative and judicial background, from settlement through emancipation. Charles Jay Wilson's "The Negro in Early Ohio" (*Ohio Archeological and Historical Quarterly* 39, 1930) is the most complete analysis of Ohio's Black Laws.

**See also** Abolition; Antislavery laws of 1777 and 1807; Black codes; Fugitive Slave Law of 1793; Fugitive Slave Law of 1850;

Missouri Compromise; New York City slave revolt; Slavery and families; Slavery and the justice system; Slavery and women; Slavery in Massachusetts; Slavery in Virginia; Underground Railroad

# Slavery

*Slavery has historically constituted a significant denial of human rights and, as practiced in the United States, laid the foundations for conflict between whites and African Americans for generations to come.*

Slavery is one of the oldest institutions of human society. Slavery was present in the earliest human civilizations, those of ancient Mesopotamia and Egypt, and continued to exist in several parts of the world through the late twentieth century.

Despite the near universality of slavery, there is no consensus regarding what distinctive practices constitute slavery. In Western society, a slave typically was a person who was owned as property by another person and forced to perform labor for the owner. This definition, however, breaks down when applied to non-Western forms of slavery. In some African societies, slaves were not owned as property by an individual but were thought of as belonging to a kinship group. The slave could be sold, but so too could nonslave members of the kinship group. In certain African societies, slaves were exempted from labor and were used solely to bring honor to the master by demonstrating his absolute power over another person.

Sociologist Orlando Patterson suggested that slavery is best understood as an institution designed to increase the power of the master or the ruling group. Slaves can fulfill this role by laboring to make the master rich, but they can also do so by bringing honor to the master. One of the defining, universal characteristics of slavery is that the slave ceases to exist as a socially meaningful person. The slave relates to society only through the master. Slavery includes many mechanisms to remove the slave from membership in any groups, such as the family, through which the slave might derive an independent sense of identity. By placing the master in a dominant position over another individual, slavery is believed to increase the honor and power of the master. The slave's status is permanent and it is typically passed down to the slave's children.

## Slavery in World History

The use of slavery was widespread in the ancient world, especially in Greece and Italy. During the classical ages of Greek and Roman society, slaves constituted about one-third of the population. Following the collapse of the Roman Empire in Western Europe during the fifth and sixth centuries, declining economic conditions destroyed the profitability of slavery and provided employers with large numbers of impoverished peasants who could be employed more cheaply than slaves. Over the next seven hundred years, slavery slowly gave way to serfdom. Although serfs, like slaves, were unfree laborers, serfs generally had more legal rights and a higher social standing than slaves.

Familiarity with the institution of slavery did not, however, disappear in Western Europe. A trickle of slaves from Eastern Europe and even from Africa continued to flow into England, France, and Germany. Western Europeans retained their familiarity with large-scale slave systems through contacts with southern Italy, Spain, and Portugal, and with the Byzantine Empire and the Muslim world, where slavery flourished. Western Europeans also inherited from their Roman forebears the corpus of Roman law, with its elaborate slave code. During the later Middle Ages, Europeans who were familiar with Muslim sugar plantations in the Near East sought to begin sugar production with slave labor on the islands of the Mediterranean.

Thus, as Western Europe entered the age of exploration and colonization, Europeans had an intimate knowledge of slavery and a ready-made code of laws to govern slaves. During the sixteenth century, as European nations sought to establish silver mines and sugar plantations in their new colonies in the Western Hemisphere, heavy labor demands led to efforts to enslave Native Americans. This supply of laborers was inadequate because of the rapid decline of the Indian population following the introduction of European diseases into the Western Hemisphere. The

*Drawing of early African slaves arriving on the shores of the New World.* (Library of Congress)

Spanish and Portuguese then turned to Africa, next most readily available source of slave laborers.

Between 1500 and 1900, European slave traders imported 9.7 million African laborers into the Western Hemisphere. Every European colony eventually used slave labor, which became the principal form of labor in the Western Hemisphere. Because the wealth of several modern nations was created by slave labor, some contemporary African Americans have claimed the right to receive reparations payments from nations such as the United States, which continue to enjoy the wealth accumulated originally by the use of slave laborers.

### Slavery and Race

The large-scale use of African slaves by European masters raised new moral issues regarding race. There is no necessary connection between slavery and race. A massive survey by Orlando Patterson of slave societies throughout history found that in three-quarters of slave societies, masters and slaves were of the same race. Slavery in the Western Hemisphere was unusual in human history because slaves were drawn almost exclusively from the black race.

In most colonies of the Western Hemisphere, the use of African slaves was accompanied by the rise of racism, which some scholars claim was a new, unprecedented phenomenon caused by slavery. Scholars seeking to understand contemporary race relations in the United States have been intrigued by the rise of prejudice in new slave societies. Did Europeans enslave Africans merely because they needed slaves and Africa was the most accessible source of slaves? If so, then prejudice probably originated as a learned association between race and subservience. Modern prejudice might be broken down through integration and affirmative action programs aimed at helping whites to witness the success of African Americans in positions of authority.

Did Europeans enslave Africans because they saw Africans as inferior persons ideally suited for slavery? If so, then contemporary racism is a deeply rooted cultural phenomenon that is not likely to disappear for generations to come. African Americans will receive justice only if the government establishes permanent compensatory programs aimed at equalizing power between the races.

Historical research has not resolved these issues. Sixteenth century Europeans apparently did view Africans as inferior beings, even before the colonization of the Western Hemisphere. These racial antipathies were minor, however, in comparison to modern racism. Emancipated slaves in recently settled colonies experienced little racial discrimination. The experience of slavery apparently increased the European settlers' sense of racial superiority over Africans.

After the slave systems of the Western Hemisphere became fully developed, racial arguments became the foundation of the proslavery argument. Supporters of slavery claimed that persons of African descent were so degraded and inferior to whites that it would be dangerous for society to release the slaves from the control of a master. In the United States, some proslavery theorists pushed the racial argument to extreme levels. In explaining the contradiction between slavery and the American ideal that all persons should be free, writers such as Josiah Nott and Samuel Cartwright claimed that African Americans were not fully human and, therefore, did not deserve all the rights belonging to humanity.

A minority of proslavery writers rejected the racial argument and the effort to reconcile slavery and American egalitarian ideals. Writers such as George Fitzhugh claimed that all societies were organized hierarchically by classes and that slavery was the most benevolent system for organizing an unequal class structure. Slavery bound together masters and slaves through a system of mutual rights and obligations. Unlike the "wage slaves" of industrial society, chattel slaves had certain access to food, clothing, shelter, and medical care, all because the master's ownership of the slaves' bodies made him diligent in caring for his property. Slavery was depicted by some proslavery theorists as the ideal condition for the white working class.

### The Antislavery Movement

From the dawning of human history until the middle of the eighteenth century, few persons appear to have questioned the morality of slavery as an institution. Although some persons had earlier raised moral objections to certain features of slavery, almost no one appears to have questioned the overall morality of slavery as a system before the middle of the eighteenth century. Around 1750, however, an antislavery movement began to appear in Britain, France, and America.

*Alexandria, Virginia, slave dealer's headquarters, around the 1850's.* (National Archives)

The sudden rise of antislavery opinion appears to be related to the rise of a humanitarian ethos during the Enlightenment that encouraged people to consider the welfare of humans beyond their kin groups. The rise of the antislavery movement was also related to the growing popularity of new forms of evangelical and pietistic religious sects such as the Baptists, Methodists, and Quakers, which tended to view slaveholding as sinful materialism and slaves as persons worthy of God's love. The rise of the antislavery movement was encouraged by the American and French Revolutions, whose democratic political philosophies promoted a belief in the equality of individuals. The rise of antislavery opinion also coincided in time with the rise of industrial capitalism. The historian Eric Williams argued in *Capitalism and Slavery* (1944) that the economic and class interests of industrial capitalists rather than the moral scruples of humanitarians gave rise to the antislavery movement.

Antislavery activism initially focused on the abolition of the Atlantic slave trade. Reformers succeeded in prompting Britain and the United States to abolish the slave trade in 1807. Other nations followed this lead over the next half century until the Atlantic slave trade was virtually eliminated.

The campaign to abolish the slave trade achieved early success because it joined together moral concerns and self-interest. Many persons in the late eighteenth and early nineteenth centuries were prepared to accept the end of the slave trade while opposing the end of slavery itself. Even slaveholders were angered by the living conditions endured by slaves on crowded, disease-infested slave ships. Some masters, in fact, attempted to justify their ownership of slaves by claiming that the conditions on their plantations were more humane than the conditions on slave-trading ships or in allegedly primitive Africa.

Some slaveholders supported the abolition of the slave trade because they realized that limiting the supply of new slaves from Africa would increase the value of the existing slave population. Finally, many persons believed that it was wrong for slave traders to deny liberty to freeborn Africans, but that it was not wrong for slave masters to exercise control over persons who were born into the status of slavery. Indeed, supporters of slavery argued that the well-being of society required masters to exercise control over persons who had no preparation for freedom and might be a threat to society if emancipated.

The campaign to eradicate slavery itself was more difficult and was accompanied by significant political upheavals and, in the case of Haiti and the United States, revolution and warfare. British reformers such as William Wilberforce, Thomas Clarkson, and Granville Sharp made, perhaps, the most significant contributions to the organization of a worldwide antislavery movement. In 1823, British activists formed the London Antislavery Committee, soon to be renamed the British and Foreign Antislavery Society. The society spearheaded a successful campaign to abolish slavery in the British Empire and, eventually, worldwide. It remained in existence in the 1990's. Known by the name Antislavery International, the society had the distinction of being the world's oldest human rights organization. Antislavery reformers were also active in the United States. From the 1830's through the 1860's, abolitionists such as William Lloyd Garrison, Wendell Phillips, and Frederick Douglass sought to arouse the moral anger of Americans against slavery. More effective, however, were politicians such as Abraham Lincoln, Charles Sumner, and Salmon P. Chase, whose antislavery message was a mixture of idealism, self-interest, and expedience.

**Emancipation of Slaves**

Beginning in the late eighteenth century and accelerating through the nineteenth century, slavery was abolished throughout the Western Hemisphere. This was followed in the late nineteenth and twentieth centuries by the legal abolition of slavery in Africa and Asia.

In evaluating the success of abolition in any society, it is necessary to distinguish between legal and de facto emancipation. Changing the legal status of a slave to that of a free person is not the same thing as freeing the slave from the control of a master. Legal emancipation often has little impact on persons held as slaves if governments fail to enforce the abolition of slavery. For example, Britain in the nineteenth century outlawed slavery in its colonies in India, the Gold Coast, Kenya, and Zanzibar. Yet, fear-

## Dates of Legal Emancipation in the United States

| State | Year | State | Year |
|---|---|---|---|
| Alabama | 1863-1865 | Missouri | 1865 |
| Arkansas | 1863-1865 | New Hampshire | 1783 |
| California | 1850 | New Jersey | 1804 |
| Connecticut | 1784 | New York | 1799 |
| Delaware | 1865 | North Carolina | 1863-1865 |
| Florida | 1863-1865 | Ohio | 1787 |
| Georgia | 1863-1865 | Oklahoma | 1866 |
| Illinois | 1787 | Oregon | 1846 |
| Indiana | 1787 | Pennsylvania | 1780 |
| Iowa | 1820 | Rhode Island | 1784 |
| Kansas | 1861 | South Carolina | 1863-1865 |
| Kentucky | 1865 | Tennessee | 1865 |
| Louisiana | 1864 | Texas | 1863-1865 |
| Maine | 1783 | Vermont | 1777 |
| Maryland | 1864 | Virginia | 1863-1865 |
| Massachusetts | 1783 | Washington, D.C. | 1862 |
| Michigan | 1787 | West Virginia | 1863 |
| Minnesota | 1858 | Western Territories | 1862 |
| Mississippi | 1863-1865 | Wisconson | 1787 |

ing a disruption of economic production in these colonies, the British government simply abstained from enforcing its own abolition laws until pressure from reformers put an end to slavery. A similar situation existed in Mauritania, where slavery was prohibited by law three separate times, in 1905, 1960, and 1980, yet the government of Mauritania enacted no penalties against masters who kept slaves in violation of the emancipation law, and the government waged no campaign to inform the slaves of their freedom. As a result, journalists and investigators for the International Labor Organisation found slavery still flourishing in Mauritania in the 1990's.

Even in societies that vigorously enforced their acts of abolition, legal emancipation was usually followed by a period of transition in which former slaves were held in a state resembling that of slavery. The Abolition of Slavery Act of 1833, which outlawed slavery in most colonies of the British Empire, provided that slaves would serve as apprentices to their former masters for a period of four to six years. In the American South after the Civil War, former slaves were subject for a time to black codes that greatly reduced the freedom of movement of African Americans and required them to work on the plantations of former slave masters. After the Civil Rights Act of 1866 and the Fourteenth Amendment outlawed such practices, southerners created the sharecropping and crop-lien systems, which allowed planters to control the labor of many African Americans through a form of debt bondage.

*Harold D. Tallant*

**Further Reading**

*Slavery and the Making of America* (New York: Oxford University Press, 2005) by James Oliver Horton and Lois E. Horton provides a detailed examination of American slavery. *The Antislavery Debate: Capitalism and Abolitionism as a Problem in Historical Interpretation* (Berkeley: University of California Press, 1992), edited by Thomas Bender, is a collection of essays that debate the question of whether the rise of industrial capitalism caused the emergence of the antislavery movement. David Brion Davis's *The Problem of Slavery in the Age of Revolution, 1770-1823* (Ithaca, N.Y.: Cornell University Press, 1975) is a Pulitzer Prize-winning study of the intellectual background of the rise of the antislavery movement. Davis's *Slavery and Human Progress* (New York: Oxford University Press, 1984) is an excellent introduction to many of the ethical issues regarding slavery organized around a discussion of changing concepts of progress. Moses I. Finley's *Ancient Slavery and Modern Ideology* (New York: Viking Press, 1980) is a study of the moral, intellectual, and social foundations of slavery by the leading expert on ancient slavery. Eric Foner's *Nothing But Free-*

*dom: Emancipation and Its Legacy* (Baton Rouge: Louisiana State University Press, 1983) is a brief but thought-provoking study of the problems associated with emancipation in several countries. Orlando Patterson's *Slavery and Social Death: A Comparative Study* (Cambridge, Mass.: Harvard University Press, 1982), the most important study of slavery in its various forms, is based on a massive survey of slave societies on all continents from the beginning of history. William D. Phillips's *Slavery from Roman Times to the Early Transatlantic Trade* (Minneapolis: University of Minnesota Press, 1985) is a highly readable historical survey of the transition from ancient slavery to modern slavery.

**See also** Abolition; Abolitionist movement and women; Agriculture; *Amistad* slave revolt; Antislavery laws of 1777 and 1807; Baptist Church; Civil War; *Clotilde* capture; Confiscation Acts of 1861 and 1862; Demographic trends; Emancipation Proclamation; Free blacks; *Groves v. Slaughter*; National Coalition of Blacks for Reparations in America; Native Americans and African Americans; New York City slave revolt; Northwest Ordinance; *Roots*; *Scott v. Sandford*; Segregation; Slavery and families; Slavery and race relations; Slavery and women; Slavery in Massachusetts; Slavery in Virginia; Stono Rebellion; Three-fifths compromise; Underground Railroad

# Slavery and families

*Despite immense obstacles, African American slaves forged strong family bonds and created communities that valued marriage, nurtured children, cared for the aged, and preserved commitment to nuclear family groups.*

Although conditions under slavery varied widely and included many humane and even loving master-slave relationships, the laws governing slavery made it impossible for slaves to enjoy secure family lives. Not only could slaveholders sell any of their slaves, regardless of family ties, but slaves could not legally marry. Moreover, any child born to a slave woman was legally a slave, even if the father was a free black or a white man. None of these deterrents to stable family life, however, kept slaves from valuing and trying to maintain family groups and kinship ties, and slaves were able, even in the face of immense obstacles, to shape a family-oriented culture that provided them emotional support, self-esteem, and a measure of autonomy from the white culture that controlled so much of their lives.

**Marriage**

Although slave marriage vows were not legally binding, slaves themselves—and most masters—recognized the commitments of those who claimed to be married. Most owners encouraged marriages: Marriage was regarded as the foundation of moral society; Moreover, family ties and responsibilities increased owners' hold on their slaves, since masters could determine whether to allow relationships to continue and could dictate the conditions under which they survived. Being able to separate spouses or family members was a powerful threat that slave owners held over their workers.

Some slaveholders arranged marriages, but most allowed their slaves to choose their own mates. Although most owners preferred that their slaves select spouses from their own holdings, they usually allowed marriages with slaves owned by others. Despite their positions of authority, owners probably worried about the ill effects of having workers discontented by thwarted love. Hence, the majority of slave marriages were marriages of love, not arrangement.

Most slaves marked their commitment by a ceremony of some sort, ranging from elaborate weddings that imitated those of whites (and were sometimes even arranged and attended by white families) to simply moving in together. Often weddings were accompanied by the folk custom of "jumping the broomstick" to see who would have the most authority in the relationship.

In wedding ceremonies, couples usually refrained from pledging to be together "till death do us part," as there was little assurance that they would have the final say in the matter. "What God has brought together, let no man put asunder" was not a realistic pronouncement at slave weddings, since owners could legally sunder couples at any time. Instead, some slaves vowed to stay married "till death or distance do us part." If slave couples were separated by the sale of one spouse, more often than not the sale was considered, realistically, tantamount to the spouse's death. Remarriage was the norm after such breakups, and children from former unions were assimilated into the new households. Nevertheless, a majority of slave marriages lasted for many years.

Most married slaves lived in single-family cabins. If husbands or wives were lucky (and, usually, light-skinned), they were perhaps assigned to work in the "big house" of the master or engage in a special craft, such as blacksmithing or carpentry. But most slaves, male and female, were field hands. Field workers usually spent from dawn to dusk, six days a week, plowing, planting, weeding, or harvesting. Some owners gave their hands Saturday afternoons off to take care of their own chores—washing clothes, hunting, making and mending clothes, making candles, repairing their cabins, or tending their own gardens. Even then, slave couples had little time to spend together. Slaves who had married "abroad"—that is, to someone not owned by the same master— might or might not have been allowed to spend weekday evenings with their spouses.

*Slave family on a southern plantation.* (Library of Congress)

## Children and Childhood

On average, slave women had around seven children. Pregnant women were often not given adequate prenatal care. Infant mortality among African Americans was greater than among whites, probably because of the lack of care and poor diets during pregnancy and early childhood. Pregnant women were typically expected to perform their normal duties to within a month of giving birth and to be back on the job a few weeks following birth. Generally, nursing mothers could leave their work long enough to feed their infants only three or four times a day, and they were expected to wean their babies at what for the time was an early age. Slave women too elderly to do field work often tended infants and young children, while older children were frequently left unsupervised.

Most slave children were allowed to have real childhoods of carefree play. They did not, however, get to spend a great deal of time with their parents, who would be away from them from dawn to dusk. Youngsters were not usually expected to work until they were eight to twelve years old, and then they were gradually assimilated into the workforce. They would, over several years, begin to be assigned duties. At first they performed light chores and spent fewer hours working than adults, but in the course of adolescence they came to take on the full workload of adults. Many children did not realize their condition of bondage until they were close to working age. Their realization sometimes came when their white playmates would go off to school without them or when the masters' children began to assume authority over them.

## Parents and Parenting

Slaves, like nineteenth century Americans in general, considered fathers to be the head of the household. Even though parents could be subjected to various humiliations at the hand of their owners and had to be deferential in public, African American families tried to preserve the dignity of parents, especially fathers, within the household. Since white owners provided slave families with food staples, clothing, and housing, many of the roles traditionally assigned to fathers were preempted by slave masters. Moreover, white masters and mistresses could discipline any slave; parents were often helpless in protecting themselves and their families from verbal and physical abuse. Some female slaves had to submit to being raped by their white masters or were even forced to live the lives of concubines. Husbands, parents, and siblings were helpless to defend their loved ones from this fate. Children were often shielded from knowledge of the worst abuses of slavery, such as rapes or whippings, but they ultimately learned of the full implications of bondage. Many slave narratives describe how youngsters were traumatized when they first witnessed a lashing or other event that made them fully cognizant of their own condition.

Although slave parents tried to shield their children from the effects of slavery, they also had to teach their children survival skills. Harsh punishments were meted out to children who violated racial codes of conduct. Children had to learn early on to be deferential in the presence of whites and to submit to the authority of even young white children. They also had to learn to protect the community in the slave quarters. Discretion and not repeating conversations they heard were of great importance. Parents whose children violated survival codes of conduct usually responded with severe punishments, including slaps, shakings, and hard spankings, for children who did not learn these survival behaviors endangered themselves, their families, and communities.

Despite the many ways slavery undermined traditional parental roles, African American parents remained providers for their families. There was enough food on most plantations, but it was not plentiful and lacked variety. Diets often lacked protein unless they were supplemented by game. Male slaves were sometimes allowed to supplement their families' food allotments by hunting, fishing, and trapping. Parents of both sexes sometimes tended personal gardens. Mothers cooked, cleaned, and sewed. Although most masters provided male slaves with blankets and clothes, women were usually given cloth and expected to make their own dresses and children's clothes. Generally, boys as well as girls wore baggy, dresslike garments until they reached the age of ten or twelve. When young boys reached this age, they were given their own chores to do and also graduated into wearing pants. With these changes, they came of age.

Parents' roles in family life revolved around the satisfaction of families' daily needs. Slave narratives reveal strong bonds of love between parents and children, especially between children and mothers. Loving home lives offered slaves a psychological buffer that offset the damages of slavery and provided a sanctuary where they could be themselves away from the scrutiny of whites. Moreover, the culture that flourished in the slave quarters fostered strong family and community values and practices that differed significantly from those of white Americans.

### African Heritage

By the mid-nineteenth century, African Americans were usually several generations removed from their African heritage, yet some Africanisms remained central to their lives. Their music retained African rhythms; their games were often adaptations of African games. Many slaves preferred folk remedies to the medicines prescribed by white practitioners.

Although most slaves became Christians, their Christianity was generally of a more exuberant kind than that of whites, and it often existed side by side with beliefs in conjuring and voodoo. Moreover, the values of the slave community did not always mirror those of the white culture that shaped so much of their lives. For example, in an era when white America demanded chastity of unmarried women, African American communities often followed the practice of many African tribes, accepting as normal some premarital sexual experimentation while expecting fidelity after marriage. Marriage to blood cousins was also usually taboo in African American communities, although it was fairly common in white society. Extended kinship networks were maintained, and the elderly were valued as they had been in Africa.

### Attitudes and Assumptions

Common assumptions about the family life of African Americans have been rooted in misperceptions that arose both during the era of slavery and in modern times. In the nineteenth century, slavery apologists and antislavery proponents alike often maintained that African Americans did not possess the same capacity for familial love as did whites, were by nature promiscuous, and were too childlike to take seriously the responsibilities of family life. These assumptions were held despite massive evidence to the contrary. Of course, such beliefs made it easier to condone slavery, especially the practice of selling individuals away from their families.

Slave owners, however, often acknowledged in practice their slaves' family feelings. As the law allowed owners to sell slaves without regard to family and kinship ties, many did so, but others took pains to keep families together—at least until economic factors outweighed their good intentions. Most owners sold slaves, even removing them from their families, if they got into serious financial trouble. In such cases, owners often arranged family breakups while parents or spouses were away to avoid emotional scenes as much as possible. Such precautions are evidence of their anticipation of heartfelt responses to their actions; records by persons who witnessed children being sold away from their parents, spouses being separated from each other, and brothers being taken away from their sisters bear testimony to the heartbreak such separations caused.

In the mid-twentieth century it was commonly believed that slavery had fostered a matriarchal structure in many modern black families, with mothers providing economic stability and fathers either emasculated or absent. By the 1970's, however, studies refuted assumptions that modern manifestations of African American family life or current dysfunctions in black families could be accounted for by slavery. Studies of the family life of slaves showed that they valued nuclear families and kinship ties. Most slave families were two-parent families, and in the years following emancipation thousands of African Americans tried desperately to reunite families forcibly separated during slavery, creating new communities with strong kinship and friendship ties that provided support networks. Such evidence suggests that the matriarchal family structures and dysfunctions found in some twentieth-century African American families have more recent origins than slavery.

## Genealogy

Family trees show that slaves often used naming patterns that emphasized kinship ties, especially in the nineteenth century. In the first two centuries of slavery in America, masters commonly assigned names to slaves they purchased and to children born as their property. Slaves, however, resisted this coopting of their identity. Many had private names used only in the slave quarters, and when allowed to name their children, slaves often followed African customs, naming offspring after events or seasons. Males were commonly named after their fathers, grandfathers, or other family members but almost never after a master, although sometimes female slaves might be given the name of a particularly favored mistress. Genealogy also reveals many slave families with racially mixed lineages. Children of slave women raped by white men were usually assimilated into their mothers' homes and raised without any acknowledgment of kinship from their white fathers.

African Americans who try to trace their family roots often have a difficult time finding records before 1870, the first year the United States census named most African Americans, since slaves were listed as numbers only. Plantation records sometimes list births, deaths, and sales; letters and diaries might shed light on family histories. Nonetheless, tracing family lines during slavery is quite difficult; tracing lineages back to African origins is usually impossible. In this respect, slavery has had an ongoing effect on African Americans' sense of family.

*Grace McEntee*

### Further Reading

Blassingame, John W. *The Slave Community: Plantation Life in the Antebellum South.* Rev. ed. New York: Oxford University Press, 1979. Classic work by the first African American to write a major study of slavery and the first to base his study mostly on accounts of former slaves.

Finkelman, Paul, ed. *Women and the Family in a Slave Society.* New York: Garland, 1989. Essays mostly published in the 1970's and 1980's that cover an array of topics dealing with marriage, family, and sexuality in southern slave cultures.

Genovese, Eugene D. *Roll, Jordan, Roll: The World the Slaves Made.* New York: Vintage, 1974. Seminal, thoroughly documented work covering all aspects of slave society and a classic that challenged and changed previous assumptions about slave culture.

Gutman, Herbert G. *The Black Family in Slavery and Freedom, 1750-1925.* New York: Vintage Books, 1976. Landmark book written to refute Daniel Patrick Moynihan's *The Negro Family in America*, which claimed that a "pathology" brought on by centuries of slavery explained "the deterioration of the Negro family" in the United States.

Kolchin, Peter. *American Slavery, 1619-1877.* New York: Hill & Wang, 1993. Traces the evolution of slavery in America and puts it in historic context with other forms of servitude.

Redford, Dorothy Spruill, with Michael D'Orso. *Somerset Homecoming: Recovering a Lost Heritage.* New York: Doubleday, 1988. First-person account of Redford's success in tracing her family's roots and what she discovered about slave families in the process.

**See also** Slave codes; Slavery; Slavery and race relations; Slavery and the justice system; Slavery and women; Slavery in Massachusetts; Slavery in Virginia

# Slavery and race relations

*The enslavement of people of African ancestry was closely connected to the development of both racial prejudice and racial inequality in the United States. The heritage of slavery prevented African Americans from entering into the mainstream of American life even after slavery was abolished. Debates over responsibility for slavery and the legacy of slavery have complicated relations between African Americans and whites.*

One of the theoretical points debated by historians is whether Europeans and Euro-Americans imposed slavery on people from Africa because they viewed Africans as inferior or whether racism came into existence as a justification for slavery. Some historians have suggested that as Europeans expanded their control over much of the world, they came into contact with many who were unlike themselves in appearance and in culture. Ethnocentrism, the tendency to see one's own group as the standard by which all others are to be judged, may have led Europeans to see the people of Asia and Africa as inferior to themselves. Thus, people from China, as well as people from Africa, were brought to the Americas as forced labor at various times.

Historians such as George Frederickson, however, have maintained that racism was a consequence rather than a cause of slavery. From this point of view, the growth of plantation economies in North and South America encouraged the importation of slave labor because these economies required large numbers of workers. Native Americans did not make good slaves because they were in their homeland and could easily escape.

Slave owners needed to justify holding other humans in bondage, according to this theory, so they argued that their slaves were childlike and needed the protection of their masters. Thus, the influential apologist for slavery Henry Hughes argued in his *Treatise on Sociology* (1854) that the simple slaves as well as the masters benefited from the arrangement.

To some extent, the relationship between slavery and racism is similar to the ancient question of whether the chicken or the egg came first. The European enslavement of Africans was probably encouraged by feelings of European superiority. Once slavery became established, though, it was necessary to justify it, and the American descendants of Europeans could comfort themselves with claims that their slaves were inferior beings.

Many of the stereotypes of African Americans developed during slavery continued to flourish well into the twentieth century. The racism of slavery outlived slavery itself; films, radio programs, and books before the Civil Rights era often portrayed black Americans as childlike, comic, servile, or dangerously unable to control themselves. The sociologist Stanford M. Lyman has observed that popular American films ranging from *Birth of a Nation* (1915) to *Gone with the Wind* (1939) drew on the racial images of slavery to portray "good" blacks as humorous, loyal, obedient family servants and "bad" blacks as rebellious and violent.

## Consequences of Master-Slave Relations

Economist Raymond S. Franklin has noted that one of the debates regarding consequences of master-slave relations concerns whether slaves and their descendants were in some way damaged by being owned and controlled. A number of historians, including Kenneth Stampp, Stanley Elkins, and William Styron, have held that being slaves left psychological scars on the slaves and damaged social institutions that slaves passed on to free black Americans. Along these lines, in 1966, Daniel Patrick Moynihan published a controversial report on the black family, in which he maintained that the experience of slavery contributed to the weakness of the black family. More recently, Harvard sociologist Orlando Patterson has claimed that the slave status undermined the roles of husband and father for black men and reinforced the central role of women in families.

Franklin observes that some historians and social thinkers have argued that the master-slave relationship actually strengthened many black social institutions by promoting the need to resist slavery. Historian Herbert Gutman, for example, offered evidence that slavery had actually strengthened black families. The historian Eric Foner has traced the origins of the black church, a central institution in African American history, to the religious activities of slaves who organized themselves into churches after emancipation.

## Geographical Consequences of Slavery

Slaves were heavily concentrated in the southern part of the United States. Even after the end of slavery, African Americans continued to be a southern population. In 1860, on the eve of the Civil War, 94 percent of the people of African ancestry in the United States were concentrated in the slave-owning states of the South. This percentage did decline notably in the years following World War I, and the descendants of slaves did move to other regions over the course of the twentieth century. Nevertheless, at the end of the century, the geographical legacy of slavery was still

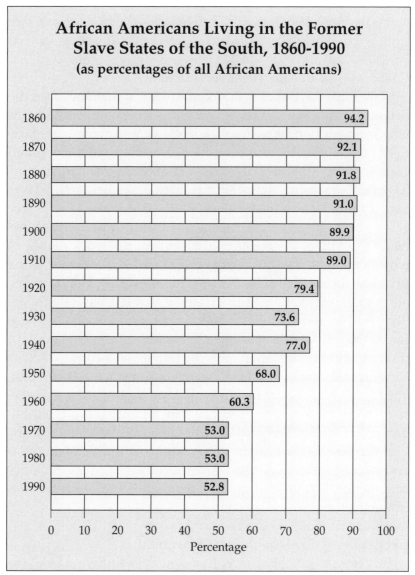

**African Americans Living in the Former Slave States of the South, 1860-1990**

(as percentages of all African Americans)

| Year | Percentage |
|------|-----------|
| 1860 | 94.2 |
| 1870 | 92.1 |
| 1880 | 91.8 |
| 1890 | 91.0 |
| 1900 | 89.9 |
| 1910 | 89.0 |
| 1920 | 79.4 |
| 1930 | 73.6 |
| 1940 | 77.0 |
| 1950 | 68.0 |
| 1960 | 60.3 |
| 1970 | 53.0 |
| 1980 | 53.0 |
| 1990 | 52.8 |

Percentage

*Source:* U.S. Census of Population and Housing, 1860-1990.

evident; the 1990 U.S. census showed a majority of the American black population residing in the South.

In many areas of the South, working as sharecroppers or low-paid wage laborers during the years following slavery, African Americans continued to do much the same sort of agricultural labor that they had performed as slaves. In order to maintain white domination, in regions with large black populations, southern whites sought to replace slavery with segregation, which placed African Americans in a separate and disadvantaged position. This kept African Americans dependent on whites and subservient to whites in a manner that was similar in many ways to the old master-slave relationship. These patterns may have even survived the years following the Civil Rights movement. As recently as the 1990's, sociologist Ruth Kornfield, looking at a rural community in Tennessee, found that patron-client relationships between white employers and black employees continued to mirror master-slave relationships.

The continuing concentration of African Americans in the South was one of the reasons that early actions of the Civil Rights movement concentrated primarily on this region. Despite the stubborn survival of many old patterns of racial inequality in this region, numbers have given African Americans in this part of the country some measure of power. In 1993, two-thirds of the black-elected officials in the United States were from the southern states. Furthermore, the major southern cities of Atlanta, Georgia; New Orleans, Louisiana; Birmingham, Alabama; and Richmond, Virginia, all had black mayors.

### The Legacy of Slavery and Urbanization

Although the South did not cease to be home to the largest proportion of African Americans, the group did shift from being heavily rural to being heavily urban. Over the course of the twentieth century, the agricultural jobs that black Americans continued to perform after slavery became increasingly unavailable as farms mechanized. In the years following World War II, African Americans moved to cities. They tended to settle in central urban areas because the U.S. government built housing projects reserved for the poor in these urban areas, and the heritage of slavery and of the system of segregation that had emerged from slavery left African Americans disproportionately poor. During the same years, whites were moving from cities to suburbs. Racism, an ideology with roots in America's centuries of slavery, contributed to the unwillingness of homeowners, real estate companies, and mortgage lenders to allow African Americans to move into homes in the suburbs.

As a result of the movement of whites to suburbs and African Americans to cities, the two groups came to live in separate places. Although schools and other public facilities ceased to be legally segregated after the 1960's, many urban neighborhoods and schools contained virtually no whites. This not only limited contact between members of the different races, but it also separated African Americans from the jobs and opportunities that became much more abundant in the suburbs. Further, even after it became easier for middle-class African Americans to move into suburban neighborhoods, the poorest were left isolated in inner cities.

### Questions of Responsibility

Professor and social commentator Shelby Steele has observed that the question of innocence is central to race relations in the United States. Many African Americans maintain that they are innocent victims of the aftermath of slavery. The problem of race relations, from this perspective, is one of achieving equality of condition for people who suffer disadvantages as a group through no fault of their own.

White Americans also frequently put forward claims of innocence. They maintain that white people alive at the end of the twentieth century, well more than a century after the end of slavery, cannot be held responsible for the legacy of slavery. Therefore, programs such as affirmative action that aim at increasing African Americans' share of positions in employment and education seek to benefit the descendants of slaves at the expense of whites who are innocent of responsibility for slavery. In discussing issues of historical responsibility, whites will often become defensive, and any assertions of black disadvantage will sometimes be seen by whites as moral accusations.

### Reparations

The issue of reparations is one of the most controversial consequences of the thorny ethical issue of historical responsibility. The term "reparations" refers to compensation paid by one nation or group of people to another for damages or losses. The United States government, for example, has made some payments to

Japanese Americans for violating their civil rights by imprisoning them during World War II.

Advocates of reparation payments for African Americans, such as the scholar Manning Marable, have argued that slavery was a massive denial of civil rights to this group. These advocates point out that slave labor built up much of the nation's wealth, allowing it to industrialize and therefore making it possible for the United States to achieve its current level of development. They point out that the descendants of slaves continue to suffer damages from slavery because African Americans have lower incomes, on average, than other Americans and tend to hold much less of the country's wealth.

Opponents of reparations maintain that while slavery is a historical source of contemporary disadvantages of African Americans, reparations would attempt to right a past injustice by penalizing present-day whites. Further, if reparations were paid to all African Americans, some rich African Americans would be receiving tax money taken from middle-class or even poor whites. Finally, opponents of reparations suggest that payments of this sort would be enormously unpopular politically and might increase racial hatred and conflict.

*Carl L. Bankston III*

**Further Reading**

George M. Frederickson's *White Supremacy: A Comparative Study in American and South African History* (New York: Oxford University Press, 1981) is a classic work on the development of racism and racial exploitation. The second chapter of Raymond S. Franklin's *Shadows of Race and Class* (Minneapolis: University of Minnesota Press, 1991) gives an excellent summary of major debates regarding the legacy of slavery. Ira Berlin's *Many Thousands Gone: The First Two Centuries of Slavery in North America* (Cambridge, Mass.: Belknap Press, 1998) is a comprehensive study of the history of American slavery and of how slavery shaped racial identities. Edward Ball considers the impact of slavery both on his own family of former slave owners and on the descendants of his family's slaves in *Slaves in the Family* (New York: Farrar, Straus & Giroux, 1998). The last work looks not only at the lingering resentment and suspicion toward local whites of the descendants of the slaves but also at the feelings of ill-defined guilt and defensiveness among the descendants of the slave owners. Clarence J. Munford gives arguments for the payment of reparations for slavery to African Americans in *Race and Reparations: A Black Perspective for the Twenty-first Century* (Trenton, N.J.: Africa World Press, 1996). On the other hand, Dinesh D'Souza's highly controversial book *The End of Racism: Principles for a Multiracial Society* (New York: Free Press, 1995) claims that whites bear no responsibility at all for contemporary racial inequality. D'Souza also denies that the history of slavery gives African Americans any moral claims as a group.

**See also** Abolition; Great Migration; Jim Crow laws; Moynihan Report; National Coalition of Blacks for Reparations in America; *Roots*; Slavery; Slavery and families; Slavery and the justice system; Slavery and women; Slavery in Massachusetts; Slavery in Virginia; Stereotypes; Stono Rebellion

# Slavery and the justice system

*Slavery defined the legal treatment of African Americans for two and one-half centuries, and the crusade against slavery gave rise to modern concepts of citizenship and civil rights.*

The first African laborers in the English colonies of North America arrived in Virginia in 1619. By the 1770's, slaves made up one-fifth of the population of the English colonies. At this time, slave labor was used in every colony, including those in the North. Only in the South, however, did slavery dominate economic life. Slaves were used primarily to grow staple crops such as tobacco and rice for exportation to Europe and the Caribbean.

### Slavery and the Territories

As Americans moved westward, the issue of whether slavery should expand into the new territories became increasingly important. Americans realized that new western states would determine the balance of political power between North and South. Congress initially divided the new territories between North and South. In the Northwest Ordinance (1787), Congress banned slavery in the lands north of the Ohio River while implicitly accepting slavery south of the Ohio. In regard to the Louisiana Purchase, the Missouri Compromise of 1820 banned slavery north of the line at 36° north latitude while allowing slavery to exist south of the line.

The Missouri Compromise resolved the issue of slavery in the territories until the Mexican War of 1846-1848 added new western lands to the United States. Subsequently, four positions emerged regarding the issue. Many northerners favored the Wilmot Proviso, a proposal to ban slavery in the territories. Other Americans favored popular sovereignty, which would allow the people of the territories to decide the issue for themselves. Some Americans favored extending the Missouri Compromise line to the Pacific coast. Many southerners believed the federal government should protect slavery in the territories.

In the 1850's, the popular sovereignty approach gained ascendancy. The Compromise of 1850 applied popular sovereignty to California, New Mexico, and Utah. The Kansas-Nebraska Act (1854) repealed the old Missouri Compromise boundary and enacted popular sovereignty for the Louisiana Purchase. The Kansas-Nebraska Act created such great controversy that the existing political alignment was shattered. Opponents of the act created a new antislavery political party, the Republican Party, while supporters of the act reconstructed the Democratic Party as a proslavery party.

Disagreements regarding slavery-related issues and sectional competition for political power led ultimately to the outbreak of the Civil War in 1861. During the war, northern military officials increasingly believed that freeing the South's slaves would severely injure the Confederacy. President Abraham Lincoln issued the Emancipation Proclamation in 1863, proclaiming that the Union army would henceforth liberate the Confederacy's slaves. In 1865, the Thirteenth Amendment to the U.S. Constitution freed all remaining slaves belonging to American citizens.

## Slavery and the U.S. Constitution

Slavery significantly influenced the writing of the U.S. Constitution. The Constitutional Convention of 1787 nearly broke up because of disagreements regarding sectional issues. Ultimately the sectional impasse was resolved with the Compromise of 1787. Direct taxes and representation in the House of Representatives were to be apportioned according to the three-fifths rule: All free people and three-fifths of the slaves were to be counted in determining a state's tax burden and congressional representation. Congress could prohibit the importation of slaves into the United States after the lapse of twenty years. States were prohibited from freeing fugitive slaves, and slaveholders were given the right to cross state boundaries to recapture fugitives. Congress was prevented from taxing exports so that slavery would not be injured by excessive taxes on the products of slave labor. Finally, to ensure that the compromise would not be abrogated, the clauses regarding the international slave trade and the three-fifths rule were declared by the Constitution to be unamendable.

As the Civil War approached, Americans debated the significance of these actions. What was the relationship between the U.S. Constitution and slavery? Before 1860, most Americans believed that the Constitution did not establish a federal right to own slaves. Slavery was thought to exist as a result of state laws, and the federal government was thought to have few constitutional powers regarding slavery. Northerners and southerners disagreed regarding the practical application of this idea. Southerners believed the federal government was increasingly intruding into matters related to slavery. They called for an end to federal interference with slavery. Northerners argued that the federal government had been indirectly providing protection to slavery for years. They called for the withdrawal of this protection.

In the 1840's and 1850's, militants on both sides developed new constitutional theories regarding slavery. Some southerners claimed that there was a federal right to own slaves, established in the fugitive slave clause and the privileges and immunities clause of the U.S. Constitution. The federal government, they said, must protect the right of citizens to own slaves in the territories. Some southern extremists argued that the federal right to own slaves was so comprehensive that even northern states could not outlaw slavery within their own boundaries. Ironically, the branch of the abolitionist movement led by William Lloyd Garrison agreed with this argument, claiming that the Constitution protected slavery and arguing that northern states should abandon this corrupt document by withdrawing from the Union.

Another branch of the abolitionist movement, led by Gerrit Smith and William Goodell, argued to the contrary that the Constitution was best read as an antislavery document. They claimed that citizenship was based on residence in the United States and that slaves therefore were citizens. The privileges and immunities clause of the Constitution, they claimed, prevented both the states and the federal government from giving unequal treatment to citizens. The due process clause of the Fifth Amendment prevented citizens from losing their liberty without due process of law. Slavery violated these principles, and judges therefore ought to declare slavery unconstitutional. While this interpretation of the Constitution seemed extreme and utopian at the time, after the Civil War, the abolitionists' constitutional ideas were incorporated into the Fourteenth Amendment.

## Fugitive Slave Laws

One of the most significant controversies regarding slavery involved fugitive slave laws. In 1793, Congress adopted legislation to enforce the fugitive slave clause of the U.S. Constitution. The Fugitive Slave Act of 1793 allowed slaveholders to obtain warrants from either state or federal courts for the rendition of fugitive slaves. In the 1820's and 1830's, several states passed personal liberty laws to prevent state officials from assisting in the recapture process. In *Prigg v. Pennsylvania* (1842), the U.S. Supreme Court upheld the constitutionality of personal liberty laws by ruling that the enforcement of fugitive slave laws rested entirely in the hands of the federal government.

Without the assistance of state officials, slaveholders found that it was difficult to recapture their slaves. Southerners clamored for federal assistance. Congress responded by passing a new

Fugitive Slave Act as a part of the Compromise of 1850. A new group of federal officials was created for the sole purpose of assisting slaveholders recapture slaves. State officials were forbidden to resist the rendition of fugitives. Even ordinary citizens could be compelled to serve in posses for the purpose of capturing fugitives. To prevent black people who were seized as fugitives from challenging their seizure, their legal rights, including the right of *habeas corpus*, were abolished.

The Fugitive Slave Act of 1850 was met with strong opposition in the North. Hundreds of fugitives, and even some free blacks, migrated to Canada to avoid seizure under the new law. Many northern communities formed vigilance committees to assist fugitives, and in a few cases northern mobs tried to rescue fugitives from the hands of government officials.

One rescue in 1854 led to a conflict between Wisconsin and the federal government. This case is notable because Wisconsin, a northern state, used states' rights arguments to challenge federal authority, a ploy normally used by southerners to defend slavery. Sherman M. Booth, an abolitionist, was arrested by federal marshals for participating in the rescue of a fugitive slave. The Wisconsin State Supreme Court twice issued writs of *habeas corpus* to free Booth from federal imprisonment and declared the federal Fugitive Slave Act to be unconstitutional. The U.S. Supreme Court in *Abelman v. Booth* (1859) reasserted the primacy of federal over state law and the right of the federal government to enforce its own laws through its own courts. The Wisconsin court accepted this decision, now believing that it did not help the antislavery cause to promote the idea of states' rights and nullification of federal law.

### Legal Treatment of Slaves

African laborers occupied an ambiguous status in the American colonies before 1660 because English law did not recognize the status of slavery. Some Africans were held as slaves; others were held as indentured servants, persons whose term of labor expired after several years. Indentured servants enjoyed certain additional legal protections since, unlike slaves, their physical bodies were not owned by their masters. After 1660, Virginia and

*The value of slaves as laborers made execution and imprisonment uneconomic punishments for wrongdoing, thereby leaving corporal punishments—such as floggings—common.* (Library of Congress)

Maryland constructed elaborate slave codes to establish the legal status of slavery. For the next two centuries, the vast majority of African Americans were slaves.

In making and enforcing slave codes, Americans recognized slaves as both people and property. As property, slaves generally had few legal rights as independent beings. Slaves could not own property, enter into contracts, sue or be sued, or marry legally. Slaves had no freedom of movement. Masters could sell their slaves without restriction, and there was no legal protection for slave families against forced separation through sale. The status of slave children was inherited from their mothers, a departure from the traditional common-law doctrine that children inherited the status of their fathers.

In some ways, the masters' property rights in slaves were limited by compelling public interest. Most southern states made it difficult for masters to free their slaves on the theory that free blacks were a nuisance to society. Most southern states also tried to prevent slaves from becoming a threat to society. State laws often required slaves to carry passes when traveling away from their masters' homes. Laws in several states prohibited slaves from living alone without the supervision of whites. In all but two states, it was illegal for anyone to teach slaves to read or write. Some states banned the use of alcohol and firearms by slaves; others outlawed trading and gambling by slaves. Although these laws were primarily a burden to the slave population, they also restricted the manner in which masters could manage and use their property.

Southern law codes occasionally recognized slaves as people as well as property. By the mid-nineteenth century, most states provided slaves with a minimal degree of protection against physical assaults by whites, although these laws were generally poorly enforced. All states outlawed the murder and harsh treatment of slaves. Although masters were occasionally put on trial for murder of their slaves, evidence suggests that most homicidal masters either received light sentences or were not punished. Laws protecting slaves against other forms of inhumane treatment (such as excessive beatings or starvation diets) were almost never enforced. In practice, masters could beat or starve their slaves with impunity. Battery of slaves by strangers was illegal and was often punished by southern courts. Rape of slaves by whites, however, was not illegal. Masters had the full legal right to rape their own slaves, although masters could charge other whites with criminal trespass for an act of rape without the master's permission.

Under the law, black people were assumed to be slaves unless they could prove otherwise, meaning that free blacks were forced always to carry legal documents certifying their freedom. Many actions, including the use of alcohol and firearms, were illegal for slaves but not for whites. Penalties for crimes were generally more severe for slaves than for whites. For slaves, capital crimes—those for which death was the penalty—included not only murder but also manslaughter, rape, arson, insurrection, and robbery. Even attempted murders, insurrections, and rapes were subject to the death penalty.

## Punishments

Despite the harshness of the law, actual executions of slaves were rare because even slave criminals were valuable property. State laws generally required governments to pay compensation to the masters of executed slaves. The fact that the labor of slaves was valuable meant that, in all states except Louisiana, imprisonment was rarely used as punishment for slave criminals. Instead, most penalties involved physical punishments such as whipping, branding, or ear-cropping, punishments which were rarely used against whites after the early nineteenth century.

While southern courts did not give black and white people equal treatment, the courts made some effort to be fair to slaves, probably because of the influence of wealthy slaveholders with an economic interest in the acquittal of their property. The proportion of slaves among those people accused of crime was about equal to the proportion of slaves in the population. Slaves appear to have been convicted at nearly the same rate as whites. Southern law codes also reflected the slaveholders' interests. Many states required that slaves have access to counsel and protected them against self-incrimination and double jeopardy. Slaves, however, could not testify in court against whites, meaning that it was nearly impossible to prosecute crimes against slaves when other slaves were the only available witnesses.

*Harold D. Tallant*

**Further Reading**

The most readable and comprehensive survey of slavery and the law is Harold M. Hyman and William M. Wiecek's *Equal Justice Under Law: Constitutional Development, 1835-1875* (New York: Harper & Row, 1982). Alan Watson's *Slave Law in the Americas* (Athens: University of Georgia Press, 1989) offers a succinct comparison of the law of slavery in several Western Hemisphere societies. Mark V. Tushnet's *The American Law of Slavery, 1810-1860: Considerations of Humanity and Interest* (Princeton, N.J.: Princeton University Press, 1981) discusses the tension within American law regarding the slaves' dual role as both property and people. The best survey of the legal treatment of slaves is Philip J. Schwarz's *Twice Condemned: Slaves and the Criminal Laws of Virginia, 1705-1865* (Baton Rouge: Louisiana State University Press, 1988).

**See also** Abolition; Emancipation Proclamation; Fugitive Slave Law of 1793; Fugitive Slave Law of 1850; Kansas-Nebraska Act; Missouri Compromise; Reconstruction; *Scott v. Sandford*; Slave codes; Slavery and families; Slavery and race relations; Slavery in Massachusetts; Slavery in Virginia; Stono Rebellion

# Slavery and women

*Although black and white women frequently found themselves at odds regarding slavery, women from both races transcended prevailing stereotypes and played an important role in the demise of this "peculiar institution."*

The first known African slaves to arrive in North America were brought to Jamestown, Virginia, in 1619. Initially, British colonists were reluctant to embrace slavery, choosing rather to use white indentured servants. As late as 1680, only about seven thousand black people could be found in all the colonies combined. In time, however, labor demands, as well as the profitability of tobacco and cotton, made slave labor an increasingly attractive economic investment for white landowners.

Not everyone, however, was happy with slavery. By the mid-eighteenth century, Pennsylvania's Quakers were denouncing slavery as immoral. By the nineteenth century, the sentiment to free the slave population was growing nationwide. The American Colonization Society was organized in 1817 with the aim of recolonizing freed slaves in Africa. Their efforts, however, were largely unsuccessful: Most freed slaves considered North America to be their home and were unwilling to go to Africa. Additionally, most masters were unwilling to free their slaves without financial compensation, and no adequate plan was ever formulated to that end.

In 1831, a Virginia slave named Nat Turner led an uprising that left some sixty white people dead. Fear of massive uprisings had been prevalent (although largely unsubstantiated) since the late eighteenth century, and Turner fulfilled the worst nightmare of slaveholders. Subsequently, many white people became more determined to control the South's slave population. To free the slaves would cost a fortune, and most white southerners feared reprisal from the black community. As a group, white women in the South were as determined as their male counterparts to keep African Americans legally subjugated.

It is important to note, however, that most southerners did not own slaves. In 1860, only about 25 percent of all southerners owned slaves. About one-half of this group owned five or fewer slaves. These figures were partially the result of the high cost of purchasing them; in the 1850's, field hands were usually sold for at least $1,500. Consequently, slave ownership served as both a gauge of personal wealth and as a social status symbol. The more slaves one possessed, the more wealth one commanded. Even those white southerners who did not own slaves had a vested interest in the South's upper class. Poorer white people could always look to the slaveholding gentry for inspiration to gain more wealth.

## Gender and Plantation Society

Throughout the early nineteenth century, American society, particularly in the South, was typically patriarchal. Most men and women lived their lives under the assumption that each gender had a distinctive "sphere." Men assumed roles of leadership and power, while women were expected to live according to the tenets of what scholars call the Cult of True Womanhood. As such, women were to be sexually chaste and pure. They were to be religiously pious, guarding society's morality by keeping their households in good order. Likewise, they were to be keepers of the home for their husbands. Finally, they were to be submissive to established authority structures.

These expectations bore especially heavy on southern women. Contrary to prevalent mythology, southern women rarely conformed to the "southern belle" stereotype, and the plantation did not shield them from a hard life. Since plantations emphasized large-scale agriculture, plantation women usually suffered from social and cultural isolation. In order to compensate for their loneliness, some wealthy women hosted extravagant social functions for which guests sometimes stayed for days. Despite their loneliness, however, plantation wives did not seek friendship from their female slaves.

In addition to rural isolation, southern women also had specific jobs to perform. Plantation wives usually supervised the slaves who worked in "the great house." Moreover, the nature of plantation agriculture demanded frequent business trips, and, in their husbands' absence, plantation wives were responsible for maintaining the entire plantation, including supervising field labor and managing the financial ledgers.

Middle-class and lower-class southern white women left few detailed accounts of their lives. Nevertheless, several things are clear. Most poor white women lived a much harder life than their plantation sisters. In addition to their family duties, such as cooking, cleaning, making clothes, and rearing children, most women worked in the fields with their husbands whenever possible. These women tended to be fiercely independent and generally refused to do certain menial tasks they deemed "servant work."

Life for slave women in the antebellum South was substantially different from life for white women. In slavery's earliest phases, black men outnumbered black women by an overwhelming margin. Sex ratios stabilized over time, however, and black women were expected to labor in the fields side by side with black men. Those who did not perform fieldwork had other chores. For example, if they were too old to perform manual labor or were specifically chosen for the task, some women supervised the young children of other slaves. In some cases, they might even watch their masters' children. Thus, unlike white women, many slave mothers were frequently denied the opportunity to rear their own children. Still others worked in the plantation home as a house servant. Such opportunities were a mixed blessing. On one hand, house servants had a higher status on the plantation than field hands. Some house servants, especially on large plantations, considered themselves to have a higher social status than poor white people. On the other hand, they generally labored under closer supervision than the other slaves, and the slightest offense could invite harsh discipline.

Most masters realized that they had an interest in promoting slave marriages, believing that married slaves were less likely to run away. The masters also valued female slaves for their ability to bear children. Slave children were likewise valuable both as part of the plantation's labor force and as a measure of control over their parents. Among slaves, it was understood that those who seemed loyal and docile were less likely to be sold, and few slaves would cause dissention on the plantation if they thought their children would be punished as a result of their actions.

Family life also added a measure of stability to the slave quarters, from the slaves' perspective. However bad plantation conditions might be, family members could always look to one another for solace. The family was one of the few places where slaves were free to be themselves, and mothers and fathers taught their children how to survive the rigors of plantation life.

Unfortunately, slave marriages had no official legal standing in white courts. Even so, both men and women sought companionship. Sometimes, men tried to marry women from neighboring plantations to avoid seeing their wives and children mistreated. The masters had the final say in such matters, however, and they generally encouraged male slaves to marry on the plantation; otherwise, determining who owned the resulting children might be problematic. Yet, it does appear that a female slave had some role in choosing who would become her husband.

Despite the benefits that marriage and family life afforded, slaves lived in constant fear. Women lived in a special kind of fear that is difficult to describe. In addition to the fear of seeing their husbands and children sold, female slaves had no protection from their masters' unwanted sexual advances. White men sometimes fathered children by their female slaves, thus creating tension between black and white women. As Mary Boykin Chesnut, a plantation mistress in South Carolina, wryly observed, "Any lady is ready to tell you who is the father of all the mulatto children in everybody's household but her own."

### Women and Abolition

As slavery became more ensconced in the social and economic fabric of early nineteenth century America, critics, many of whom were women, began calling for its demise. Among white women, Angelina and Sarah Grimké were particularly outspoken critics of "the peculiar institution." Reared in a slaveholding household in Charleston, South Carolina, the Grimké sisters came to abhor slavery in their early adulthood because of their belief that slavery was in moral opposition to God's purposes. Angelina published two forceful indictments against slavery entitled *An Appeal to the Christian Women of the South* (1836) and *An*

*Women were among the best-known leaders of the abolitionist movement. This fanciful painting depicts President Abraham Lincoln, the "Great Emancipator," meeting with Sojourner Truth, a tireless opponent of slavery.* (Library of Congress)

*Appeal to the Women of the Nominally Free States* (1837). Both sisters earned a reputation for their public lectures against slavery.

In addition to lecturing, some female abolitionists committed their sentiments to verse. Julia Ward Howe was an American poet who coedited *Commonwealth*, an abolitionist newspaper in Boston, with her husband, Samuel Gridley Howe. In 1861, she visited military camps near Washington, D.C., and received the inspiration for her most famous work, "The Battle Hymn of the Republic." It was an instant success, and Union forces soon whistled and sang the tune as they marched into battle. This song so pointedly expressed the abolitionists' righteous indignation against slavery that it was widely published in church hymnals.

Among the white women who championed abolition, however, Harriet Beecher Stowe is without peer. Her novel *Uncle Tom's Cabin* (1852) has been hailed by some as the most influential fictional work in American literary history. Stowe depicted slavery, at its worst, as a monstrous institution that would victimize even the best, most loyal slaves such as Uncle Tom by allowing them to fall into the clutches of sadistic ogres such as Simon Legree. She infuriated many southerners by implying that their form of Christianity had sinned in failing to respond to slavery's cruelty. Stowe also struck a chord with many northerners who had never considered the many negative aspects of slavery.

White women were not alone in the campaign against slavery. Several black women gained notoriety as abolitionists, particularly Harriet Tubman and Sojourner Truth. Tubman became famous as a "conductor" in the Underground Railroad, a system of individuals who helped fugitive slaves flee the South prior to the Civil War. Tubman herself had escaped from slavery in 1849, and she returned to the South nineteen times to help an estimated three hundred slaves, including her parents, secure safe passage to the North.

Likewise, Sojourner Truth became a popular antislavery lecturer in the North. Born in Hurley, New York, in 1797 as Isabella Baumtree, she ran away from her master when he refused to acknowledge New York's emancipation law of 1827. In 1843, after a series of visions, she adopted the name "Sojourner Truth" because she believed that it reflected her divine mission. Truth believed that God had ordained her to speak out against slavery. While she may not have convinced every person in her audiences of slavery's evils, few could listen to her and not be impressed by her resonant voice and oratorical skills.

### Legacy of the Abolitionist Movement

Assessing the antislavery movement can be difficult, partly because many reform efforts had overlapping objectives. Such is the case with women and abolition. Many women who favored abolition also favored equal rights for women, creating one reform movement within another. These white women tended to see the plight of black slave women in the light of their own social and political powerlessness. Consequently, they sincerely wanted to see slavery abolished, but they also wanted to better their own state.

Some male critics, notably William Lloyd Garrison, editor of the abolitionist newspaper *The Liberator,* agreed that women should have full social and political equality with men. Garrison also called for the immediate freedom of all slaves without compensation to their masters, as well as full social and political equality for freed African Americans. Many people saw Garrison as a radical, but it was his attitude toward women's rights that separated him from some of his earliest backers, particularly Arthur and Lewis Tappan. Equality for women was an issue that some abolitionists refused to address.

Ironically, as women called for equality and slave liberation, they may have been stifled most by a feminine influence. Abolitionists constituted a minority in nineteenth century America, and most women tended to stay within their own sphere. Catharine Beecher was perhaps the most outspoken proponent of distinct spheres for men and women. As she saw it, women had considerable power to shape society's morality by shaping the home. Many women chose to remain keepers of their homes rather than to fight for either abolition or women's rights.

By the end of the nineteenth century, the idea of dual spheres had assumed a new cast. Many women demanded the right to vote precisely because society needed their perceived moral influence. The experience and organizational skills learned by an earlier generation of female abolitionists, both black and white, was without doubt extremely useful to subsequent reformers.

*Keith Harper*

## Further Reading

Abzug, Robert H. *Cosmos Crumbling: American Reform and the Religious Imagination.* New York: Oxford University Press, 1994. Abzug argues that reformers, particularly abolitionists, were motivated by religious conviction.

Clinton, Catherine. *The Plantation Mistress: Woman's World in the Old South.* New York: Pantheon Books, 1982. This work focuses on plantation women. Excellent statistical data can be found in an appendix.

Fox-Genovese, Elizabeth. *Within the Plantation Household: Black and White Women of the Old South.* Chapel Hill: University of North Carolina Press, 1988. Perhaps the most comprehensive treatment of the interconnectedness between black and white women in the antebellum South.

Friedman, Jean E. *The Enclosed Garden: Women and Community in the Evangelical South, 1830-1900.* Chapel Hill: University of North Carolina Press, 1985. This multidisciplinary study argues that community, not gender, shaped the sociocultural roles of both black and white women in the South.

Genovese, Eugene D. *Roll, Jordan, Roll: The World the Slaves Made.* New York: Pantheon Books, 1974. A classic Marxist study of slavery. This work explores the extent of self-determination by African Americans while they were in bondage.

Horton, James Oliver, and Lois E. Horton. *Slavery and the Making of America.* New York: Oxford University Press, 2005.

Scott, Anne Firor. *The Southern Lady: From Pedestal to Politics, 1830-1930.* Chicago: University of Chicago Press, 1970. Scott's classic work demythologizes white Southern women.

Smith, Theophus H. *Conjuring Culture: Biblical Formations of Black America.* New York: Oxford University Press, 1994. The author explores the formation of a distinct, African American "conjure culture," with close attention to the particular role that women played in its creation.

Walters, Ronald G. *American Reformers, 1815-1860.* New York: Hill and Wang, 1978. The author explores reform as an adjustment or accommodation to nineteenth century social, economic, and political forces.

White, Deborah G. *Ar'n't I a Woman? Female Slaves in the Plantation South.* New York: W. W. Norton, 1987. White's work is one of the most thorough treatments of female slaves.

**See also** Abolitionist movement and women; Slave codes; Slavery; Slavery and families; Slavery and race relations; Slavery in Massachusetts; Slavery in Virginia

# Slavery in Massachusetts

*Legal recognition of slavery in Massachusetts Bay Colony made it an institution in Great Britain's North American colonies and helped to ensure its survival.*

From its outset, the Massachusetts Bay Colony endorsed the idea of unfree labor. One hundred and eighty indentured servants arrived with the original colonists. Subsequent food shortages led to the surviving servants' being set free in 1630. Unfree labor, however, continued on a private basis, and some white criminals were made slaves to court-appointed masters. Captives from the Pequot War of 1636-1637 were given over into slavery. Some of these captives were subsequently transported to a Puritan enclave off the coast of Nicaragua, and black slaves were introduced from there to the Massachusetts colony. The colony, however, remained without a formal endorsement of slavery until the promulgation of the Body of Liberties in 1641.

### Codifying Slave Laws

The Body of Liberties was controversial in many respects. It evolved out of the gradually weakening authority of Governor John Winthrop and his first Board of Assistants, and the emergence of the General Court as a representative body of freemen. The document was crafted and adopted by Elizabethan men who had grown up in the age of Shakespeare and the King James Bible. They were not democrats, but they had a strong sense of destiny and a healthy fear of absolute authority. In a larger sense, the document came to reflect the classic and ancient struggle between church and state.

In 1635, the General Court had appointed a committee to draw up a body of laws for the rights and duties of the colonists. This committee stalled over the church-state conflict, and another committee was impaneled in 1636. John Cotton sat on this committee. Cotton was a devout churchman who saw a government based on the theocracy of Israel and drafted a document that derived much of its authority from scripture. Cotton did, however, believe in limitations on authority. He also resisted adopting biblical statutes wholesale. Winthrop, who was lukewarm to the entire idea, called Cotton's Code, "Moses his Judicialls."

Cotton's counterpart in drawing up the code was Nathaniel Ward. Ward was a Puritan with a sense of humor and a literary bent. He later penned a humorous pamphlet of observations entitled *The Simple Cobler of Aggawam*. Like most Puritans, he was a friend to strict discipline, but he also was a foe to arbitrary authority. He could agree with Winthrop and Cotton that all law was the law of God, but with a view toward local conditions and universal morality. He insisted that the code be based on English common law rather than on the Bible. He became the chief architect and intellectual godfather of the "Massachusetts Magna Charta," the Body of Liberties. His contribution would be a government of laws and not men. The Pequot War slowed deliberations, but by 1638, the committee had a fresh start and by 1639 had ordered a document that combined Cotton's and Ward's work. The final document, which owed more to Ward than to Cotton, was adopted in November, 1641.

In many ways, the Body of Liberties was an enlightened document and certainly remarkable by seventeenth century standards. A compilation of one hundred laws, the Body of Liberties, while not democratic, allowed for wide judicial discretion and for each case to be judged on its merits. It also effectively barred the legal profession from defending anyone for pay, and it protected married women from assault. It also addressed the liberties of servants in humanitarian terms for those times. The number of lashes given to servants was limited to forty, and the capital laws were more lenient than those of England. The distinguished historian Samuel Eliot Morison wrote that the Body of Liberties was "an enlightened body of laws and of principles that would have done credit to any commonwealth in the 17th century. . . ." The one problem, however, was slavery. This bold document addressed the slavery issue thus:

> There shall never be any bond slaverie, villainage or captivitie amongst us unles it be lawfull captive, taken in just warres, and such strangers as willingly selle themselves or are sold to us. And these shall have all the liberties and Christian usages which the law of God established in Israell concerning such persons doeth morally require. This exempts none from servitude who shall be judged thereto by authoritie.

Although not a ringing endorsement of slavery, the Body of Liberties nevertheless admits of it. Thus it opened the way for the official sanction of slavery. Later and stricter codes would formalize the institution in New England on a colony-by-colony basis. The reasoning was a business decision. An early realization that the price of slaves was greater than their worth as laborers led the Yankee businessmen to market some of their slave cargoes to the plantation colonies. In the triangular trade of West Africa, the West Indies, and North America, the vast majority of slaves taken by New England traders ended up in the West Indies. Shrewd New England traders shipped rum, fish, and dairy products out; they imported slaves, molasses, and sugar. Those few slaves who were not dropped off in the West Indies or on southern plantations were taxed rather heavily. In 1705, Massachusetts imposed a duty of four pounds sterling per slave imported into the colony.

## Decline of Slavery

By 1680, Governor Simon Bradstreet estimated the number of "blacks or slaves" in the Massachusetts colony at one hundred to two hundred. Some special laws were passed restricting the movement of African Americans in white society, but the Puritans encouraged Christian conversion and honored black marriages. Slavery was mild compared to the southern kind. Slaves needed to read and write to do their jobs. Although there were occasional isolated rebellions, the slaves benefited from the New England love for learning and the strong Puritan emphasis on marriage and family.

Slavery gradually faded away in Massachusetts, perhaps because of its vague legal status. In the aftermath of the American Revolution, a national clamor for a Bill of Rights led individual colonies to adopt their own. While none expressly forbade slavery, the institution seemed at odds with the rhetoric. By 1776, the white population of Massachusetts was 343,845 and the black population was 5,249. The census of 1790 showed Massachusetts as the only state in which no slaves were listed.

As John Winthrop stated, "wee shall be as a Citty upon a Hill, the Eies of all people are uppon us; soe that if wee shall deale falsely with our god in this worke wee have undertaken and soe cause him to withdrawe his present help from us, wee shall be made a story and a by-word through the world. . . ." Despite the legalization of slavery in the Body of Liberties, slavery was never popular in Massachusetts except as incidental to trade—and the slave trade was an accepted practice by seventeenth century European standards. The Puritans themselves were products of a rigorous, harsh, isolated experience. They were humanists and intellectuals with contradictions. They prized sincerity and truthfulness, yet practiced repression and inhibition to steel themselves against life's ills. They had a strong element of individualism in their creed, believing that each person must face his maker alone. Puritan humanism thus never squared with the institution of slavery.

*Brian G. Tobin*

## Further Reading

Franklin, John Hope. *From Slavery to Freedom: A History of Negro Americans*. 3d ed. New York: Alfred A. Knopf, 1967. Classic text on the evolution of American slavery contains a chapter on "Puritan Masters."

Miller, Perry, ed. *The American Puritans: Their Prose and Poetry*. New York: Columbia University Press, 1982. Includes selected writings from John Cotton, Nathaniel Ward, and John Winthrop.

_____. *Errand into the Wilderness*. Cambridge, Mass.: The Belknap Press of Harvard University Press, 1984. A timeless source that delves into the theological underpinnings of Puritanism.

Morgan, Edmund S. *The Puritan Dilemma: The Story of John Winthrop*. Edited by Oscar Handlin. Boston: Little, Brown, 1958. A simplified view of Puritan politics, with Massachusetts Bay's first governor as the focal point.

Morison, Samuel Eliot. *Builders of the Bay Colony*. Boston: Northeastern University Press, 1981. Contains individual chapters on the Elizabethan architects of Massachusetts, including John Cotton, Nathaniel Ward, and John Winthrop.

Phillips, Ulrich B. *American Negro Slavery*. Baton Rouge: Louisiana State University Press, 1966. Rich in original source material about the development of slavery.

**See also** Slave codes; Slavery; Slavery and families; Slavery and race relations; Slavery and the justice system; Slavery and women; Slavery in Virginia

# Slavery in Virginia

*As one of the first North American colonies to institutionalize slavery
and as one of the largest and most influential colonies, Virginia established a model for slavery in the South.*

In March, 1661, the Virginia General Assembly declared that "all
children borne in this country shalbe held bond or free only according to the condition of the mother." Enacted to alleviate
confusion about the status of children with English fathers and
African mothers, this law was the first in a series of laws recognizing perpetual slavery in Virginia and equating "freedom"
with "white" and "enslaved" with "black." This law is especially
indicative of the hardening of race relations in mid-seventeenth
century Virginia society, as status in the patriarchal society of England traditionally was inherited from the father. By reversing this legal concept, perpetuation of enslavement for African
Americans was ensured for their children, whether of black or
white ancestry.

### Defining Who Were "Slaves"

Despite the extent to which the 1661 law narrowed the options
for defining Africans' status, this act did not in itself establish
slavery. Africans had two available windows through which they
could obtain freedom—conversion to Christianity and manumission (formal emancipation). In 1655, mulatto Elizabeth Key
brought a successful suit for her freedom, using as her main argument the fact that she had been baptized. In 1667, a slave named
Fernando contended that he ought to be freed because he was a
Christian and had lived in England for several years. Not only
did the court deny Fernando's appeal, but also that same year the
General Assembly took another step toward more clearly defining blacks' status, by declaring "that the conferring of baptisme
doth not alter the condition of the person as to his bondage or
freedome." Planters felt that if baptism led to freedom, they
would be without any assurance that they could retain their slave
property. The 1667 law thereby built on the earlier one to define
who would be a slave, and was clarified in 1670 and again in

1682, when the Assembly declared that any non-Christian who was brought into the colony, either by land or by sea, would be a slave for life, even if he or she later converted.

In 1691, colonial leaders provided a negative incentive to masters wishing to free their slaves by declaring that anyone who set free any "negro or mulatto" would be required to pay the costs of transporting the freedmen out of the colony within six months. Although manumissions still occurred and some free blacks managed to remain in the colony, the primary status for African Americans in Virginia was that of chattel.

### Virginia's Slave Codes

Although who was to be a slave in Virginia had now been defined, it had yet to be determined precisely what being a slave meant on a daily basis for Africans and their descendants. Be-

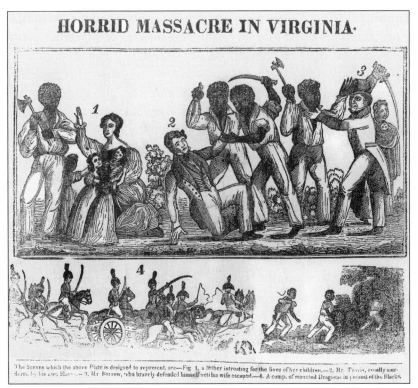

*Contemporary illustration of a slave rebellion in colonial Virginia.* (Library of Congress)

tween 1661 and 1705, nearly twenty separate laws were passed limiting, defining, and prescribing the rights, status, and treatment of African Americans. In general, these laws were designed to protect planters' slave property and to protect the order and stability of white society from an "alien and savage race."

The greater the proportion of black slaves in the overall Virginia population, the more restrictive and oppressive the laws became. Whereas Africans were only 2 percent of the total population of Virginia in 1648, they were 15 percent in 1708. In certain coastal counties, such as York, the demographic picture was even more threatening. In 1663, African Americans already made up 14 percent of the total county population; by 1701, they counted for 31 percent of the county's inhabitants. In large part, the slave codes were motivated by the growth of the black population and whites' fears of slave uprisings.

The piecemeal establishment of slavery in these separate laws culminated in 1705 in a comprehensive slave code in Virginia. This code reenacted and strengthened a number of earlier slave laws, added further restrictions and harsher punishments, and permanently drew the color line that placed African Americans at the bottom of Virginia society. Whites were prohibited from trading with, having sexual relations with, and marrying blacks. African Americans were forbidden to own Christian servants "except of their own complexion," leave their home plantation without a pass, own a gun or other weapon, or resist whites in any way.

In this society in which private property was a basic legal tenet, a slave's property was not protected: "be it enacted . . . that all horses, cattle or hoggs marked of any negro . . . shall be forfeited to the use of the poore of the parish . . . seizable by the church warden thereof." Neither was slave life or limb protected by the codes. It was legal both to kill a slave accidentally while correcting him or her, and to dismember a slave guilty of running away as a means of dissuading other slaves from trying to escape. Slaves were not allowed to assemble for prayer, for entertainment, or to bury their dead. They could not testify against white people in court and were not given the right of trial by jury. The only protection mandated in the slave code was that masters must provide adequate food, clothing, and shelter for their slaves, and that they "not give immoderate correction."

## Enforcement of the Codes

Many of these enactments lacked any means of enforcement, including the sole protection, and remained as almost dead letters in the statutes. Many of the harsher penalties for slave crimes, for example, the death penalty and maiming, were not carried out nearly as frequently as the laws suggest, because doing so would harm or destroy the master's property. Laws prohibiting slaves from trading or hiring themselves out were disregarded almost routinely. The disadvantage for slaves of this lack of enforcement was that laws prohibiting cruel treatment or defining acceptable levels of correction often were ignored as well. Where abuse was noticeably blatant, action against white offenders was taken only reluctantly, and punishments were insignificant and rare. Generally, laws in the economic and political interest of the white planter elite were enforced and respected; laws that restrained planters' pursuits were not.

To a large extent, these laws grew out of the early- to mid-seventeenth century laws regulating indentured servitude. Servants also were prohibited from having sexual relations with or marrying their masters; indentured women who became pregnant through such liaisons were fined, made to serve extra time, and had their children bound out to labor. Like slaves, servants were punished for attempting to run away or for resisting their masters. Servants also were treated harshly and exploited by ruthless masters eager to get every penny's worth of effort from their laborers.

Unlike African slaves, white indentured servants had legal rights and were protected by the laws and courts of the colony. Furthermore, white servants ultimately served out their time, became freemen and full citizens, acquired land and servants of their own, and became respected members of the community, regardless of their earlier status. Indentured servants had rights and opportunities, but African and African American slaves, by the turn of the eighteenth century, virtually had neither.

*Laura A. Croghan*

## Further Reading

Boskin, Joseph. *Into Slavery: Racial Decisions in the Virginia Colony.* Philadelphia: J. B. Lippincott, 1976. Provides a brief account of the evolution of perpetual slavery and a representative selection of relevant primary documents. Good bibliographical essays.

Catterall, Helen T., ed. *Judicial Cases Concerning American Slavery and the Negro.* 5 vols. New York: Octagon Books, 1968. Comprehensive examination of court records related to American slavery and the experiences of African Americans in slavery. Abstracts, index.

Hahn, Steven. *A Nation Under Our Feet: Black Political Struggles in the Rural South, from Slavery to the Great Migration.* Cambridge, Mass.: Belknap Press of Harvard University Press, 2003. An examination of African American political traditions dating back to the era of slavery.

Hening, William Waller, ed. *Statutes at Large: A Collection of All the Laws of Virginia.* 13 vols. New York: R & G & W Bartow, 1823. Reprint. Charlottesville: University Press of Virginia, 1969. Chronological listing of all the laws of the Virginia colony, with index.

Higginbotham, A. Leon, Jr. *In the Matter of Color: Race and the American Legal Process, the Colonial Period.* New York: Oxford University Press, 1978. Recounts the events culminating in the legal recognition of slavery in all the British mainland colonies.

Jordan, Winthrop D. *White over Black: American Attitudes Toward the Negro, 1550-1812.* New York: W. W. Norton, 1968. Examines the attitudes of British colonists toward Africans, especially concerning their religions and color. Characterizes the establishment of slavery as an "unthinking decision."

Schwartz, Philip J. *Twice Condemned: Slaves and the Criminal Laws of Virginia, 1705-1865.* Baton Rouge: Louisiana State University Press, 1988. Uses criminal trial records to examine slave resistance and whites' efforts to control threatening slave behavior. Interprets the seventeenth century as a time of adjustment or negotiation.

Shaw, Robert B. *A Legal History of Slavery in the United States.* Potsdam, N.Y.: Northern Press, 1991. Illustrates the history of slavery in terms of its legislative and judicial background, from settlement through emancipation. Early chapters discuss the evolution of early slave codes.

**See also** Abolition; Abolitionist movement and women; Slave codes; Slavery; Slavery and families; Slavery and race relations; Slavery and the justice system; Slavery and women; Slavery in Massachusetts; Stono Rebellion

# Smith v. Allwright

**The Case:** U.S. Supreme Court ruling on white primaries
**Date:** April 3, 1944
*The Supreme Court held that excluding African Americans from primaries was an unconstitutional violation of the Fourteenth and Fifteenth Amendments.*

In 1923, the Texas legislature sought to disfranchise African American voters in the state by passing a resolution that "in no event shall a Negro be eligible to participate in a Democratic primary. . . ." Since the 1890's, in Texas as in all other southern states, nomination in the Democratic primary was tantamount to election; therefore, while African Americans would be permitted to vote in the general election, they would have no meaningful role in the political process.

Almost immediately after the Texas legislature barred African Americans from participating in the Democratic primary, the National Association for the Advancement of Colored People (NAACP) secured a plaintiff, Dr. L. A. Nixon, to test the constitutionality of the legislative act. In *Nixon v. Herndon* (1927), the U.S. Supreme Court, in an opinion written by Justice Oliver Wendell Holmes, Jr., held that the Texas statute violated the equal protection clause of the Fourteenth Amendment to the U.S. Constitution by discriminating against African Americans on the basis of race. He also ruled, however, that it was unnecessary to strike down the white primary as a denial of suffrage "on account of race [or] color" repugnant to the Fifteenth Amendment.

## Texas Legislature

The Texas legislature reacted defiantly to the Supreme Court decision. On June 7, 1927, the legislature passed a new resolution granting to the state executive committees of every political party the authority to establish the qualifications of their members and to determine who was qualified to vote or otherwise participate in the party. In turn, the Democratic Party State Executive Committee limited participation in its primary to white voters in Texas.

Once again Nixon filed suit, this time against James Condon, the election officer who refused to give him a ballot in the 1928 Democratic primary. In *Nixon v. Condon* (1932), the Supreme Court struck down this new Texas statute as a violation of the equal protection clause. The vote was five to four.

The Democratic Party State Executive Committee immediately rescinded its resolution prohibiting African Americans from voting in its primary, but the state party convention voted to limit participation in its deliberations to whites, and Nixon and the NAACP, after two Supreme Court cases and an expenditure of six thousand dollars, were once more back at the beginning. In July, 1934, Richard Randolph Grovey in Houston, Texas, was refused a ballot to vote in the Democratic primary. On April 1, 1935, in *Grovey v. Townsend*, Justice Owen J. Roberts ruled that the Democratic Party was a private organization, and that its primary, although held under state law, was a party matter paid for by the Democrats. Since Roberts could find no state action in the process by which Democrats nominated their candidates, there was, he said, no violation of the Fourteenth Amendment.

There the matter rested. The primary was held not to be part of the general election, so there was presumably no relationship to the Fifteenth Amendment's protection of suffrage. Because the Democratic Party was a private organization, it was free to establish membership qualifications, and there was not sufficient state involvement to invoke the guarantees of the Fourteenth Amendment.

## A Supreme Court Reversal

It seemed there was no way to contest the validity of the Texas white primary. In 1941, however, in *United States v. Classic*, a case that ostensibly had nothing to do with African Americans or the white primary, the Supreme Court held for the first time that the right to vote was protected in a primary as well as in the general election, "where the state law has made the primary an integral part of the process of choice or where in fact the primary effectively controls the choice."

*United States v. Classic* dealt with a Louisiana primary in which there had been fraudulent returns, but otherwise there was no way to distinguish the Texas primary from the one held in the neighboring southern state. In Texas, as in Louisiana, in 1941 as in 1923, Democratic Party nomination in its primary was a virtual guarantee of election, and the general election was a mere formality.

The NAACP was back in action. Lonnie Smith, a Houston dentist and NAACP member, sued a Texas election official for five thousand dollars for refusing to give him a ballot to vote in the 1940 Democratic congressional primaries. The NAACP's legal counsel, Thurgood Marshall, and William Hastie, dean of the Howard Law School, brought *Smith v. Allwright* to the U.S. Supreme Court.

In April, 1944, mindful of southern sensibilities but intent upon overruling the nine-year-old precedent in *Grovey*, the Court chose Stanley Reed, a Democrat from Kentucky, to write its opinion. Justice Reed's opinion made it clear that the Court, except for Justice Roberts (the author of the *Grovey* decision), had concluded that the primary was an integral part of a general election, particularly in the southern states. The *Classic* decision, wrote Justice Reed, raised the issue of whether excluding African Americans from participation in the Democratic Party primary in Texas violated the Fifteenth Amendment. The answer was in the affirmative, and *Grovey v. Townsend* was expressly overruled. "If the state," Reed said, "requires a certain election procedure, prescribing a general election ballot made up of party nominees so chosen, and limits the choice of the electorate in general elections for state officers . . . to those whose names appear on such a ballot, it endorses, adopts, and enforces the discrimination against Negroes practiced by a party entrusted by Texas law with the determination of the qualifications of participants in the primary. This is state action within the meaning of the Fifteenth Amendment."

The long litigative battle against the Texas white primary seemed to be over—but it was not. In Fort Bend County, Texas, the Jaybird Democratic Party, organized after the Civil War, held primaries closed to African American voters; its candidates consistently won county offices. In spite of *Smith v. Allwright*, the Jaybirds refused to open their primary to African Americans, arguing that they did not operate under state law or use state officers or funds. Nevertheless, in *Terry v. Adams* (1953), the Supreme Court held that the Jaybird primary violated the Fifteenth Amendment, because it controlled the electoral process in Fort Bend County.

## Aftermath

It took twenty-one years for the U.S. Supreme Court to rule that the Texas white primary violated the right to vote guaranteed by the Fifteenth Amendment. It would take another twenty-one years before the Voting Rights Act of 1965 finally secured the ballot for African Americans in the South. In the interim, the fall of the white primary had the practical effect of increasing African American registrants in the southern states from approximately 250,000 in 1940 to 775,000 seven years later. African Americans were still intimidated and defrauded of their suffrage rights, but *Smith v. Allwright* was an important landmark on the road to uninhibited enfranchisement. It also was a symbol that the Supreme Court would examine the reality behind the subterfuge and act to protect African Americans in the enjoyment of their civil rights.

*David L. Sterling*

## Further Reading

Fassett, John D. *New Deal Justice: The Life of Stanley Reed of Kentucky.* New York: Vantage Press, 1994. A biography of the conservative Democratic justice who wrote the majority opinion in *Smith v. Allwright.*

Hine, Darlene Clark. *Black Victory: The Rise and Fall of the White Primary in Texas.* Millwood, N.Y.: KTO Press, 1979. An examination of the background of the white primary and the struggle to bring about its demise.

Kluger, Richard. *Simple Justice: The History of "Brown v. Board of Education" and Black America's Struggle for Equality.* New York: Alfred A. Knopf, 1976. An eminently readable analysis of another landmark Supreme Court case in African American history.

Lawson, Steven F. *Black Ballots: Voting Rights in the South, 1944-1969.* New York: Columbia University Press, 1976. Traces the development of African American enfranchisement from *Smith v. Allwright* to the Voting Rights Act of 1965 and its aftermath. Includes a chapter on the white primary.

Powledge, Fred. *Free at Last: The Civil Rights Movement and the People Who Made It.* Boston: Little, Brown, 1991. A popular account of the struggle for equality during the 1960's, with numerous human interest stories.

**See also** Civil Rights Act of 1960; Disfranchisement laws in Mississippi; Fifteenth Amendment; Fourteenth Amendment; Gerrymandering; *Grovey v. Townsend*; *Newberry v. United States*; *Nixon v. Condon*; *Nixon v. Herndon*; *United States v. Classic*; Voting Rights Act of 1965; White primaries

# Southern Christian Leadership Conference

**Identification:** Civil rights organization
**Date:** Founded in 1957
**Place:** Atlanta, Georgia; New Orleans, Louisiana; and Montgomery, Alabama

*The formation of the Southern Christian Leadership Conference (SCLC) in 1957 was the first Southwide grassroots movement dedicated to racial desegregation in the United States.*

When the Southern Christian Leadership Conference was formed in 1957, black Americans faced many obstacles to economic and political equality despite decades of piecemeal reforms. The National Association for the Advancement of Colored People (NAACP), the National Urban League, the Congress of

Racial Equality (CORE), and other advocacy organizations had achieved significant gains, but black Americans in many parts of the country were prohibited from voting and blocked by lack of education and segregationist barriers from advancing economically and socially. Particularly in the southern states, black Americans faced formidable barriers that had stood firmly and even intensified in spite of significant legal victories against segregation in interstate transportation and education. The major advocacy organizations began and operated chiefly in the North and had comparatively little impact on black southerners, who lived in perennial poverty and social ostracism.

### The SCLC and the Civil Rights Movement

The SCLC was the first large regional civil rights organization. Its distinctive role as the political arm of many black churches gave it the ability to lead direct action campaigns with the kind of massive grassroots support that had eluded the NAACP and other older advocacy organizations. Under the leadership of Dr. Martin Luther King, Jr., from 1957 to 1968, the SCLC worked with other organizations in many desegregation campaigns. Its nonviolent direct action efforts were on a scale unparalleled in previous campaigns.

*Martin Luther King, Jr., was the embodiment of the Southern Christian Leadership Conference through its early years.* (National Archives)

By 1957, numerous local desegregation campaigns had been launched without the benefit of a connecting framework. "Movement centers," as Aldon D. Morris called them, included Tallahassee, Mobile, Nashville, Birmingham, Baton Rouge, and several other cities where local leaders applied interorganizational cooperation to effect changes, usually desegregation of public transit systems. What they lacked was an organizational framework to link their efforts with those in other cities and thus achieve a broader impact on behalf of integration and racial equality. Several black leaders, notably the Reverend T. J. Jemison of Baton Rouge, the Reverend Charles Kenzie Steele of Tallahassee, and the Reverend Fred Shuttlesworth of Birmingham, expressed the need for such a larger connecting framework, especially after the important bus boycott in Montgomery, Alabama, during 1955 and 1956.

The 381-day Montgomery boycott, triggered by the bold defiance of segregated seating by a black seamstress, Rosa Parks, was the catalyst in bringing these various reform centers together. The "Montgomery way," as many termed it, had demonstrated the effectiveness of mass direct action without violence. Furthermore, it underscored the value of pooling ideas and resources to challenge laws and traditions that supported segregated public facilities such as restaurants, movie theaters, and hotels. Transportation was a particularly significant area needing attention, because many African Americans depended upon public transit to get to their jobs.

### Expanding the Struggle

Several informal groups began in late 1956 to plan a broad organization for enlarging the civil rights struggle. One of these groups included Ella Jo Baker, a perennial supporter of direct action reform, white attorney Stanley David Levison, and civil rights advocate Bayard Rustin. In New York, they formed a small group known as "In Friendship" and began to contact civil rights leaders across the South. Meanwhile, Martin Luther King, Jr., and the Reverend Ralph David Abernathy, along with others such as Joseph E. Lowery, Steele, and Jemison, met periodically in Montgomery to brainstorm on a possible southern direct action organization.

It would be a mistake to attribute this interest entirely to the Montgomery campaign or to contextual factors such as urbanization and its related tensions. The historical setting of the origins of the SCLC included these things as well as the impact of the *Brown v. Board of Education* case of May, 1954, that declared unconstitutional "separate but equal" schools, based on the 1896 *Plessy v. Ferguson* decision. The *Brown* case was a particularly encouraging factor because it showed that the Supreme Court could be a valuable ally of black reform leaders.

In early 1956, Rustin suggested to King in Montgomery the concept of a broad organization to link the various reform centers. By the end of the year, the discussions had advanced sufficiently to attempt an organization meeting. Rustin contacted Steele and others, and round-robin invitations went out from Steele, King, and Shuttlesworth to dozens of southern activists. The foundational meeting took place at the Ebenezer Baptist Church in Atlanta on January 10 and 11, 1957, with approximately sixty people, mostly black pastors, attending.

The discussions covered a wide range of topics, mostly from working papers provided by Rustin. It was agreed that the movement would be nonviolent in method and outlook and that all Americans' rights under the Constitution would be supported in order "to redeem the soul of America." The fact that many participants were ministers added to the emphasis upon faith and ethics. This basic reality of the Atlanta meeting was important in shaping the ethos of the emergent SCLC. The conference also cabled President Dwight D. Eisenhower, requesting that he or Vice President Richard Nixon travel to the South and take a strong stand in favor of civil rights. Eisenhower had already sent a civil rights package to Congress in 1956, but the administration's proposals fell short of the Atlanta delegates' expectations.

### Completing the Organization

Later meetings in New Orleans on February 14, 1957, and in Montgomery in August of the same year completed the organizational process. After experimenting with various names, the new conference arrived at its permanent name, the Southern Christian Leadership Conference, during the Montgomery meeting. Some

SCLC leaders feared that adding the word "Christian" might alienate Jews such as Stanley Levison, but King supported the new name, believing that it reflected the true nature of the organization. Levison agreed. Some of the organizers thought that the word "Christian" would lessen the likelihood that the organization would be considered radical or communist.

The Southern Christian Leadership Conference focused chiefly on basic rights for members of minorities and poor people. Its first major undertaking was a Crusade for Citizenship. Its goal was to at least double the number of registered black voters in the South. Voting rights thus became one of the major emphases of the new organization. Working in conjunction with the NAACP and other organizations, the SCLC added thousands of black voters to the voting rolls in several states. It also continued to work on behalf of ending segregated transportation, desegregating schools, and gaining broader access by African Americans to public facilities such as hotel and lunch counters.

The SCLC's loose organization was important to its distinctive role in the Civil Rights movement. Without formal individual membership, it was based on affiliates, such as local churches and activist groups like Fred Shuttlesworth's Alabama Christian Movement for Human Rights (ACMHR). Operating at first in eleven states, it linked hundreds of such entities in a way that facilitated guidance from the central headquarters while maintaining considerable local autonomy. The SCLC came into cities and towns for campaigns when invited by local leaders. As the SCLC became more experienced and efficient, these invitations were carefully planned. The Birmingham campaign of 1963, which was a highpoint of the SCLC's history, began on the basis of an invitation from Shuttlesworth's organization.

**Priorities**

The SCLC's focus was primarily on securing rights that were based on the U.S. Constitution. It was also interested, from the beginning, in economic advancement of members of minorities and perennially poor people. This aspect of the SCLC's history had not been recognized adequately. The fact that its focus on social and economic gains increased after the Selma campaign and the

Voting Rights Act of 1965 should not be taken as an indication that the SCLC came to this emphasis only in the middle 1960's. Poverty was viewed by the SCLC as a seminal cause of the political powerlessness of many black Americans, and from the beginning the organization was interested in the elimination of poverty. At the same time, King and his associates recognized that the right to vote would bring the ability to help determine political leaders and hold them accountable for such needs as jobs and housing. King sounded this note as early as the Prayer Pilgrimage of May, 1957, marking the third anniversary of the *Brown* decision. In his speech, which propelled him higher in public visibility, he gave rhythmic repetitions of the phrase "Give us the ballot," noting that if African Americans had the vote they could nonviolently eliminate many barriers to progress.

**Impact**

Thus began an important new organization dedicated to racial justice and advancement in the United States. It was quite different in key ways from the older NAACP and CORE, both of which began in the North and historically operated chiefly outside the South. The NAACP did have a strong presence in the South in 1957, but it was under attack by various groups and governments. Its distinguishing feature had always been litigation through the court system. The SCLC provided a framework for mass direct action, which many felt was urgently needed in the South. Furthermore, the SCLC was not a membership organization. It was structured around loosely linked "affiliates," such as the ACMHR, rather than individual membership.

The advent of the SCLC marked a new chapter in the history of racial and ethnic rights in the United States. Strongly grounded in local churches, it sought to bring their moral strength and organizational resources to bear upon the problems of members of minorities. With King as its president, it had an articulate spokesman who was increasingly drawing media interest. This was both an asset and a liability. King's visibility helped the young SCLC but at the same time hindered the organization's achievement of an identity apart from him. On balance, the SCLC was very significant in the continuance of the momentum gained in

Montgomery and other cities in the early and middle 1950's. For more than a decade under King, it would be a major force in massive campaigns in Birmingham, Selma, and other cities, and after 1965 would venture into the northern United States.

Nonviolence was the most characteristic mark of the SCLC's campaigns. At times it had remarkable results, not only for public policy but also for individual experiences of both black and white people. During the Birmingham campaign of 1963, for example, a group of marchers who were walking to a prayer vigil were confronted by Eugene "Bull" Connor's police and firefighters, who were wielding water hoses to stop marchers. Despite Connor's orders, those in charge of the hoses would not turn them on the unarmed and nonviolent group. They were, as Coretta Scott King later observed, disarmed by the nonviolent spirit of the demonstrators. Not hitting back, not hating, and not giving cause for increased violence were the salient features of the SCLC's new mass-based direct action.

*Thomas R. Peake*

**Further Reading**

Abernathy, Ralph David. *And the Walls Came Tumbling Down: An Autobiography*. New York: Harper & Row, 1989. This memoir by King's close friend and successor is disappointing on the formation and early development of the SCLC, but Abernathy's closeness to King and the early campaigns makes this a useful source for the context. Its chief value lies in giving one a firsthand view of what it was like to live through the Civil Rights movement in its heyday. Includes index and illustrations.

Branch, Taylor. *Parting the Waters: America in the King Years, 1954-1963*. New York: Simon & Schuster, 1988. This massive study focuses on the period from the *Brown v. Board of Education* case to the March on Washington in 1963. Its chief value lies in examining the setting in which Martin Luther King, Jr., became the leading spokesperson for racial liberation and equality. Elaborately documented and sympathetically approached, it is the first of a planned two-part series on the King years. Coverage of the founding of the SCLC is marginal, but the book is very strong on the SCLC's early campaigns. Contains notes, select bibliography, and index.

Fairclough, Adam. *To Redeem the Soul of America: The Southern Christian Leadership Conference and Martin Luther King, Jr.* Athens: University of Georgia Press, 1987. A detailed account of the early development of the SCLC and its historical context. A major focus is the changing role and attitudes of black clergy who played a pivotal role in the formation of the SCLC. Coverage of religious views and ideology is comparatively thin, but the book has valuable information on the internal dynamics of the SCLC. Contains detailed notes, chronologies, and index.

Garrow, David J. *Bearing the Cross: Martin Luther King, Jr., and the Southern Christian Leadership Conference.* New York: William Morrow, 1986. This Pulitzer Prize-winning account is thoroughly researched and elaborately documented. Although essentially biographical, Garrow's study deals with far more than King's life. It examines the campaigns, the role of the national and local governments, and the controversial personal details of King's relations with women. Although thin on the inner spiritual struggles of King and his associates, Garrow's is nevertheless the most detailed account to date of King's public career. Treatment of the SCLC's beginnings is relatively slight but useful. Contains detailed notes, illustrations, and index.

Morris, Aldon D. *The Origins of the Civil Rights Movement: Black Communities Organizing for Change.* New York: Free Press, 1984. An excellent study of the historical and institutional foundations of the Civil Rights movement. Morris examines several local centers, such as the Montgomery Improvement Association, that converged to bring about a strong southern cooperative movement. He also explores the emergence of black ministers as pivotal figures in the new activism. His coverage is basically from 1955 to 1965. The SCLC appears as the "decentralized political arm of the black church" that translated moral principles into political activism. Includes elaborate notes, bibliography, appendices, and index.

Peake, Thomas R. *Keeping the Dream Alive: A History of the Southern Christian Leadership Conference from King to the Nineteen-*

*Eighties*. New York: Peter Lang, 1987. The first comprehensive history of the SCLC from its founding to the 1980's, this work focuses on the motivations, programs, and training methods of the SCLC. It contains much biographical and institutional information as well as analysis of the SCLC's religious and political concepts. Detailed notes, bibliography, illustrations, and an index.

Ransby, Barbara. *Ella Baker and the Black Freedom Movement: A Radical Democratic Vision*. Chapel Hill: University of North Carolina Press, 2003. Discusses Baker's work with the organization.

Robinson, Jo Ann Gibson. *The Montgomery Bus Boycott and the Women Who Started It: The Memoir of Jo Ann Gibson Robinson*. Edited by David J. Garrow. Knoxville: University of Tennessee Press, 1987. A short but valuable account of the Montgomery bus boycott. Robinson, involved in the Women's Political Council that helped to organize the boycott, underscores the personal dimensions: the emotions, the hope, and the excitement of participating in these events.

**See also** Birmingham March; Black Christian Nationalist Movement; Black Power movement; Church bombings; Civil Rights Act of 1964; Civil Rights movement; Congress of Racial Equality; Freedom Summer; "I Have a Dream" speech; King assassination; Montgomery bus boycott; National Association for the Advancement of Colored People; Niagara Movement; Poor People's March on Washington; Student Nonviolent Coordinating Committee; University of Mississippi desegregation

# Southern Manifesto

**Identification:** Document signed by southern legislators renouncing the U.S. Supreme Court's 1954 *Brown v. Board of Education* decision

**Date:** Presented to Congress on March 12, 1956

*The Southern Manifesto dramatically illustrated the opposition of southern politicians to the Supreme Court's decision declaring segregation in public schools unconstitutional.*

Following the 1954 U.S. Supreme Court decision *Brown v. Board of Education*, Senate Majority Leader Lyndon B. Johnson and House Speaker Sam Rayburn, both from Texas, managed to get southern and northern Democrats to restrain themselves in response to the *Brown* decision. In 1956, however, some southern congressmen and senators were worried about being reelected if they did not oppose the decision. Southern senators, led by Strom Thurmond of South Carolina, met and drafted a resolution criticizing the Supreme Court's decision. The final draft of the resolution was presented to the U.S. Senate on March 12, 1956, by Walter George of Georgia.

Officially called the "Declaration of Constitutional Principles," the document stated that the U.S. Supreme Court had no legal basis for its decision and substituted its personal and political ideas for established law. It also criticized the Supreme Court's abuse of judicial powers and commended states that had declared their intention to resist integration by any lawful means.

The final document was signed by nineteen of the twenty-two southern senators and eighty-one southern House members. The three southern senators who did not sign the manifesto were Tennessee's Estes Kefauver and Albert Gore, Sr., and Texas's Lyndon B. Johnson.

The Southern Manifesto symbolized the open defiance of the overwhelming majority of southern congressional leaders to desegregation and gave southern segregationists hope that they could successfully resist desegregation efforts.

*William V. Moore*

**Further Reading**

Bartley, Numan V. *The Rise of Massive Resistance: Race and Politics in the South During the 1950's*. Baton Rouge: Louisiana State University Press, 1999. Details the key events and figures in the racial events of the South.

Bass, Jack, and Marilyn W. Thompson. *Ol' Strom*. Atlanta, Ga.: Longstreet, 1998. Discusses Strom Thurmond's role in the writing of the Southern Manifesto.

**See also** *Brown v. Board of Education*; Civil Rights movement; Education; Little Rock school desegregation crisis; School desegregation; White Citizens' Councils

# Sports

*Although sports are often prized by fans and participants alike as a refuge from mundane concerns, the sporting world has long provided a highly public forum for the debate and resolution of social issues. Matters of race and ethnicity have long been among the most contentious of these.*

The rise of organized sports in the mid- to late nineteenth century coincided with the drawing of the "color line" and the institution of formalized, legally sanctioned modes of discrimination in virtually all walks of American life. In sports as in most other contexts, the most virulent discrimination has typically been directed against African Americans. Although relations between whites, Latinos, Native Americans, Jews, and members of other ethnic minorities would often be strained, both on the playing fields and in the stands, such tensions historically have been relatively minor in comparison to the intense feelings aroused by the participation of black athletes.

As one baseball historian has remarked, "With the breaking of the color barrier, other ethnic identities ceased to have much meaning. . . . where the Blacks were, everybody else was just White"—a statement that encapsulates the history of race relations not only in baseball but also in most other American sports. By the latter half of the twentieth century, the integration of most sports was an accomplished fact, but other issues of race and ethnicity continued to swirl around the world of sports.

### Baseball and Discrimination in Team Sports

Baseball, the most popular and most widely played team sport of nineteenth century America, was also the first major sport to attain a secure organizational footing in North America, and in many respects, it long set the pattern for other American sports.

In the early years of organized baseball, a certain degree of racial freedom prevailed on American playing fields; although African Americans, Native Americans, and members of other ethnic minorities did not commonly compete with white players, neither was their participation formally barred. All-black teams occasionally played all-white squads, and African Americans, Latinos, and Native Americans competed with whites in front of racially mixed audiences in the earliest professional leagues.

By the waning years of the nineteenth century, however, such tolerance was becoming increasingly rare. As white America grappled with the changed legal and social status of African Americans in the post-Civil War period, segregated facilities and institutions were established in virtually all walks of American life. In 1896, the U.S. Supreme Court gave its blessing to such arrangements by endorsing the "separate but equal" doctrine in the landmark case *Plessy v. Ferguson.* Segregationists had their way in organized baseball as well, and by the century's close, African Americans had been effectively excluded from the sport's highest levels by means of an unwritten but nevertheless effective agreement among team owners and managers. (Sole responsibility for adoption of the ban is often assigned to Adrian "Cap" Anson, a star player and manager and a vocal proponent of segregation. Such an assessment, however, oversimplifies the reality; although Anson was one of the game's leading figures, he was only one among many who worked to exclude African Americans from the sport. African Americans were being systematically separated from whites in education, housing, and virtually every other arena, and the segregation of the country's most popular spectator sport was virtually inevitable.)

## Native Americans and Latinos

No such restrictions, however, were placed on the participation of Native Americans and light-skinned Latinos in organized baseball. Louis "Jud" Castro, for example, an infielder from Colombia, played in the inaugural season of the American League in 1902, and such Native Americans as Jim Thorpe and Albert "Chief" Bender had successful major league careers in the first decades of the twentieth century. As a consequence, white managers and owners made occasional attempts to pass off talented African American players as "Indians" or "Cubans"; legendary manager John McGraw, for example, tried unsuccessfully to play infielder Charlie Grant under the allegedly Cherokee name Charlie Tokohamo.

Although white teams sometimes played exhibitions against black teams, and although players of all races competed together in Latin America, the color line had been firmly drawn. For more than a half century, no openly African American players were permitted in the white professional leagues. Moreover, although light-skinned Latinos and Native Americans were not barred from the white leagues, they commonly experienced the same slights and racist treatments accorded members of ethnic minorities in all facets of American life—a fact perhaps reflected by the patronizing nicknames given even to star players; the nickname "Chief," for example, was routinely applied to Native American players, while Jewish players were often nicknamed "Moe."

In addition to Bender and Thorpe, Native American pioneers included John "Chief" Meyers, a star catcher for the New York Giants; the most successful Latino player of the early century was Adolpho "Dolf" Luque, a Cuban American pitcher also nicknamed "the Pride of Havana." (In the early part of the century, when many Americans were first- or second-generation European immigrants, ethnic identification was strong even among white players, and the achievements of athletes of Irish, Italian, German, Polish, or Jewish ancestry were celebrated by their respective communities to an extent unknown to later generations. Nicknames that called attention to a player's ethnicity were common; German American superstar Honus Wagner, for example, was known as "the Flying Dutchman.")

### Breaking the Color Line

Barred from the white leagues, African American professionals competed against one another in the Negro Leagues, a loose association of teams that flourished in the first half of the twentieth century. Negro League stars such as Oscar Charleston, Josh Gibson, Satchel Paige, and Buck Leonard were widely regarded as the equals of the best white players, but they were allowed to compete against them only in exhibitions, barnstorming tours, and foreign leagues.

In 1946, however, in a move that would have repercussions well beyond baseball or sports in general, baseball's color line was broken by Brooklyn Dodgers executive Branch Rickey, who signed Jackie Robinson, a rising star in the Negro Leagues, to a minor league contract. Robinson reached the majors the following season. Though he endured taunts and harassment both on and off the field, he quickly attained stardom (among Robinson's notable supporters was Hank Greenberg, a Jewish superstar who had long crusaded against anti-Semitism). Robinson's on-field success was matched by the remarkable dignity and restraint with which he bore the torrents of abuse directed at him, and his shining example deprived baseball's powers of any further excuse for continuing to segregate the sport. A flood of talented black players entered the white leagues, and every major league team was integrated by 1958. As a consequence, the Negro Leagues, deprived of their reason for existing, soon shriveled and disappeared.

## Football

When the color line was drawn in baseball, football was in its infancy, and professional structures did not exist. In the early years of the sport's evolution, however, a number of black players excelled at the collegiate level, often while playing for such all-black schools as Howard and Tuskegee Universities. Several black players, moreover, attained collegiate stardom at predominantly white schools; William Henry Lewis was named an All-American in 1892 and 1893 while playing for Amherst, and Paul Robeson starred for Rutgers before becoming famous as a singer and actor. When the first professional leagues were formed in the 1920's, moreover, no color line existed, and Robeson, Brown University graduate Frederick Douglass "Fritz" Pollard, and University of Iowa product Fred "Duke" Slater, among others, were among the best of the early professionals. In the early 1930's, however, professional football followed baseball's lead and excluded black players. Notable early players of other ethnic backgrounds included Jewish stars Sid Luckman and Bennie Friedman and the multitalented Native American Thorpe, whose football achievements surpassed his baseball success.

At the same time that Robinson was integrating baseball to great publicity, the established National Football League (NFL) had to fend off a challenge from the upstart All-America Football Conference, which signed a number of black players in an effort to compete with the older league. Faced with these twin pressures, the NFL owners rescinded their ban on black players. As in baseball, African Americans soon came to play important roles on every professional team.

### Basketball

Basketball, like football, was slow to develop viable professional structures. As in football, therefore, the collegiate level of play was the highest level widely available; although black teams were generally unable to play white opponents, basketball flourished at black colleges. Before the formation of solid professional leagues, traveling professional teams played all comers; among the most successful of these teams were the all-black Harlem Renaissance (or "Rens") and the Harlem Globetrotters. Both teams enjoyed success against white competition; in order, in part, to deflect hostility from white crowds, the Globetrotters learned to supplement their play with minstrel-like antics, and the team eventually evolved into an entertainment vehicle rather than a competitive unit. Jewish players and teams were also important to the rise of the sport, and such stars as Moe Goldman, Red Holtzman, and Eddie Gottlieb endured anti-Semitic taunts from opposing teams and crowds while helping to establish the basis for the first successful professional leagues.

Prior to 1950, African Americans were excluded from the National Basketball Association (NBA) and its predecessor organizations. That year, three African Americans were signed by NBA teams; within two decades, African American players would come to dominate the sport. Segregation at the college level would persist for decades, as a number of southern schools refused to use black players or to play against integrated teams. In 1966, in a game sometimes referred to as "the *Brown v. Board of Ed-*

*ucation* of college basketball," an all-black Texas Western team defeated all-white, heavily favored Kentucky for the national collegiate championship.

## Individual and Olympic Sports

Sports based on individual excellence rather than on team play have historically proven somewhat less amenable to overt racism than structured team and league sports; in addition, international competitions such as the Olympic Games have been relatively unaffected by parochial color lines. Nevertheless, issues of race have repeatedly reared their heads in international and individual sports. White boxing champions of the nineteenth and early twentieth centuries often refused to fight black competitors, and the 1908 capture of the world heavyweight championship by Jack Johnson, a flamboyant African American who flouted convention by consorting with white women, led to a prolonged search for a "Great White Hope" who could humble Johnson (who was concurrently persecuted by police).

*Heavyweight boxing champion Joe Louis sews technical-sergeant stripes onto his uniform while serving in the U.S. Army during World War II.*
(National Archives)

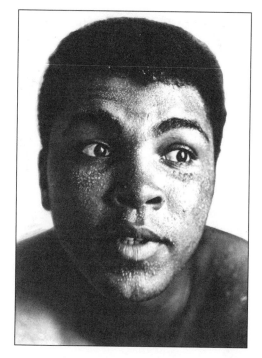

*Muhammad Ali.*
(Library of Congress)

In contrast, the midcentury heavyweight champion Joe Louis was applauded by many whites for his humility; when successors such as the irrepressible Muhammad Ali refused to defer to white sensibilities, racial alarms again were sounded. Among his many celebrated and controversial actions, Ali in 1964 became the first of many prominent black athletes to change his birth name (Cassius Clay) to a name reflecting his African heritage.

Among other individual sports, the "elitist" games of tennis and golf have proven least amenable to widescale integration. In part, this state of affairs has reflected economic realities, as relatively few minority competitors have been able to afford the club memberships and private instruction that most successful players require. Yet the intractability of racist sentiment has played an undeniable part in limiting minority success in both sports. Tennis stars of the 1950's and 1960's such as the Latino legend Pancho Gonzales and the African Americans Althea Gibson and Arthur Ashe often had to battle for permission to compete at race-restricted tournaments and clubs as did leading black golfers such as Lee Elder and Calvin Peete. Even after the resounding successes of golfing sensation Tiger Woods brought legions of new minority fans and players to the sport in the mid-1990's, country clubs across the United States—including some at which leading tournaments were held—refused to admit minority members.

International competitions such as the Olympic Games have traditionally been more open to minority participation. George Poage in 1904 became the first African American Olympic medalist, and Thorpe, generally acclaimed the world's greatest athlete, won two gold medals at the 1912 Games. In 1936, the African American track star Jesse Owens won four gold medals at the Berlin Olympics, to the chagrin of the Nazi hosts who hoped to use the Games to demonstrate Aryan supremacy. In 1968, many of the top African American athletes refused to participate in the Games, and two, sprinters John Carlos and Tommie Smith, engendered a worldwide controversy by giving a "black power salute" and refusing to acknowledge the U.S. national anthem while receiving their medals (they were subsequently stripped of their medals and removed from the Olympic team).

## Other Controversies

As the integration of most sports at the playing level became an accomplished fact, questions of race and ethnicity in the sports world came increasingly to focus on other issues. Perhaps the most persistent of these was the fact that although members of minorities had made vital contributions as athletes in every major sport, only a handful had risen to fill managerial, administrative, and executive positions. In 1987, a furor erupted when Los Angeles Dodgers executive Al Campanis—who, ironically, had been a teammate and longtime friend of Jackie Robinson—told a television interviewer that African Americans were underrepresented in front-office sports jobs because they "lack the necessities" to fill such positions. Although many commentators dismissed Campanis's remarks as the confused, out-of-context ramblings of a tired old man, the incident touched off a round of recriminations and investigations.

Although baseball and other sports appointed panels to study the situation, more than a decade later, members of minorities had yet to achieve more than token representation in the power structures of most American sports. A similar reception greeted golfer Fuzzy Zoeller's indiscreet 1997 remarks that Tiger Woods, who is partly of African American heritage, might have a preference for stereotypically "black" foods such as watermelon and fried chicken. These and other such incidents served as ongoing reminders that racial and ethnic divisions persist in the world of sports to the same extent as they do elsewhere in American society.

*Glenn Canyon*

## Further Reading

Alan H. Levy's *Tackling Jim Crow: Racial Segregation in Professional Football* (Jefferson, N.C.: McFarland & Co, 2003) provides an analysis of the segregation and integration of the National Football League. Brad Snyder's *Beyond the Shadow of the Senators: The Untold Story of the Homestead Grays and the Integration of Baseball* (Chicago: Contemporary Books, 2003) is a valuable addition to literature on African Americans and baseball. *Negro League Baseball: The Rise and Ruin of a Black Institution* (Philadelphia: University of Pennsylvania Press, 2004), by Neil Lanctot, is an excellent examination of the Negro Leagues. Calvin H. Sinnette's *Forbidden Fairways: African Americans and the Game of Golf* (Chelsea, Mich.: Sleeping Bear Press, 1998) is a welcome addition to the topic. Arthur Ashe's *A Hard Road to Glory: A History of the African American Athlete Since 1946* (New York: Warner Books, 1988) is a thorough overview of the black legacy to American sport; two companion volumes carry the discussion back to the earliest days of American history. Sociologist Harry Edwards, who was hired by major league baseball as a consultant in the wake of the Campanis incident, has written numerous thought-provoking analyses of race and sports; his groundbreaking *The Sociology of Sport* (1973) remains useful. *The Bill James Historical Baseball Abstract* (Rev. ed., New York: Villard Books, 1988) is a fascinating miscellany with many insightful comments of the history of race relations in the "national pastime." Robert Peterson's *Only the*

*Ball Was White* (Englewood Cliffs, N.J.: Prentice-Hall, 1970) was the first and is still among the best of the many histories of the Negro Leagues.

**See also** Baseball's integration; Segregation; Stereotypes

# Stereotypes

**Definition:** Popular, and usually biased, notions about African Americans held by others

*A number of stereotypes regarding African Americans, positive and negative, impair intergroup relations because they cause people to view all African Americans as being the same rather than possessing individual traits and characteristics.*

Over the years, a number of stereotypes have developed concerning African Americans. Some of these stereotypes—earth mother/mammy, natural musician, and super athlete—have basically positive connotations; however, others—Sambo, Uncle Tom, sexual predator, smart-mouthed but clever adolescent, welfare queen—have primarily negative connotations. Negative stereotypes are obviously detrimental, but even their positive counterparts are destructive and dangerous because they create the expectation that all members of a group will be able to achieve certain feats or will act in certain ways. These sorts of expectations place excessive pressure on those who cannot or do not want to live up to the stereotype.

### Early Stereotypes

During slavery, African Americans were often viewed as "Sambos," or mentally inferior, lazy people, usually cheerful and childlike, a characterization that made slavery more palatable to its practitioners. Three other early stereotypes cast African American men as sexual predators ("bucks") or Uncle Toms and women as mammies, or nurturing earth mothers. Both whites and African Americans used the term "Uncle Tom" to refer to an African American man (occasionally a woman) who gives in readily to demands made by members of the dominant white group. This term is often said to have originated with Harriet Beecher Stowe's 1852 novel *Uncle Tom's Cabin*; however, the term probably entered popular culture as a result of George L. Aiken's *Tom Shows* (1852), a crude and violent traveling show that presented caricatures of both slaves and slave owners.

The stereotypical depiction of an African American woman as a mammy, a sort of earth mother selflessly caring for children, probably originated because so many African American women cared for the children of white plantation owners. The mammy figure was popularized by Margaret Mitchell's 1936 novel *Gone with the Wind*, which was made into an Academy Award-winning movie.

Another early stereotype was the portrayal of African American men as sexual predators, or black "bucks," who would attack any white woman they encountered. This stereotype, born of white fears about the mixing of races, forced many African American men in the Deep South to be very careful in their attitude toward and dealings with white women from shortly after emancipation through the second half of the twentieth century. The

*One of the most persistent stereotypes of African American women is that of the black "mammy"— a woman selflessly devoted to caring for her white master's children.*
(Library of Congress)

---

# Black "Brute" and "Buck" Stereotypes

To help counter growing African American political power and freedoms after Reconstruction, some white southerners justified a wave of terrorism and lynching by creating new stereotypes of black male brutality. The black "brute" stereotype was a figure who was inhumanly brutal, and the "buck" was a figure who combined brutality and sexual monstrosity and who desired nothing more than to rape white women. These stereotypes found their clearest early expression in the novels of Thomas Dixon and in D. W. Griffith's 1915 film *Birth of a Nation*, which was based on Dixon's novel *The Clansman* (1905).

Although only a minority of male lynching victims were charged with rape—and many of even those allegations were false—the stereotypes were important to lynching's public defenders, who insisted that lynching was necessary to defend the supposed purity of white womanhood. One of the most important strategies for antilynching activists and organizations, such as the National Association for the Advancement of Colored People, was to attempt to undermine public support for lynching by debunking the stereotype of the black rapist. Controversy surrounding the use of black "brute" and "buck" stereotypes in a variety of modern arenas (including media and national politics) remains an important area of racial discourse in the twenty-first century.

*Jonathan Markovitz*

---

slightest suspicion of sexual relations between a black man and a white woman could mean legal problems and even physical danger (lynching) for an African American man.

### Modern Stereotypes

In the second half of the twentieth century, some of the early stereotypes diminished in intensity and others persisted in a somewhat altered form. For example, although the Sambo image faded, African Americans were still commonly believed to be mentally inferior to whites. These old stereotypes were, however, joined by new ones that were adopted and popularized by the media. Typically, the African Americans who appeared in films and television programs in the 1950's and early 1960's portrayed one-dimensional characters who embodied common stereotypes.

One stereotype that developed in this period was of the African American as a super athlete. The success of African American athletes such as baseball player Willie Mays, football star Jim Brown, and boxers such as Joe Louis and Muhammad Ali (Cassius Clay) led many Americans to believe that all African Americans possessed super athletic abilities.

Another common stereotype viewed all African Americans as having a superior sense of rhythm that produced excellent music and made them skillful dancers. Although much of the music regarded as American—jazz, blues, gospel, and rock—has its origins in African American culture and thus can be regarded as a product of African Americans, it is a mistake to project this level of musical talent onto all members of the group. Also, the stereotype ignores the historical and cultural reasons behind the creation of these musical genres. Likewise, although some African Americans possess an excellent sense of rhythm and are extremely skilled dancers, not all members of the group are similarly talented.

A common stereotype often exploited by the media is that of the street-smart, wisecracking, slightly goofy male adolescent (or young adult) African American. This cynical, know-it-all attitude is common among teenage boys or young men, but the stereotype turns it into an African American characteristic, often depicting the young black adolescent as a gang member. Of course some African American adolescents belong to gangs, but adolescents from numerous other racial and ethnic groups also join gangs.

The welfare queen—a woman who refuses to work and maintains an "upscale" lifestyle through unfair use of welfare—is a new twist on the stereotype that African Americans are slothful, childlike people. Welfare queens, usually single mothers, are depicted as lazy, perhaps immoral women who are having babies to increase the amount of their welfare check and to avoid working. In fact, in 1993, more white women were receiving welfare benefits than were African American women.

*Annita Marie Ward*

**Further Reading**

Louise Kidder discusses stereotypes in *The Psychology of Intergroup Relations: Conflict and Consciousness* (New York: McGraw-Hill, 1975). Barbara Rollock discusses the portrayal of African Americans in *The Black Experience in Children's Books* (New York: New York Public Library, 1984). Well-known journalist Carl Thomas Rowan tells what it is like to deal with racial barriers and stereotypes in *Breaking Barriers: A Memoir* (Boston: Little, Brown, 1991). Other books that deal with the African American experience and stereotypes include Frank L. Keegan's *Blacktown, USA* (Boston: Little, Brown, 1971), Gordon Parks's *Born Black* (Philadelphia: Lippincott, 1971), and Louise Meriwether's *Don't Ride the Bus on Mondays: The Rosa Parks Story* (Englewood Cliffs, N. J.: Prentice Hall, 1973).

**See also** Black Is Beautiful movement; Cowboys; Film history; Literature; Music; Slavery and race relations; Sports; Tuskegee experiment

# Stono Rebellion

**The Event:** Major slave rebellion
**Date:** September 9, 1739
**Place:** St. Paul's Parish near the Stono River, twenty miles from Charles Town, South Carolina

*The success of the Stono Rebellion triggered other slave insurrections, forcing white settlers to organize to prevent further slave uprisings.*

Conditions in South Carolina during the 1730's led to white fear of slave uprisings. The high numbers of Africans imported through Charles Town port led to legislation against Africans congregating, holding meetings, and appearing in public after night hours. Charles Town had a watch committee to guard the port city, and the rest of the colony had a white patrol system to police Africans in militia districts. South Carolina used public punishment as a deterrent.

Contrary to their intent, these white controls increasingly led to greater resistance from newly imported Africans. Cases of verbal insolence joined arson as a recurring feature of colonial life. Whites blamed illnesses and deaths on African knowledge of plants and their poisonous powers. In the 1730's, massive importations from the Congo-Angola region meant that more than half of the colony's slaves had been there fewer than ten years. Slave unrest was blamed on outside agitators—Native Americans with assistance from both the Spanish and French. Rumors of a Spanish invasion increased after the Spanish king granted liberty to African fugitive slaves in 1733.

**Prelude to Rebellion**

Tension thus was high in 1739. Then, a smallpox epidemic, coupled with the escape of slaves to Spanish Florida, led to massive loss of investments. A yellow fever epidemic hit during the summer months. In the fall, deaths decreased with the return of cool weather, but the situation was ripe for insurrection. Since Sundays afforded slaves their best opportunity for meeting in communal activities, the legislature passed the Security Act in August, 1739, requiring all white men to carry firearms to churches beginning September 29 or pay a stiff fine. News of conflict between England and Spain reached Charles Town the weekend before the uprising began, explaining why the Stono Rebellion began immediately without betrayal, caught white masters in church unarmed, and had slaves marching toward Spanish St. Augustine.

The insurrection included elements typical of early rebellions in South Carolina: total surprise, brutal killings, extensive property damage, armed fighting, and extended consequences. On the morning of September 9, 1739, twenty slaves, mostly Angolans, gathered in St. Paul's Parish near the Stono River, twenty miles from Charles Town. Led by a slave named Jemmy, the group broke into Hutchenson's store near the Stono Bridge to gather guns and ammunition. Storekeepers Robert Bathurst and Mr. Gibbs were beheaded. The slave band moved on to the Godfrey house, killing the family, gathering supplies, and burning the building. The slaves took the main road to Georgia, stopping at Wallace's Tavern but sparing the innkeeper, who was known to be a kind master. His white neighbor, however, lost his life, along with his wife and child. The band continued, sacking and burning houses on Pons Pons Road and killing all the white occupants. Slave owner Thomas Rose was successfully hidden by his slaves as the band moved through. The group's numbers grew as reluctant slaves were forced to join. Increased numbers led to diminished discipline. The group took up a banner, beat on two drums, and shouted, "Liberty!" They pursued and killed any whites they encountered.

Lieutenant Governor William Bull and four other white men were traveling to Charles Town for legislative session when they encountered the rebel slaves. They escaped to warn others. By late Sunday afternoon, the band of nearly one hundred rebel slaves stopped in an open field, showing their confidence and hoping to be joined by other slaves by morning.

Nearby, white colonists had been alerted by Sunday afternoon and had organized an armed and mounted resistance of somewhere between twenty and one hundred men. Moving to the field, the white forces caught the slaves off guard, killing or wounding at least fourteen rebels. They surrounded other rebels, who were briefly questioned before being shot to death. They released the slaves who had been forced to participate. Almost one-third of the rebelling slaves escaped the fighting. Some returned to their plantations, hoping not to be missed. Upon their return, planters cut off their heads and placed them on posts to serve as a reminder for other slaves seeking freedom.

The white colony engaged in an intensive manhunt to recapture those participants who remained at large. Whites armed themselves, and guards were posted at ferry posts. By some accounts, twenty to forty rebels were captured, hanged, disemboweled, or beaten within the two following days. Another account, a month later, reported the rebels had been stopped from doing further mischief by having been "put to the most cruel Death." The Georgia general James Oglethorpe called out rangers and American Indians, garrisoned soldiers at Palachicolas—a fort guarding the only point on the Savannah River where fugitives could cross—and issued a proclamation for whites to keep a watchful eye on any Africans.

Despite these acts of retribution and retaliation against both free African Americans and slaves, white fears did not subside.

Most whites thought persons of African descent were dangerous and possessed of a rebellious nature. By the fall of 1739,
many planters near Stono had moved their wives and children
in with other families for greater security. The Assembly placed
a special patrol along the Stono River. Outlying fugitives were
still being brought in for execution by early 1740. Finally, two fugitive slaves seeking a large reward captured the last remaining
leader, who had been at large for three years following the insurrection.

**Aftermath**

The white minority responded to the Stono Rebellion in several ways. First, the colony tightened restrictions on all African
Americans, giving South Carolina the harshest penalties of any
mainland colony. The colony also sought to improve conditions
that provoked rebellion. Finally, the colony sought to lessen the
influence of the Spanish settlement in St. Augustine as a constant
source of incitement. The war against the Spanish curbed that
stimulant. The white minority also tried to correct the numerical
racial imbalance. A prohibitive duty on new slave imports cut the
rate of importation from one thousand per year in 1730 to one
hundred per year by 1740. Collected duties went to recruit white
immigrants. The legislature required one white man present for
every ten Africans on a plantation. Fines from this infraction
went to fund additional patrols.

The government intensified efforts to control the behavior of
slaves. Through the Negro Act of 1740, the legislators shaped the
core of the South Carolina slave codes for more than a century.
Masters who failed to retain control of slaves received fines. The
right to manumit slaves was taken out of the hands of owners and
turned over to the legislature. No longer could slaves have such
personal liberties as freedom of movement, of education, of assembly, to raise food, and to earn money. Surveillance of African
American activity increased. Slaves received rewards for inform-
ing on the actions of other slaves. The legislature discouraged the
presence of free blacks in the colony.

The white minority developed several strategies of calculated
benevolence. The government assessed penalties on masters

known for excessive labor requirements or brutality of punishments for their slaves. A school was founded in Charles Town to train slaves to teach other slaves about selective Christian principles requiring submission and obedience.

These efforts did not lessen white dependency on African labor. Machines did not supplant their labor until after the American Revolution. White immigration did not increase substantially, despite offers of free land on the frontier. High duties reduced the importation of slaves, but the racial proportions varied slightly from those prior to insurrection.

The suppression of the Stono Rebellion was a significant turning point for the white minority. White factions had to cooperate to maintain the English colony. Techniques used to maintain white control shaped the race relations and history of South Carolina. The heightened degree of white repression and the reduction in African autonomy created a new social equilibrium in the generation before the American Revolution.

*Dorothy C. Salem*

## Further Reading

Aptheker, Herbert. *American Negro Slave Revolts.* Rev. ed. New York: Columbia University Press, 1969. The pioneering work on slave revolts.

Jordan, Winthrop. *White over Black: American Attitudes Toward the Negro, 1550-1812.* Chapel Hill: University of North Carolina Press, 1968. Discusses how slave revolts influenced the status of both slaves and free blacks in the United States.

Kilson, Martin. "Toward Freedom: An Analysis of Slave Revolts in the United States." *Phylon* 25 (1964): 175-189. Analyzes the distribution of slave revolts and the environments that contributed to their occurrence.

Wood, Peter H. *Black Majority: Negroes in Colonial South Carolina from 1670 Through the Stono Rebellion.* New York: W. W. Norton, 1974. Examines the patterns of white control and African resistance within the socioeconomic context of colonial South Carolina. Both a narrative and an analysis of the event and its effects on the colony.

See also *Amistad* slave revolt; New York City slave revolt; Slavery; Slavery and race relations; Slavery and the justice system; Slavery in Virginia; Turner's slave insurrection

# Strauder v. West Virginia

**The Case:** U.S. Supreme Court ruling on jury composition
**Date:** March 1, 1880
*The Supreme Court declared that exclusion of African Americans from juries was a violation of the equal protection clause of the Fourteenth Amendment.*

During the late nineteenth century, West Virginia had a statute that explicitly limited jury service to "white male persons." Strauder, a black man convicted of murder, claimed that he had not received a fair trial because of the statute. The Supreme Court agreed. Writing for a 7-2 majority, Justice William Strong explained that such a law constituted precisely the kind of discrimination that the Fourteenth Amendment was designed to prevent. Also in 1880, the Court decided three other important cases dealing with racial exclusion from juries. In *Neal v. Delaware* and *Ex parte Virginia*, it held that even if the state's laws did not exclude blacks, the actual practice of exclusion was a denial of equal protection. In *Virginia v. Rives*, however, the Court ruled that the mere absence of African Americans from juries was not in itself a violation of the Fourteenth Amendment. In effect, *Rives* allowed local officials to use their discretionary authority to exclude African Americans from juries. Although *Strauder, Ex Parte Virginia,* and *Neal* had limited impact during the Jim Crow era, they nevertheless helped prepare a constitutional foundation for the Civil Rights movement of the mid-twentieth century.

*Thomas Tandy Lewis*

See also *Batson v. Kentucky; Edmonson v. Leesville Concrete Company; Powers v. Ohio; Williams v. Mississippi*

# Student Nonviolent Coordinating Committee

**Identification:** National civil rights organization also known by
   its acronym, SNCC (pronounced "snick")
**Date:** Founded in April, 1960
**Place:** Raleigh, North Carolina
*As tensions mounted during in the mid-1960's, the Student Nonviolent
   Coordinating Committee became increasingly aggressive and even-
   tually dropped its nonviolent stance.*

In early 1960, amid a growing number of student civil rights
demonstrations, the Southern Christian Leadership Conference
(SCLC), led by Martin Luther King, Jr., encouraged students to
convene their own organization. In response to the call, a group
of student leaders, under the guidance of Ella Baker, a former administrative head of SCLC, formed the Student Nonviolent Coordinating Committee.

Committed at the outset to nonviolence, SNCC was designed
to be thoroughly democratic and to function independently from
mainstream groups, including the SCLC. It also became a biracial
organization although initially there was some concern that allowing white students to join SNCC might compromise the organization.

### Direct Action

Despite its nonviolent philosophy, SNCC was often very aggressive and confrontational in attacking segregation. The organization took on several of the more dangerous civil rights battles
including voter registration campaigns in Alabama and Mississippi. Numerous times SNCC activists were badly beaten, and in
the summer of 1964, three activists who had joined the SNCC
campaign—Michael Schwerner, Andrew Goodman, and James
Chaney—were brutally murdered by southern segregationists
including members of the Ku Klux Klan. Nevertheless, SNCC
continued its confrontational strategy.

By 1964, frustrated by the slow pace of change and apparent lack of support from the federal government, SNCC members began to splinter into two factions. One group sought to maintain the organization's original principles, and the other chose to reconsider the group's nonviolent approach. Racial tensions within the organization further divided SNCC. African American volunteers were concerned that their white counterparts were taking control of the organization, and white members were growing more critical of SNCC leadership. Amid the internal tensions, many SNCC members became increasingly radical.

During the mid-1960's, SNCC members, under the charismatic leadership of Stokely Carmichael, embraced a new creed of black power. The slogan became a call for economic self-determination and political activism as well as a symbol of black militancy. Carmichael believed that change would come only through dramatic, confrontational appeals. The evolving SNCC philosophy advocated responding to violence with violence. The increasingly strident rhetoric led some members to abandon the organization, but at the same time, it attracted new membership,

*H. Rap Brown, the leader of the Student Nonviolent Coordinating Committee in 1967, at a press conference.* (Library of Congress)

particularly radical, northern, urban African Americans. Further demonstrating its new direction, SNCC shifted its activities from voting rights and educational issues in the rural South to conditions in urban ghettos.

## Decline

SNCC, plagued by ineffective leadership and constant internal divisions, saw its membership dwindle to a handful of activists by 1968. The organization was further undermined by its entering into a formal alliance with the Black Panthers and by concern that the organization associated with other paramilitary groups. The last two SNCC chapters, Atlanta and New York, ceased operation in early 1970.

SNCC activists helped to focus the nation on the problem of institutionalized racism by taking a leading role in several major civil rights demonstrations during the 1960's. In 1961, SNCC members helped the Congress of Racial Equality (CORE) operate Freedom Rides that challenged the constitutionality of segregated interstate busing laws in the South. The rides attracted much media coverage, which brought the Civil Rights movement into middle-class white suburban homes for the first time and helped pressure President John F. Kennedy into paying more attention to civil rights issues. The rides were immediately followed by the Albany, Georgia, demonstrations, in which SNCC members sat in whites-only sections of local bus stations to test interstate transportation laws that made segregated facilities illegal.

In 1964, SNCC organized a voter registration and educational campaign in Mississippi. A biracial effort carried out by college student volunteers, the second phase of the campaign, in which young workers were to educate voters, became known as Freedom Summer. This campaign further enlightened Americans about the plight of African Americans in the South. The student volunteers who participated in the campaign were able to register more than seventeen thousand African American voters and provided more than three thousand children with educational instruction. The efforts, however, came at a price. During the summer, at least sixty-seven bombings and arson fires were directed at the volunteers. In one incident, three activists, Schwerner, Goodman, and Chaney, were killed. That same summer, SNCC helped organize the forming of the Mississippi Freedom Democratic Party, which challenged the credentials of the Mississippi delegation to the 1964 Democratic National Convention when it met to nominate Lyndon B. Johnson. SNCC members were also among the organizers and participants in most of the civil rights marches during the mid-1960's, including the March on Washington in 1963 and the march from Selma to Montgomery in 1965.

Though SNCC disbanded early in the 1970's, several of the organization's leaders and former members remained activists on both the local and national levels well into the 1970's. Among the more notable former SNCC members are James Forman, who became involved in African American economic development; John Lewis, who in 1988 won election to the House of Representatives; Charles Sherrod, who was elected mayor of Albany, Georgia; and Robert Moses, who became director of a nationwide literacy program. Other former members became involved in protesting the Vietnam War and in the women's rights movement.

*Paul E. Doutrich*

**Further Reading**

Barbara Ransby's *Ella Baker and the Black Freedom Movement: A Radical Democratic Vision* (Chapel Hill: University of North Carolina Press, 2003) discusses the impact of SNCC and Baker's work with the organization. Howard Zinn's *SNCC: The New Abolitionists* (Cambridge, Mass.: South End Press, 2002) provides a notable study of the organization. In 1998, Cheryl Lynn Greenberg edited a collection entitled *A Circle of Trust: Remembering SNCC* (New Brunswick, N.J.: Rutgers University Press, 1998). A personal memoir is available in *The River of No Return: The Autobiography of a Black Militant and the Life and Death of SNCC* (Jackson: University Press of Mississippi, 1990), by Cleveland Sellers with Robert Terrell. Clayborne Carson's *In Struggle: SNCC and the Black Awakening of the 1960's* (Cambridge, Mass.: Harvard University Press, 1995) discusses SNCC's role in the context of the Civil Rights movement in the South.

**See also** Birmingham March; "Black Manifesto"; Black Panther Party; Black Power movement; Chicago riots; Civil Rights movement; Civil rights worker murders; Congress of Racial Equality; Freedom Rides; Freedom Summer; Mississippi Freedom Democratic Party; Southern Christian Leadership Conference

# Summit Meeting of National Negro Leaders

**The Event:** Meeting between major African American leaders and President Dwight D. Eisenhower
**Date:** June, 1958
**Place:** Washington, D.C.
*This meeting between President Dwight D. Eisenhower and national African American leaders was the first and last White House conference with black leaders during the Eisenhower administration; later requests for meetings were denied.*

After five years in office and repeated requests from civil rights activists for an audience, U.S. president Dwight D. Eisenhower held a "summit meeting" in June, 1958, with four African American leaders: Dr. Martin Luther King, Jr.; A. Philip Randolph; Roy Wilkins of the National Association for the Advancement of Colored People; and Lester B. Granger of the National Urban League. The purpose of the summit was to address strategies for dealing with the approaching wave of school integration and to express concerns over the reluctance of the Eisenhower administration to support civil rights and enforce court orders mandating desegregated public schools; yet the significance of the summit lay in the fact that it was Eisenhower's first such meeting with black leaders.

The meeting itself was by all accounts brief and uneventful. The leaders presented Eisenhower with a carefully worded statement calling for increased federal visibility and involvement in advancing civil rights causes and tactfully criticized the president for his previous statement urging them to "be patient" about civil rights. Eisenhower promised the leaders that he would take their statement under consideration but responded evasively to their requests for a national conference on civil rights.

Michael H. Burchett

**See also** Black cabinet; Civil Rights movement; Congressional Black Caucus

# Swann v. Charlotte-Mecklenberg Board of Education

**The Case:** U.S. Supreme Court ruling on school integration and busing

**Date:** April 20, 1971

*The Supreme Court ruled that federal courts may order local school boards to use extensive busing plans to desegregate schools whenever racial segregation had been supported by public policy.*

The original catalyst for this case was the plan of the school board of Charlotte, Mecklenberg County, North Carolina, to close some African American schools, create attendance zones for most of the schools in the district, and allow a "freedom-of-choice" provision under which students could transfer to any school in the district, provided that they could furnish their own transportation and the school was not already filled to capacity. The litigation began on January 19, 1965, when eleven African American families, including Vera and Darius Swann and their son James, were convinced by attorney Julius L. Chambers to sue the district for relief. The plaintiffs challenged the plan on the premise that the closing of the African American schools would place the burden of desegregation on the African American students, and that the other features would only perpetuate segregation.

## The Appellate Process

In 1965, federal district court judge J. Braxton Craven rejected the plaintiff's challenge and approved the school board's plan. A year later, the Court of Appeals for the Fourth Circuit affirmed Craven's ruling. At this point, Chambers opted not to appeal to the Supreme Court, because he feared that the Court would only affirm the lower rulings under the precedents established at that time.

After the Supreme Court's ruling in *Green v. County School Board of New Kent County, Virginia* in 1968, however, Chambers decided to petition for further relief. In *Green*, the justices ruled that freedom-of-choice plans did not aid in the process of desegregation, and that other methods must be used to comply with *Brown v. Board of Education* (1954). On September 6, 1968, the *Swann* plaintiffs filed a motion for further relief in the federal district court in Charlotte. The motion came before Judge James B. McMillan. Both parties agreed that the school system fell short of achieving the unitary status required by *Green*. Two plans were submitted, one by the school board and the other by a court-appointed expert from Rhode Island College, Dr. John Finger.

Judge McMillan essentially accepted the Finger plan, which required more desegregation than the school board was willing to accept. The board plan would have closed seven schools and reassigned the students involved. Attendance zones were to be restructured to achieve greater racial balance, but the existing grade structures were left intact. Furthermore, the board plan would modify the free transfer plan into an optional majority-to-minority transfer system (students in a racial majority in one school could transfer to another where they would be in the minority).

Under the board plan, African American students would be reassigned to nine of the ten high schools in the district, thereby producing in each an African American population of between 17 and 36 percent. The tenth high school would have an African American population of 2 percent. The junior high schools would be rezoned so that all but one would have from none to 38 percent African Americans. One junior high school would have an African American population of 90 percent. Attendance at the elementary schools, however, still would be based primarily on the neighborhood concept. More than half the African American children at this level would remain in schools that were between 86 and 100 percent black.

The Finger plan used the board zoning plan for high schools, with one modification. Three hundred additional African American students would be transported to the nearly all-white Independence High School. This plan dealt similarly with the junior high schools. Nine satellite zones would be created, and inner-city African American students would be assigned to nine outlying, predominantly white junior high schools. As was typically the case, the biggest controversy concerned the elementary school students. Rather than simply relying on zoning, Finger proposed that pairing and grouping techniques be used as well, with the result that all elementary schools would have a black student proportion that would range from 9 to 38 percent. Pairing occurs when two schools, one predominantly white and one predominantly black, are combined by either sending half the students in one school to the other for all grades or by sending all the children to one school for certain grades and then to the other school for the remaining grade levels. Bus transportation would be used for the affected students. After the district court's busing order, McMillan was hanged in effigy. Crowds demonstrated at the courthouse, in front of the judge's house, and at the *Charlotte Observer*, a newspaper that had supported busing. McMillan and his family received threatening phone calls, his law office was fire-bombed by an arsonist, his car was dynamited, and his home was vandalized.

### New Appeals

The Charlotte-Mecklenburg Board of Education appealed McMillan's busing order to the Fourth Circuit Court of Appeals. The appellate court vacated McMillan's order respecting elementary schools, and affirmed his ruling only on the secondary school plans. This time, because of the *Green* case, Chambers appealed the decision to the Supreme Court.

By the time the Supreme Court ruled on *Swann* in 1971, Earl Warren had retired as Chief Justice, and President Richard Nixon (who had publicly condemned forced busing) had filled Earl Warren's seat on the Court with Warren Burger in 1969. *Swann v.*

*Charlotte-Mecklenberg Board of Education* dealt with the constitutionality of several different techniques to achieve desegregation. In writing the unanimous decision, Burger admitted that the Court had not, as of that time, provided federal district courts with comprehensive guidelines for implementing its 1954 landmark case, *Brown v. Board of Education of Topeka, Kansas*. He declared:

> Understandably, in an area of evolving remedies, those courts had to improvise and experiment without detailed or specific guidelines. This Court . . . appropriately dealt with the large constitutional principles; other federal courts had to grapple with the flinty, intractable realities of day-to-day implementation of those constitutional commands. Their efforts, of necessity, embraced a process of "trial and error," and our effort to formulate guidelines must take into account their experience.

In accepting the Finger plan, the justices ruled that federal district courts could decree as tools of desegregation the following: reasonable bus transportation, reasonable grouping of noncontiguous zones, the reasonable movement toward the elimination of one-race schools, and the use of mathematical ratios of black and white people in the schools as a starting point toward racial desegregation. Thus, the nation's highest tribunal had ruled that school districts could transport students in an effort to implement different techniques for the purpose of desegregating their schools.

*Brian L. Fife*

**Further Reading**

Barrows, Frank. "School Busing: Charlotte, N.C." *The Atlantic* 230, no. 5 (1972): 17-22. Assesses the school desegregation plan's impact on the citizens of Mecklenberg County during its implementation.

Fiss, Owen. "The Charlotte-Mecklenberg Case—Its Significance for Northern School Desegregation." *University of Chicago Law Review* 38 (1971): 697-709. Argues that the *Swann* ruling was not relegated to southern school systems, and that districts in the North would be affected as well.

Gaillard, Frye. *The Dream Long Deferred*. Chapel Hill: University of North Carolina Press, 1988. Gaillard, a reporter for the *Charlotte Observer*, documents the desegregation process in the Charlotte-Mecklenburg school district.

Goldstein, Robert D. "A *Swann* Song for Remedies: Equitable Relief in the Burger Court." *Harvard Civil Rights-Civil Liberties Law Review* 13 (1978): 1-80. Surveys three principles that the Supreme Court has applied in its review of injunctions against state officers.

Schwartz, Bernard. *Swann's Way: The School Busing Case and the Supreme Court*. New York: Oxford University Press, 1986. In interviewing members of the Supreme Court and other principal personages, Schwartz provides an inside account of the Court's decision making in *Swann*.

**See also** *Brown v. Board of Education*; Little Rock school desegregation crisis; University of Mississippi desegregation

# Sweatt v. Painter

**The Case:** U.S. Supreme Court ruling on professional school desegregation

**Date:** June 5, 1950

*This unanimous Supreme Court decision declared that the "separate but equal" standard established in* Plessy v. Ferguson *in 1896 was unattainable in higher education.*

The Supreme Court's *Plessy v. Ferguson* decision (1896) established the "separate but equal" doctrine that provided the legal justification for segregation. Civil rights organizations, including the National Association for the Advancement of Colored People (NAACP), although opposed to "separate but equal," decided to use the courts in an attempt to make sure that the "equal" part of the "separate but equal" doctrine was being enforced. In a series of cases running from 1936 to the *Sweatt* decision in 1950, the NAACP attacked the lack of law schools and graduate programs for African Americans throughout the South.

If no professional schools existed, clearly the "separate but equal" doctrine was not being met. When African Americans started seeking admission to professional schools throughout the South, many states established "overnight" law schools and professional schools in order to comply with *Plessy*. These schools were certainly separate, but were they equal? Herman Sweatt, a Houston, Texas, postal worker, applied for admission to the University of Texas Law School in 1946. He was denied admission on the grounds that Texas had just created a law school for African Americans. To avoid integration, Texas had rented a few rooms in Houston and hired two black lawyers as its faculty.

Sweatt refused to attend the "black law school," saying that it was inferior and he would be deprived of the "equal protection of the law." A unanimous Supreme Court sided with Sweatt, whose case was argued by Thurgood Marshall of the NAACP. Even if the facilities at the two Texas schools were equal, the Court concluded that inequality might exist with respect to other factors "which make for greatness in a law school." Such factors include the reputation of the faculty and administration and the prestige of the alumni. "It is difficult to believe," said Chief Justice Fred M. Vinson, Jr., "that one who had a free choice between these law schools would consider the question close."

The Court ordered that Sweatt be admitted to the University of Texas Law School. The *Sweatt* case marked the first time the Supreme Court found a black professional school to be unequal in quality. Although the Court refused to reexamine *Plessy v. Ferguson*, the decision in *Sweatt* paved the way for the NAACP to launch a direct assault in overturning *Plessy* in *Brown v. Board of Education* only four years later.

*Darryl Paulson*

**See also** *Bakke* case; *Brown v. Board of Education*; Civil Rights movement; *Keyes v. Denver School District No. 1*; National Association for the Advancement of Colored People; *Plessy v. Ferguson*; School desegregation; Segregation

# Talented Tenth

**Definition:** Term coined by W. E. B. Du Bois to denote a black intellectual elite that he hoped would provide the leadership necessary to facilitate the advancement of African Americans
**Date:** 1903

*Du Bois's idea of a Talented Tenth of black leadership reflected the changing spirit of black activism in early twentieth century America, offering a new synthesis of black protest thought that would influence the early Civil Rights movement.*

The first African American to receive a doctoral degree from Harvard University, W. E. B. Du Bois drew upon a tradition of northern-based black intellectualism predating the Civil War to promote the development of a classically trained vanguard of "leaders, thinkers, and artists" to educate and uplift oppressed, lower-class African Americans. Du Bois's Talented Tenth proposal was largely a response to accommodationists such as Booker T. Washington, who emphasized vocational education as a means for African Americans to establish themselves economically and socially in a manner nonthreatening to whites.

Originally a follower of Washington, Du Bois began to dissent from accommodationist policy when Washington's emphasis on industrial education and his influence with northern philanthropists drew resources away from southern liberal arts colleges such as Atlanta University, where Du Bois was a professor of sociology. Although Du Bois's scathing criticisms of accommodationism echoed those of other "radical" black leaders such as William Monroe Trotter, who denounced Washington as a race traitor, Du Bois's call for a Talented Tenth was essentially an elitist variation of the doctrine of self-help and racial solidarity that was at the core of accommodationism.

Like Washington, Du Bois advocated education as a means of strengthening black communities by alleviating social pathologies brought on by generations of oppression and cultural alienation. While recognizing the necessity of vocational training for young African Americans, Du Bois insisted that the true aim of education was "not to make men carpenters (but) to make car-

*W. E. B. Du Bois.* (Association for the Study of African-American Life and History)

penters men" by imbuing them with a sense of culture and an elevated awareness of their place in the world. To accomplish this, Du Bois argued, it would be necessary to maintain a small number of quality liberal-arts institutions for African Americans dedicated to developing and motivating liberally educated black teachers and professionals.

## Impact

The idea of a Talented Tenth of black leadership is significant not only as the essence of Du Bois's racial policy but also as a reflection of the changing spirit of black activism in early twentieth century America. By combining elements of accommodationism with strains of postbellum agitation, Du Bois advanced a new synthesis of black protest thought that exerted considerable influence upon the early Civil Rights movement; at the heart of this synthesis was his advocacy of leadership by the Talented Tenth.

The Niagara Movement, organized by Du Bois in 1905, consisted mainly of upper- and middle-class black intellectuals from northern states and emphasized agitation as a means of protest. In 1909, key members of the Niagara Movement, including Du

Bois, joined forces with progressive upper- and middle-class whites to establish the National Association for the Advancement of Colored People (NAACP), whose strategy of legalism and direct action relied heavily upon the leadership of attorneys and academics. Despite the success of this strategy of legalism and the prominent leadership of scholars such as Martin Luther King, Jr., enthusiasm for the idea of a Talented Tenth waned through the twentieth century as the focus of the Civil Rights movement shifted from the interests of a biracial elite to those of a predominantly black working class.

*Michael H. Burchett*

**See also** Atlanta Compromise; Black cabinet; Black colleges and universities; Civil Rights movement; Education; National Association for the Advancement of Colored People; Niagara Movement

# *Terry v. Adams*

**The Case:** U.S. Supreme Court ruling on white primaries
**Date:** May 4, 1953

*In this case, the Supreme Court clearly declared the white primary unconstitutional.*

Beginning in 1889, the Jaybird Democratic Association in Texas started the practice of holding a primary election to select candidates for the Democratic Party in order to circumvent the Fifteenth Amendment. These candidates, often uncontested, usually were elected to office. Although white voters could participate in this process, black voters were excluded. The Supreme Court, by a vote of eight to one, declared the white primaries unconstitutional. Justice Hugo L. Black announced the decision for the 8-1 majority in this case, but there was no majority opinion. Instead, there were a series of opinions issued by various justices. Black emphasized that the government could not exclude African Americans from primaries, which were the only significant elections in most southern jurisdictions. Justice Felix Frankfurter criticized the complicity of southern election officials in excluding African Americans from the process. Justice Tom C. Clark focused on the fact that the white primary was an adjunct of the state-regulated Democratic Party. In general, eight justices believed that in some way, the white primary was a public institution in violation of the Fifteenth Amendment. Only Justice Sherman Minton dissented, finding that the white primary acted simply as an interest group.

*Richard L. Wilson*

**See also** Fifteenth Amendment; Gerrymandering; Voting Rights Act of 1965; White primaries

# Thirteenth Amendment

**The Law:** Amendment to the U.S. Constitution that abolished the institution of slavery in the United States
**Date:** Ratified on December 18, 1865
*After decades of slave revolts, abolitionist struggles, and a bloody Civil War that was fought, in part, to end slavery, the Thirteenth Amendment brought a definitive end to the institution.*

The antislavery and abolition movements did not begin with the Civil War. As early as 1652, the state of Rhode Island passed antislavery legislation. In 1773, Benjamin Franklin and Dr. Benjamin Rush formed the first abolition society in America. In 1832, the New England Anti-Slavery Society was formed by newspaper editor William Lloyd Garrison, who also helped found the American Anti-Slavery Society in 1833. The Society of Friends, or Quakers, a religious group who settled early in the history of the United States, were very active in the antislavery movement. Their religion forbade the holding of slaves. Quakers primarily settled in the northern part of the country.

### Antislavery Legislation

In 1807, federal legislation was passed outlawing the importation of slaves after January 1, 1808. However, this did not end the use of slaves in the United States. The writers of the Constitution could not resolve the issue of slavery in America, and so had declared that the slave trade could end by 1808 or anytime later. Eventually, the inability of national leaders to resolve this issue would divide the nation. The Missouri Compromise of 1820 banned slavery in most of the western states and territories. This was overturned by the Supreme Court in 1857, in the infamous *Dred Scott* decision.

The split between the states was well in place at this point. Congress, in an attempt to appease pro- and antislavery proponents, adopted five provisions in the Compromise of 1850. The most notable was the Second Fugitive Slave Law, passed in 1851, which provided for slaves who escaped from the South and were found in northern antislavery states to be returned to slave owners. A great deal of violence erupted over this legislation, which led to the act's repeal on June 28, 1864. This split between the North and the South eventually resulted in the Civil War.

The abolitionist movement had fought throughout the history of the United States for an end to the institution of slavery. Robert

*Contemporary illustration of African Americans celebrating the abolition of slavery in the District of Columbia in early 1866.* (Library of Congress)

Dale Owen, an abolitionist and legislator, struggled for the emancipation of slaves and is thought to have influenced President Abraham Lincoln with his tract *The Policy of Emancipation* (1862). Another radical opponent of slavery was Wendell Phillips, a noted speaker and a graduate of Harvard Law School. He believed that the U.S. Constitution supported slavery and therefore was owed no allegiance by abolitionists. Harriet Tubman was active in the Underground Railroad, which was successful in bringing many slaves into northern states that would not return them to their owners. John Brown adopted more violent means of expressing his abolitionist sentiment. He raided the federal arsenal at Harpers Ferry, Virginia, and encouraged a slave revolt. He was eventually hanged for his fanaticism. Frederick Douglass was an important abolitionist who played a significant role in the passage toward freedom for the slaves. A runaway slave, he spoke eloquently about the need to redress the wrongs created by slavery.

As Civil War broke out, the movement placed greater pressure on President Lincoln to issue the Emancipation Proclamation. Lincoln had focused a great deal of attention on the issue of slavery during the famous Lincoln-Douglas debates. The Emancipation Proclamation was issued on September 22, 1862, well after the beginning of the Civil War. It announced that in states that had seceded from the union, all slaves would be freed effective January 1, 1863. This proclamation did not free many slaves. It did not apply to states that were part of the Union and was unenforceable in those states involved in the Confederacy. The major function of the Emancipation Proclamation was to announce to all that the Civil War was about slavery.

At the time that the Civil War began, the African American population of the United States consisted of approximately four and a half million people, four million of whom were slaves. White supremacy was the general ideology of both Southerners and Northerners. Slaves were denied such rights as the right to legal marriage, choice of residence, and education, and existed in perpetual servitude. Without significant changes in institutional structures, there was no hope of freedom.

## The Thirteenth Amendment

SECTION 1. Neither slavery nor involuntary servitude, except as a punishment for crime whereof the party shall have been duly convicted, shall exist within the United States, or any place subject to their jurisdiction.

SECTION 2. Congress shall have power to enforce this article by appropriate legislation.

### The Civil War Amendments

The Thirteenth Amendment was one of three amendments known as the Civil War amendments. The combined purpose of these three amendments was to free the slaves and promote their participation in their country. The Thirteenth Amendment states "neither slavery nor involuntary servitude, except as a punishment for crime whereof the party shall have been duly convicted, shall exist within the United States, or any place subject to their jurisdiction." One of the battles surrounding the Thirteenth Amendment in particular, and all the Civil War amendments in general, concerned the interpretation of the Tenth Amendment. The Tenth Amendment stated that no federal legislation could detract from the power of state government. Those who opposed the Thirteenth Amendment claimed that the right to allow slavery was not specifically denied in the Constitution and therefore fell within the authority of the state.

With the passage of the Thirteenth Amendment, the long fight to abolish slavery was over. The amendment was ratified on December 6, 1865, and officially announced on December 18, 1865. For some abolitionists, such as William Lloyd Garrison, the battle had been won: Slavery was ended. Others saw the Thirteenth Amendment as only a beginning.

Frederick Douglass did not have the same high hopes held by Garrison. Douglass believed that slavery would not be abolished until the former slaves acquired the right to vote. The passage of the Civil Rights Act of 1866 did not provide this right. It was not until the passage of the Fourteenth Amendment, in 1868, that citizenship and the rights thereof were guaranteed to "all persons born or naturalized in the United States." Finally, in 1870, former slaves were expressly given the right to vote. Within weeks, the first African American in the U.S. Senate, Hiram R. Revels, took his seat.

### Emancipation in the Reconstruction Era

On April 15, 1865, President Lincoln died from wounds inflicted by an assassin the night before. Vice President Andrew Johnson took over the reins of the presidency and reconstruction of the nation. Johnson, however, was not highly supportive or sympathetic to the needs of the slaves. Johnson blocked every attempt to extend rights to former slaves. In fact, Johnson vetoed most of the bills that were passed by Congress, only to have his veto overridden by a two-thirds majority of Congress. Impeachment charges eventually ensued, and Johnson was spared by only a one-vote margin. At that point, Johnson withdrew from Reconstruction activities and allowed Congress to control the process.

*African Americans marching through Richmond, Virginia, to commemorate Emancipation Day, around the turn of the twentieth century.* (Library of Congress)

One interesting note is the relationship between the woman suffrage movement and the abolition and black suffrage process. The decision over whether to support the call for the black vote divided the woman suffrage movement. Some believed that a gradual transition, in which first black men received the vote and then all women received the vote, would meet with greater success. Two such women were Lucy Stone and Julia Ward Howe. Others believed that suffrage was "all or nothing," and that women should not forsake their own cause in order to gain the vote for others. Susan B. Anthony and Elizabeth Cady Stanton were opposed to amendments that specifically referred to men and neglected suffrage for women. It was not until the passage of the Nineteenth Amendment in 1920 that women gained the long-sought suffrage.

*Sharon L. Larson*

## Further Reading

Commission on the Bicentennial of the U.S. Constitution. *1791 to 1991: The Bill of Rights and Beyond.* Washington, D.C.: Author, 1991. Discusses the history of the Constitution and each of the amendments. The abolitionist movement and passage of the Civil War amendments are discussed in relation to each other.

Franklin, John Hope. *From Slavery to Freedom: A History of Negro Americans.* 3d ed. New York: Alfred A. Knopf, 1967. Details the changes undergone by African Americans during the movement toward abolition and after they achieved citizenship.

Furnas, J. C. *The Road to Harpers Ferry.* London: Faber & Faber, 1961. An enlightening discussion of the problems created or observed in the abolitionist movement.

McKissack, Pat, and Fredrick McKissack. *The Civil Rights Movement in America from 1865 to the Present.* 2d ed. Chicago: Children's Press, 1991. Examines the progression of rights granted since the Civil War.

Owen, Robert Dale. *The Wrong of Slavery, the Right of Emancipation, and the Future of the African Race in the United States.* Philadelphia: J. B. Lippincott, 1864. Writings on the issue of slavery in the United States from an abolitionist of the slave era.

Richards, David A. J. *Conscience and the Constitution: History, Theory, and Law of the Reconstruction Amendments.* Princeton, N.J.: Princeton University Press, 1993.

Tsesis, Alexander. *The Thirteenth Amendment and American Freedom: A Legal History.* New York: New York University Press, 2004. An examination of the amendment and its tremendous impact.

**See also** Abolition; Black codes; Civil Rights Act of 1866; Civil Rights Acts of 1866-1875; *Civil Rights* cases; Civil War; Compromise of 1850; Disfranchisement laws in Mississippi; Emancipation Proclamation; Fifteenth Amendment; Fourteenth Amendment; Freedmen's Bureau; Fugitive Slave Law of 1850; Race riots of 1866; Reconstruction; Restrictive covenants; *Scott v. Sandford*; Underground Railroad

# Thomas-Hill hearings

**The Event:** Confirmation hearings of Supreme Court nominee Clarence Thomas, in which Anita Hill made charges of sexual harassment against Thomas

**Date:** October, 1991

*The hearings sparked intense national debate over issues of racism, sexism, and political gamesmanship. The public humiliation suffered by both Clarence Hill and Anita Thomas opened debate on the nature and fairness of the Senate confirmation process.*

After the resignation of Supreme Court associate justice Thurgood Marshall, the first African American to serve on the Court, President George Bush sought to fill the vacancy with another African American. Marshall, however, had been a leading advocate of the Civil Rights movement and the last staunchly liberal Supreme Court justice from the Earl Warren court era. Bush's nominee, Clarence Thomas, was his predecessor's political and philosophical opposite.

A Yale graduate, Thomas possessed a distinguished resume, including the chairmanship of the Equal Employment Opportunity Commission (EEOC) and service as a judge on the federal court of appeals. He was also one of a number of black intellectuals who challenged the merits of affirmative action. Critics charged that his tenure at the EEOC had been marked by a reluctance to pursue civil rights complaints, and his judicial record demonstrated his willingness to throw out many of the liberal decisions of the earlier Supreme Court. These were political concerns, however, in a political climate that favored Thomas's views, and no charge of unethical conduct stood up under investigation.

Anita Hill had served under Thomas at the EEOC and had maintained an amicable relationship with her former boss. During the judiciary committee's confirmation investigation, Hill confided that Thomas had pressured her for dates and made crude, sexually charged remarks to her while he was her boss. This information was leaked to the media after the judiciary committee had voted to send the nomination to the full Senate. A second hearing was convened to examine the charges.

On October 11, the first day of the second round of hearings, Thomas angrily denied the charges, and he was treated with deference by the committee. Hill, however, was barraged with accusations and insinuations by senators and witnesses. Senator Joseph Biden seemed unable to prevent the degeneration of the televised proceedings into a quasi-judicial brawl.

Thomas's characterization of the second hearing as a "high-tech lynching" provoked the greatest reaction from the African American community, outraging many African Americans with the implication that African Americans themselves and their liberal white allies were figuratively lynching an "uppity" black because of his conservatism. The viciousness of the attacks on Hill, for feminists, seemed to illustrate perfectly the very reason most victims of sexual harassment do not bring charges against their harassers.

Thomas, though confirmed, began his service on the Supreme Court tainted by Hill's accusation. Judiciary hearings operate without standards of evidence or the rules that govern court proceedings. Biden's committee could not determine the truth of the matter but could merely vote based on their impression of

Thomas's character and the political desirability of seating him on the Court.

*Janet Alice Long*

**Further Reading**
Brock, David. *The Real Anita Hill*. New York: Free Press, 1993.
Thomas, Clarence. *Confronting the Future: Selections from the Senate Confirmation Hearings and Prior Speeches*. Introduction by L. Gordon Crovitz. Washington, D.C.: Regnery Gateway, 1992.

**See also** Marshall's appointment to the Supreme Court; Politics and government

# Three-fifths compromise

**The Event:** Agreement reached in the convention that drafted the U.S. Constitution on the apportionment of congressional representation to slaveholding states
**Date:** 1787
**Place:** Philadelphia, Pennsylvania
*Northern delegates to the Constitutional Convention did not want nonvoting slave populations to be counted when congressional representation was apportioned, while southern delegates wanted slaves to be counted equally with nonslaves. The disagreement was resolved in the three-fifths compromise.*

The Constitutional Convention in 1787 adopted the three-fifths compromise, whereby five slaves were counted as three people for purposes of taxation and representation. The idea originated as part of a 1783 congressional plan to base taxation on population. Congress rejected the three-fifths idea, but delegate James Wilson of Pennsylvania resurrected it as an amendment to the Virginia plan at the Constitutional Convention.

The Wilson amendment provoked heated debate over the counting of slaves. Most northern delegates regarded slaves as property and not deserving representation, while southern delegates insisted that African Americans be counted equally with whites for purposes of representation. Northern delegates wanted slaves counted for taxation, while southern delegates disagreed.

Delegates also debated whether the Congress or a census every ten years should determine the apportionment of representatives in the national legislature. Several northern delegates wanted Congress to control apportionment because the West was developing rapidly. They considered the three-fifths idea pro-South and opposed its adoption. Southern delegates, meanwhile, threatened to reject the three-fifths idea if Congress controlled representation. Northern delegates eventually agreed to accept a census every ten years and count slaves as people rather than property, demonstrating the numerical strength of the proslavery interests. Until the Civil War, therefore, slaves were counted as three-fifths of nonslaves for purposes of taxation and representation.

*David L. Porter*

**See also** Politics and government; Slavery

# Till lynching

**The Event:** Murder of an African American youth who merely whistled at a white woman
**Date:** August 28, 1955
**Place:** Money, Mississippi
*Emmett Till's widely publicized murder helped make Americans more aware of the depth of racism that still existed in the United States.*

An African American youth, Emmett Till was born in Chicago in 1941. Shortly after he turned fourteen, his mother sent him to visit relatives in the small town of Money, Mississippi. On the afternoon of August 24, 1955, Till and a group of other teenagers went to a grocery store to buy candy and soft drinks. Till reportedly whistled at Carolyn Bryant, the wife of Roy Bryant, the store's white owner.

Early in the morning of August 28, Roy Bryant and his brother, J. W. Milam, kidnapped Till from his great uncle's home. The men beat him and shot him in the head and dumped his body in the Tallahatchie River. Till's mutilated and badly decomposed body was found three days later by a fisherman. Bryant and Milam were tried for Till's kidnapping and murder. After deliberating for only one hour, the all-white jury acquitted them. Later, Milam sold his story to *Look* magazine; in the article, he confessed to the killing. Neither Bryant nor Milam was ever convicted for Till's murder.

Till's remains were shipped to Chicago, where his mother insisted on an open-casket funeral. An estimated fifty thousand people came to see his body. Photographs of his corpse were also published in *Jet* magazine, and the murder was covered by magazines and newspapers all over the world. The murder case, and the subsequent lack of justice, is considered a major catalyst to the Civil Rights movement.

In May, 2004, the U.S. Justice Department announced that it was reopening its investigation into Till's murder. The two men tried for Till's murder decades earlier had been acquitted of all charges and had since died. However, evidence remained implicating other, still living, men in Till's lynching. The five-year federal statute of limitations had long since lapsed, but anyone charged with the murder could still be tried in a state court.

*Phyllis B. Gerstenfeld*

**Further Reading**

Metress, Christopher, ed. *The Lynching of Emmett Till: A Documentary Narrative.* Charlottesville: University of Virginia Press, 2002. A collection of diverse documents related to Till's murder.

Till-Mobley, Mamie, and Christopher Benson. *Death of Innocence: The Story of the Hate Crime That Changed America.* New York: Random House, 2003. Memoir of events related to Till's murder, written by his mother.

**See also** Civil Rights movement; Civil rights worker murders; Dyer antilynching bill; King assassination

# Turner's slave insurrection

**The Event:** Short-lived but bloody slave revolt led by Nat Turner
**Date:** 1831
**Place:** Southampton County, Virginia

*The 1831 slave revolt led by Nat Turner sent fear through the southern white community and prompted legislation prohibiting the assembly, education, and movement of plantation slaves.*

Although neither the first attempted slave rebellion nor the last during the more than two centuries of African American slavery, Nat Turner's assault against the whites in southeastern Virginia marked the only time a group of black slaves banded together to strike successfully against their white masters.

**Nat Turner**

So far as is known, Turner spent his entire life as a slave in his native Southampton County, where he had been born on October 2, 1800, on the plantation of Benjamin Turner. His mother was probably a native African, who taught him at an early age to believe that he possessed supernatural powers. He was both a mystic and oriented toward religion. In addition to possessing those traits, he could read, and historians have surmised that he learned this skill from the Turner family. Nat became a Christian through the instruction of his grandmother, Bridget, and mostly read the Bible. Perhaps because of his knowledge of the Bible, he became a Baptist preacher. Because of his mysticism, his ability to read, and his activities as a minister, Turner gained considerable influence over his fellow slaves.

Samuel Turner, Benjamin's son, inherited Nat during times of economic depression in Virginia. A newly hired overseer drove the slaves to work harder, and as a consequence, Nat ran away. Although Nat eluded capture for thirty days, he turned himself in to his owner. His return went unpunished, but in the days that followed, Nat saw that his own freedom could not be realized without his people's freedom.

Nat married a slave named Cherry in the early 1820's, and they had three children. Cherry would later conceal coded maps and lists that Turner used in his revolt, which experts have never been able to decode. When Samuel Turner died in 1822, Nat's family was broken up and sold to different families. Nat went to a neighboring farm owner, Thomas Moore. He was sold again to Joseph Travis in 1831.

Nat Turner thought of himself as an instrument of God. Between 1825 and 1830, Turner gained respect as a traveling neighborhood preacher. He became deeply religious, fasting and praying in solitude. In his own mind he had been ordained—like the prophets of old—to perform a special mission. He professed that God communicated with him through voices and signs in the heavens. On May 12, 1828, Turner heard a "great noise" and saw "white spirits" and "black spirits" battling.

### The Revolt

In February, 1831, a certain blueness in the atmosphere—a solar eclipse—persuaded him that God was announcing that the

*Contemporary drawing of Nat Turner's capture.* (Library of Congress)

time had come for the slaves to attack their white masters. Turner communicated this message to his band of followers; the rebellion ensued on August 21, when Turner and seven fellow slaves murdered the Travis family. Within twenty-four hours after the rebellion began, the band of rebels numbered seventy-five slaves. In the next two days, an additional fifty-one whites were killed. No evidence exists to indicate that Turner's movement was a part of any larger scheme. One slave, Nat Turner, used the power at his command to attempt to break his shackles and those of his followers.

Turner directed his attack toward the county seat, Jerusalem, and the weapons in its armory; he never made it. The white community responded promptly, and with an overpowering force of armed owners and militia, it routed the poorly armed slaves during the second day of the rebellion. Although he eluded capture for six weeks, Turner and all the rebels were either killed or captured and executed. Hundreds of other nonparticipating and innocent slaves were slain as a result of fright in the white community. Turner's court-appointed attorney, Thomas Gray, recorded Turner's "confessions" on November 1, and on November 11, 1831, Turner was hanged. Gray later remarked on Turner's intelligence and knowledge of military tactics.

**Aftermath**

Although Turner's revolt took place in a relatively isolated section of Virginia, the uprising caused the entire South to tremble. Many white southerners called for more stringent laws regulating slaves' behavior, such as making it a crime to teach a slave to read or write. Turner's revolt coincided with the blossoming of the abolition movement in the North, for the rebellion occurred in the same year that William Lloyd Garrison began his unremitting assault on the South's "peculiar institution." Although no one has been able to demonstrate that abolitionist activity had any influence at all on Turner, white southerners were horrified at the seeming coincidence. They described abolitionists as persons who wanted not only to end slavery but also to sponsor a massacre of southern whites. The white South stood as one against any outside interference with its system.

Although white people throughout the South looked anew at slavery, in no place did they look more closely than in Virginia. During the legislative session of 1831-1832, there occurred the most thorough public discussion of slavery in southern history prior to 1861. Only four months after Turner's revolt, the legislature appointed a committee to recommend to the state a course of action in dealing with slavery.

Those Virginians opposed to slavery made their case. They argued that slavery was a prime cause of Virginia's economic backwardness; that it injured white manners and morals; and that, as witnessed by Turner's revolt, it was basically dangerous. While they did talk about abolition as benefiting the slaves, they primarily maintained that white Virginians would reap the greatest rewards, for the African Americans, after a gradual and possibly compensated emancipation, would be removed from the state. These abolitionists, most of whom were from western Virginia (modern West Virginia), an area of few slaves, could not agree on a specific plan to accomplish their purpose. Slavery's defenders countered by boasting of Virginia's economic well-being and the good treatment and contentment of the slaves. Referring to the well-established belief in the sanctity of private property, they denied that the legislature had any right to meddle with slave property.

The Virginia legislature decided not to tamper with slavery. It rebuffed those who wanted to put Virginia on the road to emancipation. After these debates, white southerners no longer seriously considered any alternative to slavery. In the aftermath of Turner's revolt and Virginia's debate, the South erected a massive defense of its peculiar institution. That defense permeated southern politics, religion, literature, and science. Nat Turner's revolt—the only successful slave uprising in the South—heralded and confirmed the total southern commitment to black slavery. However, Turner left a profound legacy: Slaves would fight for their freedom. Turner's rebellion has inspired black activists since, including Marcus Garvey and Malcolm X.

*William J. Cooper, Jr.*
*Updated by Marilyn Elizabeth Perry*

**Further Reading**

Terry Bisson's *Nat Turner* (Los Angeles: Melrose Square, 1988) is an easy-to-read account of Nat Turner's life and motivations. Thomas R. Gray's *The Confessions of Nat Turner: The Leader of the Late Insurrection in Southampton, Va.* (1831; reprint, Miami: Mnemosyne, 1969) contains Turner's own account of his revolt, as given to an official of the court that tried him. William Styron's *Confessions of Nat Turner* (New York: Random House, 1967) is a controversial novel that aimed to show an understanding of Turner's revolt and the institution of slavery but was sharply attacked by African American intellectuals. Henry Irving Tragle's *The Southampton Slave Revolt of 1831: A Compilation of Source Material* (Amherst: University of Massachusetts Press, 1971) reprints primary source material: newspaper accounts, trial records, and other documents written at the time of the revolt.

**See also** Abolition; *Amistad* slave revolt; Harpers Ferry raid; *Liberator, The*; New York City slave revolt; Proslavery argument; Stono Rebellion

# Tuskegee Airmen

**Identification:** African American aviators who served in World War II
**Date:** 1942-1946

*African Americans have made important contributions to the military services in every war in which they have fought, but the achievements of the Tuskegee Airmen during World War II brought them previously unparalleled distinctions.*

African Americans made noteworthy gains in the military services during World War II, particularly in the U.S. Army Air Forces. Despite opposition from southern legislators, African American recruits began training at Tuskegee, Alabama. Challenged by substandard training conditions, discrimination, and segregation, the Tuskegee Airmen responded with resolve and discipline. Between 1942 and 1946, 996 African Americans received their silver wings at Tuskegee Army Air Field. Some 450 of

*Future general Benjamin O. Davis, Jr., preparing for a training flight in early 1942.* (National Archives)

these pilots flew with the 99th Fighter Squadron and later, the 332d Fighter Group. They became known as the "red tails" for the scarlet coloring on the tail and nose of their P-51B Mustang aircraft. After their baptism of fire in North Africa, the Tuskegee Airmen moved into Italy.

Their commanding officer was Colonel Benjamin O. Davis, Jr. Particularly notable is a daring strafing mission that Davis led in Austria. Despite intense group fire, Davis and his squadron destroyed or damaged thirty-five locomotives, six of which are credited to Davis himself. Around that same time, another pilot in the 332d destroyed a German destroyer single-handedly with machine guns. The Tuskegee Airmen were also the first U.S. pilots to down a German jet.

The 332d achieved lasting fame when it assumed escort duties for U.S. bombers striking deep into Germany. The 332d established a record for never losing a single bomber in approximately two hundred missions, a truly extraordinary accomplishment. The group's heroics in the air and dignity on the ground won them many medals and broke the color barriers of the U.S. military. By the end of World War II, one out of sixteen aviators in the U.S. Army Air Forces was an African American.

*Douglas W. Richmond*

**Further Reading**

Dryden, Charles W. *A-train: Memoirs of a Tuskegee Airman*. Foreword by Benjamin O. Davis, Jr. Tuscaloosa: University of Alabama Press, 1997.

Francis, Charles E. *The Tuskegee Airmen: The Men Who Changed a Nation*. 4th rev. ed. Boston: Branden, 2002.

Homan, Lynn M., and Thomas Reilly. *Black Knights: The Story of the Tuskegee Airmen*. Foreword by Louis R. Purnell. Gretna, La.: Pelican, 2001.

**See also** Buffalo soldiers; Military; World War II

# Tuskegee experiment

**The Event:** Long-term syphilis study conducted by the U.S. Public Health Service on four hundred African American men
**Date:** 1932-1972
**Place:** Tuskegee, Alabama

*During the Tuskegee experiment, scientists charted the course of the disease in men who had contracted the disease before their participation in the study. None of the men received any treatment, and at least 254 men died from the disease or its complications. Moreover, the men were told that they were receiving medical treatment, and none of them knew that they were being observed as part of an experiment on the effects of syphilis.*

It has been argued that the Tuskegee experiment was motivated by the assumption that African Americans were more susceptible than whites to syphilis, and therefore the Public Health Service was interested in studying whether this was the case and, if so, why. One critic of the study, Martin Levine, went so far as to argue that the origins of the experiment lay in a stereotypical view of black sexuality:

It was widely believed [among whites] that black racial inferiority made them a notoriously syphilis-soaked race! Their smaller brains lacked mechanisms for controlling sexual desire, causing them to be highly promiscuous. They matured earlier and consequently were sexually active; and the black man's enormous penis, with its long foreskin, was prone to venereal infections. These physiological differences meant the disease must affect the races differently. . . .

Other critics of this medical study point to it as evidence of the federal government's complicity in institutionalized racism against African Americans. Comments such as those by John Heller, the director of the Department of Venereal Diseases at the Public Health Service from 1943 to 1948, are often cited as evidence of this racism. Heller, for example, is quoted as saying of the men in the Tuskegee study that their "status did not warrant ethical debate. They were subjects, not patients: clinical material, not sick people."

For many African Americans, the Tuskegee study has come to represent verifiable evidence that institutionalized racism still exists in the United States. The study is also often cited to support possibly less verifiable claims of such racism. In the early 1990's, the Tuskegee study was often cited as supporting evidence for the AIDS conspiracy theory, which posited that the U.S. government manufactured the AIDS virus and intentionally infected people in Africa through immunization programs in order to commit genocide.

During the mid-1990's, a rumor spread through the African American community reporting that the company that made Snapple, a popular brand of bottled beverages, was owned by the Ku Klux Klan. On April 19, 1996, ABC's news magazine, *20/20*, aired a segment, narrated by journalist John Stossel, that investigated this claim. Stossel interviewed a number of people from various African American communities, many of whom believed this and other rumors, such as the U.S. government's manufacturing of the AIDS virus, and cited the Tuskegee experiment as evidence that such institutional racism has existed in the past in the United States and still existed.

*Susan Mackey-Kallis*

**See also** Brownsville incident; Stereotypes

# Twenty-fourth Amendment

**The Law:** Amendment to the U.S. Constitution that outlawed poll taxes

**Date:** Ratified on January 23, 1964

*The poll tax was an arbitrary limitation on voting rights, particularly in the South, where it was often employed to deny the franchise to African Americans and poor whites.*

On January 23, 1964, the South Dakota senate cast the deciding vote in the ratification process of the Twenty-fourth Amendment to the United States Constitution. The amendment ended the poll tax as a condition of voting in federal elections. The real function of the tax had been to deny civil rights to members of racial minorities, especially black southerners. The Twenty-fourth Amendment, passage of which began in 1962, was only one part of a larger campaign of civil rights reform that came to a head with the Civil Rights Act of 1964.

### Poll Taxes

Civil rights issues were central to the social questions that surfaced during the 1950's and 1960's. Beginning with the *Brown v. Board of Education* case in 1954, which disallowed school segregation, both courts and legislatures were engaged in the resolution of such issues. John F. Kennedy assumed office as president in 1961, at a time when the Civil Rights movement was taking on a direct-action character—undertaking mass demonstrations, civil disobedience, and occasional acts of violence—and opposition to it was being manifested in mass arrests, intimidation, and even murder. This trend convinced the new administration and its liberal supporters in Congress that the time had come to use federal legislation as well as the courts to initiate civil rights reform. The first target was the poll tax.

The poll tax, a uniform, direct, and personal tax levied upon individuals, was not a new phenomenon. It had existed in some states since the early twentieth century and in others, such as New Hampshire, since colonial times, though not as a franchise prerequisite. All states with the poll tax allowed exceptions to it:

officers and men on active militia duty, veterans, and persons with disabilities resulting from gainful occupation and whose taxable property did not exceed $500, for example. The tax was nominal in most cases for those who did have to pay, being only $1.50 or $2.00 per year. The tax was cumulative, however, so that voters who came to register after having not paid the tax for a number of years might find themselves having to pay what for many poor people would be a considerable sum. To civil rights advocates, the poll tax paralleled literacy tests as a device to limit voting rights, and they were determined that both should be abolished. Even in southern states where the poll tax was no longer used, literacy tests, closed registration lists, and straightforward intimidation were used to prevent African Americans from voting.

### The Process of Reform

The process of reform had to begin somewhere, and northern Democrats, acting upon inspiration from the Kennedy administration, began with the anti-poll tax amendment process early in 1962. There was strong opposition from a southern bloc of conservatives, mostly Democrats led by Richard B. Russell, a Democrat from Georgia, but it was not as strong as might have been expected.

The Senate majority leader was Michael H. Mansfield, a Democrat from Montana, and it was his responsibility to shepherd the legislation through the Senate. The anti-poll tax amendment itself was sponsored by Spessard L. Holland, a Democrat from Florida, whose role might have appeared surprising, since he was part of the southern bloc. Holland, however, was no friend of the poll tax in any form and had led a successful campaign to abolish it in his own state in 1937.

The Senate Judiciary Committee, chaired by Senator James O. Eastland, a Democrat from Mississippi and part of the southern bloc, had conducted hearings on the poll tax and literacy tests for weeks to little avail. On March 14, Senator Mansfield moved for Senate consideration of a bill to establish Alexander Hamilton's New York home as a national monument, to which, it was suggested, the proposed constitutional amendment could be attached. The Senate Judiciary Committee, wherein, according to liberal senators, civil rights issues tended to get lost, was effectively bypassed, and the Hamilton motion, with the expectation of its being linked to the anti-poll tax amendment, was put before the Senate.

As soon as the motion appeared on the floor, the southern conservative bloc began a "friendly" filibuster, so termed because the southerners did not go all-out to prevent the Hamilton resolution from coming to a vote. It is conceivable that the vote was considered a foregone conclusion, and the filibuster was merely for form's sake. In any event, it endured for ten days, until, apparently, the participants had run out of words. Then Senator Holland introduced the preordained motion to substitute the language of the anti-poll tax amendment for the language of the Hamilton resolution. This brought Senator Russell to his feet in protest: "We are adopting an absurd, farfetched, irrational, unreasonable, and unconstitutional method to get this amendment," he charged. Others agreed, including Jacob K. Javits, a Republican from New York, who proposed that the Senate should act against the poll tax by simple legislation, and Paul H. Douglas, a Democrat from Illinois, who warned that, the questionable manner of the adoption notwithstanding, using the amendment process could itself prove the downfall of efforts to abolish the tax.

Nevertheless, the Holland motion was put to a vote, and on March 27 it passed the Senate by a margin of seventy-seven to sixteen. An amendment to the Constitution of the United States repealing the poll tax for all federal elections was then forwarded to the House of Representatives, where it was debated, dissected, promoted, and opposed in similar manner, until it passed that chamber in August, 1962. It was then up to the states to ratify the amendment by vote of their legislatures.

## The Amendment Goes to the States

It was speculated widely during succeeding months that, on the premise that the poll-tax amendment would pass the states and greatly broaden the base of the southern electorate, the Democratic leadership would work to break the power of the southern bloc by promoting candidates who were more loyal to the national party to oppose the bloc's members in the primaries. At least thirteen congressional seats were thought to be on a target list. Needless to say, Republican Party leaders were delighted, convinced by the southerners' defiant attitude that the Democrats had outsmarted themselves.

Meanwhile, the poll-tax amendment was being considered by the states, and it was an uphill battle. The Arizona house, for example, approved the amendment in 1963, but it died in the state senate. By the end of the year, however, momentum toward ratification gathered, and by January 5, 1964, the amendment needed to be approved by only two more states. A few days later the number dropped to one, and on January 23 South Dakota's senate voted thirty-four to zero in favor of ratification. The Twenty-fourth Amendment to the Constitution was law, requiring then only the further technicality of formal certification by the General Services Administration of the federal government. South Dakota was compelled to race through its vote in order to beat out Georgia as the deciding state. There was an irony in this, as Georgia was the home of Senator Richard Russell, the most outspoken opponent of the amendment in the early days of debate on the motion.

## Impact

The poll-tax amendment symbolized the liberal determination to institute civil rights reform. There was, however, opposition of nearly equal intensity. Three political proposals made in 1963 were meant to redress—or so their advocates claimed—the eroding of states' rights by the federal government. In fact, this package aimed at countering the possible effects of impending civil rights legislation, including abolition of the poll tax. The first proposal sought to give the power to redraw congressional districts to state governments. Gerrymandering could then keep power out of the hands of members of racial minorities, even if minorities came to the polls in greater numbers after the Twenty-fourth Amendment was passed.

The second proposal placed the constitutional amendment process in the hands of the state legislatures, bypassing either

Congress or a national convention. Under this plan, a two-thirds majority of the state legislatures could propose an amendment, and a three-fourths majority could make it part of the Constitution. The third proposal sought to create a "Court of the Union" that would review Supreme Court decisions on federal-state relations and would be made up of the chief justices of the fifty states. This court would have effectively nullified the Supreme Court as the final arbiter of constitutionality in matters touching upon civil rights, because most such matters touched in turn on federal-state relations.

None of these propositions came to fruition, but the Twenty-fourth Amendment did, abolishing the poll tax in federal elections. Within two months, however, Arkansas, one of the last states to cling to the poll tax, upheld in court the state constitution's requirement of a poll tax for state and local elections. Later, a private election oversight organization found at least seven irregularities in the primary election process in Arkansas, including the fact that unauthorized persons were permitted to help count ballots. The organization discovered that, while the poll tax was no longer required for federal elections, there were many other devices available to skew elections in the way segregationists wanted.

Various avenues were taken to limit the impact of the new amendment even for federal elections. In Mississippi, state officials cracked down on minor violations of little-used aspects of the civil code as a device to intimidate members of the Congress of Racial Equality and others who were involved in voter registration drives among African Americans. Violence was used as well when African Americans congregated in anticipation of a protest march in Canton, Mississippi, in 1963. In Georgia, support for segregationist presidential candidate George Wallace led to black-white confrontations and violence. In Virginia, on the eve of the 1964 presidential election, a federal court upheld a state law requiring payment of the poll tax for the right to vote in local and state elections. Two years later, however, in *Harper v. Virginia Board of Elections*, the Supreme Court concluded that poll taxes violated the equal protection clause of the Constitution, and the last such tax was swept away.

Abolition of the poll tax was a step in the right direction, but there was a long road still to travel before voting rights for minority groups would be secure at all levels of American politics.

*Robert Cole*

**Further Reading**

Branch, Taylor. *Parting the Waters: America in the King Years, 1954-63.* New York: Simon & Schuster, 1988. A sweeping, authoritative, well-conceived, and well-written account of the Civil Rights movement, concentrating on Martin Luther King, Jr., and the Southern Christian Leadership Conference. Not an academic treatment in the conventional sense but rather intensely personal.

Kelly, Alfred H., Winifred A. Harbison, and Herman Betz. *The American Constitution: Its Origins and Development.* 6th ed. New York: W. W. Norton, 1983. Discusses in detail the Supreme Court cases and the contents of civil rights legislation, of which the Twenty-fourth Amendment was a part. It is particularly useful on those court cases that either struck down segregation rules or wiped away such voting restrictions as the poll tax and literacy tests.

Kluger, R. *Simple Justice: The History of "Brown v. Board of Education" and Black America's Struggle for Equality.* New York: Alfred A. Knopf, 1976. A study in depth of the first major step in the civil rights reform era, in which the principle of desegregation of American society was laid down. Thurgood Marshall, later a distinguished Supreme Court justice, played a central role in the developments examined here.

Matusow, A. J. *The Unraveling of America: A History of Liberalism in the 1960's.* New York: Harper & Row, 1984. This volume traces the rise and fall of American postwar liberalism, concentrating on both the successes and the failures of liberal views and policies during the era of civil rights reform.

"Poll Taxes and Literacy Texts." *The Congressional Digest* 41 (May, 1962): 131-137. A careful and detailed explanation of the background of the poll tax and the process and content of the Senate debate leading to passage of the Twenty-fourth Amendment. The article proceeds in a detached and factual manner and lists specifically the nature of poll taxes as they existed in the several states as of May, 1962.

Schlesinger, Arthur M., Jr. *A Thousand Days*. Boston: Houghton Mifflin, 1965. An inside look at the Kennedy administration with observations on aspects of Kennedy's civil rights policies, including abolition of the poll tax. Schlesinger was part of the Kennedy inner circle and an old-line Democrat. His view of the Kennedy years is not without bias; all the same, this is a masterful work and very useful.

**See also** Civil Rights Act of 1960; Civil Rights Act of 1964; Fifteenth Amendment; Politics and government; Poll taxes; Voting Rights Act of 1965; Voting Rights Act of 1975

# Underground Railroad

**Definition:** Loose network of secret routes by which fugitive slaves made their way from slave states to freedom in the North, often as far as Canada.

*Because of the Underground Railroad's inherently secretive nature, precise data on its operations do not exist, but it clearly helped to lead many thousands of slaves to freedom in the North, while keeping alive a spirit of resistance to the institution of slavery.*

Parts of the Underground Railroad may have been in place as early as 1786. By 1850, southern slave owners were claiming enormous losses of slave property to the Underground Railroad, although some scholars now believe that their claims of losses were exaggerated. It is impossible to know how many slaves made their way to freedom—estimates range from sixty to one hundred thousand people between 1800 and 1865.

### Fleeing Slavery

Many slaves reached freedom without the aid of the Underground Railroad, and many, especially those in the Deep South, did not flee north but went instead to Mexico or found refuge with the Seminole, Cherokee, or other Native American tribes.

However, the majority of fugitive slaves escaped from the border states and fled north. Usually, the most dangerous leg of their journey was reaching a station on the underground line; once there, conductors would pass them from site to site toward safety.

It was almost impossible for a runaway slave to reach freedom successfully without assistance. Most slaves had little or no knowledge of geography and fled with only vague notions of where they were headed; most left with no money and few provisions and had to risk asking strangers along the way for food, shelter, and protection from pursuers. For the most part, persons helping runaways performed impulsive acts of compassion and did not consider themselves to be part of a resistance group. In parts of the country, however, the numbers of fugitives coming through were so great that predetermined escape routes, safe houses, and plans of action were organized. In time, some Underground Railroad lines were highly organized, and at least some routes existed in most of the states between the South and Canada.

The two most frequent escape corridors were from Kentucky and Virginia into Ohio and from there north, and up the Eastern Seaboard through New England. Ohio especially was crisscrossed with routes of escape, as were western Pennsylvania and New York, eastern Indiana, and northwestern Illinois. The Middle Atlantic states and New England also had many well-established routes; lines existed west of Ohio and even, to some degree, in the South. After passage of the Fugitive Slave Law of 1850, organized aid to runaways grew, as the threats to free African Americans as well as fugitive slaves increased and more antislavery sympathizers felt the moral obligation to risk civil disobedience.

### Organization

No one knows when or how the name Underground Railroad began, although legend has it that it was coined after a frustrated slave catcher swore that the fugitives he was pursuing had disappeared as thoroughly and suddenly as if they had found an underground road. As knowledge of the existence of escape routes spread, so did the railroad terminology, with words such as "conductors," "stations," "stationkeepers," and "lines."

Conductors often used inventive means to transport fugitives safely from station to station. Many were hidden under goods or in secret compartments in wagons. A few, such as Henry "Box" Brown, were actually boxed and shipped by train or boat. At least once, slaves were hidden in carriages forming a fake funeral procession. There were so many routing options along some lines that tracing was difficult. Barns, thickets, attics, spare rooms, woodsheds, smokehouses, and cellars were used as stations. Fugitives often were disguised: A hoe could make a runaway look like a hired-out day laborer; fine clothes could disguise a runaway field hand as a servant of gentlefolk; cross-dressing could keep fugitives from matching descriptions on handbills. Mulattoes could sometimes pass as whites. Perhaps the most famous escape effected through disguise was that of husband and wife William and Ellen Craft, who, with Ellen disguised as a white southern gentleman and William as her valet, made it from Georgia to Philadelphia, where the Underground Railroad then transported them to safety. Once at a station, fugitives were given shel-

*A novel method of escape from slavery used by a few African Americans was to have themselves shipped to the North in boxes.* (Library of Congress)

ter, food, clothing, and sometimes money, as well as help in reaching the next stop.

Quakers—mostly of the Hicksite sect—played a large and early role in maintaining the Underground Railroad; in 1797, George Washington complained of Quakers helping one of his slaves escape. Other sects, such as Covenanters and Wesleyan Methodists, also contributed a number of agents. Particular locations, such as Oberlin College in Ohio, became important centers of activity. Women as well as men played active roles, especially in providing food and clothing to fugitives, and women often organized auxiliaries to support the more visible vigilance and abolitionist committees.

The role played by white antislavery sympathizers, although important, has tended to be overemphasized. In southern states, fellow slaves usually were the source of food and a hiding place for escapees. In border states, free blacks provided the most important help to fugitives, both in all-black settlements and in cities where black abolitionists worked alongside their white counterparts. Many African American churches and vigilance committees extended protection, support, and help in relocation to fugitives who reached the free states.

Whites rarely took the initiative to go south and effect escapes, but a number of former slaves returned to help friends and family flee. The most famous conductor to recruit escapees was the remarkable Harriet Tubman. Having herself escaped from slavery, she made some nineteen daring and successful trips into southern states to bring out groups of slaves, despite the forty-thousand-dollar bounty on her head. She is credited with personally leading more than three hundred slaves to safety, never losing anyone in her charge, and earned the title "the Moses of her people."

### The Busy 1850's

The period of greatest activity for the Underground Railroad was from 1850 to 1860. Among the most active white station-keepers was Levi Coffin: In thirty-five years of activism in Indiana and Ohio, Coffin helped three thousand fugitive slaves on their way north. Quaker Thomas Garrett of Wilmington, Delaware, aided several thousand fugitives over a forty-year period; he lost all of his property to court fines as a result but refused to cease his work.

Important black members of the Underground Railroad included the Reverend William H. Mitchell of Ohio, who in twelve years provided temporary shelter for thirteen hundred fleeing slaves; Robert Purvis of Philadelphia, Pennsylvania; William Whipper of Columbia, Pennsylvania; Henry Highland Garnet of New York; Lewis Hayden of Boston, Massachusetts; Frederick Douglass of Rochester, New York; and William Wells Brown of Buffalo, New York.

However, most of those who hid, fed, transported, and otherwise aided fugitive slaves have remained anonymous. Likewise, records about the fugitives themselves are scarce. Following the Civil War, several prominent activists published memoirs about their Underground Railroad activities that included accounts of some of the slaves they aided. Black stationkeeper William Still of Philadelphia kept notes on almost seven hundred fugitives he helped, providing valuable statistics. His records indicate that 80 percent of runaways were male and that significant numbers of house servants as well as field hands fled. However, the names and profiles of the vast majority of the thousands of men, women, and children who braved the hazards of flight in desperate bids for freedom remain unknown.

*Grace McEntee*

**Further Reading**

Several important contributions have been made to the literature on the Underground Railroad including Tom Calarco's *The Underground Railroad in the Adirondack Region* (Jefferson, N.C.: McFarland & Co., 2004), Keith P. Griffler's *Front Line of Freedom: African Americans and the Forging of the Underground Railroad in the Ohio Valley* (Lexington: University Press of Kentucky, 2004), William J. Switala's *Underground Railroad in Pennsylvania* (Mechanicsburg, Pa.: Stackpole Books, 2001), Switala's *Underground Railroad in Delaware, Maryland, and West Virginia* (Mechanicsburg, Pa.: Stackpole Books, 2004), and Ann Hagedorn's *Beyond the River: The Untold Story of the Heroes of the Underground Railroad* (New

York: Simon & Schuster, 2002). Henrietta Buckmaster's *Let My People Go: The Story of the Underground Railroad and the Growth of the Abolition Movement* (Boston: Beacon Press, 1941) discusses the Underground Railroad within the broader context of the growth of antislavery sentiment. Levi Coffin's *Reminiscences of Levi Coffin* (New York: Arno Press, 1968) is an important primary source; this work reprints his third edition of 1898. Larry Gara's *The Liberty Line: The Legend of the Underground Railroad* (Lexington: University of Kentucky Press, 1961) counters popular notions that exaggerate the role of white abolitionists and underplay blacks' contributions in helping fugitive slaves. Wilbur H. Siebert's *The Underground Railroad from Slavery to Freedom* (1898; reprint, New York: Arno Press, 1968) is a landmark history of much value. William Still's *The Underground Railroad* (1872; reprint, Chicago: Johnson, 1972) is a vast collection of narratives and sketches, focusing on the fugitives' stories.

**See also** Abolition; American Anti-Slavery Society; Antislavery laws of 1777 and 1807; Fugitive Slave Law of 1793; Fugitive Slave Law of 1850; National Council of Colored People; *North Star, The*; Slave codes; Slavery; Thirteenth Amendment

# Understanding tests

**Definition:** Forms of literacy tests requiring prospective voters to demonstrate their understanding of portions of documents such as the U.S. and state constitutions

*Understanding tests were used to practice racial discrimination in voter registration. The Supreme Court ruled on such tests several times before they were prohibited by the Voting Rights Act of 1965.*

In an effort to circumvent the Fifteenth Amendment, which gave the right to vote to African Americans, many southern states, beginning in the latter part of the nineteenth century, used poll taxes and literacy requirements to prevent African Americans from registering to vote. Part of the literacy requirement in some states was the passing of understanding tests, which commonly required prospective voters to read and explain a provision of the U.S. Constitution or the state constitution. Voting registrars sometimes had discretion to choose the passage to be interpreted and judge the adequacy of the explanation given. The discretion vested in registrars provided the opportunity for widespread discrimination against African American voters.

The Supreme Court confronted the issue of literacy tests several times. In *Lassiter v. Northampton County Board of Elections* (1959), the Court upheld the use of literacy tests on the grounds that they had some relationship to intelligent voter choices. The Court did say, however, that should a state law give election officials complete discretion to determine whether prospective voters understood the constitutional passages they were given to interpret, that law might be unconstitutional. The Court subsequently did hold such a law unconstitutional in *Louisiana v. United States* (1965). Because of the difficulty in determining when literacy tests were being used to perpetuate racial discrimination, Congress suspended their use in the Voting Rights Act of 1965.

*Daryl R. Fair*

**See also** Civil Rights movement; Fifteenth Amendment; *Lassiter v. Northampton County Board of Elections*; Voting Rights Act of 1965

# United Negro College Fund

**Identification:** Privately funded education assistance organization created to help African American students attain college educations

**Date:** Established on April 25, 1944

*Since its foundation, the United Negro College Fund has played a major role in assisting students and helping to support predominantly black colleges and universities, which produce more than 25 percent of all African American college graduates.*

Under the direction of Frederick D. Patterson, president of Tuskegee Institute, the United Negro College Fund (UNCF) was established in 1944, with twenty-seven member colleges and a combined enrollment of fourteen thousand students. The goal was to become one of the world's leading education assistance organizations. With a few exceptions, most UNCF member institutions had been founded by religious societies from the North after the Civil War and before the turn of the century. Located principally in the Southeast and in eastern Texas, these institutions operate with a variety of organizational structures and program offerings.

Since its inception, UNCF has grown to become the oldest and most successful African American higher-education assistance organization. In 1998, UNCF provided support for a consortium of forty-one private, accredited four-year black colleges and universities. UNCF raises operating money for its member schools so that they can maintain the highest academic standards and prepare their students for demanding professions and careers. Although these institutions constitute only about 3 percent of all colleges and universities in the United States, they graduate more than one-quarter of all African Americans who earn the baccalaureate degree and nearly 40 percent of African Americans who later earn a doctoral degree. These graduates help build a stronger nation as community leaders and educators and in numerous other vocations.

*Alvin K. Benson*

**See also** Ashmun Institute; Black colleges and universities; Education

# United States Commission on Civil Rights

**Identification:** Federal commission created by the Civil Rights Act of 1957
**Date:** Created in 1957
**Place:** Washington, D.C.
*The reports and studies of the Commission on Civil Rights have been an important factor in the passage of major civil rights legislation.*

The U.S. Commission on Civil Rights was created in 1957 by Congress as part of the Civil Rights Act of 1957. It consisted of six members, appointed by the president and approved by Congress. The original purpose of the agency was to monitor civil rights (particularly violations of voting rights in the South), issue reports, and then disband, but Congress has continuously renewed its mandate. The Commission on Civil Rights (abbreviated as CRC, for Civil Rights Commission) was created in the wake of the 1954 Supreme Court decision in *Brown v. Board of Education*. In this case, the Court decided that separate facilities for black and white students in public education were unconstitutional. A year later, in *Brown II*, the Court ruled that schools must integrate with "all deliberate speed." No specific timetable was given, however, for fear of further alienating southern whites.

The CRC helped lay the foundation for the civil rights legislation of the 1960's. The commission's mandate involved investigating voting rights violations, collecting and studying voting data related to denials of equal protection under the law, and appraising federal laws and policies as they related to equal protection. In addition to creating the CRC, the 1957 Civil Rights Act made the civil rights component in the Justice Department a division, and empowered the U.S. attorney general to initiate civil court proceedings to enforce voting rights. The 1957 statute gave the attorney general the power to intervene only on a case-by-case basis, which was tedious, as there were thousands of cases of voting rights violations.

### Civil Rights Legislation

During Dwight D. Eisenhower's administration, the Commission on Civil Rights investigated voting rights violations in eight southern states and found no fewer than a hundred counties using discriminatory measures against African Americans. The Civil Rights Act of 1960 was passed as a result of the CRC's 1959 report. Although the CRC had recommended that Congress pass legislation authorizing federal registrars in obstructionist districts, the act provided only court-appointed referees to oversee and resolve alleged voting rights abuses. Continuing studies by the CRC would assist in more powerful legislation in 1964 and 1965.

The 1964 Civil Rights Act was instrumental in the desegregation of public facilities in a still-segregated South. Based on ongoing concerns and studies by the CRC in education, voting, and employment, and influenced by the intensifying Civil Rights movement and the March on Washington in 1963, the 1964 act forbade racial discrimination in public facilities, voting registration procedures, and employment. The act empowered the attorney general to intervene and take civil action in cases of racial discrimination in public accommodations. It also cut federal funds to school districts that discriminated and created the Equal Employment Opportunity Commission to oversee discrimination complaints in the workplace.

The 1965 Voting Rights Act is the most powerful legislation in the area of suffrage, and it eliminated virtually all remaining loopholes. The act effectively took the process of voter registration out of the hands of states and localities, providing federal machinery for this process. The legislation also forbade literacy tests in most instances. In addition, a preclearance mechanism (often called Section 5) was put in place that required political districts to submit proposed changes in elections or districts to the federal government for approval. A "clean record" provision was instituted, allowing political districts to be removed from coverage of the preclearance provision if no discrimination or voting irregularities have been found for the previous ten years.

The CRC has played a vital role in the extension of the 1965 Voting Rights Act and thus in continued suffrage among African Americans in the Deep South. One of the most controversial areas of the act, the preclearance provision, was challenged by southerners. Testimony by the CRC revealed that southern states, and particularly Mississippi, were seeking to subvert the intent of the act and dilute the black vote and black political victories. Legislatures did this by racial gerrymandering of political districts, going to at-large systems of municipal elections, developing multimember districts, and consolidating black and white counties. The CRC was instrumental in the extension of Section 5 and the drafting of other provisions of the 1970 Voting Rights Act. Reports by the commission would play an important role in the 1975 and 1982 extensions of the act as well.

## Challenges and Impact

A major challenge to the commission came in the early 1980's, after it issued a 1981 statement entitled *Affirmative Action in the 1980's*, which advocated quotas to ensure the hiring of members of minorities. President Ronald Reagan strongly opposed the recommendations and removed three of the CRC's commissioners, appointing more conservative commissioners. A lawsuit ensued, and in 1983 Reagan was ordered by the courts to reinstate the commissioners he had fired. Also in 1983, the commission was reorganized by a compromise congressional act (Reagan had vowed to veto an act routinely renewing the commission) to consist of eight members chosen by the president and Congress. The commission was criticized from many quarters in the 1980's, partly for appearing to succumb to various political pressures, and many of its leaders, including Clarence Pendleton, were controversial. In the early 1990's, it began to resume the more active role it had played in the past.

Originally intended as a watchdog agency, the Commission on Civil Rights has been essential as a bipartisan fact-finding body and a resource for both Congress and the president in developing legislation. While its early charge was in the area of voting rights, it has conducted numerous studies and provided congressional testimony in education, housing, racial segregation, employment discrimination, and denial of civil rights on the basis of race, creed, color, religion, national origin, sex, age, or disability.

*Mfanya D. Tryman*

## Further Reading

Among the best sources for information on the CRC are Gerald David Jaynes and Robin M. Williams, Jr., eds., *A Common Destiny: Blacks and American Society* (Washington, D.C.: National Academy Press, 1989); Theodore Eisenberg's article "Civil Rights Commission," in *Civil Rights and Equality: Selections from the Encyclopedia of the American Constitution* (New York: Macmillan, 1989); Frank R. Parker, *Black Votes Count* (Chapel Hill: University of North Carolina Press, 1990); Steven F. Lawson, *Running for Freedom* (New York: McGraw-Hill, 1991); Hugh Davis Graham, *Civil Rights and the Presidency* (New York: Oxford University Press,

1992); Charles S. Bullock III and Charles M. Lamb, *Implementation of Civil Rights Policy* (Monterey, Calif.: Brooks/Cole, 1984); and Gertrude Ezorsky, *Racism and Justice* (Ithaca, N.Y.: Cornell University Press, 1991).

**See also** *Brown v. Board of Education*; Civil Rights Act of 1957; Civil Rights Act of 1960; Civil Rights Act of 1964; Civil Rights Act of 1968; Civil Rights Act of 1991; Civil Rights Acts of 1866-1875; Civil Rights movement; Voting Rights Act of 1965

# United States v. Classic

**The Case:** U.S. Supreme Court ruling on white primaries
**Date:** May 26, 1941
*Overturning its 1921 decision, the Supreme Court held that Congress has the power to regulate primaries whenever state law makes them an integral part of the process for electing candidates to federal office.*

Two decisions of the U.S. Supreme Court, in 1921 and 1935, gave southern states the authority to exclude African Americans from voting in primary elections. These decisions were important because the South was dominated by the Democratic Party from the end of Reconstruction until the middle of the twentieth century. If African Americans could not vote in the Democratic primary, they were denied any real choice in the selection of elected officials.

In 1921, the Supreme Court ruled in *Newberry v. United States* that Congress did not have the authority to regulate primary elections. At issue was a Michigan senatorial primary race between Henry Ford and Truman Newberry in which Newberry alleged that he was the victim of vote fraud. The *Newberry* case provided the opportunity for southern states to pass white primary laws, since the Court declared that such elections fell outside constitutional protection. In *Grovey v. Townsend* (1935), the Court ruled that state party conventions could exclude African Americans from primaries without violating the Constitution. In the battle to eliminate the white primary, the U.S. Justice Department had to persuade the Supreme Court to overturn the *Newberry* decision. *United States v. Classic* provided the opportunity to reverse *Newberry*. Although the *Classic* case did not involve racial discrimination or the white primary, it did involve the relationship of the primary to the election process.

Vote fraud was a common feature of Louisiana elections. While investigating charges of fraud by the heirs of former governor and senator Huey Long, the Justice Department discovered that Patrick Classic, an opponent of the Long faction, had engaged in altering and falsely counting votes. Classic, invoking the *Newberry* decision, argued that primaries were beyond federal control.

Reversing *Newberry*, the U.S. Supreme Court declared that the Constitution protected the right to vote in primaries as well as general elections. This was certainly true in Louisiana, the Court stated, "where the state law has made the primary an integral part of the procedure of choice, or where in fact the primary effectively controls the choice."

The reversal of *Newberry* by the *Classic* decision provided the framework for the final attack on white primaries. It was evident that in the one-party South, whoever won the Democratic primary won the general election. Only three years after the *Classic* decision, the National Association for the Advancement of Colored People (NAACP) successfully challenged the white primaries in *Smith v. Allwright*. Without the *Classic* decision, the assault on the white primaries would have been delayed for years.

**See also** *Grovey v. Townsend*; National Association for the Advancement of Colored People; *Newberry v. United States*; *Smith v. Allwright*; Voting Rights Act of 1965; White primaries

# *United States v. Cruikshank*

**The Case:** U.S. Supreme Court ruling on federal enforcement of civil rights and states' rights
**Date:** March 27, 1876

*Drawing on narrow interpretations of the Fourteenth and Fifteenth Amendments, the Supreme Court severely limited the authority of the federal government to protect the civil rights of African Americans.*

In 1875, William Cruikshank and two other men were convicted in a federal court of participating in the lynching of two African Americans. The 1870 Reconstruction statute under which they were convicted was broadly written to make it unlawful to interfere with most rights of citizens. The constitutional authority claimed for this federal statute was the Fourteenth Amendment. Cruikshank and his codefendants, who were charged with interfering with the right and privilege "peaceably to assemble," argued that the Fourteenth Amendment does not authorize the federal government to establish so broad a criminal statute because the amendment was written to limit state governments, not private persons.

In 1876, the U.S. Supreme Court, in an opinion written by Chief Justice Morrison R. Waite, unanimously agreed with Cruikshank. The Fourteenth Amendment, which establishes citizenship and then says, "No State shall make or enforce any law which shall abridge the privileges or immunities of citizens of the United States," applies in the first instance to state, not private, action. Private action such as the lynching in which Cruikshank participated may be punished by the federal government only if it can be shown that the intent was to deprive a specific constitutional right—and even then the indictment must specify the intent very narrowly. The decision effectively sanctioned the lynchings of African Americans for the next few decades.

*Robert Jacobs*

**See also** Civil Rights Acts of 1866-1875; *Civil Rights* cases; Dyer antilynching bill; Lynching

# *United States v. Reese*

**The Case:** U.S. Supreme Court ruling on the right to vote and the
Fifteenth Amendment
**Date:** March 27, 1876
*The Supreme Court voided part of the 1870 Enforcement Act, claiming
that voting was a privilege, not a right.*

*United States v. Reese* (1876) marked the first major test of voting
rights under the Fifteenth Amendment, which had been passed
in 1870 and stated that the right to vote "shall not be denied or
abridged by the United States or by any State on account of race,
color, or previous condition of servitude." A Kentucky voting official was indicted for refusing to let an African American, who
had offered to pay his poll tax, vote in a municipal election. The
U.S. Supreme Court, by an 8-1 margin, declared unconstitutional
the Enforcement Act of 1870, the law on which the indictment
was based. The Enforcement Act provided penalties for obstructing or hindering persons from voting in an election. In the majority decision delivered by Chief Justice Morison R. Waite, the Supreme Court ruled that the U.S. Congress had overreached its
powers by seeking to punish the denial of voting rights on any
grounds and could only legislate against discrimination based on
race.

According to the U.S. Supreme Court, the Fifteenth Amendment did not confer the right of suffrage on anyone but merely
prohibited the United States from excluding a person from voting because of race, color, or previous condition of servitude. The
ruling made it constitutionally possible for southern states to
deny the right to vote on any grounds except race, thus allowing the use of poll taxes, literacy tests, good character tests, understanding clauses, and other devices to disfranchise African
Americans.

*David L. Porter*

**See also** Disfranchisement laws in Mississippi; Fifteenth Amendment; Poll taxes

# United Steelworkers of America v. Weber

**The Case:** U.S. Supreme Court ruling on affirmative action
**Date:** June 27, 1979

*In this case, the U.S. Supreme Court ruled that an employer could estab-
lish voluntary programs, including quotas, to eliminate a manifest
racial imbalance, even without evidence that the employer had previously discriminated.*

Title VII of the Civil Rights Act of 1964 made it unlawful "to discriminate against any individual because of his race, color, religion, sex, or national origin." Based on this law, President
Lyndon B. Johnson issued Executive Order 11246, which required
all companies doing business with the federal government to
take "affirmative action" to eliminate discrimination. Shortly
thereafter, federal agencies began to use "numerical imbalance"
as *prima facie* evidence of invidious discrimination, and they encouraged employers to use numerical goals, timetables, and sometimes quotas to advance the employment opportunities of underrepresented minorities and women.

In the Equal Employment Opportunity Act of 1972, the majority of Congress rejected Senator Samuel Ervin's amendment that
would have barred all "preferential treatment," but the law did
not make clear how far employers were expected to go. Meanwhile, lower courts were endorsing strict quotas in situations
where intentional discrimination was proven.

### Earlier Court Decisions

In a 1976 case, *McDonald v. Santa Fe Transportation Company*,
the Court ruled unanimously that Title VII forbade discrimination against whites as well as members of minorities, but this
case avoided the question of whether employers might sometimes use affirmative-action programs that presented comparative disadvantages for whites. In the famous *Regents of the
University of California v. Bakke* case (1978), the Court decided
against rigid quotas in education. Many people expected the

Court to take a similar position on questions of employment opportunity.

The Kaiser Corporation aluminum and chemical plant of Gramercy, Louisiana, had never made employment decisions explicitly on the basis of race, but African Americans were not represented in the plant in proportion to their percentage in the local population, especially in the higher-paying craft positions. Because Kaiser Corporation did business with the federal government, its employment practices were examined by the Office of Federal Contracts Compliance. The agency was naturally critical of the fact that although African Americans made up 39 percent of the local workforce they occupied fewer than 2 percent of the craft positions at the Gramercy plant. Fourteen other Kaiser plants were found to have similar patterns of black employment.

Because a costly legal challenge appeared likely, the Kaiser Corporation and the United Steelworkers of America jointly agreed to begin "voluntary" affirmative-action programs for the fifteen plants, including both goals and quotas. In the Kaiser plant, there was to be a special program to train craft workers, with thirteen positions the first year. Admission to the program was based on seniority, but at least half the positions were reserved for African Americans even if they had less seniority. This quota was to continue until the number of African Americans was commensurate with their percentage in the local labor force.

Brian Weber, who had been active in union affairs, was a white employee who had five years of experience at the Gramercy plant. Disappointed not to receive one of the thirteen positions, he became angry when he learned that two African Americans with less seniority had been admitted to the program. After reading the Civil Rights Act, he decided to sue both the company and the union on the grounds that Title VII prohibited employment practices that favored one race over another.

In 1977, a federal district court ruled in Weber's favor, and the following year he again received a favorable judgment from the Fifth Circuit Court of Appeals. At the appeals court, however, Justice John Wisdom dissented from the argument that statistical disproportion created a presumptive case of discrimination that merited remediation, and he referred to the fact that Congress in 1972 had not banned preferential treatment. The Supreme Court agreed to a writ of *certiorari*, and the Court listened to oral arguments on March 28, 1979. Justice Louis Powell, who was recovering from surgery, did not participate in the case, and Justice John Paul Stevens did not participate for unstated reasons.

### The Supreme Court's Ruling

On June 27, the Court announced a five-to-two decision that reversed the lower courts. The senior member of the majority, Justice William Brennan, Jr., decided to write the controversial opinion, and he was joined by Justices Harry Blackmun, Potter Stewart, Thurgood Marshall, and Byron White, with Blackmun writing a concurring opinion. Stewart's vote was a surprise and seemed to contradict his position in similar cases. Chief Justice Warren Burger and Justice William Rehnquist both dissented and wrote strongly worded opinions.

Speaking for the majority, Brennan stressed the narrowness of the decision, indicating that the Court was not ruling on all possible forms of preferential treatment. He argued that Weber's case was based on a "literal" interpretation of Title VII, but that the "spirit" or purpose of the law had to be considered within the framework of its legislative history. Since the goal of Title VII was to promote "the integration of blacks into the mainstream of American society," the law should not be used to prohibit reasonable means designed to achieve that end. Since section 703(j) stated that the statute was not to be interpreted "to require" preferential treatment, Brennan concluded that this wording gave an employer the freedom to institute a voluntary program.

In defending the Kaiser program, Brennan presented three principles. First, the program did "not unnecessarily trammel the interests of the white employees," because they were not discharged or barred from future advancement. Second, the plan was a "temporary measure" that would end when the specific target had been achieved. Third, the program did not aim for a permanent quota but was a limited measure "to eliminate a manifest racial imbalance." Brennan implied that programs violating these principles would likely be declared invalid.

Justice Blackmun's concurring opinion accepted the majority outcome but took a less expansive approach to Title VII. Rather than emphasizing the voluntary nature of the Kaiser program, Blackmun followed Justice Wisdom's contention that statistical imbalance was evidence of an "arguable violation" of the law, allowing employers "to make reasonable responses without fear of liability." Finally, he noted that if the Court had "misperceived" the intent of Congress, this could be corrected easily by legislative action.

In his thirty-seven page dissent, Justice Rehnquist emphasized the actual language of the 1964 law, criticizing Brennan's method of stressing the goals at the expense of the literal words of the law. He noted that Section 703(j) was joined to Section 703(e), with the latter explicitly prohibiting any classifications that might deprive an individual of equal opportunity because of race or sex. He also quoted extensively from supporters of the law during the eighty-three-day debate in the Senate, including Senator Hubert Humphrey's statement that Title VII "forbids discrimination against anyone on account of race." Rehnquist charged that the majority holding was "a *tour de force* reminiscent not of jurists . . . but of escape artists such as Houdini."

In a more restrained dissent, Chief Justice Burger declared that the majority opinion "effectively rewrites Title VII to achieve what it regards as a desirable result." He declared that he would be inclined to allow preferential treatment if he were a member of a legislative body, but that it was incompatible with the principle of separation of powers for the Court to rule "contrary to the explicit language of the statute." In looking for the "spirit" of a law, he asked: "How are judges expected to ascertain the purpose of a law except through the words Congress used and the legislative history of the statute's evolution?"

## Impact

When the *Weber* decision was announced, it created much controversy. Defenders included most civil rights groups and officials of the administration of President Jimmy Carter. Some supported the ruling because of the assumption that preferential treatment and numerical remedies were necessary to counteract the "institutional racism" that was endemic in American society, and others believed that such policies were justified in order to compensate for the socioeconomic disadvantages of African Americans and members of other minorities. In contrast, critics of affirmative action feared that the *Weber* ruling would give a green light to quotas and "reverse discrimination," with innocent whites being punished for past injustices for which they were not responsible. Jewish organizations such as B'nai B'rith were especially outspoken in their disagreement, for historically quotas had been used to place limits on opportunities for Jews.

Formally, the *Weber* ruling was limited to voluntary programs of racial preference for private businesses that had manifest racial imbalance when compared with the local labor force. It did not draw a clear line of demarcation between permissible and impermissible forms of affirmative action. Since the majority chose to ignore the fact that Kaiser Corporation and the union were acting because of federal pressure under Executive Order 11246, the ruling did not address the constitutionality of this kind of state action, but the silence of the Court on this crucial issue appeared to give tacit approval. Informed observers generally agreed that there was unlikely to be an epidemic of voluntary affirmative action without the "prodding" of governmental agencies.

During the 1980's, the Court, although becoming more conservative, made decisions that generally were consistent with the key points of *Weber*. In *Fullilove v. Klutznick* (1980), the majority upheld a congressional public works law that stipulated that 10 percent of contracts had to be reserved for minority-owned businesses. When there was evidence that either public or private employers had demonstrated bad faith in the employment of members of minorities, the Court supported the right of lower courts to impose rigid quotas. In several cases, the Court allowed statistical evidence of racial or sexual imbalance to be used as one of the indicators of possible discrimination. When employees lost their jobs because of economic difficulties, however, the Court did not permit racial quotas to determine who was to be laid off. Despite public opposition to preferential treatment, by the early 1990's it appeared very unlikely that *Weber* would be reversed.

A quarter of a century after the passage of the Civil Rights Act of 1964, African Americans and members of other minorities had made a number of gains in the realm of employment, although statistics made it clear that they were far from achieving parity with whites. By that time, the vast majority of Americans said that they agreed with the goal of equal opportunity, but there was no consensus on the goal of equality of outcomes. Few observers denied that African Americans continued to face negative stereotypes and discrimination, and race relations did not seem to be improving for the better. The principles of the *Weber* decision continued to elicit emotional debates.

*Thomas Tandy Lewis*

## Further Reading

Brennan, William, Harry Blackmun, Warren Burger, and William Rehnquist. *"United Steelworkers of America v. Weber." Supreme Court Reporter* 99 (1982): 2721-2753. The complete text of both the majority and dissenting opinions, with a short introduction and summary of the facts of the case. The same texts are found in *United States Reports* and *United States Supreme Court Reports, Lawyers' Edition*.

Cohen, Carl. "Justice Debased: The *Weber* Decision." *Commentary* 68 (September, 1979): 45-53. Written just after the decision, Cohen calls Brennan's opinion an "unbelievably obtuse reading" of the law, showing callousness to ordinary working-class people. The one redeeming feature of the decision is Blackmun's statement that Congress has ultimate power in the matter.

_____. "Why Racial Preference Is Illegal and Immoral." *Commentary* 67 (June, 1979): 40-52. Giving an excellent account of the circumstances of *Weber*, this legal and philosophical analysis argues that individual rights should not be sacrificed for the benefit of the well-being of ethnic groups. Cohen reflects the traditional Jewish opposition to quotas.

Eastland, Terry, and William J. Bennett. *Counting by Race: Equality from the Founding Fathers to "Bakke" and "Weber."* New York: Basic Books, 1979. A historical summary with an emphasis on the change from the goal of individual equality of opportunity to that of "numerical parity" for groups. The authors are very critical of the majority opinion in the *Weber* case.

Edwards, Harry. "Affirmative Action or Reverse Discrimination: The Head and Tail of *Weber*." *Creighton Law Review* 13 (1979-1980): 713-766. A detailed and scholarly analysis that defends affirmative action but criticizes Brennan's opinion for not concentrating more on the 1972 law. Edwards argues that remedial action is not a form of discrimination, even if innocent parties pay a price.

Greenwalt, Kent. *Discrimination and Reverse Discrimination*. New York: Alfred A. Knopf, 1982. About two-thirds of this convenient little book is composed of Supreme Court opinions and other primary material, with an excellent introduction that defends racial preference. This is designed primarily as a text for college courses.

Gross, Barry. *Discrimination in Reverse: Is Turnabout Fair Play?* New York: New York University Press, 1978. Deals with the philosophical and ethical issues of preferential treatment, with limited material on the legal questions. The book considers such a policy to be ethically wrong and contrary to the goal of equal justice.

Meltzer, Bernard. "The *Weber* Case: The Judicial Abrogation of the Antidiscrimination Standard in Employment." *The University of Chicago Law Review* 47 (Spring, 1980): 423-466. Includes a helpful history of affirmative action and a good analysis of the case. Meltzer believes that the goal of equal outcomes for groups will aggravate racial conflict and obstruct the ends of the Fourteenth Amendment. Meltzer's views should be compared with those of Harry Edwards.

Urofsky, Melvin. *A Conflict of Rights: The Supreme Court and Affirmative Action*. New York: Charles Scribner's Sons, 1991. About a fifth of this excellent book deals with the history of affirmative action, and the rest is devoted to *Johnson v. Transportation Agency* in 1987. In contrast to most works, Urofsky's presents a balanced and sympathetic evaluation of the opposing viewpoints on the controversial topic.

**See also** *Adarand Constructors v. Peña*; Affirmative action; *Bakke* case; *Fullilove v. Klutznick*

# Universal Negro Improvement Association

**Identification:** Short-lived national organization dedicated to advancing international black consciousness and racial pride
**Date:** Founded in May, 1917
**Place:** New York, New York

*Founded by Jamaican immigrant Marcus Garvey, the Universal Negro Improvement Association was an important precursor to the civil rights and black nationalist movements of the 1950's and 1960's.*

In March, 1916, a young black Jamaican, Marcus Garvey, arrived in New York City. He had come to the United States in the hope of securing financial help for the Universal Negro Improvement Association (UNIA), which he had founded in Jamaica two years earlier. After delivering his first public speech in Harlem in May, Garvey began a long speaking tour that took him through thirty-eight states. In May, 1917, he returned to Harlem and—with the help of his secretary and future wife, Amy Ashwood—organized the first American chapter of the UNIA. Though hardly noticed at the time, this infant organization was a significant first step in the growth of black nationalism in the United States. Within a few years, the UNIA would claim millions of members and hundreds of branches throughout the United States, the Caribbean region, and Africa, and Garvey would be one of the most famous black people in the world.

## Marcus Garvey

Garvey was born in St. Ann's Bay, Jamaica, in 1887. He claimed to be of pure African descent. His father was a descendant of the maroons, or Jamaican slaves, who successfully revolted against their British masters in 1739. During his early years, Garvey gradually became aware that his color was considered by some in his society to be a badge of inferiority. Jamaica, unlike the United States, placed the mulatto in a higher caste as a buffer against the unlettered black masses. This reality caused a sense of racial isolation and yet pride to grow in the young black man.

By his twentieth birthday, Garvey had started a program to change the lives of black Jamaicans. While working as a foreman in a printing shop in 1907, he joined a labor strike as a leader. The strike, quickly broken by the shop owners, caused Garvey to lose faith in reform through labor unions. In 1910, he started publishing a newspaper, *Garvey's Watchman*, and helped form a political organization, the National Club. These efforts, which were not particularly fruitful, gave impetus to Garvey's visit to Central America where he was able to observe the wretched conditions of black people in Costa Rica and Panama.

Garvey's travels as a black Ulysses finally led him to London, the center of the British Empire. There the young man met Dusé Mohamed Ali, an Egyptian scholar, who increased the young Jamaican's knowledge and awareness of Africa. During his stay in England, Garvey also became acquainted with the plight of African Americans through reading Booker T. Washington's *Up from Slavery* (1901). Washington's autobiography raised questions in Garvey's mind

*Students at Tuskegee Institute, whose achievements drew Marcus Garvey to the United States, where he wished to study Booker T. Washington's schemes for racial uplift.* (Library of Congress)

I asked, where is the black man's Government? Where is his King and his Kingdom? Where is his President, his country and his ambassador, his army, his navy, his men of big affairs? I could not find them, and then I declared, I will help to make them.

Returning to Jamaica in 1914, Garvey created a self-help organization for black people to which he gave the imposing title, the Universal Negro Improvement and Conservation Association and African Communities League. This new organization, renamed the Universal Negro Improvement Association, based its philosophy on the need to unite "all people of Negro or African parentage." The goals of the UNIA were to increase racial pride, to aid black people throughout the world, and "to establish a central nation for the race." Garvey, elected the first president of UNIA, realized that black people would have to achieve these goals without assistance from white people. This self-help concept, similar to the philosophy (but not the practice) of Booker T. Washington, led Garvey to propose a black trade school in Kingston, Jamaica, similar to Washington's Tuskegee Institute. The idea did not attract wide support and Garvey was temporarily frustrated.

### Garvey's Arrival in the United States

In 1915 Garvey decided to come to the United States in order to seek aid for his Jamaica-based organization. Although he had corresponded with Booker T. Washington, Washington had died before Garvey arrived in the United States in 1916. Garvey went directly to Harlem, which in the early twentieth century was becoming a center of black culture.

The lives of African Americans were rapidly changing in the first two decades of the twentieth century. Metropolitan areas in the North were experiencing mass migrations of African Americans from the South. In New York City, for example, the black population increased from 91,709 in 1910 to 152,467 in 1920. African Americans were attracted by the promise of jobs and by the possibility of escaping the rigid system of segregation in the South.

African Americans found, however, that they could not escape racism simply by moving. Northern whites also believed in the racial inferiority of African Americans and opposed black competitors for their jobs. The new immigrants, like their foreign-born counterparts, were crowded into the northern ghettos without proper housing or the possibility of escape. Racial violence broke out in several northern cities. The North proved not to be a utopia for African Americans.

**Founding of the UNIA**

These harsh realities aided Garvey in establishing the UNIA in New York. The population of Harlem was not attracted to the accommodationist philosophy of Booker T. Washington or the middle-class goals of the National Association for the Advancement of Colored People. Indeed, urban African Americans were wary of all prophets, even Garvey; but the young Jamaican was able to obtain support from the Jamaican immigrants in Harlem, who felt isolated, and he established a branch of UNIA there in 1917. At first, the organization encountered difficulties. Local politicians tried to gain control of it, and Garvey had to fight to save its autonomy. The original branch of the UNIA was dissolved, and a charter was obtained from the state of New York which prevented other groups from using the organization's name. By 1918, under Garvey's exciting leadership, the New York chapter of the UNIA boasted 3,500 members. By 1919, Garvey optimistically claimed two million members for his organization throughout the world and 200,000 subscribers for his weekly newspaper, *The Negro World*.

In an effort to promote the economic welfare of African Americans under the auspices of the UNIA, Garvey established in 1919 two joint stock companies—the Black Star Line, an international commercial shipping company, and the Negro Factories Corporation, which was to "build and operate factories . . . to manufacture every marketable commodity." Stock in these companies was sold only to black investors. The Black Star Line was to establish commerce with Africa and transport willing emigrants "back to Africa."

Although both companies were financial failures, they gave many black people a feeling of dignity. As a result of his promotional efforts in behalf of the Black Star Line, the federal government, prodded by rival black leaders, had Garvey indicted for fraudulent use of the mails in 1922. He was tried, found guilty, and sent to prison in 1923. Although his second wife, Amy Jacques Garvey, worked to hold the UNIA together, it declined rapidly. In 1927, Garvey was released from prison and deported as an undesirable alien. He returned to Jamaica, and then went to London and Paris and tried to resurrect the UNIA, but with little success. He died in poverty in London in 1940. Although a poor businessman, Garvey was a master propagandist and popular leader who made a major contribution toward race consciousness and pride among black people in the United States and throughout the world.

In 2005, a vestige of the UNIA still remained in operation and even maintained an interactive Web site. The modern organization continues to honor Garvey's legacy and the goals of the original organization.

*John C. Gardner*
*Updated by R. Kent Rasmussen*

## Further Reading

Cronon, E. David. *Black Moses: The Story of Marcus Garvey and the Universal Negro Improvement Association*. Madison: University of Wisconsin Press, 1955. This first scholarly biography of Garvey remains the best introduction to his life.

Garvey, Amy Jacques. *Garvey and Garveyism*. 1963. Reprint. New York: Collier, 1976. Intimate memoir of Garvey written by his widow two decades after his death.

Garvey, Marcus. *Philosophy and Opinions of Marcus Garvey*. Edited by Amy Jacques-Garvey, with new introduction by Robert A. Hill. New York: Atheneum, 1992. This classic collection of Garvey's speeches and writings was assembled by his wife during the early 1920's, while Garvey was fighting mail-fraud charges. Hill's new introduction places the work in a broad historical perspective.

Hill, Robert A., et al., eds. *The Marcus Garvey and Universal Negro Improvement Association Papers*. 9 vols. Berkeley: University of California Press, 1983-1996. The most extensive collection of original documents by and about Garvey and his movement, this set is the best starting point for all research on the UNIA.

Hill, Robert A., and Barbara Bair, eds. *Marcus Garvey: Life and Lessons*. Berkeley: University of California Press, 1987. Collection of Garvey's most didactic writings, including autobiographical material that he wrote in 1930. A long appendix includes biographies of figures important in his life.

Lewis, Rupert, and Maureen Warner-Lewis, eds. *Garvey: Africa, Europe, the Americas*. Kingston, Jamaica: Institute of Social and Economic Research, University of the West Indies, 1986. Collection of original research papers on international aspects of Garveyism.

**See also** Atlanta Compromise; Black nationalism; Great Migration; Nation of Islam; National Association for the Advancement of Colored People; Niagara Movement; Pan-Africanism; *Plessy v. Ferguson*

# University of Mississippi desegregation

**The Event:** Admission of the first African American student to the traditional segregated University of Mississippi
**Date:** October, 1962
**Place:** Oxford, Mississippi

*The enrollment of the first African American student at the University of Mississippi provoked a national controversy.*

In January, 1961, James Meredith, a native Mississippian and an Air Force veteran attending Jackson State College, one of Mississippi's all-black colleges, decided to transfer to the University of Mississippi, affectionately called "Ole Miss." His application was rejected because, Ole Miss officials maintained, Jackson State was not an approved Southern Association Secondary School and because Meredith did not furnish letters of recommendation from University of Mississippi alumni. On May 31, 1961, he filed a lawsuit against the university, charging that he had been denied admission because of his race. In its 114-year history, the University of Mississippi had never admitted an African American student.

## Meredith's Legal Victory

A federal district court judge dismissed Meredith's suit, but in June, 1962, a U.S. court of appeals ruled that Meredith had been rejected from Ole Miss "solely because he was a Negro," a ruling based on the *Brown v. Board of Education* school desegregation case of 1954. The court ordered the university to admit Meredith, and the ruling was upheld by Justice Hugo L. Black of the U.S. Supreme Court. On September 13, Mississippi governor Ross Barnett delivered a televised speech and stated, "No school will be integrated in Mississippi while I'm governor." A week later, the board of trustees of Ole Miss appointed Governor Barnett as the university's registrar, and he personally blocked Meredith from registering for courses that same day.

Throughout Meredith's court appeals, the U.S. Department of Justice had been monitoring the case. Attorney General Robert F. Kennedy, the brother of President John F. Kennedy, made more than a dozen phone calls to Governor Barnett, hoping to persuade him to allow Meredith to matriculate and thereby avoid a confrontation between the state of Mississippi and the federal government. The attorney general had provided Meredith with federal marshals to protect him as he attempted to register.

On September 24, the court of appeals that initially had heard Meredith's case again ordered the Board of Higher Education of Mississippi to allow Meredith to register. The following day, Meredith reported to the registrar's office in the university's Lyceum Building, but again Governor Barnett was there to block his registration. During a phone conversation with Attorney General Kennedy that same day, Barnett declared that he would never agree to allow Meredith to attend the University of Mississippi. When Kennedy reminded Barnett that he was openly defying a court order and could be subject to penalty, Barnett told Kennedy that he would rather spend the rest of his life in prison than allow Meredith to enroll.

On September 26, Meredith again tried to register for courses, and for the third time, Governor Barnett turned him away. Two days later, the court of appeals warned Barnett that if he continued to block Meredith's admission to Ole Miss, the governor would be found in contempt of court, arrested, and fined ten thousand dollars per day. On Saturday, September 29, Governor Barnett appeared at a university football game and proudly announced,

> I love Mississippi, I love her people, her customs! And I love and respect her heritage. Ask us what we say, it's to hell with Bobby K!

That evening, President Kennedy called Governor Barnett and told him that the federal government would continue to back Meredith until Ole Miss admitted him. Under direct pressure from the president, Barnett began to reconsider. Finally, he agreed to allow Meredith to register on Sunday, September 30, when, the governor surmised, few students and news reporters would be milling around the campus. On Sunday evening, Meredith arrived at the Lyceum Building protected by three hundred marshals, armed in riot gear and equipped with tear gas.

As Meredith and his escorts approached the campus, a group of twenty-five hundred students and other agitators attempted to block their passage. The crowd began to shout and throw bricks and bottles at the federal marshals, who retaliated with tear gas. Some of the protesters were armed with guns and began firing random shots. One federal marshal was seriously wounded by a bullet in the throat. Two onlookers, Paul Guihard, a French journalist, and Roy Gunter, a jukebox repairman, were shot and killed by rioters.

### Kennedy's National Address

On Sunday evening, while Mississippians rioted on the university campus, President Kennedy addressed the nation on television. The Meredith crisis had captured the country's and news media's attention, and the president attempted to show Mississippians and other U.S. citizens that his administration's commitment to civil rights was serious and unwavering. He reminded his audience that "Americans are free . . . to disagree with the law but not to disobey it. For in a government of laws and not of men, no man, however prominent or powerful, and no mob, however

*James Meredith on his first day as a student at the University of Mississippi.* (Library of Congress)

unruly or boisterous, is entitled to defy a court of law." He told Mississippians, "The eyes of the nation and all the world are upon you and upon all of us. And the honor of your university—and state—are in the balance."

The situation at the University of Mississippi was deteriorating. The federal marshals, low on tear gas, requested additional help to control the unruly mob. President Kennedy federalized Mississippi National Guardsmen and ordered them to Oxford. At dawn on Monday morning, the first of five thousand troops began arriving at Oxford to restore order. During the evening's rioting, more than one hundred people were injured and about two hundred were arrested, only twenty-four of whom were Ole Miss students.

On Monday morning, October 1, at 8:30 A.M., Meredith again presented himself at the Lyceum Building to register. He was closely guarded by federal marshals, and National Guardsmen continued patrolling the Ole Miss campus and Oxford's streets. Meredith, dressed impeccably in a business suit, registered for classes and began his matriculation at the University of Mississippi. "I am intent on seeing that every citizen has an opportunity of being a first-class citizen," Meredith told a reporter the next day. "I am also intent on seeing that citizens have a right to be something if they work hard enough."

During his tenure at the University of Mississippi, Meredith was often the target of insults and threats. Federal marshals remained with him during his entire time at the university. On August 18, 1963, Meredith graduated from the university with a bachelor of arts degree in political science. After a year of study in Africa, Meredith enrolled at Columbia University of Law. In 1966, the year before he completed his law degree, Meredith was wounded by a sniper's gunshot during a voter registration march from Tennessee to Mississippi.

### Meredith's Impact

As a result of his successful effort to desegregate Ole Miss, Meredith became one of the heroes of the Civil Rights movement. In his "Letter from Birmingham Jail" (1963), Martin Luther King, Jr., states that "One day the South will recognize its real heroes. They will be the James Merediths, courageously and with a majestic sense of purpose facing jeering and hostile mobs and the agonizing loneliness that characterizes the life of the pioneer."

Meredith's victory at the University of Mississippi was a key triumph for the Civil Rights movement during the 1960's. Within two years, the University of Alabama, the University of Georgia, and other southern colleges and universities that had prevented African Americans from enrolling were also desegregated, as the era of overt segregation in U.S. institutions of higher learning came to an end.

The Meredith case also convincingly demonstrated that the federal government would use its power to end racial segregation in the South. Despite Governor Barnett's defiance, President Kennedy and his attorney general were able to force the state of Mississippi to comply with a federal court order, signaling that the South would be unable to block the subsequent wave of federal legislation designed to void the region's segregation laws.

*James Tackach*

**Further Reading**

Russell H. Barrett's *Integration at Ole Miss* (Chicago: Quadran-gle Press, 1965) discusses Meredith's attempt to integrate the Uni-versity of Mississippi. James H. Meredith's *Three Years in Missis-sippi* (Bloomington: Indiana University Press, 1966) is Meredith's own story of his years at Ole Miss. Arthur M. Schlesinger, Jr.'s *Robert Kennedy and His Times* (Boston: Houghton Mifflin, 1978) details Kennedy's involvement in the Meredith case. Sanford Wexler's *The Civil Rights Movement: An Eyewitness History* (New York: Facts on File, 1993) devotes a chapter to Meredith's integra-tion of Ole Miss.

**See also** Black Power movement; *Brown v. Board of Education*; Civil Rights movement; Council of Federated Organizations; Freedom Summer; Little Rock school desegregation crisis; Mont-gomery bus boycott; Southern Christian Leadership Conference; *Swann v. Charlotte-Mecklenberg Board of Education*

# Vietnam War

**The Event:** U.S. military involvement in Vietnam's civil war
**Date:** 1960's-1973
**Place:** Southeast Asia

*American involvement in the war in Vietnam yielded disparate results for African Americans who served there. On one hand, it was the first time that African Americans were fully integrated into the armed services. On the other, African American casualties were dis-proportionately greater than those suffered by white soldiers and were a significantly higher percentage than that of African Ameri-cans in the United States population. These discrepancies were mir-rored at home in the conflicting attitudes of leaders of the Civil Rights movement and the African American population in general.*

African Americans have fought in all the foreign wars in which the United States has been involved. Before the Vietnam War, most served in the Army, and all had been segregated into sepa-rate units. Not until World War II were African Americans allowed to join the Marines. Even after the services were integrated by Executive Order 9981 in 1948, the officer corps remained almost entirely white, and African Americans had few opportunities for promotion. Nevertheless, some African Americans stayed in the military services and advanced in the ranks. By the 1960's, the armed forces were among the few truly integrated institutions in American society, and many African Americans found more opportunities in the military services than in civilian life.

During the Vietnam War, the draft system helped to increase the number of African Americans in military service. College students were eligible for deferments from the draft; because fewer African Americans than whites were college students, a disproportionate number of them were drafted. Sixteen percent of draftees during the war were African Americans, although African Americans represented only 12 percent of the total U.S. population. Most African American servicemen during the war served in Army and Marine combat units, often on the front lines.

Some critics have charged that during the Vietnam War, African American soldiers were given the most dangerous combat assignments. Although fewer than 13 percent of the U.S. soldiers in Vietnam were African Americans, they constituted 20 percent of the Army's fatalities between 1961 and 1966. However, these figures may be misleading, as many African American soldiers volunteered to join the elite combat units, which offered higher pay, greater chances for promotion, and greater respect of others in the military, while also being involved in some of the most dangerous missions.

At the time of the Vietnam War, women could not serve in combat roles. However, African Americans joined other women as army and air force nurses, as military personnel in noncombat positions, and in such civilian jobs as teachers, aid workers, and in government offices in Vietnam.

### African American Leaders Speak Out

African American leaders have historically generally supported service in the military. However, as awareness and anger regarding discrimination throughout the United States grew, more leaders and soldiers questioned why citizens who were denied their rights at home should be sent to fight for the rights of citizens of other countries. The more radical factions of the Civil Rights movement further argued that members of an oppressed minority in the United States should not agree to kill members of an oppressed minority in a nation such as Vietnam.

In 1964, African Americans backed Lyndon B. Johnson for president overwhelmingly. Many initially refrained from criticizing his conduct of the Vietnam War because he had supported civil rights and voting rights legislation, and his Great Society program promised to lift the economically disadvantaged from poverty and other social ills. Critics noted, however, that Johnson's war policies drained away the money that could have been used to support these programs.

Radicals such as Eldridge Cleaver, Stokely Carmichael, and Malcolm X urged African Americans to refuse to serve in the Vietnam War. The moderate civil rights leader and winner of the Nobel Peace Prize, Martin Luther King, Jr., at first shied away from criticizing the Vietnam War. However, in April, 1967, he delivered his "Beyond War" speech, adding a highly respected voice to the growing criticism of the war. Another prominent African Ameri-

*Draft lottery conducted during the Vietnam War. One of the most controversial aspects of the war was the public perception that the draft itself discriminated against African Americans.* (Library of Congress)

can critic was heavyweight boxing champion Muhammad Ali, who refused induction into the Army because of his religious beliefs. He was not granted conscientious objector status; instead, he was convicted of draft evasion, sentenced to prison, and stripped of his boxing title. However, his title was later restored.

During the early years of the Vietnam War, racial tensions in the military were muted, but as the Civil Rights movement and antiwar protests converged to increase polarity in the United States, divisions in the armed services mirrored societal chasms. At the start of American involvement in the war, many of the African Americans in the military had been career soldiers who had had little contact with the Civil Rights movement at home. As the war lengthened, more young African American soldiers arrived from the ghettos and housing projects of the cities in which civil rights protests were growing. African American soldiers began to band together, studying black history and culture, using special signs and handshakes, and calling themselves blood brothers, or "bloods."

### Distinguished African American Servicemen

The Army's 173rd Airborne Brigade, paratroopers known as the "Sky Soldiers," comprised mainly African Americans, and was considered by many to be one of the best units in Vietnam for its bravery in ferocious battles. Milton Olive and Lawrence Joel, both Sky Soldiers, were two of the twenty African Americans who received the U.S. Medal of Honor, the highest U.S. military award for bravery in battle. Colin Powell, who served two tours in Vietnam with the infantry, went on to become a general, chairman of the Joint Chiefs of Staff, and U.S. secretary of state.

*Irene Struthers Rush*

### Further Reading

Appy, Christian. *Patriots: Vietnam War Remembered from All Sides.* New York: Penguin Books, 2003.

David, Jay, and Elaine Crane, eds. *The Black Soldier from the American Revolution to Vietnam.* New York: William Morrow, 1971.

Nalty, Bernard C. *Strength for the Fight: A History of Black Americans in the Military.* New York: Simon & Schuster, 1989.

Terry, Wallace. *Bloods: An Oral History of the Vietnam War by Black Veterans.* New York: Random House, 1984.

**See also** Civil Rights movement; Civil War; Military; Military desegregation; World War II

# Voting Rights Act of 1965

**The Law:** Federal law expanding the government's authority to increase black voter registration and participation in states in which African Americans had been subjected to discrimination

**Date:** Signed into law on August 16, 1965

*Passage of this law was a major step in the enfranchisement of African Americans. In 1966, the U.S. Supreme Court upheld the provisions of the act, justifying the extension of federal power by noting the existence of exceptional conditions. The act had a major impact on African American participation in the political process in the South.*

At the turn of the twentieth century, southern states adopted numerous devices designed to disfranchise African Americans and poor whites. The most common device was the literacy test, which required prospective voters to read, write, and interpret any part of the U.S. Constitution or state constitution. The inclusion of an interpretation requirement meant that registrars could reject literate African Americans by deeming their interpretations incorrect. Other devices included the white primary, which excluded African Americans from voting in the Democratic Party primary, and poll taxes, which excluded many poor people, both black and white.

Because of these devices, only about 3 percent of African Americans were registered to vote in the South in 1940. By 1956 the percentage had increased to 25 percent of the black voting-age population. In contrast, 60 percent of the white voting-age population was registered. Efforts by African Americans to register intensified during the Civil Rights movement, and by November, 1964, approximately 43 percent of voting-age African Americans

*Promotion of universal suffrage has been a principle of the National Association for the Advancement of Colored People since its inception in the early twentieth century.* (Library of Congress)

in the South were registered. This registration, however, was uneven. In the Deep South, especially in the rural areas, black registration was significantly lower. For example, the average black registration rate in Alabama, Georgia, Louisiana, and South Carolina was approximately 22 percent while in Mississippi the figure was less than 7 percent.

### The Struggle for Voting Rights

Efforts to increase the registration of African Americans in the southern states involved a variety of organizations, including the Voter Education Project of the Southern Regional Council, the Congress of Racial Equality (CORE), the Student Nonviolent Coordinating Committee (SNCC), and the Southern Christian Leadership Conference (SCLC). The most important campaign occurred in Selma, Alabama, in 1965. In the fall of 1964 only 335 out of more than 15,000 African Americans of voting age were registered in Dallas County, Alabama. In Dallas County, registration was allowed only two days a month. Applicants had to fill in more than fifty blanks on a form, write a part of the Constitution from dictation, read four parts of the Constitution and answer four questions about what they had read, answer four questions on the working of government, and swear loyalty to both the state of Alabama and the United States.

Following several months of demonstrations and efforts, civil rights activists held a march from Selma to Montgomery, Alabama. State troopers and sheriff's posse men attacked marchers when they attempted to cross the Edmund Pettus Bridge in Selma, and approximately one hundred marchers were injured. National outrage over the attacks led to approval of the Voting Rights Act in August, 1965, by a vote of 328 to 74 in the House of Representatives and by a 79-18 vote in the Senate. On August 6, 1965, President Lyndon B. Johnson signed the bill into law, referring to it as "one of the most monumental laws in the entire history of American freedom."

**Provisions**

Upon the request of President Johnson, Attorney General Nicholas Katzenbach designed an exceptionally strong act. Its purpose was to enforce section 2 of the Fifteenth Amendment, which forbade states or political subdivisions from applying a voter prerequisite to deny or abridge on account of race or color the right of any citizen of the United States to vote. The previous Civil Rights Acts passed in 1957, 1960, and 1964 contained provisions designed to end voter discrimination; however, their impact was limited because they required a case-by-case approach in seeking remedies. In addition, these acts did not allow the federal government to intervene on behalf of those subject to discrimination.

The 1965 Voting Rights Act included several provisions designed to overcome the shortcomings of the previous acts. First, section 4 of the act included a formula that targeted areas where discrimination was greatest and where federal government intervention in voter registration could be of the most help. The targeted areas were those that required a literacy test or similar test for registration prior to November 1, 1964, and where fewer than 50 percent of the eligible voters were either registered to vote or had actually voted in the 1964 presidential election. This provision affected the entire states of Alabama, Alaska, Georgia, Louisiana, Mississippi, South Carolina, and Virginia as well as twenty-six counties in North Carolina and one county in Arizona. In these areas, the Voting Rights Act eliminated for five years the use of literacy tests and other such devices as a prerequisite for registration. On August 7, 1965, Attorney General Katzenbach suspended the tests in these places. Later, in 1965 and 1966, additional counties in North Carolina and Arizona as well as one county each in Hawaii and Idaho were also targeted.

Section 5 of the act included a preclearance provision that required state and local governments covered by the triggering formula to submit any proposed changes in voting laws or practices that had not been in force on November 1, 1964, to the Justice Department or the federal district court in Washington, D.C. This was designed to prevent these governments from developing new techniques designed to limit African American participation in voting.

Under provisions in sections 6 and 7 of the act, the attorney general could send federal voter examiners in to gather names of eligible voters and present them to local officials, who were required to register them. Under section 8 of the law, the attorney general could also send observers or poll watchers to oversee elections to ensure that African Americans were permitted to vote and their votes were counted. During the first ten years of the act, examiners were sent to approximately sixty counties in the South, most of which were in Mississippi or Alabama. An estimated 15 percent of the African Americans who registered in this period were registered by these examiners. The federal government also assigned more than 6,500 poll watchers during the same period.

Section 3 gave the courts the authority to send federal registrars and poll watchers to locales outside covered jurisdictions if the attorney general or private parties brought suits. Section 10 instructed the attorney general to challenge the constitutionality of the poll tax as a prerequisite for voting in state and local elections. Section 11 prohibited anyone "acting under color of law" from preventing qualified voters from voting or intimidating, threatening, or coercing voters; it also prohibited voting fraud in federal elections. Section 12 stipulated punishment for violation of someone's voting rights. Finally, section 14 provided a detailed definition of voting.

## Legal Challenges to the Act

South Carolina sued to test the legality of the Voting Rights Act of 1965. In *South Carolina v. Katzenbach* (1966), the Supreme Court unanimously upheld the major provisions of the law. In its decision, the Court recognized that the act represented an uncommon extension of federal power; however, it justified these powers by noting that exceptional conditions could justify legislative measures that might otherwise be deemed inappropriate.

Other court cases followed concerning provisions of the act. In *Harper v. Virginia Board of Elections* (1966), the Court declared the poll tax for state and local elections unconstitutional. This overturned the Court's 1937 decision in *Breedlove v. Suttles*, which stated that a poll tax did not violate the Constitution.

Although African American voter registration increased significantly, some southern locales used a variety of more subtle techniques to limit the impact of black voters. These techniques included withholding information from black voters, failing to provide assistance to illiterate voters, purging voting rolls, disqualifying voters on technical grounds, requiring separate registration for different types of elections, moving polling places, and failing to provide adequate voting facilities in black precincts. Efforts were also made to dilute the impact of African American voters, which resulted in more court cases.

In *Allen v. Board of Elections* (1969), the Court examined the issue of dilution of black voters in Mississippi when the state moved from single-member districts to at-large elections. The Court held that the Voting Rights Act gave a broad interpretation to the right to vote and stated that voting included all actions necessary to make a vote effective. This greatly increased the importance of section 5 of the Voting Rights Act and resulted in many more challenges to proposed changes in election procedures in covered jurisdictions. For example, between 1965 and 1969 the Justice Department objected to only six proposed changes. By the end of 1989, 2,335 changes had been objected to under section 5.

In *White v. Regester* (1973), the Court unanimously agreed that multimember districts in the Texas counties of Bexar and Dallas were unconstitutional based on the totality of the circumstances, which included the cultural and economic realities of African Americans and Mexicans as well as the multimember districts. In general, this decision resulted in multimember districts being replaced by single-member districts.

In 1980, however, in *Mobile v. Bolden*, the Court held that the Fifteenth Amendment applied only to access to the ballot, not vote dilution, and that the Fourteenth and Fifteenth Amendments required a showing of purpose to discriminate. This decision was a setback for voting rights. However, in 1986 the Court gave explicit guidelines for dilution in *Thornburg v. Gingles*. In this North Carolina case, the Court provided a three-part test for determining if multimember districts resulted in dilution: The minority group had to be sufficiently large and geographically compact to constitute a majority in at least one single-member district; the minority group had to tend to vote as a bloc; and the majority group had to vote sufficiently as a bloc to enable it to normally defeat the minority's preferred candidate.

**Impact**

Overall, despite manipulation and court challenges, the Voting Rights Act had a significant impact on the South. Within one month of its passage, more than 27,000 new African American voters were registered by federal examiners in Alabama, Louisiana, and Mississippi alone. By 1968 black registration in the South increased from 2 million to 3.3 million. In the seven states originally covered by the act, African American registration increased from 29.3 percent in March, 1965, to 56.6 percent by 1972. By 1988 black registration in the eleven states of the South stood at 63.7 percent; in the five Deep South states, it was 65.2 percent.

Increased registration made African Americans important actors in the political process in many parts of the South and resulted in a significant rise in the number of black elected officials. In 1968 there were only 248 black elected officials in the South, but this number rose to 2,601 in 1982 and to 4,924 in 1993.

The Voting Rights Act was renewed in 1970, 1975, and 1982. Each time it was expanded, and it is now applicable to the entire United States. Some of the major additions to the act included extending the franchise to eighteen-year-olds, adding bilingual provisions that required voting information and ballots to be printed not only in English but also in other languages appropriate for local citizens, and creating a provision for minority access and influence districts. Therefore, the Voting Rights Act not only increased the federal government's role in voting but also resulted in significant increases in participation in the political process.

*William V. Moore*

**Further Reading**

Davidson, Chandler, ed. *Minority Vote Dilution.* Washington, D.C.: Howard University Press, 1984.

Elliott, Ward E. *The Rise of Guardian Democracy: The Supreme Court's Role in Voting Rights Disputes, 1845-1969.* Cambridge, Mass.: Howard University Press, 1974.

Garrow, David J. *Protest at Selma: Martin Luther King, Jr., and the Voting Rights Act of 1965.* New Haven, Conn.: Yale University Press, 1978.

Grofman, Bernard, and Chandler Davidson, eds. *Controversies in Minority Voting: The Voting Rights Act in Perspective.* Washington, D.C.: Brookings Institution, 1992.

Kotz, Nick. *Judgment Days: Lyndon Baines Johnson, Martin Luther King, Jr., and the Laws That Changed America.* Boston: Houghton Mifflin, 2005.

**See also** Civil Rights Act of 1960; Civil Rights Act of 1964; Civil Rights movement; Fifteenth Amendment; Gerrymandering; *Gomillion v. Lightfoot*; Grandfather clauses; *Harper v. Virginia Board of Elections*; *Katzenbach v. McClung*; *Mobile v. Bolden*; *Newberry v. United States*; *Nixon v. Condon*; Politics and government; Poll taxes; *Shaw v. Reno*; *Smith v. Allwright*; *Terry v. Adams*; Twenty-fourth Amendment; Understanding tests; Voting Rights Act of 1975; White primaries; *Williams v. Mississippi*; *Yarbrough, Ex parte*

# Voting Rights Act of 1975

**The Law:** Federal law abolishing the use of literacy tests for
voters

**Date:** Signed into law on August 6, 1975

*By eliminating discriminatory and often arbitrarily applied literacy
tests, the Voting Rights Act of 1975 expanded voting rights to large
numbers of poorly educated citizens and members of language minorities throughout the United States.*

Civil rights became a central concern of American politics in the
1960's. Strong civil rights acts were passed during that decade,
and none was more important for the extension of voting rights
in particular than the Voting Rights Act of 1965. The 1975 extension of this act included a ban on literacy tests for members of language minorities. Many consider these acts to be the most important extensions of suffrage rights ever granted by Congress. In
American history, the only actions that surpass the 1965 and 1975
voting rights acts in importance for extending voting rights are
the Fifteenth (1870) and Nineteenth (1920) amendments to the
U.S. Constitution, respectively prohibiting denial of voting rights
on the basis of race, color, or previous servitude and granting the
vote to women.

By the mid-1960's, the number of demonstrations by civil
rights groups had grown considerably. Violence surrounding
even the "peaceful" demonstrations had intensified their impact.
President Lyndon B. Johnson had hoped that the states would address voting rights problems within their own borders. The federal government attempted to assist states by removing some of
the obstacles to voting rights. One clear example was President
Johnson's leadership in securing the passage of the Twenty-
fourth Amendment in 1964, outlawing the use of poll taxes as a
necessary prerequisite to voting in federal elections. This was a
major step in encouraging members of minorities to exercise their
voting rights.

**The Need for New Legislation**

Although the Twenty-fourth Amendment was a major electoral breakthrough, it had the same shortcoming as the civil rights acts Congress approved in 1957, 1960, and 1964: It left the federal government in a passive role in the crucial area of voter registration. The voting rights acts of 1965, 1970, and 1975 overcame this critical shortcoming.

The history of the Voting Rights Act of 1965 is also the history of the Voting Rights Act of 1975, since the later action was an extension of the earlier act. The 1965 act largely was forced on President Johnson and others who hoped that the federal government could avoid direct intervention in what historically had been a local prerogative. Public opinion grew intolerant and impatient after a series of bloody demonstrations. By most accounts, the decisive event that led to congressional action in 1965 was the Freedom March from Selma to Montgomery, Alabama. The Reverend Martin Luther King, Jr., organized this march to protest the registration process in Dallas County. Like other marches during this period, it drew marchers from the entire nation. What distinguished this particular march was the violence that erupted when Governor George Wallace called out state troopers to stop the march. The clash between marchers and troopers resulted in the death of two marchers and severe injuries to scores of others.

This conflict produced an outburst of demonstrations and protest across the nation. The cries for an end to this violence forced President Johnson to introduce a comprehensive voting rights bill to the U.S. Congress. The final version of this bill, which Johnson signed into law on August 6, 1965, ended literacy tests in the states of Alabama, Georgia, Louisiana, Mississippi, South Carolina, and Virginia and in thirty-nine counties in North Carolina.

The other key provision of the Voting Rights Act of 1965 was the authorization of federal examiners to conduct registration and federal observers to oversee elections. The states and counties within the affected jurisdictions also had to submit any changes in their election laws and procedures to federal examiners for clearance. The literacy provision affected southern states primarily, but the broader jurisdiction of the act affected states in every region of the nation.

## The 1970 Act

The voting rights act was due for renewal in 1970. In June of that year, Congress extended the act and made some significant changes. The major changes in the 1970 amendments were a ban on literacy tests in all states, prohibition of long-term residency requirements for voting in presidential elections, and establishment of eighteen as the legal age for voting in national elections. Like the 1965 act, this legislation had a five-year life.

The 1970 act created two distinct legal categories, general and special. The general provisions dealt with literacy tests, voting age, residency requirements, and penalties for interfering with voting rights. The general provisions were permanent laws which were applied nationally. The special provisions, like those in the 1965 act, were selectively applied to areas where such provisions were deemed necessary. States or counties were subjected to the special provisions if they had any test or device established as a prerequisite to either registration or voting and had less than half of the registered voters participate in the presidential elections of 1964 or 1968. The courts could also apply the special provisions to other electoral districts if the attorney general successfully brought suit against them for violating the Fifteenth Amendment.

Areas subjected to the special provisions were placed under additional federal controls. There was a provision for the suspension of literacy and other test devices beyond the ban. Federal examiners were assigned to these areas to conduct registration drives, and federal observers were sent into these areas to monitor elections. In addition, similar to the 1965 act, these areas had to submit any changes in voting laws or procedures to the federal government for clearance. The special provisions could be lifted from a state or county if it successfully filed suit in a three-judge federal district court in Washington, D.C. Such suits had to convince the court that the voter tests or devices in use were not discriminatory.

### Renewing the 1970 Act

As with the 1965 act, the 1970 amendments required reconsideration and renewal after five years. In preparation for this renewal, the U.S. Commission on Civil Rights prepared an extensive report for the president and Congress in January of 1975. The report, *The Voting Rights Act: Ten Years After,* set the tone for the congressional debate that was to follow. In general, the report found that minority participation in the electoral process had increased significantly since 1965. Discriminatory practices, however, were still hampering minority registration and voting. The report suggested a number of changes, the most controversial of which were its recommendation of a ten-year extension of the act and its call for greater attention to members of language minorities, or those who did not speak English.

In February, the House Judiciary Subcommittee on Civil and Constitutional Rights began hearings on extending the Voting Rights Act. Although many different bills were introduced in both the House and the Senate, the one that worked its way successfully through both chambers was H.R. 6219. After swift movement through the committee system, this bill passed the House of Representatives on June 4 by a 341-70 vote.

Efforts to stall this bill when it was sent to the Senate proved unsuccessful. Senator James O. Eastland, chair of the Senate Judiciary Committee and a strong opponent of the bill, put off action until mid-July. The tactics used by Senator Eastland proved unsuccessful when the Senate leadership under Mike Mansfield, managed to bring the House bill directly to the Senate floor. When it appeared that the bill's opponents would stall it on the Senate floor, Majority leader Mansfield and Majority whip Robert Byrd skillfully passed two cloture motions (limiting debate) to get the bill passed.

After considerable parliamentary maneuvering, the Senate leadership managed to get seventeen proposed amendments rejected or tabled. The one area where the bill's opponents succeeded was an amendment that limited the extension to seven years instead of ten. Once this issue was settled, the Senate passed the bill by a vote of 77-12.

The House quickly made some expedient rules changes which allowed it to accept the Senate version of the bill without going to a conference committee. The House then voted 346 to 56 to accept the Senate version and sent the bill to President Gerald Ford.

President Ford signed the voting rights extension (PL 9473) on August 6, 1975.

## Impact

The passage of the Voting Rights Act of 1975 extended the rights secured by the initial 1965 act through August 6, 1982. This portion of the act, Title I, added little to the previous legislation. The most significant changes were the result of Titles II and III of the 1975 act. Title II of the new act expanded the basic protection of the old legislation to members of certain language minorities: persons of Spanish heritage, American Indians, Asian Americans, and Alaskan natives. Federal observers could be sent into areas if more than 5 percent of the voting-age population was identified by the Census Bureau as a single language minority, election material for the 1972 presidential election was printed in English only, or less than half of the voting-age citizens had voted in the 1974 presidential election.

As with the earlier acts, areas could be removed from Title II jurisdiction by appealing their case successfully to the federal district court in Washington, D.C. They had to prove that their election laws had posed no barrier to voting over the past ten years.

The provisions in Title III of this act required certain jurisdictions, those with at least 5 percent non-English-speaking populations, to conduct bilingual elections. The interesting twist to this provision was that areas could drop the bilingual elections if they could prove that the illiteracy rate among their language minority had dropped below the national illiteracy rate. States and their subdivisions could free themselves from these federal regulations by improving the educational opportunities for members of their language minorities.

The primary accomplishment of this legislation was that it gave access to the electoral process to a significant number of members of language minorities. It also expanded voting rights enforcement to numerous jurisdictions outside the South. The Justice Department identified 513 political jurisdictions in thirty states that provided bilingual elections in 1976. All of these bilingual elections were a direct result of the Voting Rights Act of 1975.

The number of electoral districts required to seek clearance for changes in their election laws increased by 279 after this enactment.

Many people believe the 1975 Voting Rights Act to be the most significant expansion of suffrage rights outside the South since the passage of the Nineteenth Amendment. It was clearly the most significant ever for members of language minorities.

*Donald V. Weatherman*

**Further Reading**

"Controversy over Extension of the Federal Voting Rights Act." *Congressional Digest* 54 (June/July, 1975): 163-192. One of the best summaries of the arguments both for and against the voting rights extension. It contains edited versions of speeches presented in Congress as well as position papers presented by interest groups on both sides of the issue.

Lawson, Steven. *Black Ballots: Voting Rights in the South, 1944-1969.* New York: Columbia University Press, 1976. A valuable resource on the development of the black suffrage movement. Especially useful for people interested in the obstacles that confronted reform-minded individuals during the two decades that preceded the major legislative breakthroughs of the mid-1960's. Contains a complete list of references and a thorough index.

Matthews, Donald, and James W. Prothro. *Negroes and the New Southern Politics.* New York: Harcourt, Brace & World, 1966. A good general resource with an especially helpful bibliography. Chapter 10 has an especially illustrative discussion of some of the frustrations that grew out of the Civil Rights movement after significant legislative successes.

Stanley, Harold W. *Voter Mobilization and the Politics of Race: The South and Universal Suffrage, 1952-1984.* New York: Praeger, 1987. A good general resource on the impact of suffrage reform in the South. Its main shortcoming is that it does not cover the impact of this legislation outside that region. Shows the complexity of this topic within the South.

U.S. Commission on Civil Rights. *The Voting Rights Act: Ten Years After.* Washington, D.C.: U.S. Government Printing Office,

1975. One of the best resources on this topic. Readily available at any library with government documents. A fine brief history of the impact of the voting rights acts of 1965 and 1970, combined with recommendations for extension in 1975. This report was the focal point of the debate in Congress in 1975.

**See also** Gerrymandering; Politics and government; Twenty-fourth Amendment; Voting Rights Act of 1965

# Washington v. Davis

**The Case:** U.S. Supreme Court ruling on employment discrimination
**Date:** June 7, 1976

*The Supreme Court ruled that plaintiffs must show a discriminatory intent, not merely a disparate impact, to prevail under the equal protection requirements of the Fifth and Fourteenth Amendments.*

In 1970 African American plaintiffs challenged the constitutionality of a hiring and promotion policy of the District of Columbia police department. They objected to the use of Test 21, which attempted to measure verbal skills and reading ability, because African American applicants failed the test at a rate four times that of white applicants. They were encouraged by *Griggs v. Duke Power Company* (1971), when the Supreme Court interpreted Title VII so that employers had to demonstrate the business necessity of any employment policies having a disparate impact on members of racial minorities. The plaintiffs in the *Washington* case had to rely on the Fifth Amendment because at the time they filed suit Title VII did not apply to governmental agencies.

By a 7-2 vote, the Court upheld the use of the examination. Justice Byron R. White's opinion for the majority emphasized that an employment practice is not unconstitutional "solely because it has a racially disproportionate impact." Citing numerous precedents, White concluded that the Court had employed the "purposeful discrimination" test when examining claims of a constitutional violation.

Addressing the questions of when and how one might infer discriminatory intent, White wrote that disproportionate impact was "not irrelevant," but that it had to be considered within the context of the totality of relevant facts. The Constitution did not require scientific proof that requirements were related to job performance, but employers had to show that there was a reasonable relationship between the two. White found that Test 21 was neutral on its face and rationally related to the legitimate governmental purpose of improving the communication skills of police officers.

The *Washington* decision did not disturb the Court's earlier rulings in regard to Title VII of the Civil Rights Act of 1964, prohibiting many employment requirements that had a disproportionate effect on members of minorities. It also actually had little influence in regard to the racial effects of employment requirements because Title VII was expanded to include governmental employees in 1972. The decision was important, however, for nonemployment cases such as *McCleskey v. Kemp* (1987), in which the Court disregarded statistical studies when examining the constitutionality of capital punishment.

*Thomas Tandy Lewis*

**See also** *Griggs v. Duke Power Company*; *McCleskey v. Kemp*

# Washington, D.C., riots

**The Event:** Racial unrest that erupted in the nation's capital
**Date:** November 22, 1962; August 1-3, 1967
**Place:** Washington, D.C.
*The events were short-lived but had a profound impact on the country as a whole during the Civil Rights movement.*

Although much of the attention during the Civil Rights movement in the 1960's focused on the South, racial tension also existed in the North, especially in urban areas such as Washington, D.C. The 1962 riot broke out at a football game between two long-time rival high schools, one white and the other African American, and spilled over into the streets. In 1967, other seemingly minor incidents set off a riot.

On November 22, 1962, two high school football rivals met for a fifth consecutive annual Washington, D.C., championship game. These schools were St. John's, a mostly white Catholic high school, and Eastern, a mainly African American public school. During the game, a player ejected for roughness returned to the field and began fighting. His own teammates subdued him, but his actions began a chain reaction. The fighting spread quickly from the field into the crowd, the parking lots, and surrounding streets. A total of thirty-four people were injured before the police brought it under control.

In 1967, a citywide riot occurred. Earlier that summer, many civil rights leaders, including Martin Luther King, Jr., had warned of possible disorders in several cities including Washington, D.C., but their warnings were largely ignored. Although some accused these leaders of giving people reasons to riot, Federal Bureau of Investigation director J. Edgar Hoover acknowledged there was no direct evidence supporting this belief. The violence broke out on August 1. The riot started with sporadic fires set mainly in African American neighborhoods. This was followed by rioters throwing rocks and bottles at police officers and firefighters responding to the blaze. In one area, two roaming gangs shot at police. The turmoil subsided on August 3.

After the 1967 racial unrest in Washington and other cities, President Lyndon B. Johnson appointed Illinois governor Otto Kerner head of the National Advisory Commission on Civil Disorders, known as the Kerner Commission, to study the reasons for the riots and growing racial tension in the nation. The commission eventually concluded that the United States was being divided into two societies, one white and the other black. The commission concluded that the urban areas of the nation faced a downward trend unless action was taken to relieve discriminatory conditions. This gave rise to a new attitude that brought about new government legislation.

*Robert Sullivan*

**Further Reading**

See Richard and Beatrice K. Hofstadter's *Great Issues in American History* (1982) for extensive materials on racial problems of the 1960's and the attempted solutions. The Kerner Commission Report published in 1968 also contains important information.

**See also** Chicago riots; Chisholm's election to Congress; New York riots; Newark riot; Watts riot

# Watts riot

**The Event:** Racially motivated civil disturbances that reached such a level of violence that National Guard troops were employed to regain control
**Date:** August, 1965
**Place:** Los Angeles, California

*The outbreak of racial violence on August 11, 1965, shattered the summer calm of Los Angeles, California, and eroded the elation felt by many people when President Lyndon B. Johnson had signed the 1965 Voting Rights Act into law only five days earlier. Official investigations confirmed that the causes of the upheaval were deeply rooted in the conditions of ghetto life in the sprawling metropolis. In less immediate terms, however, the upsurge of anarchistic energy stemmed from the existence of intolerable tensions in relations between whites and blacks within U.S. society.*

The Watts area of Los Angeles in 1965 provided a perfect setting for racial conflict. The neighborhood had long been the center of African American life in the city. As a result, Watts offered its inhabitants full exposure to the hazards of ghetto existence. More than 30 percent of the workforce was unemployed. Approximately 14 percent of the population was functionally illiterate. The black residents of Watts faced serious barriers in their pursuit of better housing, more remunerative jobs, and improved education. Separated from white society, Watts was a storehouse of combustible material on the southeast side of Los Angeles.

## Beginnings

A minor clash between police and African American residents caused the explosion that ripped through Watts. Along the edge of the ghetto, on the night of August 11, a California Highway Patrol officer arrested two young African Americans for reckless driving. While the officer administered a sobriety test, a hostile crowd gathered. The confrontation led to more arrests. Finally, the police departed amid a hail of rocks thrown by irate African Americans. Rumors of police brutality spread through Watts. In the hours before midnight, a full-scale riot developed. Automobiles traveling through the ghetto were pelted with rocks and bottles. Police moved back into the area at 11:00 P.M., but flurries of violence continued throughout the night.

After a day filled with tension, the rioters returned to the streets on the night of August 12. Commercial buildings were set ablaze, and firemen who responded to the alarms were greeted with rocks and gunfire. California state officials received reports that estimated the number of rioters at eight thousand. The police were unable to prevent widespread burning and looting.

The upheaval reached its climax on the night of August 13. Crowds of angry African Americans surged through Watts. Arsonists began the systematic destruction of whole city blocks in the ghetto. Police and firemen faced added peril from snipers who took up positions in the ruins. At its height, the riot encompassed an area of more than fifty blocks.

## Reaction

In the early hours of August 14, law enforcement officers began to regain control of the streets. At the request of city officials, National Guard troops joined the Los Angeles Police Department in battling the rioters. Ultimately, nearly fourteen thousand members of the National Guard entered the fray. Burning and looting continued sporadically, but the presence of fully armed soldiers in large numbers gradually restored quiet to the riot-torn area. A dusk-to-dawn curfew went into effect on Saturday night, August 14. Three days later the curfew was lifted, and most of the National Guard troops left the city. Amid the rubble, the people of Watts returned to their everyday concerns. The six days of rioting had wreaked widespread destruction on the African American neighborhood. Thirty-four deaths were reported, and police made more than three thousand arrests. Property damage reached the forty-million-dollar mark, as 288 businesses and private buildings and 14 public buildings were damaged and/or looted, and 1 public and 207 private buildings were destroyed.

Yet the most significant harm caused by the riot was beyond specific assessment. In the realm of race relations, the outbreak of violence exacerbated tensions between black and white people throughout the United States. Watts became the first chapter in a history of race riots that included upheavals in Detroit, Michigan, and Newark, New Jersey, in 1967, and Washington, D.C., in 1968. Faced with repeated outbreaks of violence, the Civil Rights movement, with its emphasis on civil disobedience and interracial cooperation, suffered a significant setback in the short run. Beginning with the explosion at Watts, U.S. race relations entered a new, more ominous phase.

The riot did not, however, mean the end of nonviolent direct action or the total reversal of the multiracial cooperation that had brought important legal victories for desegregation in the United States. The history of civil rights reform after 1965 was marked by a growing realization that the socioeconomic conditions in which African Americans, Mexican Americans, and members of other minorities lived could not be ignored in the quest for social justice and personal fulfillment for all U.S. citizens. The last major effort by civil rights leader Dr. Martin Luther King, Jr.—who visited Watts at the time of the rioting and asked the insurgents to change their motto from "Burn, baby, burn" to "Build, baby, build"—was a Poor People's Campaign that was implemented two months after his assassination on April 4, 1968.

*John G. Clark*
*Updated by Thomas R. Peake*

**Further Reading**

The Governor's Commission on the Los Angeles Riots' *Violence in the City: An End or a Beginning?* (Los Angeles: Author, 1965) focuses on the details and location of damage, with useful maps. Thomas R. Peake's *Keeping the Dream Alive: A History of the*

*Southern Christian Leadership Conference from King to the Nineteen-Eighties* (New York: Peter Lang, 1987) includes extensive material on the urban riots and post-1965 efforts to deal with social problems in big-city ghettos. David O. Sears and John B. McConahay's *The Politics of Violence: The New Urban Blacks and the Watts Riot* (Boston: Houghton Mifflin, 1973) reviews the history of the crisis, the views and actions of urban blacks, and official reactions. The Watts Writers' Workshop's *From the Ashes: Voices of Watts*, edited and with an introduction by Budd Schulberg (New York: New American Library, 1967), contains writings by residents of Watts during the time of the 1965 riots and their aftermath, showing their frustrations as well as their hopes for better answers to social, personal, and economic problems.

**See also** Chicago riots; Congress of Racial Equality; "I Have a Dream" speech; Los Angeles riots; Miami riots; National Advisory Commission on Civil Disorders; New York riots; Newark riot; Race riots of 1943; Race riots of 1967; Race riots of the twentieth century; Washington, D.C., riots

# West Indians

**Definition:** Americans of West Indian, or Caribbean, origins or ancestry

*The success of black West Indian Americans in the United States has drawn the attention of sociologists and other scholars and created some conflict with other African Americans.*

Black West Indian immigrants from the former British West Indian Islands, Belize and Guyana, and their U.S.-born descendants, a small group among the African American population, have achieved considerable economic, educational, and political success in the United States relative to other African Americans. Notable conservatives such as economist Thomas Sowell of Stanford's Hoover Institution and author Dinesh D'Souza contend that this group's relative success in part demonstrates the error in attributing the economic and social plight of some African Americans exclusively to racism. The group's exceptionalism has also been noted by sociologists such as Stephen Steinberg in *The Ethnic Myth: Race, Ethnicity, and Class in America* (1981) and Reynolds Farley and Walter Allen in *The Color Line and the Quality of Life in America* (1989).

The portrayal of exceptionalism is only part of this group's profile. Structural shifts in the U.S. economy mean that segments of this community will face severe sociopsychological adjustments to migration, coupled with constricted assimilation into American society. Pressures against full assimilation are greater for lower-class West Indians. Typically, middle- and upper-class professionals alternate between a more inclusive West Indian American or particularistic African American identity, and the lower/working class chooses a more ethnically focused, West Indian identity.

Most of the West Indian immigrants arrived in the United States in the late nineteenth and early twentieth centuries. In 1924, restrictive immigration legislation effectively halted immigration from the islands. Most of the immigrants settled in the Northeast, creating urban ethnic communities in Miami, Boston, Newark (New Jersey), Hartford (Connecticut), and New York City; they settled in Brooklyn and formed ethnic enclaves in East Flatbush, Flatbush, Crown Heights, Canarsie, and Midwood districts.

## West Indian Exceptionalism

Generally, West Indian immigrants have been perceived as models of achievement for their frugality, emphasis on education, and ownership of homes and small businesses. Economist Sowell argued that the group's successes, including those of famous members such as General Colin Powell, derived from a distinctive cultural capital source and an aggressive migrant ideology, legacies of their native lands. Home ownership and economic entrepreneurship were financed partly by using a cultural source of capital, an association called *susu* (known in West Africa as *esusu*), that first reached the West Indian societies during slavery. A *susu* facilitates savings, small-scale capital formation, and micro lending. These traditional associations have been incorporated into mainstream financial organizations such as credit un-

*Actor Sidney Poitier, at left in this scene from the 1967 film* In the Heat of the Night, *was born in Florida; however, his parents were West Indian, and he was raised in the Bahamas.* (Museum of Modern Art, Film Stills Archive)

ions and mortgage and commercial banks as they adapt to serve the needs of West Indian Americans.

Demographer Albert Murphy, in a report for Medgar Evers College's Caribbean Research Center in New York, found that in 1990, 29.1 percent of West Indian Americans had a bachelor's degree or higher degree, compared with the U.S. average of 20.3 percent. In addition, their median household income in 1989 was $28,000, compared with $19,750 for African Americans overall and $31,435 for whites.

### Political and Social Incorporation

Early immigrants such as Pan-Africanists Edward Blyden and Marcus Garvey and poet activist Claude McKay were among the first West Indian Americans to become well-known and well-respected figures. Other famous West Indian Americans are Congresswoman Shirley Chisholm; Franklin Thomas, former head of the Ford Foundation; federal judge Constance Baker Motley; Nobel laureate Derek Walcott; and actor Sidney Poitier. Activist Stokely Carmichael, Deputy U.S. Attorney General Eric Holder, and Earl Graves, businessman and publisher of *Black Enterprise*, have made impressive efforts on behalf of African Americans.

From the 1930's to the 1960's, West Indian American politicians were elected with the help of the African American vote; many of the West Indians, believing their stay in the United States to be temporary, did not become citizens and were thus ineligible to vote. In the 1970's, this trend changed, and two congressional districts in New York with heavy concentrations of West Indians became represented by African Americans. However, West Indians Americans, becoming increasingly dissatisfied with African American representation, have been fielding their own candidates in state and local elections in New York, Connecticut, and New Jersey. These efforts have been aided by the fact that since 1993, when legislation less favorable to the immigrant population was passed, West Indian Americans have been acquiring U.S. citizenship in greater numbers.

## Differential Assimilation

At the beginning of the twentieth century, West Indian Americans and African Americans held negative stereotypes of each other and rarely interacted socially. In the 1930's, 1940's, and 1950's, the children of some West Indian immigrants downplayed their ethnicity and attempted to integrate into the African American community, but both groups' images of each other changed slowly. Powell, in his autobiography, *My American Journey* (1995), recalls his African American father-in-law's reaction when he proposed marriage to his daughter Alma: "All my life I've tried to stay away from those damn West Indians and now my daughter's going to marry one!"

The late 1960's, with its emphasis on racial solidarity and group identity, eroded much of the conflict between African Americans and West Indian Americans and supplanted it with black nationalist sentiments and identity. In the late twentieth century, many West Indian Americans were caught in an identity crisis, unsure of whether they should be West Indians with a strong ethnic orientation, African Americans with a focus on their racial identity, or "West Indian Americans" with a more hybrid identity. Class pressures play influential roles in this identity dilemma. Lower- and working-class West Indian Americans have strong affiliations with their ethnicity and its cultural symbols, using the ethnic community as a "structural shield" in their coping repertoire. However, a growing segment of West Indian American professionals regard themselves as West Indian Americans because this identity unites the more desirable choices by eliminating obstacles to their ultimate assimilation as Americans. In addition, this community is not monolithic, and class divisions segment the group as well as influence its responses to racism and other societal challenges.

*Aubrey W. Bonnett*

**Further Reading**

*Black Identities: West Indian Immigrant Dreams and American Realities* (Cambridge, Mass.: Harvard University Press, 1999), by Mary C. Waters, and *Crosscurrents: West Indian Immigrants and Race* (New York: Oxford University Press, 1999), by Milton Vickerman, both examine the West Indian immigrant experience in the United States. Ira De Augustine Reid's *The Negro Immigrant: His Background, Characteristics, and Social Adjustment, 1899-1937* (New York: Columbia University Press, 1939) is a classic study of the early pioneers. Other excellent sources are Aubrey W. Bonnett's *Institutional Adaptation of West Indian Immigrants to America* (Washington, D.C.: University Press of America, 1982), Philip Kasinitz's *Caribbean New York: Black Immigrants and the Politics of Race* (Ithaca, N.Y.: Cornell University Press, 1992), Ransford W. Palmer's *Pilgrims from the Sun: West Indian Migration to America* (New York: Twayne Publishers, 1995), Irma Watkins-Owens's *Blood Relations: Caribbean Immigrants and the Harlem Community, 1900-1930* (Bloomington: Indiana University Press, 1996), Robert Carr's *Black Nationalism in the New World: Reading the African-American and West Indian Experience* (Durham, N.C.: Duke University Press, 2002), and Calvin Holder's "The Rise of the West Indian Politicians in New York City," in *Afro-Americans in New York Life and History* (4, 1980).

**See also** Cubans and African Americans; Haitians; Jamaicans; Pan-Africanism

# White Citizens' Councils

**Identification:** Prosegregation bodies that arose in the American South following the U.S. Supreme Court's 1954 decree that public schools must be racially integrated

**Date:** First councils formed during the summer of 1954

*The highly popular White Citizens' Councils led the fight to prevent integration throughout the South during the mid-1950's.*

On May 17, 1954, the U.S. Supreme Court ruled in *Brown v. Board of Education* that racial segregation of public schools was unconstitutional. This decision held special significance in the South, where African American students traditionally attended separate, poorly funded schools. Many southern communities were outraged at this threat to what they regarded as white privilege. In response, white citizens quickly organized to impede attempts at integration. The White Citizens' Councils became a prominent force in this resistance movement.

The inspiration for organized white resistance came from a strident speech delivered by Tom Brady, a Mississippi circuit court judge, shortly after the Supreme Court's decision. Later expanded into a ninety-page tract titled *Black Monday*, Brady's speech was distributed widely and served as a rallying cry for concerned white citizens. Robert B. Patterson, a plantation manager, responded by organizing influential citizens of Indianola, Mississippi, into the first chapter of the White Citizens' Council. Other chapters quickly sprung up, predominantly in communities that possessed small white populations and where civil rights organizations were active.

The councils' memberships largely consisted of middle-class whites who possessed influence in their communities, such as business owners, lawyers, judges, bankers, politicians, and doctors. The councils were viewed as the "respectable" alternative to violent segregationist groups such as the Ku Klux Klan. Determined to present their members as responsible, upstanding citizens, they publicly encouraged legal acts of resistance. Often they used propaganda to educate the public. The propaganda typically attempted to unify white communities into fighting integration by linking it to communism, depicting African Americans as inferior, and disparaging leading civil rights organizations. Nevertheless, some councils used more disturbing and underhanded means of achieving their ends. For example, in his book *The Fiery Cross* (1987), Wyn Wade reported that a council in Mississippi retaliated against a group of African Americans who supported integration by prominently publishing their names and addresses in a local newspaper. As a result, some of the African Americans lost their jobs; others were intimidated into moving from the town.

By 1956, membership in the councils reached a peak of between 250,000 and 300,000 southerners. At this time, a sufficient number of council chapters had been established to prompt the creation of a national organization called the Citizens' Councils of America.

Despite the grassroots attempts of middle-class southerners to defend their racist traditions, their efforts ultimately failed. By the early 1960's, the influence of the White Citizens' Councils had dwindled in the face of the gains made by the Civil Rights movement and by the rising popularity of the Ku Klux Klan. Nonetheless, the councils did demonstrate that appeals to racial division could resonate powerfully in the political arena. Thus, they served as forerunners to later neo-Confederate organizations such as the Council of Conservative Citizens.

*Beth A. Messner*

**Further Reading**

Diamond, Sara. "Organized Resistance to Preserve Segregation." In *Roads to Dominion: Right-Wing Movements and Political Power in the United States*. New York: Guilford Press, 1995. Diamond chronicles the development and influence of right-wing thought in the United States and helps readers understand the place of the White Citizens' Councils within this larger movement.

McMillen, Neil R. *The Citizens' Council: Organized Resistance to the Second Reconstruction, 1954-1964*. Urbana: University of Illinois Press, 1971. Perhaps the most definitive treatise on the White

Citizens' Councils, this text discusses the organization's inception, evolution, and eventual decline.

Wade, Wyn. *The Fiery Cross: The Ku Klux Klan in America*. New York: Simon & Schuster, 1987. Although primarily a discussion of the Ku Klux Klan, there is some discussion about the role of the White Citizens' Councils in the prosegregation movement.

**See also** *Brown v. Board of Education*; Civil Rights movement; Ku Klux Klan; Little Rock school desegregation crisis; Montgomery bus boycott; School desegregation; Southern Manifesto

# White primaries

**Definition:** Elections designed to exclude African Americans from voting

*In cases on which it ruled from 1927 to 1953, the U.S. Supreme Court declared white primaries to be unconstitutional state actions that are prohibited by the equal protection clause of the Fourteenth Amendment.*

In *Newberry v. United States* (1921), the Supreme Court declared that primaries were not constitutionally protected as elections and could not be controlled by Congress. Although African Americans could not be prevented from voting in federal elections, southern legislatures used *Newberry* to prohibit African Americans from voting in primaries. In the southern states, which were dominated by the Democratic Party, the only significant competition occurred at the primary level, within the party. Thus, inability to participate in a primary in these states meant effective disfranchisement.

The first challenge to the white primary, *Nixon v. Herndon* (1927), resulted in a unanimous decision for the African American plaintiff. Justice Oliver Wendell Holmes held that the Texas white primary law violated the equal protection clause of the Fourteenth Amendment. In *Nixon v. Condon* (1932), the Court invalidated a Texas Democratic Party executive committee order excluding African Americans from voting in primaries. However, in *Grovey v. Townsend* (1935), a unanimous Court ruled that white primaries were the elections of a private organization and not forbidden as state action. *United States v. Classic* (1941), dealing with corrupt voting in Louisiana, held that primaries selecting nominees for federal office were protected.

Applying *Classic*, the Court reversed *Grovey* in *Smith v. Allwright* (1944). *Terry v. Adams* (1953) invalidated the preprimary of the Jaybird Democratic Association as a denial of equal protection and removed the final institutional obstacle to African American voting.

*Gilbert Morris Cuthbertson*

**See also** Fifteenth Amendment; Gerrymandering; Grandfather clauses; *Grovey v. Townsend*; *Nixon v. Condon*; *Nixon v. Herndon*; Politics and government; Poll taxes; *Smith v. Allwright*; *Terry v. Adams*; *United States v. Classic*; Voting Rights Act of 1965

# Wilder's election to Virginia governorship

**The Event:** Election of the first African American state governor since Reconstruction
**Date:** November 7, 1989
**Place:** Virginia

*L. Douglas Wilder became the first elected African American governor nearly 125 years after the end of the Civil War; however, his tenure as governor brought little substantive change in Virginia, and his legacy is difficult to assess.*

The 1989 contest for the governor's mansion in Virginia was destined to receive an unusual amount of attention both within the state and around the country. The election offered the possibility of producing the first elected black governor in the former capital of the Confederacy. In addition, there were few other contests of national importance in 1989 to attract the interest of the news media. Each of the candidates spent more than $6 million in the general election campaign. History was made when, on November 7, 1989, Democrat L. Douglas Wilder was elected governor of Virginia.

## Nomination

Wilder, the incumbent lieutenant governor, received the Democratic nomination without challenge. He had proven his ability to win a statewide election when he became lieutenant governor in 1985, demonstrating that he could attract white voters in a state whose electorate was 80 percent white. Wilder received the full support of the state Democratic Party and of outgoing governor Gerald L. Baliles and the less-than-enthusiastic endorsement of U.S. senator Charles S. Robb. There was friction between Wilder and Robb, but Robb did support Wilder's candidacy.

Marshall Coleman, the Republican gubernatorial candidate, had scored a come-from-behind victory in a hotly contested and often acrimonious three-man race for his party's nomination. For the first time, state Republicans employed a primary election to choose their candidate, and the Coleman campaign was noted for its strong negative content. Coleman had lost the 1981 gubernatorial election and was denied the Republican nomination for lieutenant governor in 1985, but he was resurrected politically in 1989.

By the 1980's, America had witnessed an increasing number of successful African American candidates at the local and state legislative levels. Many of America's largest cities had elected black mayors. The number of African Americans in statewide office and at the national level, however, remained low. At the time of Wilder's election, African Americans held fewer than 2 percent of the nation's elective offices. Most of those were in jurisdictions with a majority of black residents.

Wilder's candidacy was seen, then, as extremely important for civil rights in America. Wilder himself was viewed as a model for other black candidates. His campaign was not based on race. His campaign strategy was to portray himself as a moderate alternative to the extremely conservative Coleman.

Although Wilder's politics were clearly more moderate than the positions favored by former presidential candidate Jesse Jackson, Wilder may have benefited from Jackson's experience. Black candidates, who have often been dismissed by voters on the basis of their race, may have been taken more seriously after Jackson's campaigns in 1984 and, particularly, 1988. Opponents and the media, however, still struggled with the issues surrounding black candidacies. Heavy criticism of a black candidate could lead to charges of racism, while ignoring or emphasizing the race of a black candidate could be viewed as patronizing.

**The Election Campaign**

In 1989, African Americans faced major electoral hurdles, not the least of which was the misleading nature of public opinion polls in black-white contests. Usually reliable, polls in elections in which a black candidate faced a white candidate tended to overestimate the strength of the black candidates by several percentage points. This phenomenon was evident in the Wilder election as well as in the New York City mayoral campaign of David Dinkins and the unsuccessful California gubernatorial campaign of Los Angeles mayor Tom Bradley. Experts speculated that the effect might be caused by racism, low turnout among black voters, fear of those polled of appearing racist, or their attempt to offer what might be perceived as the "correct answer."

Although Wilder faced many of these problems, his candidacy also posed problems for his opponent. The race factor was virtually absent from the campaigns of both candidates. Coleman's campaign was relatively negative but was careful not even to allude to the question of race. The only exception to this came late in the campaign, when Coleman complained publicly that he was the victim of a media double standard in which Wilder was not seriously questioned regarding several ethics issues raised by Coleman. Coleman, conversely, was frequently questioned about his position on abortion. The implication was that Wilder was getting preferential treatment from the press because he was black.

For his part, Wilder was equally careful not to raise the race issue. He did discuss his background, but he chose to emphasize how far Virginia had come in matters of race. His attempt to run as a moderate also prevented him from running as a "black" candidate. In his television advertisements, Wilder was usually surrounded by whites. His issue emphasis was almost solely on abortion, on which issue he endorsed a woman's right to choose. His theme was summed up by his campaign motto, "I trust the women of Virginia."

One of Wilder's most popular campaign advertisements used conservative rhetoric to take a prochoice position. In the advertisement, a narrator claimed that "Doug Wilder believes the government shouldn't interfere in your right to choose. He wants to keep politicians out of your personal life. Don't let Marshall Coleman take us back." This strategy effectively made Wilder look at least moderate, if not conservative, and it may well have been a subtle reference to the overt racism of Virginia's past.

Wilder avoided some more controversial issues. There was no discussion of funding abortions for the poor. Wilder also chose not to associate himself with Jesse Jackson or the National Organization for Women's Molly Yard, emphasizing that he had not requested any help from outside the state.

### Wilder's Background

Wilder's qualifications and experience were never questioned. The grandson of slaves, Wilder grew up in a middle-class family in segregated Richmond. He excelled in the segregated schools, and he was graduated from Virginia Union College in Richmond. After winning a Bronze Star for his actions during the Korean War, he attended law school at Howard University. In 1959, Wilder was the only African American to pass the Virginia bar exam, and he soon opened his own law practice.

Wilder rose rapidly within his profession, and in 1969 he entered politics, winning a seat in the Virginia senate. Two white candidates split the white vote, allowing Wilder to win by a narrow margin. He worked diligently and established a reputation as a powerful individual in Virginia politics. Initially a liberal, Wilder moderated his positions and issues over time. By 1985, he was ready for a run for lieutenant governor, and some clever political maneuvering placed him on the Democratic ticket with Gerald Baliles. Successful grassroots campaigning enabled him to win that election and position himself for the gubernatorial race in 1989.

With his election as lieutenant governor, Wilder became only the second African American elected to a major statewide office since Reconstruction. (Former Republican senator Edward Brooke of Massachusetts was the first. P. B. S Pinchback was acting governor of Louisiana for forty-three days in 1873 but was never elected to that position.)

**Election**

On November 7, 1989, Wilder eked out a narrow victory over Marshall Coleman, capturing 50.1 percent of the votes cast. Nearly 1.8 million Virginians voted in the contest, which set records both for the total number of voters and for the 66.5 percent of registered voters who cast a ballot. While his margin of victory was considerably narrower than those of the Democratic nominees for lieutenant governor and attorney general, Wilder had once again fooled the political pundits and accomplished what seemed to be impossible. Many experts attributed his victory to heavy turnout among black voters and his popularity among women, but it should be remembered that Wilder took more than 40 percent of the votes cast by whites and more than 40 percent of the votes cast by men.

The impact of Wilder's election was felt in three specific areas: the national stature and reputation of Wilder himself, the nation's and the state's view of Virginia, and the possible long-term effects on black candidates nationwide. Wilder's election propelled him into the national spotlight. He came to be seen by many as a national spokesperson for African Americans and as a viable candidate for the 1992 Democratic presidential nomination. Wilder welcomed this notoriety and spent much time preparing and delivering speeches around the country.

Perceptions of Virginia also changed virtually overnight. The state had changed dramatically in the previous two decades, but the changes had gone largely unnoticed. An urbanized corridor running from northern Virginia through Richmond into Tidewater produced more than 60 percent of the voters. Many of these voters had migrated to Virginia, many from the North, and they voted disproportionately for Wilder. The rural areas of Virginia, which had dominated the state's politics, now accounted for less than one-third of the state's votes. These major demographic changes made Virginia politically more like a Middle Atlantic state than a southern state. Virginia politics would still be considered conservative nationally, but the state had moderated considerably in twenty years.

The lessons of the election for other black candidates were mixed. Wilder's victory showed that an African American willing to run as a mainstream, moderate, nonthreatening candidate could win a statewide election. This contrasted sharply with the liberal approach taken by Jesse Jackson. Jackson's philosophy was successful within the Democratic Party, where liberals wielded considerable power, but Wilder's strategy seemed much more likely to be successful in general elections.

Other lessons were drawn from the election. The journey for a minority candidate was still a long and difficult one. Wilder had many advantages in the campaign. He was the heir apparent to two popular Democratic administrations, he won the party's nomination unopposed, and he was supported by a united party. His campaign was well financed. He ran a strategic campaign, played the issues correctly, and was opposed by a relatively weak opponent. Despite all these advantages, he won by an extremely narrow margin.

## Impact

Combined with the election of David Dinkins as the first black mayor of New York City, Wilder's win was seen by some as the vanguard of more political successes by African Americans. Andrew Young's losing campaign for the governorship of Georgia the following year caused much of that optimism to disappear.

The effects of the Wilder victory on Virginia politics and public policy are difficult to assess. There were still relatively few black politicians in the state. Policy, too, remained largely unchanged. Governor Wilder was prevented from proposing any governmental initiatives by a continuing budget crisis that allowed him to show his fiscal conservative stripes through a steadfast refusal to raise taxes and an insistence on serious budget cuts. The consequence of these actions was a decline in Wilder's popularity within the state and a rise in his stock nationally. Wilder's legacy seemed likely to be the subject of debate for years to come.

*Harry L. Wilson*

**Further Reading**

Bond, Julian. *Black Candidates: Southern Campaign Experiences*. Atlanta: Southern Regional Council, 1968. A recounting of the experiences of several candidates for state and local office in the South in the 1960's. Provides an interesting context for the Wilder election and exemplifies the changes in the South and the nation with regard to race relations.

Broh, C. Anthony. *A Horse of a Different Color: Television's Treatment of Jesse Jackson's 1984 Presidential Campaign*. Washington, D.C.: Joint Center for Political Studies, 1987. A thorough and insightful discussion of how the media covered the first serious black presidential candidate. Points out clearly the disadvantages and advantages of being a black candidate.

Edds, Margaret. *Claiming the Dream*. Chapel Hill, N.C.: Algonquin Books, 1990. A chronological journalistic recounting and analysis of the 1989 gubernatorial campaign focusing primarily on Wilder.

Lichter, S. Robert, et al. *The Video Campaign: Network Coverage of the 1988 Primaries*. Washington, D.C.: American Enterprise Institute, 1988. A brief, useful analysis of how television news covered the presidential candidates in 1988. Makes good use of statistics to present a clear and easily understood argument regarding who was treated well by the media and why.

Sabato, Larry J. "Virginia's National Election for Governor." In *Virginia Government and Politics*, edited by Thomas R. Morris and Weldon Cooper. Charlottesville: University Press of Virginia, 1990. An excellent discussion of the national and state implications of the 1989 gubernatorial election by the leading expert on Virginia state politics. Sabato provides both statistical and anecdotal analyses of the campaign and election.

Shapiro, Walter. "Breakthrough in Virginia." *Time* 134 (November 20, 1989): 54-57. Emphasizes the moderate politics and personal nature of Wilder's campaign and victory. Wilder is seen as a politician, not as a black politician.

Wilson, Harry L. "Media Treatment of Black Candidates: The 1989 Virginia Gubernatorial Campaign." *Virginia Social Science Journal* 26 (Winter, 1991): 82-90. An analysis of newspaper and television coverage in southwestern Virginia of the election. Concludes that although most news stories were neutral, those that were not were likely to be positive if about Wilder and negative if about Coleman.

Yancey, Dwayne. *When Hell Froze Over.* Dallas: Taylor, 1988. Journalist Yancey traces Wilder's rise to power from his humble beginnings in Richmond to his election to lieutenant governor in 1985. Reveals the political Wilder who seeks and uses power.

**See also** Chisholm's election to Congress; Jackson's run for the presidency; Politics and government; Voting Rights Act of 1965

# Williams v. Mississippi

**The Case:** U.S. Supreme Court ruling on jury composition
**Date:** April 25, 1898

*In* Williams v. Mississippi, *the Supreme Court ignored a ruling it had made a dozen years earlier and upheld the murder conviction of an African American in a trial in which no African Americans served on the jury.*

Williams, an African American from Mississippi, had been convicted of murder by an all-white jury. Williams argued, in line with *Yick Wo v. Hopkins* (1886), that his indictment and conviction by all-white grand and petit juries violated the Fourteenth Amendment's equal protection clause. At the time in Mississippi, African Americans were effectively excluded from jury service because only qualified voters could serve, and poll taxes and literacy tests rendered most African Americans unable to vote. The Court distinguished *Yick Wo* and its principle that a racially fair law could be voided if it was administered in a discriminatory manner from the facts of this case, saying that Williams did not prove that the actual practice of Mississippi's suffrage laws was unfair. As a result of this ruling, other southern states quickly followed Mississippi and passed laws designed to prevent African Americans from voting. White primaries, poll taxes, and literacy tests became common in the South until white primaries were banned in the 1940's and discriminatory voting practices were stopped by the 1964 and 1965 Voting Rights Acts.

*Richard L. Wilson*

**See also** *Batson v. Kentucky*; Council of Federated Organizations; *Edmonson v. Leesville Concrete Company*; Fourteenth Amendment; *Powers v. Ohio*; *Strauder v. West Virginia*; Voting Rights Act of 1965

# *Wisconsin v. Mitchell*

**The Case:** U.S. Supreme Court ruling on freedom of speech
**Date:** June 11, 1993

*The Supreme Court upheld the constitutionality of a state law that increased the sentence for a crime in which the defendant intentionally selected the victim on the basis of race, national origin, religion, sexual orientation, or similar characteristics.*

Following a showing of the 1988 film *Mississippi Burning*, several African American men and boys congregated at an apartment complex to talk about the film. After a discussion of a scene in the film in which a young African American boy is beaten by a white man, the accused, Todd Mitchell, asked those who joined him outside if they were ready to go after a white man.

Walking on the opposite side of the street and saying nothing, fourteen-year-old Gregory Riddick approached the complex. Mitchell selected three individuals from the group to go after Riddick. The victim was beaten, and his tennis shoes were stolen.

In a Kenosha, Wisconsin, trial court, Mitchell was convicted as a party to the crime of aggravated battery. By Wisconsin law, this crime carried a maximum prison sentence of two years. Mitchell's sentence was extended to four years, however, under a state statute commonly known as the "hate crimes" statute. This statute provided for sentence extensions if it could be determined that the victim was selected because of his or her race, religion, color, disability, sexual orientation, national origin, or ancestry.

Mitchell appealed his conviction and the extended sentence. His conviction was upheld by the court of appeals, but the Supreme Court of Wisconsin reversed the decision of the appellate court. Wisconsin's Supreme Court held that the "hate crimes" statute violated the defendant's First Amendment protection for freedom of speech because it was unconstitutionally overbroad and punished only what the state legislature found to be offensive. Moreover, the state supreme court believed that this statute would have a "chilling effect" on a citizen's freedom of speech; that is, a citizen would fear reprisal for actions that might follow the utterance of prejudiced or biased speech.

The U.S. Supreme Court reversed the state court's decision. Chief Justice William H. Rehnquist wrote the opinion in this unanimous decision. The Court held that Mitchell's First Amendment rights to free speech had not been violated.

The Court pointed out that the statute was not aimed at speech but at conduct, which is not protected by the First Amendment. The Court also addressed the concern about the "chilling effect" of the statute, finding that such would not be the case and that the state supreme court's hypothesis was far too speculative to be entertained. This decision indicates that the U.S. Supreme Court appears ready to uphold legislation designed to enhance punishment for criminal acts based on bigotry and bias without making bigoted or biased speech itself a crime.

*Donna Addkison Simmons*

**See also** *R.A.V. v. City of St. Paul*

# World War II

**The Event:** Worldwide conflict that the United States entered after Japan's attack on Pearl Harbor

**Date:** United States entered the war on December 8, 1941; Japan's surrender ended the war on August 14, 1945

*Despite segregation and widespread discrimination, African Americans made important contributions to the American war effort. By linking racism at home with fascism abroad, civil rights activists promoted a "Double V" strategy—a victory against oppression at home as well as abroad.*

The Selective Service Act of 1940, which initiated a military draft, forbade racial discrimination in the recruitment and training of men, but it continued the traditional policy of segregation. When black leaders protested, President Franklin D. Roosevelt announced a policy of seeking to use African Americans in numbers approximately equal to their proportion of the national population, which was about 10 percent. Soon thereafter, Roosevelt promoted Colonel Benjamin O. Davis, Sr., to brigadier general, making him the first African American to hold this rank. He also appointed Judge William Hastie as a civilian aid to the secretary of war.

## The Home Front

As U.S. involvement in the war approached and defense industries grew, African Americans grew dismayed by their lack of employment opportunities in businesses contracting with the government. Hoping to promote change, A. Philip Randolph and other black leaders organized the March on Washington movement in early 1941, hoping to involve 150,000 protesters. Roosevelt persuaded the organizers to call off the demonstration in exchange for his issuing Executive Order 8802, which formally prohibited discrimination in defense industries because of "race, creed, color, or national origin." To implement its provisions, the order created the Fair Employment Practices Committee (FEPC), the first federal agency devoted to combating racial discrimination.

Although the FEPC lacked enforcement powers, the booming defense industries soon had such a need for labor that African Americans increasingly secured factory jobs. They constituted only 3 percent of American defense workers in 1942, but that proportion increased to 8 percent by 1945. In the automobile industry, representation of African Americans grew to about 12 percent of the United Auto Workers in Detroit. With the growth of job opportunities in the North and California, more than a half-million African Americans migrated out of the South.

Many instances of ugly racial violence occurred during the war years. Authorities reported fourteen instances of racially inspired lynchings, with two black soldiers among the victims. In 1943 alone, researchers at Fisk University recorded 242 instances of racial fighting in forty-seven cities. The most destructive conflict took place in Detroit, where a minor skirmish among teenagers escalated into bitter fighting in which at least twenty-five African Americans and nine white Americans were killed. A few weeks later, in Harlem, a disagreement between a black soldier and a white police officer set off a race riot that resulted

*Marine recruits negotiating an obstacle course during their training.* (National Archives)

in six deaths, 550 arrests, and five million dollars in property damage.

## The War Front

During the course of the nearly four years that the United States fought in the war, almost one million African Americans served in the armed services. About half of them served overseas, in the European and Pacific theaters of the war. Nevertheless, due mostly to disparities in education and health, African Americans represented less than 6 percent of the military in 1942. Denied equal opportunities for combat service, they were assigned disproportional numbers of mundane tasks in areas such as supply and support. When Walter White, the secretary of the National Association for the Advancement of Colored People, investigated the morale of black soldiers abroad, he found that one of their most common complaints was that the backbreaking work of unloading supplies was often as dangerous to soldiers as fighting on the front lines.

Despite these limitations, significant numbers of African Americans engaged in combat, often with great distinction. The most famous of them were the seven hundred pilots trained at the Tuskegee Air Force Base. These Tuskegee Airmen, as they were known, flew 15,533 sorties and destroyed 261 enemy planes. Sixty-six of the pilots were killed in action. In 1945, the 332d Fighter Group, commanded by Benjamin O. Davis, Jr., received a Presidential Unit Citation, and eighty of its pilots were awarded the Distinguished Flying Cross. This impressive record proved that African Americans, when given the chance, could become skilled pilots.

In 1942, the Army reactivated two traditionally all-African American infantry divisions: the Ninety-second (buffalo soldiers) and the Ninety-third (Blue Helmets). Soldiers of the Ninety-second Division, who were deployed in Italy, received more than 12,000 decorations. The Ninety-third Division fought in many bloody battles in the Solomon Islands, Treasury Island, and the Philippines in the South Pacific. Another unit, the highly decorated Back Panthers of the 761st Tank Battalion, engaged in some of the fiercest fighting at the Battle of the

*Enlisted men on their way to the Pacific theater of the war celebrate news of Japan's surrender.* (National Archives)

Bulge, after which they helped breech the Siegfried line and captured seven German towns. Nominated many times for a Presidential Unit Citation, the 761st finally received the award in 1978.

Late in 1944, General Dwight Eisenhower approved a limited experiment of using racially integrated units. The experiment utilized African Americans who volunteered to fight with white troops. Out of 5,000 volunteers, 2,500 men were selected and organized into 37 platoons of 40 men each, which were then attached to white units containing 200 white soldiers. The integrated units fought in the Battle of the Bulge as well as on German soil. Although white officers reported that the experiment was an unqualified success, it was quietly discontinued at the end of the war because of fears of undermining white southern support for a postwar military draft.

Many African Americans viewed a tragedy that occurred at the Navy base at Port Chicago, California, in 1944 as an illustration of the problem of unequal treatment in the military. While black sailors were loading ammunition there, the ammunition cargos of two ships exploded, killing 320 men, including 202 African Americans. When ordered to resume loading several weeks later, 258 black sailors refused to obey and called for improved safety procedures. The Navy court charged 50 of the sailors with mutiny and charged the remainder with lesser offenses. Those convicted of mutiny were sentenced to fifteen years in prison but were granted amnesty after the war. Controversy over the incident had one positive result: The loading of ammunition ceased being a "blacks only" assignment.

Frequently the efforts of African Americans to oppose discrimination and segregation led to clashes on military bases. In July, 1944, for instance, Army lieutenant Jackie Robinson, the future baseball star, disobeyed a command to sit in the back of a military bus at Fort Hood, Texas. He was court-martialed but acquitted because the court ruled that the command had violated the Army's antidiscriminatory policies in transportation. At Freeman Field, Indiana, more than a hundred black officer trainees were arrested and disciplined in 1945 for entering a club reserved for white officers. Second Lieutenant Roger Terry was court-martialed and convicted of brushing against a superior officer when entering the club—a conviction that was not overturned until 1995.

### Demobilization

Black soldiers returning home, even if wounded in action, continued to experience invidious discrimination in employment, education, and political rights. Even German prisoners of war held in the United States were treated with more respect and dignity. Conservative white southerners were ready to use violence against anyone challenging the Jim Crow system. In a highly publicized incident of 1946, Army veteran Isaac Woodward was attacked and blinded by policemen. President Harry S. Truman, incensed to learn of such events, created the President's Committee on Civil Rights, which was charged with investigating discrimination and making proposals for change. Progress would be slow, but World War II helped put the issue of equal rights on the national agenda.

*Thomas Tandy Lewis*

**Further Reading**

Hargrove, Hondon. *Buffalo Soldiers in Italy: Black Americans in World War II*. New York: McFarland, 2003.

Homan, Lynn, and Thomas Reilly. *Black Knights: The Story of the Tuskegee Airmen*. Gretna, La.: Pelican Press, 2001.

Honey, Maureen. *Bitter Fruit: African American Women in World War II*. Jackson: University Press of Mississippi, 1999.

Moore, Christopher. *Fighting for America: Black Soldiers—the Unsung Heroes of World War II*. New York: Random House, 2004.

Morehouse, Maggie. *Fighting the Jim Crow Army: Black Men and Women Remember World War II*. New York: Rowman & Littlefield, 2002.

Savage, Barbara. *Broadcasting Freedom: Radio, War, and the Politics of Race, 1938-1948*. Chapel Hill: University of North Carolina Press, 1999.

Takaki, Ronald. *Double Victory: A Multicultural History of America in World War II*. New York: Little, Brown, 2000.

Wilkerson, Martha, and Dominic Capaci. *Layered Violence: The Detroit Rioters of 1943*. Jackson: University Press of Mississippi, 1991.

Wynn, Neil. *The Afro-American and the Second World War*. London: P. Elek, 1976.

**See also** Defense industry desegregation; Military; Military desegregation; Tuskegee Airmen; Vietnam War

# Yarbrough, Ex parte

**The Case:** U.S. Supreme Court ruling on voting rights
**Date:** March 3, 1884

*This 1884 decision is the only nineteenth century case in which the Supreme Court allowed the federal government to enforce the Fifteenth Amendment by punishing private individuals for obstructing a citizen's right to vote.*

In *Ex parte Yarbrough*, also known as the *Ku Klux Klan* case, Jasper Yarbrough and his fellow Klansmen were convicted in federal court of using violence against an African American, Berry Saunders, to prevent him from voting in a federal election. The Supreme Court unanimously upheld the conviction. Justice Samuel F. Miller broadly interpreted the Fifteenth Amendment as a guarantee that a citizen must not be prevented from voting in federal elections because of his race. In *James v. Bowman* (1903), however, the Court ignored *Yarbrough* and held that congressional enforcement of the Fifteenth Amendment was limited to state action.

*Thomas Tandy Lewis*

**See also** Fifteenth Amendment; Voting Rights Act of 1965

# Bibliography

## List of Categories

General Reference . . . . . . 1027
History . . . . . . . . . . . . 1030
Affirmative Action. . . . . . 1035
African Americans and
    Other Minorities . . . . . 1038
Civil Rights. . . . . . . . . 1040
Civil Rights Law . . . . . . . 1046
Crime . . . . . . . . . . . . . 1047
Desegregation . . . . . . . 1048
Economics . . . . . . . . . . 1050
Education. . . . . . . . . . . 1051
Employment and Labor. . . 1053
Family and Community. . . 1054
Hate and White
    Supremacy . . . . . . . . 1055
Housing. . . . . . . . . . . . 1058
Martin Luther King, Jr. . . . 1059
The Media . . . . . . . . . . 1060
Military . . . . . . . . . . . . 1062
Politics . . . . . . . . . . . . 1062
Religion and the Black
    Church. . . . . . . . . . . 1064
Slavery . . . . . . . . . . . . 1067
The South and
    Segregation . . . . . . . 1074

## General Reference

Allen, Bonnie. *We Are Overcome: Thoughts on Being Black in America*. New York: Crown, 1995.

America, Richard F. *Paying the Social Debt: What White America Owes Black America*. Westport, Conn.: Praeger, 1993.

Armour, Jody David. *Negrophobia and Reasonable Racism: The Hidden Costs of Being Black in America*. New York: New York University Press, 1997.

Asante, Molefi Kete. *The Afrocentric Idea*. Philadelphia: Temple University Press, 1987.

_____. *Afrocentricity*. Trenton, N.J.: Africa World Press, 1988.

Berry, Mary Frances, and John Blassingame. *Long Memory: The Black Experience in America*. New York: Oxford University Press, 1982.

Blauner, Bob. *Black Lives, White Lives: Three Decades of Race Relations in America*. Berkeley: University of California Press, 1989.

Boxill, Bernard R. *Blacks and Social Justice*. Totowa, N.J.: Rowman & Allanheld, 1984.

Brooks, Roy L. *Rethinking the American Race Problem*. Berkeley: University of California Press, 1990.

Broussard, Albert S. *Black San Francisco: The Struggle for Racial Equality in the West, 1900-1954.* Lawrence: University Press of Kansas, 1993.

Brown, Tony. *Black Lies, White Lies: The Truth According to Tony Brown.* New York: Wm. C. Morrow, 1995.

Clark, Kenneth B. *Dark Ghetto: Dilemmas of Social Power.* New York: Harper & Row, 1965.

Cleaver, Eldridge. *Soul on Ice.* New York: McGraw-Hill, 1968.

Coleman, Jonathan. *Long Way to Go: Black and White in America.* New York: Atlantic Monthly Press, 1997.

Collier, Peter, and David Horowitz. *The Race Card: White Guilt, Black Resentment, and the Assault on Truth and Justice.* Rocklin, Calif.: Prima Publishing, 1997.

Croucher, Sheila. *Imagining Miami.* Charlottesville: University Press of Virginia, 1997.

Cruse, Harold. *Plural but Equal: A Critical Study of Blacks and Minorities in America's Plural Society.* New York: William Morrow, 1987.

Davis-Adeshoté, Jeanette, et al. *Black Survival in White America: From Past History to the Next Century.* Orange, N.J.: Bryant and Dillon, 1995.

Dorman, James H., and Robert R. Jones. *The Afro-American Experience.* New York: Wiley, 1974.

Du Bois, W. E. B. *The Souls of Black Folk.* 1903. Reprint. New York: Vintage Books, 1990.

Dunn, Marvin. *Black Miami in the Twentieth Century.* Tallahassee: University of Florida Press, 1997.

Dvorak, Katharine L. *An African American Exodus.* Brooklyn, N.Y.: Carlson, 1991.

Gaillard, Frye. *The Dream Long Deferred.* Chapel Hill: University of North Carolina Press, 1988.

Goldschmid, Marcel L., ed. *Black Americans and White Racism: Theory and Research.* New York: Holt, Rinehart and Winston, 1970.

Gubar, Susan. *Racechanges: White Skin, Black Face in American Culture.* New York: Oxford University Press, 1997.

Guerrero, Ed. *Framing Blackness.* Philadelphia: Temple University Press, 1993.

Hacker, Andrew. *Two Nations: Black and White, Separate, Hostile, Unequal*. New York: Charles Scribner's Sons, 1992.

Johnson, Charles S. *The Negro in American Civilization: A Study of Negro Life and Race Relations in the Light of Social Research*. New York: Henry Holt, 1930.

Jordan, Winthrop D. *White over Black: American Attitudes Toward the Negro, 1550-1812*. 1968. Reprint. New York: W. W. Norton, 1995.

Keyes, Alan L. *Masters of the Dream: The Strength and Betrayal of Black America*. New York: William Morrow, 1995.

Long, Richard A. *African Americans: A Portrait*. New York: Crescent Books, 1993.

Lyman, Stanford M. *The Black American in Sociological Thought*. New York: Putnam, 1972.

McWilliams, Carey. *Brothers Under the Skin*. Rev. ed. Boston: Little, Brown, 1964.

Miller, Arthur G., ed. *In the Eye of the Beholder: Contemporary Issues in Stereotyping*. New York: Praeger, 1982.

Mills, Charles W. *Blackness Visible: Essays on Philosophy and Race*. Ithaca, N.Y.: Cornell University Press, 1998.

Munford, Clarence J. *Race and Reparations: A Black Perspective for the Twenty-first Century*. Trenton, N.J.: Africa World Press, 1996.

Myrdal, Gunnar. *An American Dilemma: The Negro Problem and American Democracy*. New York: Harper & Row, 1944. Reprint. New York: McGraw-Hill, 1964.

Nash, Gary B. *Forbidden Love: Secret History of Mixed Race America*. New York: H. Holt, 1999.

Parsons, Talcott, and Kenneth B. Clark, eds. *The Negro American*. Boston: Houghton Mifflin, 1966.

Pettigrew, Thomas F. *A Profile of the Negro American*. Princeton, N.J.: D. Van Nostrand, 1964.

Pieterse, Jan Nederveen. *White on Black*. New Haven, Conn.: Yale University Press, 1992.

Ploski, Harry A., and James Williams, eds. *The Negro Almanac: A Reference Work on the African American*. Detroit, Mich.: Gale Research, 1989.

Rosenblatt, Paul, Terri A. Karis, and Richard D. Powell. *Multiracial Couples: Black and White Voices*. Thousand Oaks, Calif.: Sage Publications, 1995.

Shipler, David K. *A Country of Strangers: Blacks and Whites in America*. New York: Knopf, 1997.

Sigelman, Lee, and Susan Welch. *Black Americans' Views of Racial Inequality*. Cambridge, England: Cambridge University Press, 1991.

Silberman, Charles E. *Crisis in Black and White*. New York: Vintage Books, 1964.

Smith, Lillian. *Killers of the Dream*. New York: W. W. Norton, 1949.

Steele, Shelby. *A Dream Deferred: The Second Betrayal of Black Freedom in America*. New York: HarperCollins, 1998.

Thernstrom, Stephan, and Abigail Thernstrom. *America in Black and White: One Nation Indivisible*. New York: Random House, 1997.

West, Cornell. *Race Matters*. New York: Random House, 1993.

_____. *Restoring Hope: Conversations on the Future of Black America*. Boston: Beacon Press, 1997.

Williamson, Joel. *New People: Miscegenation and Mulattoes in the United States*. Baton Rouge: Louisiana State University Press, 1995.

Wonkeryor, Edward Lama. *On Afrocentricity, Intercultural Communication, and Racism*. Lewiston, N.Y.: Edwin Mellin Press, 1998.

## History

Anderson, Eric, and Alfred A. Moss, Jr., eds. *The Facts of Reconstruction: Essays in Honor of John Hope Franklin*. Baton Rouge: Louisiana State University Press, 1991.

Bell, Howard Holman. *A Survey of the Negro Convention Movement, 1830-1861*. New York: Arno Press, 1969.

Blight, David W. *Race and Reunion: The Civil War in American Memory*. Cambridge, Mass.: Belknap Press of Harvard University Press, 2001.

Bonnett, Aubrey W., and G. Llewellyn Watson, eds. *Emerging Perspectives on the Black Diaspora*. Lanham, Md.: University Press of America, 1990.

Brown, Richard H. *The Missouri Compromise: Political Statesmanship or Unwise Evasion?* Boston: D. C. Heath, 1964.

Carter, Dan T. *Scottsboro: A Tragedy of the American South*. Rev. ed. Baton Rouge: Louisiana State University Press, 1979.

_____. *When the War Was Over: The Failure of Self-Reconstruction in the South, 1865-1867*. Baton Rouge: Louisiana State University Press, 1985.

Chalmers, Allan Knight. *They Shall Be Free*. Garden City, N.Y.: Doubleday, 1951.

Collins, Bruce. *The Origins of America's Civil War*. New York: Holmes & Meier, 1981.

Conniff, Michael L., and Thomas J. Davis. *Africans in the Americas: A History of the Black Diaspora*. New York: St. Martin's Press, 1994.

Cox, LaWanda. *Lincoln and Black Freedom: A Study in Presidential Leadership*. Columbia: University of South Carolina Press, 1981.

Cox, LaWanda, and John H. Cox. *Politics, Principle, and Prejudice: Dilemma of Reconstruction America, 1865-1866*. New York: Free Press, 1963.

Cronon, E. David. *Black Moses: The Story of Marcus Garvey and the Universal Negro Improvement Association*. Madison: University of Wisconsin Press, 1955.

Crouch, Barry A. *The Freedmen's Bureau and Black Texans*. Austin: University of Texas Press, 1992.

Dykstra, Robert R. *Bright Radical Star: Black Freedom and White Supremacy on the Hawkeye Frontier*. Cambridge, Mass.: Harvard University Press, 1993.

Etcheson, Nicole. *Bleeding Kansas: Contested Liberty in the Civil War Era*. Lawrence: University Press of Kansas, 2004.

Foner, Eric. *Nothing But Freedom: Emancipation and Its Legacy*. Baton Rouge: Louisiana State University Press, 1983.

_____. *Reconstruction: America's Unfinished Revolution*. New York: Harper & Row, 1988.

Franklin, John Hope. *The Emancipation Proclamation*. Garden City, N.Y.: Doubleday, 1963.

_____. *Reconstruction: After the Civil War*. Chicago: University of Chicago Press, 1961.

Franklin, John Hope, and Alfred A. Moss, Jr. *From Slavery to Freedom: A History of African Americans*. 7th ed. New York: McGraw-Hill, 1994.

Frazier, Thomas R., ed. *Afro-American History: Primary Sources*. New York: Harcourt, Brace & World, 1970.

Garvey, Amy Jacques. *Garvey and Garveyism*. 1963. Reprint. New York: Collier, 1976.

Garvey, Marcus. *Philosophy and Opinions of Marcus Garvey*. Edited by Amy Jacques-Garvey, with new introduction by Robert A. Hill. New York: Atheneum, 1992.

Guelzo, Allen C. *Lincoln's Emancipation Proclamation: The End of Slavery in America*. New York: Simon & Schuster, 2004.

Hamilton, Holman. *Prologue to Conflict: The Crisis and Compromise of 1850*. New York: W. W. Norton, 1964.

Harlan, Louis R. *Booker T. Washington: The Making of a Black Leader, 1856-1901*. New York: Oxford University Press, 1972.

_____. *Booker T. Washington: The Wizard of Tuskegee, 1901-1915*. New York: Oxford University Press, 1983.

_____. *Booker T. Washington in Perspective: Essays of Louis R. Harlan*. Edited by Raymond W. Smock. Jackson: University Press of Mississippi, 1988.

Hill, Robert A., and Barbara Bair, eds. *Marcus Garvey: Life and Lessons*. Berkeley: University of California Press, 1987.

Holt, Michael. *The Political Crisis of the 1850's*. New York: W. W. Norton, 1978.

Hornsby, Alton, Jr. *Chronology of African-American History*. Detroit, Mich.: Gale Research, 1991.

Keegan, Frank L. *Blacktown, U.S.A*. Boston: Little, Brown, 1971.

Kellogg, Charles Flint. *NAACP: A History of the National Association for the Advancement of Colored People*. Baltimore: Johns Hopkins University Press, 1964.

Kusmer, Kenneth L., ed. *Black Communities and Urban Development in America, 1720-1990*. New York: Garland, 1991.

Lanctot, Neil. *Negro League Baseball: The Rise and Ruin of a Black Institution*. Philadelphia: University of Pennsylvania Press, 2004.

Lasch-Quinn, Elisabeth. *Black Neighbors: Race and the Limits of Reform in the American Settlement House Movement, 1890-1945*. Chapel Hill: University of North Carolina Press, 1993.

Leckie, William H. *The Buffalo Soldiers: A Narrative of the Negro Cavalry in the West*. Norman: University of Oklahoma Press, 1967.

Lemann, Nicholas. *The Promised Land: The Great Black Migration and How It Changed America*. New York: Alfred A. Knopf, 1991.

Lewis, David Levering. *W. E. B. Du Bois: Biography of a Race, 1868-1919*. New York: Henry Holt, 1993.

Lewis, Rupert, and Maureen Warner-Lewis, eds. *Garvey: Africa, Europe, the Americas*. Kingston, Jamaica: Institute of Social and Economic Research, University of the West Indies, 1986.

Lofgren, Charles A. *The Plessy Case: A Legal-Historical Interpretation*. New York: Oxford University Press, 1987.

Lubiano, Wahneema, ed. *The House That Race Built: Black Americans, U.S. Terrain*. New York: Pantheon, 1997.

McPherson, James M. *The Battle Cry of Freedom: The Civil War Era*. Oxford, England: Oxford University Press, 1988.

_____. *The Negro in the Civil War*. New York: Vintage Books, 1965.

_____. *Ordeal by Fire: The Civil War and Reconstruction*. 2d ed. New York: McGraw-Hill, 1992.

_____. *The Struggle for Equality: Abolitionists and the Negro in the Civil War and Reconstruction*. Princeton, N.J.: Princeton University Press, 1964.

Magdol, Edward. *A Right to the Land: Essays on the Freedmen's Community*. Westport, Conn.: Greenwood Press, 1977.

Mathurin, Owen Charles. *Henry Sylvester Williams and the Origins of the Pan-African Movement, 1869-1911*. Westport, Conn.: Greenwood Press, 1976.

Meier, August. *Negro Thought in America, 1880-1915: Racial Ideologies in the Age of Booker T. Washington*. Ann Arbor: University of Michigan Press, 1988.

Miller, Loren. *The Petitioners: The Story of the Supreme Court of the United States and the Negro*. New York: Pantheon Books, 1966.

Moses, Wilson Jeremiah. *The Golden Age of Black Nationalism, 1850-1925*. New York: Oxford University Press, 1978.

Nieman, Donald G. *Promises to Keep: African-Americans and the Constitutional Order, 1776 to the Present*. New York: Oxford University Press, 1991.

Norris, Clarence, and Sybil D. Washington. *The Last of the Scottsboro Boys*. New York: Putnam, 1979.

Oates, Stephen B. *Our Fiery Trial: Abraham Lincoln, John Brown, and the Civil War Era*. Amherst: University of Massachusetts Press, 1979.

Ovington, Mary White, et al. *Black and White Sat Down Together: The Reminiscences of an NAACP Founder.* New York: Feminist Press of City University of New York, 1996.

Patterson, Haywood, and Earl Conrad. *Scottsboro Boy.* Garden City, N.Y.: Doubleday, 1950.

Quarles, Benjamin. *Lincoln and the Negro.* New York: Oxford University Press, 1962.

_____. *The Negro in the Civil War.* Boston: Little, Brown, 1953.

Rabinowitz, Howard N., and George W. Frederickson. *Race Relations in the Urban South, 1865-1890.* New York: Oxford University Press, 1996.

Rhym, Darren. *The NAACP.* Philadelphia: Chelsea House, 2002.

Richardson, Heather Cox. *The Death of Reconstruction: Race, Labor, and Politics in the Post-Civil War North, 1865-1901.* Cambridge, Mass.: Harvard University Press, 2001.

Rymer, Russ. *American Beach: A Saga of Race, Wealth, and Memory.* New York: HarperCollins, 1998.

Shropshire, Kenneth L., and Kellen Winslow. *In Black and White: Race and Sports in America.* New York: New York University Press, 1996.

Simon, Scott. *Jackie Robinson and the Integration of Baseball.* Hoboken, N.J.: J. Wiley & Sons, 2002.

Snyder, Brad. *Beyond the Shadow of the Senators: The Untold Story of the Homestead Grays and the Integration of Baseball.* Chicago: Contemporary Books, 2003.

Stampp, Kenneth, ed. *The Causes of the Civil War.* Rev. ed. Englewood Cliffs, N.J.: Prentice-Hall, 1974.

_____. *The Era of Reconstruction, 1865-1877.* New York: Alfred A. Knopf, 1965.

Tygiel, Jules. *Baseball's Great Experiment: Jackie Robinson and His Legacy.* New York: Vintage, 1984.

Van Deburg, William L., ed. *Modern Black Nationalism: From Marcus Garvey to Louis Farrakhan.* New York: New York University Press, 1997.

Walther, Eric H. *The Shattering of the Union: America in the 1850's.* Wilmington, Del.: Scholarly Resources, 2004.

Waugh, John C. *On the Brink of Civil War: The Compromise of 1850 and How It Changed the Course of American History.* Wilmington, Del.: Scholarly Resources, 2003.

Wood, Peter H. *Black Majority: Negroes in Colonial South Carolina from 1670 Through the Stono Rebellion.* New York: W. W. Norton, 1974.


**Affirmative Action**

Anderson, Terry H. *The Pursuit of Fairness: A History of Affirmative Action.* New York: Oxford University Press, 2004.

*Annals of the American Academy of Political and Social Science* 523 (September, 1992). Special issue, Affirmative Action Revisited.

Ball, Howard. *The Bakke Case: Race, Education, and Affirmative Action.* Lawrence: University Press of Kansas, 2000.

Beckwith, Francis J., and Todd E. Jones, eds. *Affirmative Action: Social Justice or Reverse Discrimination?* Amherst, N.Y.: Prometheus, 1997.

Benokraitis, Nijole, and Joe R. Feagin. *Affirmative Action and Equal Opportunity: Action, Inaction, Reaction.* Boulder, Colo.: Westview Press, 1978.

Bolick, Clint. *The Affirmative Action Fraud: Can We Restore the American Civil Rights Vision?* Washington, D.C.: Cato Institute, 1996.

Bowen, William G., and Derek Bok. *The Shape of the River: Long-Term Consequences of Considering Race in College and University Admissions.* Princeton, N.J.: Princeton University Press, 1998.

Bowie, Norman E., ed. *Equal Opportunity.* Boulder, Colo.: Westview Press, 1988.

Burstein, Paul. "Affirmative Action, Jobs, and American Democracy: What Has Happened to the Quest for Equal Opportunity?" *Law and Society Review* 26, no. 4 (1992): 901-922.

Carter, Stephen L. *Reflections of an Affirmative Action Baby.* New York: Basic Books, 1992.

Cohen, Carl. *Naked Racial Preferences: The Case Against Affirmative Action.* Lanham, Md.: Madison Books, 1995.

Delgado, Richard. *The Coming Race War? And Other Apocalyptic Tales of America After Affirmative Action and Welfare.* New York: New York University Press, 1996.

Dworkin, Ronald. "What Did *Bakke* Really Decide?" In *A Matter of Principle*. Cambridge, Mass.: Harvard University Press, 1985.

Eastland, Terry. *Ending Affirmative Action: The Case for Colorblind Justice*. New York: Basic Books, 1996.

Edley, Christopher F., Jr. *Not All Black and White: Affirmative Action, Race, and American Values*. New York: Hill & Wang, 1996.

Ezorsky, Gertrude. *Racism and Justice: The Case for Affirmative Action*. Ithaca, N.Y.: Cornell University Press, 1991.

Fiscus, Ronald J. *The Constitutional Logic of Affirmative Action*. Durham, N.C.: Duke University Press, 1992.

Fullinwider, Robert. *The Reverse Discrimination Controversy*. Totowa, N.J.: Rowman and Littlefield, 1980.

Glazer, Nathan. *Affirmative Discrimination: Ethnic Inequality and Public Policy*. New York: Basic Books, 1975.

Gray, W. Robert. *The Four Faces of Affirmative Action: Fundamental Answers and Actions*. Westport, Conn.: Greenwood Press, 2001.

Greene, Kathanne W. *Affirmative Action and Principles of Justice*. New York: Greenwood Press, 1989.

Greenwalt, Kent. *Discrimination and Reverse Discrimination*. New York: Alfred A. Knopf, 1983.

Horne, Gerald. *Reversing Discrimination: The Case for Affirmative Action*. New York: International, 1992.

Jackson, Charles C. "Affirmative Action: Controversy and Retrenchment." *The Western Journal of Black Studies* 16, no. 4 (Winter, 1992).

Jones, Augustus J. *Affirmative Talk, Affirmative Action: A Comparative Study of the Politics of Affirmative Action*. New York: Praeger, 1991.

Kahlenberg, Richard D. *The Remedy: Class, Race, and Affirmative Action*. New York: BasicBooks, 1996.

Leonard, Jonathan. "The Federal Anti-Bias Effort." In *Essays on the Economics of Discrimination*, edited by Emily P. Hoffman. Kalamazoo, Mich.: W. E. Upjohn Institute, 1991.

Lerner, Robert, and Althea K. Nigai. *Racial Preferences in Undergraduate Enrollment at the University of California, Berkeley, 1993-1995: A Preliminary Report*. Washington, D.C.: Center for Equal Opportunity, 1996.

Lynch, Frederick R. *The Diversity Machine: The Drive to Change the "White Male Workplace."* New York: Free Press, 1996.

McCormack, Wayne. *The "Bakke" Decision: Implications for Higher Education Admissions.* Washington, D.C.: American Council on Education and the Association of American Law Schools, 1978.

McWhirter, Darien A. *The End of Affirmative Action: Where Do We Go from Here?* New York: Carol Publishing Group, 1996.

Maguire, Daniel. *A Case for Affirmative Action.* Dubuque, Iowa: Shepherd, 1992.

Post, Robert, and Michael Paul Rogin, eds. *Race and Representation: Affirmative Action.* New York: Zone Books, 1998.

Pusser, Brian. *Burning Down the House: Politics, Governance, and Affirmative Action at the University of California.* Albany: State University of New York Press, 2004.

Roberts, Paul Craig, and Lawrence M. Stratton, Jr. *The New Color Line: How Quotas and Privilege Destroy Democracy.* Washington, D.C.: Regnery, 1995.

Rosenfeld, Michel. *Affirmative Action and Justice: A Philosophical and Constitutional Inquiry.* New Haven, Conn.: Yale University Press, 1991.

Sindler, Allan P. *Bakke, Defunis, and Minority Admissions: The Quest for Equal Opportunity.* New York: Longman, 1978.

Sowell, Thomas. *Preferential Policies: An International Perspective.* New York: William Morrow, 1990.

Steinberg, Stephen. *Turning Back: The Retreat from Racial Justice in American Thought and Policy.* Boston: Beacon Press, 1995.

Stohr, Greg. *A Black and White Case: How Affirmative Action Survived Its Greatest Legal Challenge.* Princeton: Bloomberg Press, 2004.

Swain, Carol M., ed. *Race Versus Class: The New Affirmative Action Debate.* Lanham, Md.: University Press of America, 1996.

Thernstrom, Abigail. *Whose Votes Count? Affirmative Action and Minority Voting Rights.* Cambridge, Mass.: Harvard University Press, 1987.

U.S. Commission on Civil Rights. *Affirmative Action in the 1980's: Dismantling the Process of Discrimination: A Statement of the United States Commission on Civil Rights.* Washington, D.C.: Author, 1981.

Urofsky, Melvin I. *A Conflict of Rights: The Supreme Court and Affirmative Action*. New York: Charles Scribner's Sons, 1991.

Wise, Tim J. *Affirmative Action: Racial Preference in Black and White*. New York: Routledge, 2005.

Zelnick, Bob. *Backfire: A Reporter's Look at Affirmative Action*. Chicago: Henry Regnery, 1996.

## African Americans and Other Minorities

Abelmann, Nancy, and John Lie. *Blue Dreams: Korean Americans and the Los Angeles Riots*. Cambridge, Mass.: Harvard University Press, 1995.

Adams, Maurianne, and John Bracey, eds. *Strangers and Neighbors: Relations Between Blacks and Jews in the United States*. Amherst: University of Massachusetts Press, 1999.

Berman, Paul, ed. *Blacks and Jews: Alliance and Arguments*. New York: Delacorte Press, 1994.

Bonnett, Aubrey W. *Institutional Adaptation of West Indian Immigrants to America*. Washington, D.C.: University Press of America, 1982.

Brock, Lisa, and Digna Castañeda Fuertes, eds. *Between Race and Empire: African-Americans and Cubans Before the Cuban Revolution*. Philadelphia: Temple University Press, 1998.

Collum, Danny Duncan. *Black and White Together: The Search for Common Ground*. Maryknoll, N.Y.: Orbis Books, 1996.

Daughtry, Herbert D., Sr. *No Monopoly on Suffering: Blacks and Jews in Crown Heights*. Trenton, N.J.: Africa World Press, 1997.

Diner, Hasia R. *In the Almost Promised Land: American Jews and Blacks, 1919-1935*. Westport, Conn.: Westview, 1977.

Forbes, Jack D. *Black Africans and Native Americans: Color, Race, and Caste in the Evolution of Red-Black Peoples*. Urbana: University of Illinois Press, 1993.

Halliburton, R., Jr. *Red over Black: Black Slavery Among the Cherokee Indians*. Westport, Conn.: Greenwood Press, 1977.

Helg, Aline. *Our Rightful Share: The Afro-Cuban Struggle for Equality, 1886-1912*. Chapel Hill: University of North Carolina Press, 1995.

Hentoff, Nat, ed. *Black Anti-Semitism and Jewish Racism*. New York: Richard W. Baron, 1969.

Hoover, Dwight W. *The Red and the Black*. Chicago: Rand McNally, 1976.

Joyce, Patrick D. *No Fire Next Time: Black-Korean Conflicts and the Future of America's Cities*. Ithaca, N.Y.: Cornell University Press, 2003.

Kasinitz, Philip. *Caribbean New York: Black Immigrants and the Politics of Race*. Ithaca, N.Y.: Cornell University Press, 1992.

Katz, William Loren. *Black Indians: A Hidden Heritage*. New York: Atheneum, 1986.

Kaufman, Jonathan. *Broken Alliance: The Turbulent Times Between Blacks and Jews in America*. New York: Scribner's, 1988.

Kim, Claire Jean. *Bitter Fruit: The Politics of Black-Korean Conflict in New York City*. New Haven: Yale University Press, 2000.

Kim, Kwang Chung, ed. *Koreans in the Hood: Conflict with African Americans*. Baltimore: Johns Hopkins University Press, 1999.

Laguerre, Michel S. *Diasporic Citizenship: Haitian Americans in Transnational America*. New York: St. Martin's Press, 1998.

Lerner, Michael, and Cornel West. *Jews and Blacks: Let the Healing Begin*. New York: G. P. Putnam's Sons, 1995.

Lieberson, Stanley. *A Piece of the Pie: Blacks and White Immigrants Since 1880*. Berkeley: University of California Press, 1980.

Littlefield, Daniel F., Jr. *Africans and Creeks: From the Colonial Period to the Civil War*. Westport, Conn.: Greenwood Press, 1979.

_____. *Africans and Seminoles: From Removal to Emancipation*. Westport, Conn.: Greenwood Press, 1978.

Melnick, Jeffrey. *Black-Jewish Relations on Trial: Leo Frank and Jim Conley in the New South*. Jackson: University Press of Mississippi, 2000.

Miller, Jake. *The Plight of Haitian Refugees*. New York: Praeger, 1984.

Min, Pyong Gap. *Caught in the Middle: Korean Merchants in America's Multiethnic Cities*. Berkeley: University of Calfornia Press, 1996.

Ownby, Ted, ed. *Black and White Cultural Interaction in the Antebellum South*. Jackson: University Press of Mississippi, 1993.

Palmer, Ransford W. *Pilgrims from the Sun: West Indian Migration to America*. New York: Twayne Publishers, 1995.

Phillips, William M., Jr. *An Unillustrious Alliance: The African American and Jewish American Communities*. Westport, Conn.: Greenwood Press, 1991.

Piatt, Bill, et al. *Black and Brown in America: The Case for Cooperation*. New York: New York University Press, 1997.

Salzman, Jack, and Cornel West, eds. *Struggles in the Promised Land: Towards a History of Black-Jewish Relations in the United States*. New York: Oxford University Press, 1997.

Schorsch, Jonathan. *Jews and Blacks in the Early Modern World*. New York: Cambridge University Press, 2004.

Stepick, Alex. *Haitian Refugees in the U.S.* London: Minority Rights Group, 1982.

_____. *Pride Against Prejudice: Haitians in the United States*. Boston: Allyn and Bacon, 1998.

Vickerman, Milton. *Crosscurrents: West Indian Immigrants and Race*. New York: Oxford University Press, 1998.

Waldinger, Roger. *Still the Promised City? African-Americans and the New Immigrants in Post-Industrial New York*. Cambridge, Mass.: Harvard University Press, 1996.

Waters, Mary C. *Black Identities: West Indian Immigrant Dreams and American Realities*. Cambridge, Mass.: Harvard University Press, 1999.

Watkins-Owens, Irma. *Blood Relations: Caribbean Immigrants and the Harlem Community, 1900-1930*. Bloomington: Indiana University Press, 1996.

Williams, Richard E. *Hierarchical Structures and Social Value: The Creation of Black and Irish Identities in the United States*. Cambridge, England: Cambridge University Press, 1990.

Zéphir, Flore. *The Haitian Americans*. Westport, Conn.: Greenwood Press, 2004.

## Civil Rights

Abernathy, Ralph. *And the Walls Came Tumbling Down*. New York: Harper & Row, 1989.

Ashmore, Harry S. *"Civil Rights and Wrongs": A Memoir of Race and Politics, 1944-1996*. Rev. and expanded ed. Columbia: University of South Carolina Press, 1997.

Bartley, Numan V. *The Rise of Massive Resistance: Race and Politics in the South During the 1950's*. Baton Rouge: Louisiana State University Press, 1969.

Bass, Patrik Henry. *Like a Mighty Stream: The March on Washington, August 28, 1963*. Philadelphia: Running Press, 2002.

Bates, Daisy. *The Long Shadow of Little Rock: A Memoir*. New York: David McKay, 1962.

Blaustein, Albert P., and Robert L. Zangrando, eds. *Civil Rights and the American Negro: A Documentary History*. New York: Trident Press, 1968.

Bloom, Jack D. *Class, Race, and the Civil Rights Movement*. Bloomington: Indiana University Press, 1987.

Blossom, Virgil T. *It Has Happened Here*. New York: Harper and Brothers, 1959.

Blumberg, Rhoda L. *Civil Rights: The 1960's Freedom Struggle*. Boston: Twayne, 1984.

Breitman, George, Herman Porter, and Baxter Smith. *The Assassination of Malcolm X*. New York: Pathfinder Press, 1976.

Burk, Robert Frederick. *The Eisenhower Administration and Black Civil Rights*. Knoxville: University of Tennessee Press, 1984.

Burns, W. Haywood. *The Voices of Negro Protest in America*. New York: Oxford University Press, 1963.

Carmichael, Stokely, and Charles V. Hamilton. *Black Power: The Politics of Liberation in America*. New York: Random House, 1967.

Carmichael, Stokely, with Ekwueme Michael Thelwell. *Ready for Revolution: The Life and Struggles of Stokely Carmichael (Kwame Ture)*. New York: Scribner, 2003.

Carson, Clayborne. *In Struggle: SNCC and the Black Awakening of the 1960's*. Cambridge: Mass.: Harvard University Press, 1981.

_____. *Malcolm X: The FBI Files*. New York: Carroll & Graff, 1991.

Carson, Clayborne, et al., eds. *Eyes on the Prize Civil Rights Reader: Documents, Speeches, and Firsthand Accounts from the Black Freedom Struggle, 1954-1990*. New York: Penguin, 1991.

Chappell, David L. *Inside Agitators: White Southerners in the Civil Rights Movement*. Baltimore: Johns Hopkins University Press, 1994.

Chong, Dennis. *Collective Action and the Civil Rights Movement.* Chicago: University of Chicago Press, 1991.

Churchill, Ward, and Jim Vander Wall. *Agents of Repression: The FBI's Secret Wars Against the Black Panther Party and the American Indian Movement.* Boston: South End Press, 1988.

Clark, John Henrick, ed. *Malcolm X: The Man and His Times.* Trenton, N.J.: African World Press, 1990.

Cleaver, Kathleen, and George Katsiaficas, eds. *Liberation, Imagination, and the Black Panther Party: A New Look at the Panthers and Their Legacy.* New York: Routledge, 2001.

Collier-Thomas, Bettye, and V. P. Franklin, eds. *Sisters in the Struggle: African American Women in the Civil Rights-Black Power Movement.* New York: New York University Press, 2001.

Couto, Richard A. *Ain't Gonna Let Nobody Turn Me Round: The Pursuit of Racial Justice in the Rural South.* Philadelphia: Temple University Press, 1991.

Crawford, Vicki L., Jacqueline Anne Rouse, and Barbara Woods, eds. *Women in the Civil Rights Movement: Trailblazers and Torchbearers, 1941-1965.* Bloomington: Indiana University Press, 1993.

Dees, Morris. *The Gathering Storm.* New York: HarperCollins, 1996.

Dees, Morris, with Steve Fiffer. *A Season for Justice: The Life and Times of Civil Rights Lawyer Morris Dees.* New York: Maxwell Macmillan International, 1991.

D'Emilio, John. *The Civil Rights Struggle: Leaders in Profile.* New York: Facts On File, 1979.

Dierenfield, Bruce J. *The Civil Rights Movement.* New York: Pearson Longman, 2004.

Dittmer, John. *Local People: The Struggle for Civil Rights in Mississippi.* Urbana: University of Illinois Press, 1994.

Draper, Alan. *Conflict of Interests: Organized Labor and the Civil Rights Movement in the South, 1954-1968.* Ithaca, N.Y.: ILR Press, 1994.

Dunbar, Leslie W. *Minority Report: What Has Happened to Blacks, American Indians, and Other Minorities in the Eighties.* New York: Pantheon, 1984.

Early, Gerald L. *This Is Where I Came In: Black America in the 1960's.* Lincoln: University of Nebraska Press, 2003.

Farmer, James. *Freedom—When?* New York: Random House, 1965.

_____. *Lay Bare the Heart: The Autobiography of the Civil Rights Movement.* New York: New American Library, 1985.

Finch, Minnie. *The NAACP: Its Fight for Justice.* Metuchen, N.J.: Scarecrow Press, 1981.

Forman, James. *The Making of Black Revolutionaries.* 1972. 2d ed. Washington, D.C.: Open Hand, 1985.

Freyer, Tony. *The Little Rock Crisis: A Constitutional Interpretation.* Westport, Conn.: Greenwood Press, 1984.

Garrow, David J., ed. *We Shall Overcome: The Civil Rights Movement in the United States in the 1950's and 1960's.* 3 vols. Brooklyn, N.Y.: Carlson, 1989.

Graham, Hugh Davis. *The Civil Rights Era: Origins and Development of National Policy.* New York: Oxford University Press, 1990.

Harvey, James C. *Black Civil Rights During the Johnson Administration.* Jackson: University and College Press of Mississippi, 1973.

Higham, John, ed. *Civil Rights and Social Wrongs: Black-White Relations Since World War II.* University Park: Pennsylvania State University Press, 1997.

Hill, Herbert, and James E. Jones, Jr., eds. *Race in America: The Struggle for Equality.* Madison: University of Wisconsin Press, 1993.

Hill, Lance. *The Deacons for Defense: Armed Resistance and the Civil Rights Movement.* Chapel Hill: University of North Carolina Press, 2004.

Jonas, Gilbert. *Freedom's Sword: The NAACP and the Struggle Against Racism in America, 1909-1969.* Foreword by Julian Bond. New York: Routledge, 2005.

Jones, Charles E., ed. *The Black Panther Party (Reconsidered).* Baltimore: Black Classic Press, 1998.

Kosof, Anna. *The Civil Rights Movement and Its Legacy.* New York: Watts, 1989.

Lee, Taeku. *Mobilizing Public Opinion: Black Insurgency and Racial Attitudes in the Civil Rights Era.* Chicago: University of Chicago Press, 2002.

Levine, Daniel. *Bayard Rustin and the Civil Rights Movement*. New Brunswick, N.J.: Rutgers University Press, 2000.

Levy, Peter B. *The Civil Rights Movement*. Westport, Conn.: Greenwood Press, 1998.

Ling, Peter J., and Sharon Monteith, eds. *Gender and the Civil Rights Movement*. New Brunswick, N.J.: Rutgers University Press, 2004.

McClymer, John F., ed. *Mississippi Freedom Summer*. Belmont, Calif.: Thomson/Wadsworth, 2004.

McKissack, Pat, and Fredrick McKissack. *The Civil Rights Movement in America from 1865 to the Present*. 2d ed. Chicago: Children's Press, 1991.

McMillen, Neil R. *The Citizens' Council: Organized Resistance to the Second Reconstruction, 1954-1964*. Urbana: University of Illinois Press, 1971.

McWhorter, Diane. *Carry Me Home: Birmingham, Alabama, the Climactic Battle of the Civil Rights Revolution*. New York: Simon & Schuster, 2001.

Malcolm X. *By Any Means Necessary: Speeches, Interviews and a Letter by Malcolm X*. Edited by George Breitman. New York: Pathfinder, 1970.

Malcolm X with Alex Haley. *The Autobiography of Malcolm X*. New York: Ballantine Books, 1965.

Marsh, Charles. *God's Long Summer: Stories of Faith and Civil Rights*. Princeton, N.J.: Princeton University Press, 1997.

Meier, August, and Elliot Rudwick. *CORE: A Study in the Civil Rights Movement, 1942-1968*. Urbana: University of Illinois Press, 1975.

Meredith, James H. *Three Years in Mississippi*. Bloomington: Indiana University Press, 1966.

Meriwether, Louise. *Don't Ride the Bus on Mondays: The Rosa Parks Story*. Englewood Cliffs, N.J.: Prentice Hall, 1973.

Miller, Marilyn. *The Bridge at Selma*. Morristown, N.J.: Silver Burdett, 1985.

Morris, Aldon B. *The Origins of the Civil Rights Movement: Black Communities Organizing for Change*. New York: Free Press, 1984.

Newton, Huey P. *To Die for the People*. New York: Random House, 1972.

_____. *War Against the Panthers: A Study of Repression in America*. 1980. Reprint. New York: Harlem River Press, 1996.

Oppenheimer, Martin. *The Sit-In Movement of 1960*. Brooklyn, N.Y.: Carlson, 1989.

O'Reilly, Kenneth. *Racial Matters: The FBI's Secret File on Black America, 1960-1972*. New York: Free Press, 1989.

Powledge, Fred. *Free at Last? The Civil Rights Movement and the People Who Made It*. Boston: Little, Brown, 1991.

Price, Steven D., comp. *Civil Rights, 1967-68*. Vol. 2. New York: Facts On File, 1973.

Record, Wilson, and Jane Cassels Record, eds. *Little Rock, U.S.A.* San Francisco: Chandler, 1960.

Riches, William T. Martin. *The Civil Rights Movement: Struggle and Resistance*. New York: Palgrave Macmillan, 2004.

Robinson, Jo Ann Gibson. *The Montgomery Bus Boycott and the Women Who Started It: The Memoir of Jo Ann Gibson Robinson*. Knoxville: University of Tennessee Press, 1987.

Rothschild, Mary Aickin. *A Case of Black and White: Northern Volunteers and the Southern Freedom Summers, 1964-1965*. Westport, Conn.: Greenwood Press, 1982.

Sargent, Frederic O. *The Civil Rights Revolution: Events and Leaders, 1955-1968*. Foreword by Bill Maxwell. Jefferson, N.C.: McFarland & Co., 2004.

Seale, Bobby. *Seize the Time: The Story of the Black Panther Party and Huey P. Newton*. New York: Random House, 1968.

Sitkoff, Harvard. *The New Deal for Blacks: The Emergence of Civil Rights as a National Issue*. New York: Oxford University Press, 1978.

_____. *The Struggle for Black Equality, 1954-1980*. New York: Hill and Wang, 1993.

Weisbrot, Robert. *Freedom Bound: A History of America's Civil Rights Movement*. New York: W. W. Norton, 1990.

Wexler, Sanford. *The Civil Rights Movement: An Eyewitness History*. New York: Facts On File, 1993.

Williams, Juan. *Eyes on the Prize: America's Civil Rights Years, 1954-1965*. New York: Viking, 1987.

Young, Andrew. *An Easy Burden: The Civil Rights Movement and the Transformation of America*. New York: HarperCollins, 1996.

Zinn, Howard. *SNCC: The New Abolitionists*. Cambridge, Mass.: South End Press, 2002.

**Civil Rights Law**

Abernathy, Charles F. *Civil Rights and Constitutional Litigation: Cases and Materials*. 2d ed. St. Paul, Minn.: West, 1992.

Abernathy, M. Glenn. *Civil Liberties Under the Constitution*. 5th ed. Columbia: University of South Carolina Press, 1989.

Bardolph, Richard, ed. *The Civil Rights Record: Black Americans and the Law, 1849-1870*. New York: Thomas Crowell, 1970.

Bell, Derrick A., Jr. *Race, Racism, and American Law*. 2d ed. Boston: Little, Brown, 1980.

Berman, Daniel M. *A Bill Becomes a Law: Congress Enacts Civil Rights Legislation*. New York: Macmillan, 1966.

Berry, Mary Frances. *Black Resistance/White Law: A History of Constitutional Racism in America*. Rev. ed. New York: Penguin, 1994.

Curtis, Michael Kent. *No State Shall Abridge*. Durham, N.C.: Duke University Press, 1986.

Davidson, Chandler, and Bernard Grofman, eds. *Quiet Revolution in the South: The Impact of the Voting Rights Act, 1965-1990*. Princeton, N.J.: Princeton University Press, 1994.

Flagg, Barbara J. *Was Blind, but Now I See: White Race Consciousness and the Law*. New York: New York University Press, 1998.

Grofman, Bernard, and Chandler Davidson, eds. *Controversies in Minority Voting: The Voting Rights Act in Perspective*. Washington, D.C.: Brookings Institution, 1992.

Halpern, Steven C. *On the Limits of the Law: The Ironic Legacy of Title VI of the 1964 Civil Rights Act*. Baltimore: Johns Hopkins University Press, 1995.

Hoemann, George H. *What God Hath Wrought: The Embodiment of Freedom in the Thirteenth Amendment*. New York: Garland Press, 1987.

Hyman, Harold M., and William M. Wiecek. *Equal Justice Under Law: Constitutional Development, 1835-1875*. New York: Harper & Row, 1982.

Klarman, Michael J. *From Jim Crow to Civil Rights: The Supreme Court and the Struggle for Racial Equality*. New York: Oxford University Press, 2004.

Kull, Andrew. *The Color-Blind Constitution.* Cambridge, Mass.: Harvard University Press, 1992.

Labb, Ronald M., and Jonathan Lurie. *The Slaughterhouse Cases: Regulation, Reconstruction, and the Fourteenth Amendment.* Lawrence: University Press of Kansas, 2003.

Lively, Donald E. *The Constitution and Race.* New York: Praeger, 1992.

Nelson, William. *The Fourteenth Amendment.* Cambridge, Mass.: Harvard University Press, 1988.

Perry, Michael J. *We the People: The Fourteenth Amendment and the Supreme Court.* New York: Oxford University Press, 1999.

Reams, Bernard D., Jr., and Paul E. Wilson, eds. *Segregation and the Fourteenth Amendment in the States: A Survey of State Segregation Laws, 1865-1953, Prepared for United States Supreme Court in re Brown vs. Board of Education of Topeka.* Buffalo, N.Y.: W. S. Hein, 1975.

Roberts, Ronald S. *Clarence Thomas and the Tough Love Crowd: Counterfeit Heroes and Unhappy Truths.* New York: New York University Press, 1995.

Tsesis, Alexander. *The Thirteenth Amendment and American Freedom: A Legal History.* New York: New York University Press, 2004.

Tushnet, Mark V. *Making Civil Rights Law: Thurgood Marshall and the Supreme Court, 1936-1961.* New York: Oxford University Press, 1994.

U.S. Commission on Civil Rights. *The Voting Rights Act: Unfulfilled Goals.* Washington, D.C.: Government Printing Office, 1981.

Whalen, Charles, and Barbara Whalen. *The Longest Debate: A Legislative History of the 1964 Civil Rights Act.* Washington, D.C.: Seven Locks Press, 1985.

## Crime

Cole, David. *No Equal Justice: Race and Class in the American Criminal Justice System.* New York: New Press, 1999.

Free, Marvin, Jr. *African Americans and the Criminal Justice System.* New York: Garland, 1996.

Fukarai, Hirosaki, Edgar W. Butler, and Richard Krooth. *Race and the Jury: Racial Disenfranchisement and the Search for Justice.* New York: Plenum, 1993.

Gibbs, Jewelle Taylor. *Race and Justice: Rodney King and O.J. Simpson in a House Divided*. San Francisco: Jossey-Bass, 1996.

Hutchinson, Earl Ofari. *The Crisis in Black and Black*. Los Angeles: Middle Passage Press, 1998.

Kennedy, Randall. *Race, Crime, and the Law*. New York: Pantheon Books, 1997.

Khalifah, H. Khalif, ed. *Rodney King and the L.A. Rebellion: Analysis and Commentary by Thirteen Best-Selling Black Writers*. Hampton, Va.: U.B. & U.S. Communications Systems, 1992.

Owens, Tom, with Rod Browning. *Lying Eyes: The Truth Behind the Corruption and Brutality of the LAPD and the Beating of Rodney King*. New York: Thunder's Mouth Press, 1994.

Paul, Arnold, ed. *Black Americans and the Supreme Court Since Emancipation: Betrayal or Protection?* New York: Holt, Rinehart and Winston, 1972.

Pinderhughes, Howard. *Race in the Hood: Conflict and Violence Among Urban Youth*. Minneapolis: University of Minnesota Press, 1997.

## Desegregation

Armor, David J. *Forced Justice: School Desegregation and the Law*. New York: Oxford University Press, 1995.

Barnes, Catherine A. *Journey from Jim Crow: The Desegregation of Southern Transit*. New York: Columbia University Press, 1981.

Barrett, Russell H. *Integration at Ole Miss*. Chicago: Quadrangle Press, 1965.

Brooks, Roy L. *Integration or Separation? A Strategy for Racial Equality*. Cambridge, Mass.: Harvard University Press, 1996.

Clark, E. Culpepper. *The Schoolhouse Door: Segregation's Last Stand at the University of Alabama*. New York: Oxford University Press, 1993.

Cohodas, Nadine. *The Band Played Dixie: Race and the Liberal Conscience at Ole Miss*. New York: Free Press, 1997.

Hochschild, Jennifer L. *The New American Dilemma: Liberal Democracy and School Desegregation*. New Haven, Conn.: Yale University Press, 1984.

Hughes, Larry W., William M. Gordon, and Larry W. Hillman. *Desegregating American Schools*. New York: Longman, 1980.

Jacoby, Tamar. *Someone Else's House: America's Unfinished Struggle for Integration*. New York: Free Press, 1998.

Jones, Leon. *From Brown to Boston: Desegregation in Education, 1954-1974*. Metuchen, N.J.: Scarecrow Press, 1979.

Klein, Woody, ed. *Toward Humanity and Justice: The Writings of Kenneth B. Clark, Scholar of the 1954 "Brown v. Board of Education" Decision*. Foreword by John Hope Franklin. Westport, Conn.: Praeger, 2004.

Kluger, Richard. *Simple Justice: The History of "Brown v. Board of Education" and Black America's Struggle for Equality*. New York: Alfred A. Knopf, 1976.

Kohn, Howard. *We Had a Dream: A Tale of the Struggles for Integration in America*. New York: Simon & Schuster, 1998.

Loevy, Robert D. *To End All Segregation: The Politics of the Passage of the Civil Rights Act of 1964*. Lanham, Md.: University Press of America, 1990.

Metcalf, George R. *From Little Rock to Boston: The History of School Desegregation*. Westport, Conn.: Greenwood Press, 1983.

Molotch, Harvey. *Managed Integration: Dilemmas of Doing Good in the City*. Berkeley: University of California Press, 1972.

Patterson, Orlando. *The Ordeal of Integration: Progress and Resentment in America's "Racial" Crisis*. Washington: Civitas/Counterpoint, dist. by Publishers Group West, 1997.

Schwartz, Bernard. *Swann's Way: The School Busing Case and the Supreme Court*. New York: Oxford University Press, 1986.

Small, Stephen. *Racialized Barriers: The Black Experience in the United States and England in the 1980's*. London: Routledge, 1994.

Wicker, Tom. *Tragic Failure: Racial Integration in America*. New York: William Morrow, 1996.

Wilkinson, J. Harvie, III. *From "Brown" to "Bakke": The Supreme Court and School Integration: 1954-1978*. New York: Oxford University Press, 1979.

Wolters, Raymond. *The Burden of "Brown": Thirty Years of School Desegregation*. Knoxville: University of Tennessee Press, 1984.

Ziegler, Benjamin, ed. *Desegregation and the Supreme Court*. Boston: D. C. Heath, 1958.

## Economics

Banner-Haley, Charles T. *The Fruits of Integration: Black Middle-Class Ideology and Culture, 1960-1990*. Jackson: University Press of Mississippi, 1994.

Becker, Gary S. *The Economics of Discrimination*. 2d ed. Chicago: University of Chicago Press, 1971.

Benjamin, Lois. *The Black Elite: Facing the Color Line in the Twilight of the Twentieth Century*. Chicago: Nelson-Hall, 1991.

Bonacich, Edna. "A Theory of Middleman Minorities." *American Sociological Review* 38 (October, 1973): 583-594.

Burman, Stephen. *The Black Progress Question: Explaining the African American Predicament*. Newbury Park, Calif.: Sage Publications, 1995.

Carnoy, Martin. *Faded Dreams: The Politics and Economics of Race in America*. New York: Cambridge University Press, 1994.

Farley, Reynolds. *Blacks and Whites: Narrowing the Gap?* Cambridge, Mass.: Harvard University Press, 1984.

Feagin, Joe R., and Melvin P. Sikes. *Living with Racism: The Black Middle Class Experience*. Boston: Beacon Press, 1994.

Franklin, Raymond S., and Solomon Resnik. *The Political Economy of Racism*. New York: Holt, Rinehart and Winston, 1973.

Frazier, E. Franklin. *Black Bourgeoisie*. Glencoe, Ill.: Free Press, 1957.

Gans, Herbert. *The Urban Villagers*. Rev. ed. New York: Free Press, 1982.

Jaynes, Gerald D., and Robin M. Williams, eds. *A Common Destiny: Blacks and American Society*. Washington, D.C.: National Academy Press, 1988.

Levitan, Sar A., William B. Johnston, and Robert Taggart. *Still a Dream: The Changing Status of Blacks Since 1960*. Cambridge, Mass.: Harvard University Press, 1975.

Lewis, W. Arthur. *Racial Conflict and Economic Development*. Cambridge, Mass.: Harvard University Press, 1985.

Light, Ivan. *Immigrant Entrepreneurs: Koreans in Los Angeles*. Berkeley: University of California Press, 1988.

Mandle, Jay R. *Not Slave, Not Free: The African American Economic Experience Since the Civil War*. Durham, N.C.: Duke University Press, 1992.

Oliver, Melvin L., and Thomas M. Shapiro. *Black Wealth, White Wealth: A New Perspective on Racial Inequality*. New York: Routledge, 1995.

Perlo, Victor. *Economics of Racism U.S.A.: Roots of Black Inequality*. 2d ed. New York: International Publishers, 1976.

Pinkney, Alphonso. *The Myth of Black Progress*. New York: Cambridge University Press, 1984.

Shapiro, Thomas M. *The Hidden Cost of Being African American: How Wealth Perpetuates Inequality*. New York: Oxford University Press, 2004.

Smith, James P., and Finis R. Welch. *Closing the Gap: Forty Years of Economic Progress for Blacks*. Santa Monica, Calif.: Rand Corporation, 1986.

Squires, Gregory D. *Capital and Communities in Black and White: The Intersections of Race, Class, and Uneven Development*. Albany: State University of New York Press, 1994.

Wilson, William Julius. *The Declining Significance of Race: Blacks and Changing American Institutions*. Chicago: University of Chicago Press, 1978.

**Education**

Atkinson, Pansye S. *Brown vs. Topeka—an African American's View: Desegregation and Miseducation*. Chicago: African American Images, 1993.

Barnett, Marqueritz R., ed. *Readings on Equal Education*. New York: AMS Press, 1984.

Bell, Derrick. *Silent Covenants: "Brown v. Board of Education" and the Unfulfilled Hopes for Racial Reform*. New York: Oxford University Press, 2004.

_____, ed. *Shades of Brown: New Perspectives on School Desegregation*. New York: Teachers College Press, 1980.

Bond, Horace Mann. *Education for Freedom: A History of Lincoln University*. Princeton, N.J.: Princeton University Press, 1976.

Brown, M. Christopher, II, and Kassie Freeman, eds. *Black Colleges: New Perspectives on Policy and Practice*. Westport, Conn.: Praeger, 2004.

Clotfelter, Charles T. *After "Brown": The Rise and Retreat of School Desegregation*. Princeton, N.J.: Princeton University Press, 2004.

Fairclough, Adam. *Teaching Equality: Black Schools in the Age of Jim Crow.* Athens: University of Georgia Press, 2001.

Feagin, Joe R., et al. *The Agony of Education: Black Students at White Colleges and Universities.* New York: Routledge, 1996.

Formisano, Ronald P. *Boston Against Busing: Race, Class, and Ethnicity in the 1960's and 1970's.* Chapel Hill: University of North Carolina Press, 1991.

Gill, Walter. *Issues in African American Education.* Nashville, Tenn.: One Horn Press, 1991.

Graglia, Lino A. *Disaster by Decree: The Supreme Court Decisions on Race and the Schools.* Ithaca, N.Y.: Cornell University Press, 1976.

Hill, Leven, ed. *Black American Colleges and Universities.* Detroit, Mich.: Gale Research, 1994.

Jones-Wilson, Faustine C. *The Encyclopedia of African American Education.* Westport, Conn.: Greenwood Press, 1996.

Kozol, Jonathan. *Death at an Early Age: The Destruction of the Hearts and Minds of Negro Children in the Boston Public Schools.* Boston: Houghton, Mifflin, 1967.

Lefkowitz, Mary. *Not Out of Africa: How Afrocentrism Became an Excuse to Teach Myth.* New York: Basic Books, 1996.

Margo, Robert A. *Race and Schooling in the South, 1880-1950: An Economic History.* Chicago: University of Chicago Press, 1990.

Mwadilitu, Mwalimi I. [Alexander E. Curtis]. *Richard Allen: The First Exemplar of African American Education.* New York: ECA Associates, 1985.

Ogletree, Charles J., Jr. *All Deliberate Speed: Reflections on the First Half Century of "Brown v. Board of Education."* New York: W. W. Norton & Co., 2004.

Roebuck, Julian, and Komanduri Murty. *Historically Black Colleges and Universities: Their Place in American Higher Education.* Westport, Conn.: Praeger, 1993.

Rossell, Christine H., and Willis D. Hawley, eds. *The Consequences of School Desegregation.* Philadelphia: Temple University Press, 1983.

Samuels, Albert L. *Is Separate Unequal? Black Colleges and the Challenge to Desegregation.* Lawrence: University Press of Kansas, 2004.

Williams, Juan, and Dwayne Ashley with Shawn Rhea. *I'll Find a Way or Make One: A Tribute to Historically Black Colleges and Universities.* New York: Amistad/HarperCollins, 2004.

Wollenberg, Charles. *All Deliberate Speed: Segregation and Exclusion in California Schools, 1855-1975.* Berkeley: University of California Press, 1976.

**Employment and Labor**

Blumrosen, Alfred. *Modern Law: The Law Transmission System and Equal Employment Opportunity.* Madison: University of Wisconsin Press, 1993.

Davis, George, and Glegg Watson. *Black Life in Corporate America: Swimming in the Mainstream.* New York: Doubleday, 1985.

*Equal Employment Opportunity Act of 1972.* Washington, D.C.: U.S. Government Printing Office, 1972.

Fernandez, John P., and Jules Davis. *Race, Gender, and Rhetoric: The True State of Race and Gender Relations in Corporate America.* New York: McGraw-Hill, 1999.

Hartigan, John A., and Alexandra K. Wigdor, eds. *Fairness in Employment Testing: Validity Generalizations, Minority Issues, and the General Aptitude Test Battery.* Washington, D.C.: National Academy Press, 1989.

Kent, Ronald C., et al. *Culture, Gender, Race, and U.S. Labor History.* Westport, Conn.: Greenwood Press, 1993.

Newman, Katherine S. *No Shame in My Game: The Working Poor in the Inner City.* New York: Knopf and the Russell Sage Foundation, 1999.

Practising Law Institute. *The Civil Rights Act of 1991: Its Impact on Employment Discrimination Litigation.* New York: Author, 1992.

Royster, Deirdre A. *Race and the Invisible Hand: How White Networks Exclude Black Men from Blue-Collar Jobs.* Berkeley: University of California Press, 2003.

Sedmak, Nancy J. *Primer on Equal Employment Opportunity.* 6th ed. Washington, D.C.: Bureau of National Affairs, 1994.

Shulman, Steven, and William Darity, Jr., eds. *The Question of Discrimination: Racial Inequality in the U.S. Labor Market.* Middletown, Conn.: Wesleyan University Press, 1989.

Singer, M. *Diversity-Based Hiring: An Introduction from Legal, Ethical, and Psychological Perspectives*. Brookfield, Vt.: Ashgate, 1993.

Stith, Anthony, and Tonya A. Martin, eds. *Breaking the Glass Ceiling: Racism and Sexism in Corporate America—the Myths, the Realities and the Solutions*. Orange, N.J.: Bryant & Dillon, 1996.

Turner, Margery Austin, Michael Fix, and Raymond J. Struyk. *Opportunities Denied: Discrimination in Hiring*. Washington, D.C.: Urban Institute, 1991.

Twomey, David. *Equal Employment Opportunity Law*. 2d ed. Cincinnati: South-Western Publishing, 1990.

U.S. Equal Employment Opportunity Commission. *EEOC Compliance Manual*. Chicago: Commerce Clearing House, 1995.

Wilson, William Julius. *When Work Disappears: The World of the New Urban Poor*. New York: Knopf, 1996.

## Family and Community

Billingsley, Andrew. *Black Families in White America*. Englewood Cliffs, N.J.: Prentice-Hall, 1968.

Blackwell, James. *The Black Community: Diversity and Unity*. New York: Harper & Row, 1975.

David, Jay, ed. *Growing Up Black: From Slave Days to the Present, Twenty-five African-Americans Reveal the Trials and Triumphs of Their Childhoods*. New York: Avon Books, 1992.

Frazier, Edward Franklin. *The Negro Family in the United States*. Chicago: University of Chicago Press, 1939.

Griffin, John Howard. *Black Like Me*. Boston: Houghton Mifflin, 1961.

Haizlip, Shirlee Taylor. *The Sweeter the Juice*. New York: Simon & Schuster, 1994.

Hamblin, Ken. *Pick a Better Country: An Unassuming Colored Guy Speaks His Mind About America*. New York: Simon & Schuster, 1996.

Hill, Robert, ed. *Research on the African-American Family: A Holistic Perspective*. Westport, Conn.: Auburn House, 1993.

Horton, James Oliver. *Free People of Color: Inside the African American Community*. Washington, D.C.: Smithsonian Institution Press, 1993.

Jewell, K. Sue. *Survival of the African American Family: The Institutional Impact of U.S. Social Policy*. Westport, Conn.: Praeger, 2003.

McAdoo, Harriette Pipes, ed. *Black Families*. 3d ed. Thousand Oaks, Calif.: Sage, 1997.

McCall, Nathan. *Makes Me Wanna Holler: A Young Black Man in America*. New York: Random House, 1994.

Page, Clarence. *Showing My Color: Impolite Essays on Race and Identity*. New York: HarperCollins, 1996.

Parks, Gordon. *Born Black*. Philadelphia: Lippincott, 1971.

Staples, Robert. *Black Families at the Crossroads*. San Francisco: Jossey-Bass, 1993.

Warner, Lee H. *Free Men in an Age of Servitude: Three Generations of a Black Family*. Lexington: University Press of Kentucky, 1992.

### Hate and White Supremacy

Alexander, Charles C. *The Ku Klux Klan in the Southwest*. Norman: University of Oklahoma Press, 1995.

Almaguer, Tomás. *Racial Fault Lines: The Historical Origins of White Supremacy in California*. Berkeley: University of California Press, 1994.

Baird, Robert M., and Stuart E. Rosenbaum, eds. *Bigotry, Prejudice and Hatred: Definitions, Causes, and Solutions*. Buffalo, N.Y.: Prometheus Books, 1992.

Bennett, Lerone, Jr. *Confrontation: Black and White*. Baltimore: Penguin, 1966.

Boesel, David, and Peter H. Rossi, eds. *Cities Under Siege: An Anatomy of the Ghetto Riots, 1964-1968*. New York: Basic Books, 1971.

Bridges, Tyler. *The Rise of David Duke*. Jackson: University Press of Mississippi, 1994.

Brundage, W. Fitzhugh. *Lynching in the New South: Georgia and Virginia, 1880-1930*. Urbana: University of Illinois Press, 1993.

_____, ed. *Under Sentence of Death: Lynching in the South*. Chapel Hill: University of North Carolina Press, 1997.

Button, James W. *Black Violence: Political Impact of the 1960's Riots*. Princeton, N.J.: Princeton University Press, 1978.

Cannon, Lou. *Official Negligence: How Rodney King and the Riots Changes Los Angeles and the LAPD*. New York: Times Books, 1998.

Capeci, Dominic J., Jr. *The Harlem Riot of 1943*. Philadelphia: Temple University Press, 1977.

Chalmers, David M. *Hooded Americanism: The First Century of the Ku Klux Klan*. 3d ed. Durham, N.C.: Duke University Press, 1987.

Cobbs, Elizabeth H., and Petric J. Smith. *Long Time Coming: An Insider's Story of the Birmingham Church Bombing That Rocked the World*. Birmingham, Ala.: Crane Hill, 1994.

Connery, Robert, ed. *Urban Riots*. New York: Vintage Books, 1969.

Daniels, Jessie. *White Lies: Race, Class, Gender and Sexuality in White Supremacist Discourse*. New York: Routledge, 1997.

Davis, Daryl. *Klan-Destine Relationships: A Black Man's Odyssey in the Ku Klux Klan*. Far Hills, N.J.: New Horizon Press, 1998.

Dray, Philip. *At the Hands of Persons Unknown: The Lynching of Black America*. New York: Random House, 2002.

Feagin, Joe R., and Harlan Hahn. *Ghetto Revolts*. New York: Macmillan, 1973.

Feldberg, Michael. *The Philadelphia Riots of 1844: A Study of Ethnic Conflict*. Westport, Conn.: Greenwood Press, 1975.

Fine, Sidney. *Violence in the Model City: The Cavanaugh Administration, Race Relations and the Detroit Riot of 1967*. Ann Arbor: University of Michigan Press, 1989.

Finkelman, Paul, ed. *Lynching, Racial Violence, and Law*. New York: Garland, 1992.

Frederickson, George M. *White Supremacy: A Comparative Study in American and South African History*. New York: Oxford University Press, 1980.

Gale, Dennis E. *Understanding Urban Unrest: From Reverend King to Rodney King*. Newbury Park, Calif.: Sage Publications, 1996.

Gates, Henry Louis, Jr., ed. *Speaking of Race, Speaking of Sex: Hate Speech, Civil Rights, and Civil Liberties*. New York: New York University Press, 1994.

Ginzburg, Ralph. *100 Years of Lynchings*. Baltimore: Black Classic Press, 1997.

Gooding-Williams, Robert, ed. *Reading Rodney King/Reading Urban Uprising*. New York: Routledge, 1993.

Grimshaw, Allen D. *Racial Violence in the United States*. Chicago: Aldine Publishing, 1969.

Horne, Gerald. *Fire This Time: The Watts Uprising and the 1960's*. Charlottesville: University Press of Virginia, 1995.

Howard, Walter T. *Lynchings: Extralegal Violence in Florida During the 1930's*. London: Susquehanna University Press, 1995.

Kennedy, Stetson. *I Rode with the Ku Klux Klan: The Klan Unmasked*. Gainesville: University Presses of Florida, 1990.

Kotlowitz, Alex. *The Other Side of the River: A Story of Two Towns, a Death, and America's Dilemma*. New York: Nan A. Talese, 1998.

Kronenwetter, Michael. *United They Hate: White Supremacist Groups in America*. New York: Walker, 1992.

Lee, Alfred McClung. *Race Riot, Detroit 1943*. 1943. Reprint. New York: Octagon Books, 1968.

Levin, Jack, and Jack McDevitt. *Hate Crimes: The Rising Tide of Bigotry and Bloodshed*. New York: Plenum Press, 1993.

Los Angeles Times editors. *Understanding the Riots: Los Angeles Before and After the Rodney King Case*. Los Angeles: Los Angeles Times, 1992.

McGovern, James R. *Anatomy of a Lynching: The Killing of Claude Neal*. Baton Rouge: Louisiana State University Press, 1982.

MacLean, Nancy. *Behind the Mask of Chivalry: The Making of the Second Ku Klux Klan*. New York: Oxford University Press, 1994.

Madhubuti, Haki R., ed. *Why L.A. Happened: Implications of the '92 Los Angeles Rebellion*. Chicago: Third World Press, 1993.

Markovitz, Jonathan. *Legacies of Lynching: Racial Violence and Memory*. Minneapolis: University of Minnesota Press, 2004.

National Advisory Commission on Civil Disorders [Kerner Commission]. *Report*. New York: Bantam, 1968.

Pinkney, Alphonso. *Lest We Forget: White Hate Crimes, Howard Beach, and Other Racial Atrocities*. Chicago: Third World Press, 1994.

Porter, Bruce, and Marvin Dunn. *The Miami Riot of 1980: Crossing the Bounds*. Lexington, Mass.: D. C. Heath, 1984.

Raper, Arthur. *The Tragedy of Lynching*. New York: Arno Press, 1969.

Ridgeway, James. *Blood in the Face: The Ku Klux Klan, Aryan Nations, Nazi Skinheads, and the Rise of a New White Culture.* Rev. ed. New York: Thunder's Mouth Press, 1995.

Ruiz, Jim. *The Black Hood of the Ku Klux Klan.* San Francisco: Austin & Winfield, 1998.

Sears, David O., and John B. McConahay. *The Politics of Violence: The New Urban Blacks and the Watts Riot.* Boston: Houghton Mifflin, 1973.

Smith, John David, ed. *Disfranchisement Proposals and the Ku Klux Klan.* New York: Garland, 1993.

Southern Poverty Law Center, comp. *The Ku Klux Klan: A History of Racism and Violence.* 4th ed. Montgomery, Ala.: Klanwatch, 1991.

Stanton, Bill. *Klanwatch: Bringing the Ku Klux Klan to Justice.* New York: Weidenfeld, 1991.

Tolnay, Stewart E., and E. M. Beck. *A Festival of Violence: An Analysis of Southern Lynchings, 1882-1930.* Urbana: University of Illinois Press, 1995.

Trelease, Allen W. *White Terror: The Ku Klux Klan Conspiracy and the Southern Reconstruction.* Baton Rouge: Louisiana State University Press, 1995.

Turner, John. *The Ku Klux Klan: A History of Racism and Violence.* Montgomery, Ala.: Southern Poverty Law Center, 1982.

Wade, Wyn Craig. *The Fiery Cross: The Ku Klux Klan in America.* New York: Simon & Schuster, 1987.

Zangrando, Robert. *The NAACP Crusade Against Lynching, 1909-1950.* Philadelphia: Temple University Press, 1980.

## Housing

Bullard, Charles, J. Eugene Grigsby III, and Charles Lee, eds. *Residential Apartheid: The American Legacy.* Los Angeles: UCLA Center for Afro-American Studies, 1994.

Ellen, Ingrid Gould. *Sharing America's Neighborhoods: The Prospects for Stable Racial Integration.* Cambridge, Mass.: Harvard University Press, 2000.

Haar, Charles M. *Suburbs Under Siege: Race, Space, and Audacious Judges.* Princeton, N.J.: Princeton University Press, 1996.

Harrison, M. L. *Housing, "Race," Social Policy, and Empowerment.* Brookfield: Avebury, 1995.

Kirp, David L., John Dwyer, and Larry Rosenthal. *Our Town: Race, Housing, and the Soul of Suburbia.* New Brunswick, N.J.: Rutgers University Press, 1996.

Kushner, James A. *Fair Housing: Discrimination in Real Estate, Community Development, and Revitalization.* New York: McGraw-Hill, 1983.

Metcalf, Georg. *Fair Housing Comes of Age.* New York: Greenwood Press, 1988.

Schwemm, Robert G., ed. *The Fair Housing Act After Twenty Years.* New Haven, Conn.: Yale Law School, 1989.

Yinger, John. *Closed Doors, Opportunities Lost: The Continuing Costs of Housing Discrimination.* New York: Russell Sage Foundation, 1995.

**Martin Luther King, Jr.**

Ansbro, John J. *Martin Luther King, Jr.: The Making of a Mind.* Maryknoll, N.Y.: Orbis Books, 1982.

Branch, Taylor. *Parting the Waters: America in the King Years, 1954-1963.* New York: Simon & Schuster, 1988.

_____. *Pillar of Fire: America in the King Years, 1963-65.* New York: Simon & Schuster, 1998.

Burns, Stewart. *To the Mountaintop: Martin Luther King, Jr.'s Sacred Mission to Save America, 1955-1968.* New York: HarperSanFrancisco, 2004.

Clark, Kenneth B., ed. *The Negro Protest: James Baldwin, Malcolm X, Martin Luther King Talk with Kenneth B. Clark.* Boston: Beacon Press, 1963.

Colaiaco, James A. *Martin Luther King, Jr.: Apostle of Militant Nonviolence.* New York: St. Martin's Press, 1988.

Fairclough, Adam. *Martin Luther King, Jr.* Athens: University of Georgia Press, 1990.

_____. *To Redeem the Soul of America: The Southern Christian Leadership Conference and Martin Luther King, Jr.* Athens: University of Georgia Press, 1987.

Frady, Marshall. *Martin Luther King, Jr.* New York: Penguin Group, 2002.

Frank, Gerold. *An American Death: The True Story of the Assassination of Dr. Martin Luther King, Jr.* Garden City, N.Y.: Doubleday, 1972.

Garrow, David J. *Bearing the Cross: Martin Luther King, Jr., and the Southern Christian Leadership Conference.* New York: William Morrow, 1986.

_____. *Protest at Selma: Martin Luther King, Jr., and the Voting Rights Act of 1965.* New Haven, Conn.: Yale University Press, 1978.

Hanigan, James P. *Martin Luther King, Jr., and the Foundations of Nonviolence.* Lanham, Md.: University Press of America, 1984.

Hansen, Drew D. *The Dream: Martin Luther King, Jr., and the Speech That Inspired a Nation.* New York: Ecco, 2003.

King, Martin Luther, Jr. *Stride Toward Freedom: The Montgomery Story.* New York: Harper & Row, 1958.

Kotz, Nick. *Judgment Days: Lyndon Baines Johnson, Martin Luther King, Jr., and the Laws That Changed America.* Boston: Houghton Mifflin, 2005.

Lewis, David L. *King: A Critical Biography.* New York: Praeger, 1970.

Ling, Peter J. *Martin Luther King, Jr.* New York: Routledge, 2002.

McPhee, Penelope, and Flip Schulke. *King Remembered.* New York: Pocket Books, 1986.

Oates, Stephen B. *Let the Trumpet Sound: The Life of Martin Luther King, Jr.* New York: Harper & Row, 1982.

Peake, Thomas R. *Keeping the Dream Alive: A History of the Southern Christian Leadership Conference from King to the Nineteen-Eighties.* New York: Peter Lang, 1987.

Sunnemark, Fredrik. *Ring Out Freedom! The Voice of Martin Luther King, Jr., and the Making of the Civil Rights Movement.* Bloomington: Indiana University Press, 2004.

Ward, Brian, and Tony Badger. *The Making of Martin Luther King and the Civil Rights Movement.* New York: New York University Press, 1996.

## The Media

Bogle, Donald. *Blacks in American Films and Television.* New York: Garland Publishing, 1988.

_____. *Bright Boulevards, Bold Dreams: The Story of Black Hollywood*. New York: One World Ballantine Books, 2005.

_____. *Primetime Blues: African Americans on Network Television*. New York: Farrar, Straus and Giroux, 2001.

_____. *Toms, Coons, Mulattoes, Mammies, and Bucks*. New York: Continuum, 1992.

Campbell, Christopher P. *Race, Myth, and the News*. Thousand Oaks, Calif.: Sage Publications, 1995.

Center for Integration and Improvement of Journalism. *News Watch: A Critical Look at People of Color*. San Francisco: San Francisco State University Press, 1994.

Chideya, Farai. *Don't Believe the Hype: Fighting Cultural Misinformation About African Americans*. New York: Plume, 1995.

Cripps, Thomas. *Slow Fade to Black: The Negro in American Film, 1900-1942*. New York: Oxford University Press, 1993.

_____. *Making Movies Black: The Hollywood Message Movie from World War II to the Civil Rights Era*. New York: Oxford University Press, 1993.

Dennis, Everette E., and Edward C. Pease, eds. *The Media in Black and White*. New Brunswick, N.J.: Transaction, 1997.

Gabriel, John. *Whitewash: Racialized Politics and the Media*. New York: Routledge, 1998.

Gates, Henry Louis, Jr. *The Signifying Monkey: A Theory of Afro-American Literary Criticism*. New York: Oxford University Press, 1988.

Gershoni, Yekutiel. *Africans on African-Americans: The Creation and Uses of an African-American Myth*. New York: New York University Press, 1997.

Hill, George, Lorraine Raglin, and Chas Floyd Johnson. *Black Women in Television*. New York: Garland Publishing, 1990.

Hutchinson, Janis Faye, ed. *Cultural Portrayals of African Americans: Creating an Ethnic/Racial Identity*. Westport, Conn.: Bergin & Garvey, 1997.

Lhamon, W. T., Jr. *Raising Cain: Blackface Performance from Jim Crow to Hip Hop*. Cambridge, England: Cambridge University Press, 1998.

Lusane, Clarence. *Race in the Global Era: African Americans at the Millennium*. Boston: South End Press, 1997.

Mintz, Sidney W., and Richard Price. *The Birth of African-American Culture*. Boston: Beacon Press, 1992.

Rocchio, Vincent F. *Reel Racism: Confronting Hollywood's Construction of Afro-American Culture*. Boulder, Colo.: Westview Press, 2000.

Ross, Karen. *Black and White Media: Black Images in Popular Film and Television*. Cambridge, Mass.: Polity Press, 1996.

Torres, Sasha, ed. *Living Color: Race and Television in the United States*. Durham, N.C.: Duke University Press, 1998.

Tyler, Bruce Michael. *From Harlem to Hollywood: The Struggle for Racial and Cultural Democracy, 1920-1943*. New York: Garland, 1992.

**Military**

Bogart, Leo. *Social Research and Desegregation of the United States Army*. Chicago: Markham, 1969.

Brandt, Nat. *Harlem at War: The Black Experience in WWII*. Syracuse, N.Y.: Syracuse University Press, 1996.

Dalifiume, Richard. *Desegregation of the U.S. Armed Forces: Fighting on Two Fronts, 1939-1953*. Columbia: University of Missouri Press, 1969.

Mershon, Sherie, and Steven L. Schlossman. *Foxholes and Color Lines: Desegregating the U.S. Armed Forces*. Baltimore: Johns Hopkins University Press, 1998.

Moskos, Charles C. *All That We Can Be: Black Leadership and Racial Integration the Army Way*. New York: Basic Books, 1996.

Nalty, Bernard C. *Strength for the Fight: A History of Black Americans in the Military*. New York: Free Press, 1986.

Stillman, Richard. *Integraton of the Negro in the U.S. Armed Forces*. New York: Frederick A. Praeger, 1968.

U.S. Department of Defense. Office of the Deputy Assistant Secretary of Defense for Civilian Personnel Policy/Equal Opportunity. *Black Americans in Defense of Our Nation*. Washington, D.C.: Government Printing Office, 1991.

**Politics**

Conti, Joseph G., and Brad Stetson. *Challenging the Civil Rights Establishment: Profiles of a New Black Vanguard*. Westport, Conn.: Praeger, 1993.

Cross, Theodore. *The Black Power Imperative: Racial Inequality and the Politics of Nonviolence*. New York: Faulkner, 1984.

Dawson, Michael C. *Behind the Mule: Race and Class in African-American Politics*. Princeton, N.J.: Princeton University Press, 1994.

Faryna, Stan, Brad Stetson, and Joseph G. Conti, eds. *Black and Right: The New Bold Voice of Black Conservatives in America*. Westport, Conn.: Greenwood, 1997.

Gilroy, Paul, and Houston A. Baker. *There Ain't No Black in the Union Jack: The Cultural Politics of Race and Nation*. Chicago: Chicago University Press, 1991.

Ginzberg, Eli, and Alfred S. Eichner. *Troublesome Presence: Democracy and Black Americans*. New Brunswick, N.J.: Transaction, 1993.

Hahn, Steven. *A Nation Under Our Feet: Black Political Struggles in the Rural South, from Slavery to the Great Migration*. Cambridge, Mass.: Belknap Press of Harvard University Press, 2003.

Hine, Darlene Clark. *Black Victory: The Rise and Fall of the White Primary in Texas*. Millwood, N.Y.: KTO Press, 1979.

Jewell, K. Sue. *From Mammy to Miss America and Beyond: Cultural Images and the Shaping of U.S. Social Policy*. New York: Routledge, 1993.

Lawson, Steven F. *Black Ballots: Voting Rights in the South, 1944-1969*. New York: Columbia University Press, 1976.

_____. *In Pursuit of Power: Southern Blacks and Electoral Politics, 1965-1982*. New York: Columbia University Press, 1985.

McKissick, Floyd B. *Three-fifths of a Man*. New York: Macmillan, 1969.

Marable, Manning. *Beyond Black and White: Transforming African-American Politics*. New York: Verso, 1995.

_____. *Race, Reform, and Rebellion: The Second Reconstruction in Black America, 1945-1991*. Jackson: University Press of Mississippi, 1991.

Merelman, Richard M. *Representing Black Culture: Racial Conflict and Cultural Politics in the United States*. New York: Routledge, 1995.

Norton, Philip. *Black Nationalism in America*. Hull, Humberside, England: Department of Politics, University of Hull, 1983.

Ogbar, Jeffrey O. G. *Black Power: Radical Politics and African American Identity.* Baltimore: Johns Hopkins University Press, 2004.

Orfield, Gary, and Carol Ashkinaze. *The Closing Door: Conservative Policy and Black Opportunity.* Chicago: University of Chicago Press, 1991.

Perkins, Joseph, ed. *A Conservative Agenda for Black Americans.* Washington, D.C.: Heritage Foundation, 1990.

Persons, Georgia A., ed. *Dilemmas of Black Politics: Issues of Leadership and Strategy.* New York: HarperCollins, 1993.

Reed, Adolph L. *The Jesse Jackson Phenomenon: The Crisis of Purpose in Afro-American Politics.* New Haven, Conn.: Yale University Press, 1986.

Singh, Robert. *The Farrakhan Phenomenon: Race, Reaction, and the Paranoid Style in American Politics.* Washington, D.C.: Georgetown University Press, 1997.

Smith, T. Alexander, and Lenahan O'Connell. *Black Anxiety, White Guilt, and the Politics of Status Frustration.* Westport, Conn.: Praeger, 1997.

Sonenshein, Raphael J. *Politics in Black and White: Race and Power in Los Angeles.* Princeton, N.J.: Princeton University Press, 1993.

Swain, Carol M. *Black Faces, Black Interests: The Representation of African Americans in Congress.* Cambridge, Mass.: Harvard University Press, 1993.

Tate, Katherine. *From Protest to Politics: The New Black Voters in American Elections.* Cambridge, Mass.: Harvard University Press, 1994.

Walton, Hanes, Jr. *Black Politics.* Philadelphia: J. B. Lippincott, 1972.

## Religion and the Black Church

Allen, Richard. *The Life, Experience, and Gospel Labors of the Right Reverent Richard Allen.* 1833. Reprint. Nashville, Tenn.: Abingdon Press, 1983.

Angell, Stephen W., ed., and Anthony B. Pinn. *Social Protest Thought in the African Methodist Episcopal Church, 1862-1939.* Knoxville: University of Tennessee Press, 2000.

Campbell, James T. *Songs of Zion: The African Methodist Episcopal Church in the United States and South Africa.* New York: Oxford University Press, 1995.

Chireau, Yvonne, and Nathaniel Deutsch, eds. *Black Zion: African American Religious Encounters with Judaism.* New York: Oxford University Press, 2000.

Cone, James H. *Black Theology and Black Power.* New York: Seabury Press, 1969.

_____. *A Black Theology of Liberation.* 20th anniversary ed. Maryknoll, N.Y.: Orbis Books, 1990.

Dodson, Jualynne E. *Engendering Church: Women, Power, and the AME Church.* Lanham, Md.: Rowman & Littlefield, 2002.

Evans, James H., Jr. *Spiritual Empowerment in Afro-American Literature.* Lewiston, N.Y.: Edwin Mellen, 1987.

Findlay, James F., Jr. *Church People in the Struggle: The National Council of Churches and the Black Freedom Movement, 1950-1970.* New York: Oxford University Press, 1993.

Fitts, LeRoy. *A History of Black Baptists.* Nashville, Tenn.: Broadman Press, 1985.

Frazier, E. Franklin, and C. Eric Lincoln. *The Negro Church in America: The Black Church Since Frazier.* New York: Schocken Books, 1974.

George, Carol V. R. *Segregated Sabbaths: Richard Allen and the Rise of Independent Black Churches, 1760-1840.* New York: Oxford University Press, 1973.

Harvey, Paul. *Redeeming the South: Religious Cultures and Racial Identities Among Southern Baptists, 1865-1925.* New York: Oxford University Press, 1997.

Lee, Martha F. *The Nation of Islam: An American Millenarian Movement.* Lewiston, N.Y.: Edwin Mellen Press, 1988.

Lincoln, C. Eric. *The Black Muslims in America.* Rev. ed. Boston: Beacon Press, 1973.

Lincoln, C. Eric, and Lawrence H. Mamiya. *The Black Church in the African-American Experience.* Durham, N.C.: Duke University Press, 1990.

Little, Lawrence S. *Disciples of Liberty: The African Methodist Episcopal Church in the Age of Imperialism, 1884-1916.* Knoxville: University of Tennessee Press, 2000.

Luker, Ralph E. *The Social Gospel in Black and White: American Racial Reform, 1885-1912.* Chapel Hill: University of North Carolina Press, 1991.

Marsh, Clifton E. *From Black Muslims to Muslims: The Transition from Separatism to Islam, 1930-1980.* Metuchen, N.J.: Scarecrow Press, 1984.

Mitchell, Henry H. *Black Church Beginnings: The Long-Hidden Realities of the First Years.* Grand Rapids, Mich.: W. B. Eerdmans, 2004.

Muhammad, Elijah. *The Supreme Wisdom.* 2 vols. Brooklyn: Temple of Islam, 1957.

Mukenge, Ida Rousseau. *The Black Church in Urban America.* Lanham, Md.: University Press of America, 1983.

Nelson, Timothy J. *Every Time I Feel the Spirit: Religious Experience and Ritual in an African American Church.* New York: New York University Press, 2005.

Paris, Peter J. *The Social Teaching of the Black Churches.* Philadelphia: Fortress Press, 1985.

Phillips, C. H. *The History of the Colored Methodist Episcopal Church in America.* 1898. Reprint. New York: Arno Press, 1972.

Pinn, Anthony B. *The Black Church in the Post-Civil Rights Era.* Maryknoll, N.Y.: Orbis Books, 2002.

Sernett, Milton C. *Afro-American Religious History: A Documentary Witness.* Durham, N.C.: Duke University Press, 1985.

Seymour, Robert E., Jr. *"Whites Only": A Pastor's Retrospective on Signs of the New South.* Valley Forge, Pa.: Judson Press, 1991.

Smith, Theophus H. *Conjuring Culture: Biblical Formations of Black America.* New York: Oxford University Press, 1994.

Turner, Richard Brent. *Islam in the African American Experience.* Bloomington: Indiana University Press, 1997.

Wesley, Charles. *Richard Allen: Apostle of Freedom.* Washington, D.C.: Associated Publishers, 1935.

White, Vibert L., Jr. *Inside the Nation of Islam: A Historical and Personal Testimony by a Black Muslim.* Gainesville: University Press of Florida, 2001.

Williams, Juan, and Quinton Dixie. *This Far by Faith: Stories from the African-American Religious Experience.* New York: William Morrow, 2003.

Wilmore, Gayraud S., ed. *African American Religious Studies: An Interdisciplinary Anthology.* Durham, N.C.: Duke University Press, 1989.

_____. *Black Religion and Black Radicalism.* 3d ed. Rev. and enlarged. Maryknoll, N.Y.: Orbis Books, 1998.

## Slavery

Abbott, Richard H. *Cotton and Capital: Boston Businessmen and Antislavery Reform, 1854-1868.* Amherst: University of Massachusetts Press, 1991.

Angle, Paul M., ed. *Created Equal? The Complete Lincoln-Douglas Debates of 1858.* Chicago: University of Chicago Press, 1958.

Aptheker, Herbert. *American Negro Slave Revolts.* 1943. Rev. ed. New York: Columbia University Press, 1969.

Ball, Edward. *Slaves in the Family.* New York: Farrar, Straus & Giroux, 1998.

Barber, John Warner. *A History of the Amistad Captives.* New York: Arno Press, 1969.

Barnes, Gilbert Hobbs. *The Antislavery Impulse: 1830-1844.* New York: Harcourt, Brace & World, 1964.

Bender, Thomas, ed. *The Antislavery Debate: Capitalism and Abolitionism as a Problem in Historical Interpretation.* Berkeley: University of California Press, 1992.

Berlin, Ira. *Many Thousands Gone: The First Two Centuries of Slavery in North America.* Cambridge, Mass.: Belknap Press, 1998.

Berlin, Ira, et al. *Slaves No More: Three Essays on Emancipation and the Civil War.* Cambridge, England: Cambridge University Press, 1992.

Blackburn, Robin. *The Overthrow of Colonial Slavery, 1776-1848.* New York: Verso, 1988.

Blassingame, John W. *The Slave Community: Plantation Life in the Antebellum South.* New York: Oxford University Press, 1972.

Blassingame, John W., and John R. McKivigan, eds. *The Frederick Douglass Papers.* Series 1, *Speeches, Debates, and Interviews.* Vol. 3, *1855-1863.* New Haven, Conn.: Yale University Press, 1991.

Blight, David W., ed. *Passages to Freedom: The Underground Railroad in History and Memory*. Washington, D.C.: Smithsonian Books in association with the National Underground Railroad Freedom Center, Cincinnati, Ohio, 2004.

Bontemps, Arna, ed. *Great Slave Narratives*. Boston: Beacon Press, 1969.

Boskin, Joseph. *Into Slavery: Racial Decisions in the Virginia Colony*. Philadelphia: J. B. Lippincott, 1976.

Boyer, Richard O. *The Legend of John Brown: A Biography and a History*. New York: Alfred A. Knopf, 1972.

Buckmaster, Henrietta. *Let My People Go: The Story of the Underground Railroad and the Growth of the Abolition Movement*. Boston: Beacon Press, 1941.

Campbell, Stanley. *The Slave Catchers: Enforcement of the Fugitive Slave Law, 1850-1860*. Chapel Hill: University of North Carolina Press, 1970.

Catterall, Helen T., ed. *Judicial Cases Concerning American Slavery and the Negro*. 5 vols. New York: Octagon Books, 1968.

Curtin, Philip D. *The Atlantic Slave Trade*. Madison: University of Wisconsin Press, 1969.

Daniel, Pete. *The Shadow of Slavery: Peonage in the South, 1901-1969*. Urbana: University of Illinois Press, 1972.

Davis, David Brion. *The Problem of Slavery in the Age of Revolution, 1770-1823*. Ithaca, N.Y.: Cornell University Press, 1975.

_____. *The Problem of Slavery in Western Culture*. Ithaca, N.Y.: Cornell University Press, 1966.

_____. *Slavery and Human Progress*. New York: Oxford University Press, 1984.

Duberman, Martin, ed. *The Antislavery Vanguard: New Essays on the Abolitionists*. Princeton, N.J.: Princeton University Press, 1965.

Elkins, Stanley M. *Slavery: A Problem in American Institutional and Intellectual Life*. Chicago: University of Chicago Press, 1959.

Eltis, David, and James Walvin, eds. *The Abolition of the Atlantic Slave Trade: Origins and Effects in Europe, Africa, and the Americas*. Madison: University of Wisconsin Press, 1981.

Faust, Drew Glipin. *The Ideology of Slavery: Proslavery Thought in the Antebellum South, 1830-1860*. Baton Rouge: Louisiana State University Press, 1981.

Filler, Louis. *The Crusade Against Slavery, 1830-1860*. New York: Harper & Row, 1960.

Finkelman, Paul, ed. *Slavery and the Founders: Race and Liberty in the Age of Jefferson*. Armonk, N.Y.: M. E. Sharpe, 1996.

Finley, Moses I. *Ancient Slavery and Modern Ideology*. New York: Viking Press, 1980.

Fogel, Robert. *Without Consent or Contract: The Rise and Fall of American Slavery*. New York: W. W. Norton, 1989.

Franklin, Raymond S. *Shadows of Race and Class*. Minneapolis: University of Minnesota Press, 1991.

Friedman, Lawrence J. *Gregarious Saints: Self and Community in American Abolitionism, 1830-1870*. New York: Cambridge University Press, 1982.

Frost, J. William, ed. *The Quaker Origins of Antislavery*. Norwood, Pa.: Norwood Editions, 1980.

Gara, Larry. *The Liberty Line: The Legend of the Underground Railroad*. Lexington: University of Kentucky Press, 1961.

Genovese, Eugene D. *Roll, Jordan, Roll: The World the Slaves Made*. New York: Pantheon Books, 1974.

_____. *The Slaveholders' Dilemma: Freedom and Progress in Southern Conservative Thought, 1820-1860*. Columbia: University of South Carolina Press, 1992.

Giddings, Joshua R. *The Exiles of Florida: Or, The Crimes Committed by Our Government Against the Maroons Who Fled from South Carolina and Other Slave States, Seeking Protection Under Spanish Laws*. 1858. Reprint. Gainesville: University of Florida Press, 1964.

Goldwin, Robert A., and Art Kaufman. *Slavery and Its Consequences: The Constitution, Equality, and Race*. Washington, D.C.: American Enterprise Institute Press, 1988.

Goodheart, Lawrence, Richard D. Brown, and Stephen Rabe, eds. *Slavery in American Society*. 3d ed. Lexington, Mass.: Heath, 1993.

Goodman, Paul. *Of One Blood: Abolitionism and the Origins of Racial Equality*. Berkeley: University of California Press, 1998.

Gordon-Reed, Annette, et al. *Slavery and the American South: Essays and Commentaries*. Edited by Winthrop D. Jordan. Jackson: University Press of Mississippi, 2003.

Gutman, Herbert. *The Black Family in Slavery and Freedom, 1750-1925*. New York: Pantheon, 1976.

Hagedorn, Ann. *Beyond the River: The Untold Story of the Heroes of the Underground Railroad*. New York: Simon & Schuster, 2002.

Harris, Marvin. *Patterns of Race Relations in America*. New York: Walker, 1964.

Harrold, Stanley. *The Rise of Aggressive Abolitionism: Addresses to the Slaves*. Lexington: University Press of Kentucky, 2004.

Hoetink, H. *Slavery and Race Relations in the Americas: Notes on Their Nature and Nexus*. New York: Harper & Row, 1973.

Holzer, Harold, ed. *The Lincoln-Douglas Debates: The First Complete, Unexpurgated Text*. New York: HarperCollins, 1993.

Horowitz, David. *Uncivil Wars: The Controversy over Reparations for Slavery*. San Francisco: Encounter Books, 2002.

Horton, James Oliver, and Lois E. Horton. *Slavery and the Making of America*. New York: Oxford University Press, 2005.

Howard, Warren S. *American Slavers and the Federal Law: 1837-1862*. Berkeley: University of California Press, 1963.

Huggins, Nathan Irvin. *Slave and Citizen: The Life of Frederick Douglass*. Boston: Little, Brown, 1980.

James, Sydney V. *A People Among Peoples: Quaker Benevolence in Eighteenth Century America*. Cambridge, Mass.: Harvard University Press, 1963.

Jeffrey, Julie Roy. *The Great Silent Army of Abolitionism: Ordinary Women in the Antislavery Movement*. Chapel Hill: University of North Carolina Press, 1998.

Jenkins, William S. *Pro-Slavery Thought in the Old South*. Chapel Hill: University of North Carolina Press, 1935.

Johnson, Walter. *Soul by Soul: Life Inside the Antebellum Slave Market*. Cambridge, Mass.: Harvard University Press, 1999.

Kolchin, Peter. *American Slavery: 1619-1877*. New York: Hill & Wang, 1993.

Kraditor, Aileen S. *Means and Ends in American Abolitionism: Garrison and His Critics on Strategy and Tactics, 1834-1850*. New York: Vintage Books, 1970.

Kraut, Alan M., ed. *Crusaders and Compromisers: Essays on the Relationship of the Antislavery Struggle to the Antebellum Party System*. Westport, Conn.: Greenwood Press, 1983.

Levine, Alan J. *Race Relations Within Western Expansion*. Westport, Conn.: Praeger, 1996.

Litwack, Leon F. *Been in the Storm So Long: The Aftermath of Slavery*. New York: Alfred A. Knopf, 1979.

_____. *North of Slavery: The Negro in the Free States: 1790-1860*. Chicago: University of Chicago Press, 1961.

McGary, Howard, and Bill E. Lawson. *Between Slavery and Freedom: Philosophy and American Slavery*. Bloomington: Indiana University Press, 1992.

McKivigan, John R. *The War Against Proslavery Religion: Abolitionism and the Northern Churches, 1830-1865*. Ithaca, N.Y.: Cornell University Press, 1984.

MacLeod, Duncan J. *Slavery, Race, and the American Revolution*. London: Cambridge University Press, 1974.

McManus, Edgar J. *A History of Negro Slavery in New York*. Syracuse, N.Y.: Syracuse University Press, 1966.

Martin, Christopher. *The "Amistad" Affair*. New York: Abelard-Schuman, 1970.

Martin, Waldo E. *The Mind of Frederick Douglass*. Chapel Hill: University of North Carolina Press, 1984.

Mayer, Henry. *All on Fire: William Lloyd Garrison and the Abolition of Slavery*. New York: St. Martin's Press, 1998.

Melish, Joanne Pope. *Disowning Slavery: Gradual Emancipation and "Race" in New England, 1780-1860*. Ithaca, N.Y.: Cornell University Press, 1998.

Meltzer, Milton, ed. *Frederick Douglass, in His Own Words*. San Diego, Calif.: Harcourt, Brace, 1995.

Merrill, Walter M. *Against Wind and Tide: A Biography of William Lloyd Garrison*. Cambridge, Mass.: Harvard University Press, 1963.

Morgan, Edmund S. *American Slavery, American Freedom: The Ordeal of Colonial Virginia*. New York: W. W. Norton, 1975.

Morris, Thomas D. *Free Men All: The Personal Liberty Laws of the North, 1780-1861*. Baltimore: Johns Hopkins University Press, 1974.

Mullin, Michael. *Africa in America: Slave Acculturation and Resistance in the American South and the British Caribbean, 1736-1831*. Urbana: University of Illinois Press, 1992.

Newman, Richard S. *The Transformation of American Abolitionism: Fighting Slavery in the Early Republic*. Chapel Hill: University of North Carolina Press, 2002.

Nye, Russel B. *William Lloyd Garrison and the Humanitarian Reformers*. Boston: Little, Brown, 1955.

Oakes, James. *The Ruling Race: A History of American Slaveholders*. New York: Alfred A. Knopf, 1982.

_____. *Slavery and Freedom: An Interpretation of the Old South*. New York: Alfred A. Knopf, 1990.

Owen, Robert Dale. *The Wrong of Slavery, the Right of Emancipation, and the Future of the African Race in the United States*. Philadelphia: J. B. Lippincott, 1864.

Owens, William A. *Black Mutiny: The Revolt on the Schooner "Amistad."* Philadelphia: Pilgrim Press, 1968.

Patterson, Orlando. *Slavery and Social Death: A Comparative Study*. Cambridge, Mass.: Harvard University Press, 1982.

_____. *The Sociology of Slavery*. Rutherford, N.J.: Fairleigh Dickinson University Press, 1975.

Perry, Lewis, and Michael Fellman, eds. *Antislavery Reconsidered: New Perspectives on the Abolitionists*. Baton Rouge: Louisiana State University Press, 1979.

Peterson, Merrill D. *John Brown: The Legend Revisited*. Charlottesville: University of Virginia Press, 2002.

Phillips, Ulrich B. *American Negro Slavery*. Baton Rouge: Louisiana State University Press, 1966.

Phillips, William D. *Slavery from Roman Times to the Early Transatlantic Trade*. Minneapolis: University of Minnesota Press, 1985.

Quarles, Benjamin. *Black Abolitionists*. New York: Oxford University Press, 1969.

Rawley, James A. *The Transatlantic Slave Trade: A History*. New York: W. W. Norton, 1981.

Reynolds, David S. *John Brown, Abolitionist: The Man Who Killed Slavery, Sparked the Civil War, and Seeded Civil Rights*. New York: Alfred A. Knopf, 2005.

Richards, Leonard L. *The Slave Power: The Free North and Southern Domination, 1780-1860*. Baton Rouge: Louisiana State University Press, 2000.

Rogers, William B. *"We Are All Together Now": Frederick Douglass, William Lloyd Garrison, and the Prophetic Tradition.* New York: Garland, 1995.

Schwartz, Philip J. *Twice Condemned: Slaves and the Criminal Laws of Virginia, 1705-1865.* Baton Rouge: Louisiana State University Press, 1988.

Shaw, Robert B. *A Legal History of Slavery in the United States.* Potsdam, N.Y.: Northern Press, 1991.

Siebert, Wilbur H. *The Underground Railroad from Slavery to Freedom.* 1898. Reprint. New York: Arno Press, 1968.

Smith, John D. *Black Slavery in the Americas: An Interdisciplinary Bibliography, 1865-1980.* 2 vols. Westport, Conn.: Greenwood Press, 1982.

Sorin, Gerald. *Abolitionism: A New Perspective.* New York: Praeger, 1972.

Stampp, Kenneth M. *The Peculiar Institution: Slavery in the Ante-Bellum South.* New York: Alfred A. Knopf, 1956.

Stewart, James Brewer. *Holy Warriors: The Abolitionists and American Slavery.* New York: Hill & Wang, 1976.

_____. *William Lloyd Garrison and the Challenge of Emancipation.* Arlington Heights, Ill.: Harlan Davidson, 1992.

Still, William. *The Underground Railroad.* 1872. Reprint. Chicago: Johnson, 1972.

Stuckey, Sterling. *Slave Culture.* New York: Oxford University Press, 1987.

Styron, William. *Confessions of Nat Turner.* New York: Random House, 1967.

Thomas, John L. *The Liberator: William Lloyd Garrison, a Biography.* Boston: Little, Brown, 1963.

Tise, Larry E. *Proslavery: A History of the Defense of Slavery in America, 1701-1840.* Athens: University of Georgia Press, 1987.

Tushnet, Mark V. *The American Law of Slavery, 1810-1860: Considerations of Humanity and Interest.* Princeton, N.J.: Princeton University Press, 1981.

Washington, Booker T. *Up from Slavery.* 1901. Reprint. New York: Gramercy Books, 1993.

Watson, Alan. *Slave Law in the Americas.* Athens: University of Georgia Press, 1989.

White, Shane. *Somewhat More Independent: The End of Slavery in New York City, 1770-1810*. Athens: University of Georgia Press, 1991.

Wilson, Carol. *Freedom at Risk: The Kidnapping of Free Blacks in America, 1780-1865*. Lexington: University Press of Kentucky, 1994.

Winbush, Raymond A., ed. *Should America Pay? Slavery and the Raging Debate on Reparations*. New York: Amistad, 2003.

Woodward, C. Vann. *American Counterpoint: Slavery and Racism in the North-South Dialogue*. Boston: Little, Brown, 1971.

Zilversmit, Arthur. *The First Emancipation: The Abolition of Slavery in the North*. Chicago: University of Chicago Press, 1967.

### The South and Segregation

Baer, Hans A., and Yvonne Jones, eds. *African Americans in the South: Issues of Race, Class, and Gender*. Athens: University of Georgia Press, 1992.

Bartley, Numan V. *The New South: 1945-1980*. Baton Rouge: Louisiana State University Press, 1995.

Bayor, Ronald H. *Race and the Shaping of Twentieth-Century Atlanta*. Chapel Hill: University of North Carolina Press, 1996.

Clinton, Catherine. *The Plantation Mistress: Woman's World in the Old South*. New York: Pantheon Books, 1982.

Davis, Allison, Burleigh B. Gardner, and Mary R. Gardner. *Deep South: A Social Anthropological Study of Caste and Class*. Chicago: University of Chicago Press, 1941.

Dollard, John. *Caste and Class in a Southern Town*. New Haven, Conn.: Yale University Press, 1947.

Fossett, Mark A., and Therese Siebert. *Long Time Coming: Racial Inequality in the Nonmetropolitan South, 1940-1990*. Boulder, Colo.: Westview Press, 1997.

Fox-Genovese, Elizabeth. *Within the Plantation Household: Black and White Women of the Old South*. Chapel Hill: University of North Carolina Press, 1988.

Goldfield, David R. *Black, White, and Southern: Race Relations in Southern Culture, 1940 to the Present*. Baton Rouge: Louisiana State University Press, 1990.

_____. *Region, Race, and Cities: Interpreting the Urban South*. Baton Rouge: Louisiana State University Press, 1997.

Hale, Grace Elizabeth. *Making Whiteness: The Culture of Segregation in the South, 1890-1940.* New York: Pantheon, 1998.

McLaurin, Melton A. *Separate Pasts: Growing Up White in the Segregated South.* Athens: University of Georgia Press, 1987.

McMillen, Neil R. *Dark Journey: Black Mississippians in the Age of Jim Crow.* Urbana: University of Illinois Press, 1990.

Newby, I. A. *Jim Crow's Defense.* Baton Rouge: Louisiana State University Press, 1965.

Odum, Howard W. *Race and Rumors of Race: The American South in the Early Forties.* Baltimore: Johns Hopkins University Press, 1997.

Packard, Jerrold M. *American Nightmare: The History of Jim Crow.* New York: St. Martin's Press, 2002.

Perman, Michael. *Struggle for Mastery: Disfranchisement in the South, 1888-1908.* Chapel Hill: University of North Carolina Press, 2001.

Stokes, Melvyn, and Rick Halpern, eds. *Race and Class in the American South Since 1890.* Providence, R.I.: Berg, 1994.

Williamson, Joel. *A Rage for Order: Black-White Relations in the American South Since Emancipation.* New York: Oxford University Press, 1986.

Wilson, Theodore B. *The Black Codes of the South.* Tuscaloosa: University of Alabama Press, 1965.

Woods, Jeff. *Black Struggle, Red Scare: Segregation and Anti-communism in the South, 1948-1968.* Baton Rouge: Louisiana State University Press, 2003.

Woodward, C. Vann. *The Strange Career of Jim Crow.* Afterword by William S. McFeely. New York: Oxford University Press, 2002.

# Time Line of African American History

| Year | Event |
|------|-------|
| 1619 | First Africans are brought to the colony of Virginia as indentured servants. |
| 1641 | Massachusetts Bay Colony recognizes the legality of slavery. |
| 1662 | Virginia legislature rules that children of unions of slave and free parents are slave or free according to their mothers' status. |
| 1664 | Maryland enacts the first law outlawing marriage between white women and black men. |
| 1688 | Pennsylvania Mennonites protest slavery. |
| 1691 | Virginia law restricts manumissions to prevent the growth of a free black class. |
| 1712 | Slave revolt in New York results in the execution of twenty-one slaves and the suicides of six others. |
| 1723 | Virginia denies African Americans the right to vote. |
| 1739 | South Carolina slaves rise up in Stono Rebellion (September 9). |
| 1775 | First abolitionist organization in the United States, the Pennsylvania Society for the Abolition of Slavery, is formed (April 14). |
| 1784 | First African American Masonic lodge is founded in Boston. |
| 1786 | Underground Railroad is started. |
| 1787 | The U.S. Constitution drafted in Philadelphia does not mention slavery by name but contains several clauses alluding to the existence of slaves and the slave trade. |
| 1787 | Free African Society is founded in Pennsylvania. |
| 1787 | Northwest Ordinance, governing the organization of the Northwest Territories, disallows slavery in the territories (July 13). |
| 1793 | Virginia outlaws entry of free African Americans into the state. |

| Year | Event |
|------|-------|
| 1793 | Federal Fugitive Slave Act requires the return of escaped slaves to their owners. |
| 1793 | Invention of the cotton gin encourages the spread of slavery in the South. |
| 1808 | Federal government bans importation of slaves into the United States, but illegal importation continues. |
| 1816 | American Colonization Society is founded. |
| 1816 | African Methodist Episcopal Church is founded (April 9). |
| 1820 | Congress enacts the Missouri Compromise, under which Missouri is admitted to the Union as a slave state, Maine is admitted as a free state, and slavery is prohibited in the remaining territories north of Missouri's southern boundary (March 3). |
| 1821 | African Methodist Episcopal Zion Church is founded. |
| 1827 | First African American newspaper, *Freedman's Journal*, begins. |
| 1831 | Nat Turner leads major slave insurrection in Virginia. |
| 1831 | Abolitionist William Lloyd Garrison begins publishing *The Liberator* (January 1). |
| 1832 | New England Anti-Slavery Society is organized. |
| 1833 | American Anti-Slavery Society is founded (December). |
| 1839 | Slaves being transported aboard the Spanish ship *Amistad* revolt and take control of the ship. |
| 1841 | Supreme Court's decision in *Groves v. Slaughter* holds that an amendment to Mississippi's state constitution that bans bringing slaves into the state for sale is not valid in the absence of legislation to enforce it (March 10). |
| 1843 | Sojourner Truth begins giving abolitionist lectures. |
| 1847 | Frederick Douglass publishes *The North Star* in Rochester, New York. |
| 1850 | Congress passes new Fugitive Slave Act to facilitate the return of slaves who flee from the South to the North. |
| 1850 | Compromise of 1850 allows for California's admission to the Union as a nonslave state (September 20). |

| Year | Event |
|------|-------|
| 1852 | Harriet Beecher Stowe publishes *Uncle Tom's Cabin*, a novel that attacks slavery. |
| 1853 | National Council of Colored People is founded in Rochester, New York (July 6). |
| 1854 | Congress passes the Kansas-Nebraska Act, a compromise between pro- and antislavery positions (May 30). |
| mid-1850's | Free-soil and proslavery factions fighting in Kansas—a period known in history as "Bleeding Kansas." |
| 1857 | Ashmun Institute (later Lincoln University) is founded in Pennsylvania (January 1). |
| 1857 | Supreme Court's *Scott v. Sandford* decision declares that slaves are not citizens of the United States and that the Missouri Compromise is unconstitutional (March 6-7). |
| 1859 | Capture of the slave ship *Clotilde* ends the delivery of slaves to the United States from abroad. |
| 1859 | Abolitionist John Brown is hanged after his October raid on the federal arsenal at Harpers Ferry, Virginia (December 2). |
| 1861 | Armed fighting in the Civil War begins (April). |
| 1861 | Congress passes first Confiscation Act to confiscate all property, including slaves, used in the Confederate war effort (August). |
| 1862 | Congress's second Confiscation Act declares that seized slaves will not be returned to their Confederate owners and will later be freed (July). |
| 1863 | President Abraham Lincoln issues the Emancipation Proclamation, declaring slaves in states still in rebellion against the Union to be free (January 1). |
| 1863 | Draft riots erupt in New York City after the federal government enacts its first military conscription act (July). |
| 1865 | As southern states begin to enforce black codes, which severely limit liberties of newly freed African Americans, Radical Republicans in Congress began planning Reconstruction policies. |

| Year | Event |
|------|-------|
| 1865 | Federal government creates the Freedmen's Bureau to assist African Americans make the transition from slavery to freedom (March 3). |
| 1865 | Civil War ends with Confederate commander Robert E. Lee's formal surrender at Appomatox (April 9). |
| 1865 | Ratification of the Thirteenth Amendment to the U.S. Constitution prohibits slavery or other involuntary servitude (December 18). |
| 1866 | Ku Klux Klan is founded in Tennessee. |
| 1866 | Congress enacts the Civil Rights Act of 1866, declaring that persons born in the United States are, without regard to race, citizens of the United States entitled to equal protection of the law (April 9). |
| 1868 | Ratification of the Fourteenth Amendment grants citizenship to all persons born in the United States, without regard to race, and requires states to accord individuals equal protection of the law and due process of the law (July). |
| 1870 | Ratification of the Fifteenth Amendment guarantees the right to vote without regard to race, color, or previous condition of servitude (February). |
| 1871 | Congress enacts the Ku Klux Klan Act in an attempt to restrain the violence perpetrated by the organization. |
| 1873 | White terrorists kill more than sixty African Americans in Colfax, Mississippi (April 13). |
| 1875 | Congress enacts the Civil Rights Act of 1875, prohibiting racial discrimination in transportation, hotels, inns, theaters, and places of public amusement (March 1). |
| 1875 | Angry white mob kills more than twenty African Americans in Clinton, Mississippi (September 4-6). |
| 1876 | Supreme Court's decision in *United States v. Cruikshank* limits the authority of the federal government to protect the civil rights of African Americans. (March 27). |

| Year | Event |
|------|-------|
| 1876 | Racially divisive fighting erupts between Republicans and Democrats during the months leading up to the presidential election in Charleston, South Carolina (September-November). |
| 1877 | Compromise of 1877 awards the presidency to Rutherford B. Hayes in return for a Republican promise to withdraw the last Union troops from the South, thus ending Reconstruction (January). |
| 1880 | Supreme Court's decision in *Strauder v. West Virginia* holds that excluding African Americans from juries is a violation of the Fourteenth Amendment's equal protection clause (March 1). |
| 1881 | Booker T. Washington founds the Tuskegee Institute. |
| 1883 | Supreme Court's *Civil Rights* cases ruling declares the Civil Rights Act of 1875 unconstitutional (October 15). |
| 1884 | *Ex parte Yarbrough* is the Supreme Court's only nineteenth century decision that allows the federal government to enforce the Fifteenth Amendment by punishing private individuals for obstructing a citizen's right to vote (March 3). |
| 1890 | Supreme Court's decision in *Louisville, New Orleans, and Texas Railway Company v. Mississippi* upholds Mississippi law requiring segregated accommodations on railroads (March 3). |
| 1892 | Colored Women's League is founded in Washington, D.C. (June). |
| 1895 | Booker T. Washington offers his Atlanta Compromise in an address delivered at the Atlanta Exposition (September 18). |
| 1896 | National Association of Colored Women is founded. |
| 1896 | Supreme Court's *Plessy v. Ferguson* decision establishes the separate but equal doctrine by holding that a legally mandated provision for separate railway cars for whites and blacks does not violate the equal protection clause (May 18). |

| Year | Event |
| --- | --- |
| 1899 | In its *Cumming v. Richmond County Board of Education* decision, the Supreme Court refuses to enforce the "equal" stipulation in the separate but equal doctrine governing segregated schools (December 18). |
| 1904 | W. E. B. Du Bois articulates the concept of the "Talented Tenth." |
| 1905 | Niagara Movement, predecessor of the National Association for the Advancement of Colored People, is organized with the help of W. E. B. Du Bois. |
| 1906 | Troop of African American soldiers are unfairly blamed for a shooting incident in Brownsville, Texas (August 13). |
| 1910-1930's | More than one million African Americans move from the South to northern states in the Great Migration. |
| 1910 | National Association for the Advancement of Colored People (NAACP) is founded (May). |
| 1911 | National Urban League is organized to protect the rights of African Americans who migrate to northern cities from the South (September 29). |
| 1915 | Supreme Court's *Guinn v. United States* decision invalidates state voter literacy requirements intended to prevent African Americans from voting (June 21). |
| 1916 | Marcus Garvey arrives in the United States from Jamaica and becomes a leading advocate of black nationalism. |
| 1917 | Jamaican immigrant Marcus Garvey founds the first North American branch of his Universal Negro Improvement Association in New York City (May). |
| 1917 | Supreme Court's *Buchanan v. Warley* decision strikes down state laws mandating racial segregation in housing (November 5). |
| 1920's-1935 | Harlem Renaissance sees a flowering of black culture and racial pride. |
| 1925 | Brotherhood of Sleeping Car Porters is founded. |
| 1927 | Supreme Court's *Nixon v. Herndon* decision finds unconstitutional the exclusion of blacks from voting in state Democratic primaries (March 7). |

| Year | Event |
| --- | --- |
| 1929 | L. C. Dyer introduces antilynching bill in Congress. |
| 1930 | Wallace Fard founds the Nation of Islam in Detroit, Michigan. |
| 1931 | Trial of the Scottsboro Nine begins in Alabama. |
| 1932-1972 | U.S. Public Health Service conducts long-term study at Tuskegee, Alabama, of African American men afflicted with syphilis who think they are receiving treatment for their condition. |
| 1935 | Mary McLeod Bethune founds the National Council of Negro Women. |
| 1935 | Supreme Court's decision in *Grovey v. Townsend* accepts the right of political parties to exclude African Americans from voting in primaries (April 1). |
| 1938 | Supreme Court's *Missouri ex rel. Gaines v. Canada* decision holds that refusal of a state to allow African Americans to attend a state's only public law school violates the equal protection clause (December 12). |
| 1939 | NAACP creates the Legal Defense and Educational Fund to oppose racially discriminatory laws, and Thurgood Marshall takes charge of these efforts. |
| 1939 | Contralto Marian Anderson performs from the steps of Washington, D.C.'s Lincoln Memorial (January 2). |
| 1941 | In response to A. Philip Randolph's call for African Americans to march on Washington to protest racial discrimination in the armed forces, defense industries, and federal employment generally, President Franklin D. Roosevelt issues Executive Order 8802, which temporarily establishes the Fair Employment Practices Committee (June 25). |
| 1941 | United States enters World War II after Japan's surprise attack on Pearl Harbor (December 8). |
| 1942-1946 | Black pilots who train for service in the U.S. Army Air Forces at Tuskegee, Alabama, become known as the Tuskegee Airmen. |
| 1942 | James Farmer and students at the University of Chicago establish the Congress of Racial Equality (CORE; June). |

| Year | Event |
| --- | --- |
| 1943 | First sit-in demonstrations protesting segregation in Chicago (May-June). |
| 1944 | Supreme Court's *Smith v. Allwright* decision finds that exclusion of African Americans from participation in party primaries violates the Constitution (April 3). |
| 1944 | United Negro College Fund is founded (April 25). |
| 1946 | President Harry S. Truman issues an executive order establishing the President's Committee on Civil Rights (December 5). |
| 1947 | Jackie Robinson becomes the first African American in modern times to play Major League Baseball. |
| 1947 | Journey of Reconciliation attracts national attention to the civil rights work of the Congress of Racial Equality (April 9-23). |
| 1948 | Supreme Court's *Shelley v. Kraemer* decision holds that the Constitution prevents state courts from enforcing racially restrictive real estate covenants (May 3). |
| 1948 | President Harry S. Truman signs Executive Order 9981 prohibiting racial discrimination in the armed forces and other federal employment (July 26). |
| 1950 | Supreme Court's *Sweatt v. Painter* decision holds that Texas's attempt to establish a separate law school for blacks rather than admit black applicants to the University of Texas Law School violates the equal protection clause. On the same day, the Court's decision in *McLaurin v. Oklahoma State Regents for Higher Education* overrules Oklahoma's policy of maintaining segregated programs for African Americans in a public university graduate school (June 5). |
| 1953 | Supreme Court's decision in *Terry v. Adams* outlaws white primaries (May 4). |
| 1954 | Supreme Court's *Brown v. Board of Education* decision finds that racial segregation in public schools violates the equal protection clause (May 17). |
| 1954 | First White Citizens' Councils form, in reaction to *Brown v. Board of Education* (summer). |

| Year | Event |
| --- | --- |
| 1955 | Supreme Court issues a second opinion in the *Brown v. Board of Education* case (*Brown II*), requiring desegregation of public schools "with all deliberate speed." |
| 1955 | Rosa Parks's defiance of segregated seating rules on a Montgomery, Alabama, bus touches off a year-long bus boycott. |
| 1955 | Fifteen-year-old African American Emmett Till is murdered in Mississippi after allegedly flirting with a white woman; a jury ultimately acquits two white men charged with his murder (August 28). |
| 1956 | Most southern members of Congress sign the "Southern Manifesto" denouncing the Supreme Court's *Brown v. Board of Education* decision (March 12). |
| 1957 | Martin Luther King, Jr., and other African American leaders found the Southern Christian Leadership Conference (SCLC). |
| 1957 | Congress passes the first civil rights act since Reconstruction, banning discrimination in public places based on race, color, religion, or national origin. |
| 1957 | After Arkansas's governor uses National Guard troops to block African American children from entering Little Rock's Central High School, President Dwight D. Eisenhower federalizes the guard and mobilizes additional federal armed forces to ensure that the school is peacefully integrated (September). |
| 1958 | President Dwight D. Eisenhower meets with national African American leaders in the Summit Meeting of National Negro Leaders (June). |
| 1958 | Supreme Court's decision in *Cooper v. Aaron* directs that fear of violence is not an acceptable excuse for delaying school desegregation (September 12). |
| 1960 | Supreme Court's decision in *Gomillion v. Lightfoot* strikes down gerrymandering in Tuskegee, Alabama. |
| 1960 | Student sit-ins begin at lunch counters in Greensboro, North Carolina (February-July). |

| Year | Event |
| --- | --- |
| 1960 | Student Nonviolent Coordinating Committee (SNCC) is founded (April). |
| 1960 | Congress passes the Civil Rights Act of 1960, which expands protections of voting rights (May 6). |
| 1961 | President John F. Kennedy issues an executive order that establishes the Equal Employment Opportunity Commission and requires businesses with government contracts to take "affirmative action" in the equal treatment of employees. |
| 1961 | Freedom rides sponsored by CORE test the ban on segregation in interstate buses; riders are beaten, and a bus is burned in Birmingham, Alabama (May-August). |
| 1962 | President John F. Kennedy signs an executive order banning racial discrimination in federally financed housing. |
| 1962 | Voter registration drives begin in southern states under the direction of the Council of Federated Organizations (COFO). |
| 1962 | James Meredith enrolls in the University of Mississippi over the defiant protests of Governor Ross R. Barnett and in the face of mob violence. |
| 1963 | Birmingham March to protest segregation is sponsored by the SCLC (April 4-May 7). |
| 1963 | First African Liberation Day is celebrated (May 25). |
| 1963 | Medgar W. Evers, the field secretary for the Mississippi NAACP, is assassinated (June 12). |
| 1963 | March on Washington is sponsored by civil rights, labor, and religious organizations; featured speaker Martin Luther King, Jr., delivers his "I Have a Dream" speech (August 28). |
| 1963 | Four African American girls are killed when a bomb explodes at the Sixteenth Street Baptist Church in Birmingham, Alabama (September 15). |

| Year | Event |
|------|-------|
| 1964 | Council of Federated Organizations (COFO), a group of associated civil rights groups, organizes the Freedom Summer project to register African Americans to vote in Mississippi. |
| 1964 | Mississippi Freedom Democratic Party is founded in Jackson, Mississippi. |
| 1964 | Ratification of the Twenty-fourth Amendment prohibits poll taxes in federal elections (January 23). |
| 1964 | Civil rights workers James Chaney, Michael Schwerner, and Andrew Goodman are murdered near Philadelphia, Mississippi (June). |
| 1964 | Congress passes the Civil Rights Act of 1964, which prohibits racial, religious, sexual, and other forms of discrimination in a variety of contexts (July 2). |
| 1964 | Supreme Court's *Heart of Atlanta Motel v. United States* decision upholds the power of Congress to prohibit racial discrimination in privately owned hotels and inns (December 14). |
| 1965 | Moynihan Report attempts to explain the high levels of poverty in African American communities. |
| 1965 | Malcolm X is assassinated in New York City (February 21). |
| 1965 | Martin Luther King, Jr., leads a march from Selma to Montgomery, Alabama, to protest voting discrimination (March). |
| 1965 | Congress passes the Voting Rights Act. |
| 1965 | Watts riot flares in Los Angeles (August). |
| 1966 | Stokely Carmichael takes over leadership of SNCC and coins the phrase "Black Power" to advocate more militant responses to continued racial discrimination. |
| 1966 | Supreme Court's decision in *Harper v. Virginia Board of Elections* outlaws poll taxes (March 24). |
| 1966 | Black Panther Party is organized in Oakland, California, by Bobby Seale and Huey P. Newton (October). |

| Year | Event |
|------|-------|
| 1967 | Summer race riots disrupt more than thirty northern cities. |
| 1967 | Supreme Court's *Loving v. Virginia* decision holds that a state law barring interracial marriages is unconstitutional. |
| 1967 | President Lyndon Johnson appoints Thurgood Marshall to the U.S. Supreme Court (June 13). |
| 1968 | Republic of New Africa is founded in Detroit, Michigan. |
| 1968 | Kerner Commission (National Advisory Committee on Civil Disorders) releases its report concerning urban riots, claiming as key reasons white racism and increasing racial and economic stratification (February). |
| 1968 | Campus police in Orangeburg, South Carolina, kill three African American students (February 8). |
| 1968 | Martin Luther King, Jr., is assassinated in Memphis, Tennessee, a few days after leading a protest march for striking sanitation workers (April 4). |
| 1968 | Congress passes the Civil Rights Act of 1968, which prohibits discrimination in the sale and rental of housing and in home financing (April 11). |
| 1968 | Poor People's March on Washington attempts to broaden the Civil Rights movement into a nonracial national campaign to reduce poverty (April 28-May 13). |
| 1968 | Supreme Court's *Green v. County School Board of Kent County* decision finds that a "freedom of choice" plan adopted by a Virginia school district does not satisfy its obligation to desegregate its schools (May 27). |
| 1968 | Supreme Court's *Jones v. Alfred H. Mayer Co.* decision finds that Congress has the power to prohibit racial discrimination in housing sales (June 17). |
| 1968 | Shirley Chisholm of New York is the first African American woman elected to Congress (November 5). |
| 1969 | Supreme Court's *Alexander v. Holmes County Board of Education* decision requires southern school boards to desegregate their schools immediately. |

| Year | Event |
|------|-------|
| 1969 | Militant black leaders issue "Black Manifesto," calling for white churches and synagogues to pay reparations to African Americans for the hardships of slavery (April 26). |
| 1969 | League of Revolutionary Black Workers is founded in Detroit, Michigan (June). |
| 1970 | Black members of Congress form the Congressional Black Caucus. |
| 1971 | National Black Women's Political Leadership Caucus is founded. |
| 1971 | In *Griggs v. Duke Power Company*, the Supreme Court bans non-job-related tests that might unfairly screen minorities (March 8). |
| 1971 | Supreme Court's *Swann v. Charlotte-Mecklenburg Board of Education* decision authorizes busing to desegregate the school district (April 20). |
| 1971 | Supreme Court's *Griffin v. Breckenridge* decision upholds a federal law punishing racially motivated assaults on public highways (June 7). |
| 1972 | Congress passes Equal Employment Opportunity Act, which prohibits government agencies and educational institutions from discriminating in hiring, firing, promotion, compensation, and admission to training programs (March 13). |
| 1973 | Supreme Court's decision in *Keyes v. Denver School District No. 1*, its first school desegregation case involving a major city outside the South, holds that a district-wide busing plan is an appropriate remedy for rectifying deliberately segregated schools (June 21). |
| 1974 | Combahee River Collective is founded. |
| 1974 | In *Milliken v. Bradley*, the Supreme Court holds that federal judges may not order the busing of students across school district lines (July 25). |

| Year | Event |
|------|-------|
| 1975 | Supreme Court's *Albemarle Paper Company v. Moody* rules that employers guilty of racial discrimination in screening tests must compensate harmed employees with back pay. |
| 1975 | Congress passes the Voting Rights Act of 1975, which abolishes the use of literacy tests for voters (August 6). |
| 1976 | Alex Haley publishes *Roots*. |
| 1976 | Supreme Court's *Washington v. Davis* decision holds that laws having a disproportionately burdensome effect on racial minorities are not subject to the same rigorous review as laws purposefully discriminating on grounds of race (June 7). |
| 1978 | Supreme Court's *Bakke* case decision rules against the use of quotas to achieve racial balance in colleges and universities but allows an applicant's race to be considered in the admissions process. |
| 1979 | Supreme Court's *United Steel Workers of America v. Weber* decision upholds the ability of private employers to adopt affirmative action plans (June 27). |
| 1980 | Race riots leave eighteen people dead in Miami after four Miami police officers are acquitted of charges of beating a black insurance executive to death (May 17-23). |
| 1980 | In *Fullilove v. Klutznick*, the Supreme Court upholds minority set-aside contracts established by Congress for federal programs (July 2). |
| 1983 | Jesse Jackson founds the Rainbow Coalition. |
| 1985 | Philadelphia city government bombs a residential neighborhood to evict MOVE squatters (May 13). |
| 1986 | Supreme Court's *Batson v. Kentucky* decision holds that a prosecutor's attempt to disqualify possible jurors because of their race violates the equal protection clause of the Fourteenth Amendment. |
| 1986 | Holiday honoring Martin Luther King, Jr., is celebrated officially for the first time. |
| 1987 | National Coalition of Blacks for Reparations in America is founded. |

| Year | Event |
| --- | --- |
| 1987 | Three white teenagers are convicted of manslaughter following a racially motivated attack on three black men in the Howard Beach section of New York City a year earlier. |
| 1987 | Supreme Court's *McCleskey v. Kemp* decision holds that mere proof of a racially disproportionate impact of death penalty sentences on African Americans does not violate the Constitution (April 22). |
| 1988 | Fair Housing Amendments Act establishes a procedure for imposing fines for those found guilty of housing discrimination based on race, color, sex, religion, or national origin. |
| 1988 | Jesse Jackson runs a strong second in the race for the Democratic nomination for the presidency. |
| 1988 | Congress passes the Civil Rights Restoration Act, restricting federal funding to institutions that discriminate on the basis of race, gender, disability or age, reversing a 1984 Supreme Court decision that narrowed the scope of federal antidiscrimination laws (March 22). |
| 1989 | Supreme Court's *Richmond v. J. A. Croson, Co.* decision holds that state and local affirmative action programs must be subject to "strict scrutiny," a constitutional standard requiring the most compelling government justifications. |
| 1989 | Following a 1988 federal court ruling that Mississippi judicial districts must be redrawn, voters elect five black trial court judges. |
| 1989 | In *Martin v. Wilks*, the Supreme Court allows white firefighters in Birmingham, Alabama, to challenge a 1981 court-approved affirmative action program designed to increase minority representation and promotion (June 12). |
| 1989 | Black honor student Yusuf Hawkins is killed in the predominantly Italian Brooklyn neighborhood of Bensonhurst when he and three friends are assaulted by about thirty white men (August 23). |

| Year | Event |
| --- | --- |
| 1989 | Douglas Wilder is the first African American to be elected a state governor—in Virginia—in U.S. history (November 7). |
| 1990 | Milwaukee, Wisconsin, school board votes to open two schools for blacks utilizing a special curriculum focusing on black culture and featuring programs designed to develop self-esteem and personal responsibility. |
| 1990 | President George Bush vetoes the Civil Rights Act, which would have overturned five recent Supreme Court rulings making it more difficult to win discrimination lawsuits against employers. |
| 1990 | Under a new law, the Justice Department begins collecting statistics on hate crimes in order to determine if changes in federal law are needed. |
| 1990 | Black activists boycott Korean American supermarkets in Brooklyn following charges that a black customer had been assaulted in one of the stores. |
| 1991 | President George Bush signs the Civil Rights Bill, making it easier for employees to sue employers for discrimination, but only after changes are made to a vetoed 1990 bill that might have created racial quotas. |
| 1991 | Clarence Thomas succeeds Thurgood Marshall as the second black Supreme Court justice, despite protests from civil rights groups decrying his opposition to affirmative action programs and busing for school desegregation. |
| 1991 | National Civil Rights Museum, dedicated to the 1950's and 1960's struggle for racial equality in the United States, is opened in Memphis, Tennessee. |
| 1991 | Studies by the Urban Institute find that hiring and housing discrimination against blacks is "widespread and entrenched." |
| 1991 | Killing of a young Guyanese immigrant by a Jewish driver leads to the retaliatory murder of an Australian scholar by black youths and prompts four days of rioting in Brooklyn's Crown Heights neighborhood. |

| Year | Event |
| --- | --- |
| 1991 | Los Angeles police officers beat Rodney King after stopping him for a driving violation in an incident caught on videotape by a bystander (March 3). |
| 1991 | Supreme Court's decision in *Powers v. Ohio* holds that prosecutors cannot use peremptory challenges to exclude African Americans from criminal trial juries (April 1). |
| 1991 | Supreme Court's decision in *Edmonson v. Leesville Concrete Company* extends an earlier ruling to rule that potential jurors may not be peremptorily excluded from civil trials on the basis of their race (June 3). |
| 1991 | Congress passes the Civil Rights Act of 1991, which outlaws employment discrimination (November 21). |
| 1992 | U.S. Department of Education determines that the admissions policy of the University of California at Berkeley's law school violates the Civil Rights Act of 1964 by comparing prospective candidates only against others in their own racial group. |
| 1992 | In *United States v. Fordice*, the Supreme Court rules that remnants of segregation remain in the Mississippi system of higher education and that positive steps must be taken to remedy such segregation. |
| 1992 | Four Los Angeles police officers are acquitted of charges stemming from the 1991 beating of Rodney King, touching off five days of rioting in Los Angeles that result in more than fifty deaths and $1 billion in property damage (April 29). |
| 1992 | In *R.A.V. v. City of St. Paul*, the Supreme Court unanimously rules that a St. Paul, Minnesota, law making the use of racist language a criminal offense is a violation of First Amendment guarantees of free speech (June 22). |
| 1993 | Los Angeles police officers Stacey Koon and Laurence Powell are sentenced to prison for violating the civil rights of Rodney King in a 1991 beating incident. |
| 1993 | In *Wisconsin v. Mitchell*, the Supreme Court rules that states can punish racially motivated crimes more harshly than similar crimes not motivated by bias (June 11). |

| Year | Event |
|------|-------|
| 1994 | Seventy-three-year-old white supremacist Byron De La Beckwith is convicted of the 1963 murder of civil rights leader Medgar Evers and is sentenced to life in prison. |
| 1994 | Flagstar Company agrees to pay $45.7 million in a class-action settlement stemming from 4,300 racial bias complaints against its Denny's restaurant chain. |
| 1994 | Federal jury orders the city of Los Angeles to pay Rodney King $3.8 million in damages stemming from his 1991 beating by white police officers. |
| 1995 | Delegates to the annual convention of Southern Baptists, the nation's largest Protestant denomination, pass a resolution denouncing racism and apologizing for "historic acts of evil such as slavery." |
| 1995 | Supreme Court's *Adarand Constructors v. Peña* decision requires that in federal contracts based on affirmative action, set-asides are valid only when those benefiting have suffered actual discrimination in the past. |
| 1995 | Maryland Democratic representative Kweisi Mfume becomes chief executive of the NAACP following longstanding controversies over improper financial practices of former directors William F. Gibson, Benjamin Chavis, and Benjamin L. Hooks. |
| 1995 | O. J. Simpson's acquittal of the 1994 murder of his wife and a companion divides the country along racial lines (October 3). |
| 1995 | Approximately 700,000 people, mostly African American men, attend Louis Farrakhan's Million Man March, a Washington, D.C., rally highlighting male family responsibilities and addressing problems plaguing the black community in America (October 16). |
| 1996 | California voters approve Proposition 209, designed to end all forms of affirmative action in "the operation of public employment, public education, or public contracting." |
| 1996 | Wave of church burnings begins sweeping the South. |

| Year | Event |
| --- | --- |
| 1996 | U.S. Fifth Circuit Court of Appeals rules, in *Hopwood v. Texas*, that the University of Texas Law School may not consider race as a factor in its admissions process. |
| 1996 | President Bill Clinton signs the Church Arson Prevention Act, making destruction of religious property "on the basis of race, color, or ethnicity" a federal crime. |
| 1996 | Texaco Incorporated agrees to pay $176.1 million to settle a discrimination suit filed on behalf of 1,500 current and former black employees. |
| 1996 | Oakland, California, school board determines that the English dialect spoken by many African Americans is a separate language (Ebonics) based upon West African roots, thus qualifying for federal funds approved for bilingual education. |
| 1997 | National Church Arson Task Force, appointed by President Clinton in 1996, reports that racism was only one of many factors contributing to more than four hundred church fires that had been set during the 1990's. |
| 1997 | President Bill Clinton launches a year-long debate on race relations in America by appointing black historian John Hope Franklin to lead a panel consisting of three whites, two blacks, one Hispanic, and one Korean American. |
| 1997 | Winnie Madikizela-Mandela speaks at the Million Woman March, a Philadelphia rally organized to unify African American women against common community and family problems (October 25). |
| 1999 | Mistaken killing of an African immigrant by New York City police provokes public outrage. |
| 1999 | African American farmers win a lawsuit against the U.S. Department of Agriculture for discriminating against them in awarding loans in the past. |
| 2000 | Coca-Cola Company agrees to pay $192.5 million to settle a discrimination suit filed on behalf of an estimated 2,000 black employees. |

| Year | Event |
| --- | --- |
| 2000 | South Carolina's legislature votes to remove the Confederate flag from the statehouse in response to protests and boycotting efforts launched by the NAACP. |
| 2001 | Newly elected president George W. Bush makes Colin Powell the first African American secretary of state. |
| 2002 | Slavery Reparations Coordinating Committee reveals plans to sue corporations that have profited from slavery. |
| 2003 | Supreme Court's *Grutter v. Bollinger* decision holds that race can be used as a standard in school admissions. |
| 2004 | Kweisi Mfume resigns as chief executive officer of the NAACP. |
| 2004 | U.S. Justice Department announces that it is reopening its investigation into the 1955 murder of Emmett Till in Mississippi. |
| 2005 | Total African American population is about 36 million people. |
| 2005 | Condolezza Rice succeeds Colin Powell as U.S. secretary of state and becomes the first African American woman to hold that post. |

*John Powell and the Editors*

# Notable Figures in African American History

**Abernathy, Ralph David** (1926-1990): Christian minister and civil rights activist. Abernathy was a close friend of Martin Luther King, Jr., when both took Baptist pastorates in Montgomery, Alabama, around 1951. He helped to coordinate the Montgomery bus boycott in 1955 and to organize the Southern Christian Leadership Conference (SCLC) in 1957. After King's assassination, he became president of the SCLC (1968-1977). In 1977, he ran unsuccessfully for Congress. The year before he died, he published a controversial autobiography, *And the Walls Came Tumbling Down* (1989), which included details of King's extramarital affairs.

**Ali, Muhammad** (1942-    ): Professional boxing champion. Born Cassius Marcellus Clay, Jr., Ali started boxing at an early age in Louisville, Kentucky, and won an Olympic gold medal as a light-heavyweight in 1960. In 1964, he converted to the Black Muslim religion and changed his name from Clay to Ali. He won the world heavyweight boxing championship four times (1964, 1967, 1974, 1978). He was stripped of his title when he refused induction into the U.S. Army in 1967, but the U.S. Supreme Court reversed the draft evasion conviction in 1971. Ali became a symbol of black pride during the 1960's and remained an icon into the twenty-first century.

**Allen, Richard** (1760-1831): Founder of the African Methodist Episcopal Church. After gaining his freedom from slavery when he was twenty-one, Allen became the first African American ordained by the Methodist Society but was denied the right to worship at a predominantly white church in Philadelphia, so he founded his own church, which was later granted legal independence from the white church. In 1830, Allen led the first meeting of what would become the Negro Convention Movement.

**Anderson, Marian** (1897-1993): Contralto. Raised in Philadelphia, Anderson studied music from an early age and earned an international reputation while performing throughout Europe during the 1930's. On her return to the United States, her stature was immense; however, she became the focus of an embarrassing incident in 1939, when the Daughters of the American Revolution refused her permission to sing in Philadelphia's Constitution Hall because she was black. When first Lady Eleanor Roosevelt learned of the matter, she arranged for Anderson to perform on the steps of the Lincoln Memorial in Washington, D.C. The incident immortalized Anderson as a symbol of African American oppression. Anderson continued performing until 1965 and earned a long list of distinctions.

**Angelou, Maya** (1928-    ): Novelist, poet. Born Marguerite Johnson, Angelou worked as a nightclub singer in New York and San Francisco, as an editor for the English-language *Arab Observer* in Cairo, Egypt, and as a teacher of music and drama in Ghana. She became a national figure with the publication of the first volume of her autobiography, *I Know Why the Caged Bird Sings* (1970), which detailed her experiences with southern racism and sexual abuse. She was nominated for an Emmy Award for her performance as Nyo Boto in the television series *Roots* (1977). In 1993, she was invited to read her poem "On the Pulse of Morning" at the inauguration of President Bill Clinton.

**Asante, Molefi Kete** (1942-    ): Scholar. Born Arthur Lee Smith, Jr., he legally changed his name in 1975. After receiving a doctoral degree in communications from the University of California at Los Angeles (UCLA) in 1968, he taught at Purdue, UCLA, the State University of New York, Howard University, and Temple University and was named director of the Center for Afro-American Studies at UCLA. His more than two dozen books include *Afrocentricity: The Theory of Social Change* (1980), *African Culture: The Rhythms of Unity* (1985), and *The Historical and Cultural Atlas of African-Americans* (1991). He was also a founding editor of the *Journal of Black Studies*.

**Baker, Josephine** (1903-1986): Civil rights activist. After graduating as valedictorian with a bachelor's degree from Shaw Boarding School in 1927, she moved to New York City, where she became deeply involved with progressive politics. In 1931, she became director of the Young Negroes Cooperative League, which provided reasonably priced food to its members during the Depression. She also worked with the literacy program of the Works Progress Administration. During the 1940's, she set up and directed branch offices of the National Association for the Advancement of Colored People. She moved to Atlanta, Georgia, to work with the Southern Christian Leadership Conference in 1958 and was an unofficial adviser to the Student Nonviolent Coordinating Committee during the 1960's. She also helped organize the Mississippi Freedom Democratic Party and raised money for freedom fighters in Rhodesia (Zimbabwe) and South Africa. (Not to be confused with the singer Josephine Baker, 1903-1975).

**Baldwin, James Arthur** (1924-1987): Author and playwright. Baldwin has often been praised for his ability to make readers feel the destructive power of racial prejudice on both black and white people. His books include two autobiographical works, *Notes of a Native Son* (1955) and *Nobody Knows My Name* (1961); several powerful novels, including *Go Tell It on the Mountain* (1953), *Another Country* (1962), and *Just Above My Head* (1979); and a number of plays, including *Blues for Mister Charlie* (1964) and *The Amen Corner* (1964). He spent the final years of his life in France, where he was made commander of the Legion of Honor, France's highest civilian honor.

**Baraka, Amiri** (1934-    ): Poet and playwright. Born LeRoi Jones, Baraka founded *Yugen* magazine and Totem Press in 1958 and the Black Arts Repertory Theater in 1964. He achieved fame with his honest treatment of racism in plays such as *Dutchman* (1964), *The Slave* (1966), and *Four Revolutionary Plays* (1968). He was also a leading spokesperson for the Black Power movement in Newark, New Jersey, where he headed the activist Temple of Kawaida. In 1972, he chaired the National Black Political Convention.

**Bethune, Mary McLeod** (1875-1955): Educator. After teaching at various schools in Georgia and Florida, Bethune founded the Daytona Educational and Industrial School for Negro Girls in 1904 and McLeod Hospital in 1911. In 1922, her Daytona school merged with the Cookman Institute to become Bethune-Cookman College, of which she served as president until 1942. During the 1920's, she served on conferences under Herbert Hoover. She also served as director of the Division of Negro Affairs of the National Youth Administration (1936-

1944), was special assistant to the secretary of war during World War II, and was a special adviser on minority affairs to President Franklin D. Roosevelt (1935-1944). Bethune also played important roles in the National Urban League, National Association for the Advancement of Colored People, and the National Council of Negro Women.

**Bond, Julian** (1940-      ): Georgia politician and civil rights activist. A student founder of the Committee on Appeal for Human Rights, Bond attracted the attention of Martin Luther King, Jr., and helped found the Student Nonviolent Coordinating Committee, of which he was the first director of communications (1961-1966). A Democrat, he was elected to the Georgia house of representatives (1965-1975) and the Georgia senate (1975-1987). He helped found the Southern Poverty Law Center in 1971, served as president of the Atlanta branch of the National Association for the Advancement of Colored People (NAACP; 1974-1989), and became chairman of the NAACP in 1998. Bond also hosted the television program *America's Black Forum* and narrated the Public Broadcasting Service civil rights series *Eyes on the Prize.*

**Bradley, Thomas** (1917-1998): California politician. Bradley held various positions with the Los Angeles Police Department from 1940 to 1961 and earned a law degree in the 1950's. In 1963, he became the first African American elected to the Los Angeles City Council and was also the first African American elected the city's mayor in 1973, despite the fact that African Americans constituted a small minority of the city's voters. While serving four terms as mayor, he also ran for governor of California twice (1982, 1986). Bradley also was a founding member of the Black Achievers Committee of the National Association for the Advancement of Colored People.

**Braun, Carol Moseley** (1947-      ): Illinois politician. Braun was an assistant U.S. attorney for the northern district of Illinois (1973-1977) and served as an Illinois state representative (1979-1987), in which position she established a reputation as an ardent supporter of civil rights legislation. After serving as Cook County recorder of deeds (1987-1993), she became the first African American woman to be elected to the U.S. Senate, in which she served one term (1993-1999).

**Brooke, Edward W.** (1919-    ): Massachusetts politician and former state attorney general who, in 1966, became the first African American elected to a full term in the U.S. Senate since Reconstruction. A liberal Democrat, Brooke was reelected in 1972. After losing his bid for a third term in 1978, he returned to practicing law and became a lobbyist in Washington, D.C.

**Brown, H. Rap** (1943-    ): Civil rights activist. Brown became leader of the Student Nonviolent Coordinating Committee in 1967. The following year he was charged with inciting a riot in Cambridge, Maryland, and was convicted of carrying a gun across state lines. In 1969, he published *Die Nigger Die* (1969) while serving a prison term for a robbery conviction. After converting to Islam, he changed his name to Jamil Abdullah Al-Amin and became the leader of Community Mosque in Atlanta, Georgia.

**Brown, John** (1800-1859): White abolitionist. Brown joined anti-slavery forces in Kansas in 1855 and murdered five proslavery advocates in 1856 in retaliation for a previous massacre. After establishing a plan for a slave refuge state, he led a band that seized the federal arsenal at Harpers Ferry, Virginia, in 1859, hoping to incite a slave insurrection. Convicted of treason and hanged, he later became an icon of the abolitionist movement.

**Bruce, Blanche Kelso** (1841-1898): Mississippi politician. Born a slave, Bruce built a fortune as a plantation owner after the Civil War and served in various local and state positions in Mississippi during Reconstruction. He was a U.S. senator from Mississippi (1875-1881), and became the first African American to serve a full term in the Senate. He was also a staunch defender of black, Chinese, and American Indian rights. After Reconstruction, he worked with the U.S. register of the treasury (1881-1889, 1895-1898) and as recorder of deeds for the District of Columbia (1889-1895).

**Bunche, Ralph** (1904-1971): Diplomat and scholar. A former head of the political science department of Howard University, Bunche served as senior social analyst for the Office of the Coordinator of Information in African and Far Eastern Affairs and with the African section of the Office of Strategic Services during World War II. Recognized as an expert on colonial affairs, he joined the U.S. State Department in 1944 and served as delegate or adviser to nine international conferences over the next four years. After serving as chief assistant on the United Nations Palestine Commission, he became the first African American to receive the Nobel Peace Prize in 1950, for his role in the Arab-Israeli cease-fire of 1948-1949. Bunche also served as U.N. undersecretary of Special Political Affairs (1957-1967) and undersecretary general of the United Nations (1968-1971).

**Carmichael, Stokely** (1941-1998): Trinidad-born political activist. After attending Howard University, Carmichael became an accomplished organizer for the Student Nonviolent Coordinating Committee (SNCC) of which he was elected chair in 1966. He popularized the phrase "black power" and became known for radical positions that led to his expulsion from SNCC in 1968. He joined the Black Panther Party in 1968, but resigned the following year and moved to Guinea in West Africa, where he became a supporter of Pan-Africanism. In 1978, he changed his name to Kwame Toure, in honor of the West African nationalist leaders Sékou Touré and Kwame Nkrumah.

**Chavis, Benjamin** (1948-    ): Civil rights activist. After training as a theologian, Chavis became a civil rights organizer for the Southern Christian Leadership Conference and the United Church of Christ. In 1971, he was indicted as one of the Wilmington Ten for the firebombing of a store in Wilmington, Delaware. He was convicted but was granted parole, and his conviction was reversed in 1980. Five years later, he was appointed executive director of the Commission for Racial Justice, and he served as executive director of the National Association for the Advancement of Colored People (1993-1994)—a position from which he was forced to resign because of a financial scandal. In 1995, he served as national director of the Million Man March.

**Chisholm, Shirley** (1924-2005): New York Democratic politician. After an early career in child care and education, Chisholm was elected New York State assemblywoman in 1964. In 1969, she became the first African American woman elected to the U.S. House of Representatives, where she served until 1983. She also cofounded the National Political Congress of Black Women. Her autobiography is titled *Unbossed and Unbought* (1970).

**Cleaver, Eldridge** (1935-1998): Civil rights activist. After serving a prison sentence from 1958 to 1966, Cleaver joined the Black Panther Party and became one of the most vocal proponents of the doctrine of black power. His memoir *Soul on Ice* (1968) became one of the most powerful statements of that movement. After becoming involved in a 1968 shooting, Cleaver fled to Algeria. He returned to the United States in 1975 and espoused more conservative views.

**Cone, James** (1938-    ): Theologian. A faculty member at Union Theological Seminary since 1969, Cone provided a systematic case for divine support of the black liberation struggle in the United States and elsewhere. His many books include *Black Theology and Black Power* (1969), *For My People: Black Theology and the Black Church* (1984), and *Martin and Malcolm and America: A Dream or a Nightmare?* (1991).

**Cosby, Bill** (1937-    ): Actor and comedian. By the mid-1960's, Cosby was playing top nightclubs with his comedy routine and regularly appearing on television. In 1965, he became the first African American star of a prime-time television series, *I Spy*, for which he won Emmy Awards (1965-1968). Throughout the 1970's, he appeared in films and television shows and in Las Vegas, Reno, and Tahoe nightclubs. His television sitcom *The Cosby Show* (1985-1992) presented upper-middle-class black family life to mainstream American audiences and was the top-rated show of its time. Cosby also earned five Grammy Awards and wrote *Fatherhood* (1986) and *Time Flies* (1987). A quiet but forceful advocate of African American education, Cosby donated twenty million dollars to Spellman College in 1988. In 2004, Cosby received national attention for his outspoken criticisms of the values and parenting skills of many low-income African Americans, whom he accused of neglecting their responsibilities as parents by raising their children to think of themselves as victims of racism.

**Crummell, Alexander** (1819-1898): Christian minister and author. After earning a degree at Cambridge University in England, Crummell served as professor of mental and moral science at the College of Liberia (1853-1873) in West Africa and was minister of St. Luke's Protestant Episcopal Church in Washington, D.C. (1876-1898). In 1897, he helped found the

American Negro Academy. His many books include *Future of Africa* (1862) and *Africa and America* (1892).

**Davis, Angela** (1944-    ): Political activist and scholar. After an extensive education at Brandeis University, the Sorbonne, and the University of Frankfurt, Davis took a teaching job at the University of California at Los Angeles (UCLA). In 1969, she joined the Communist Party. She later became involved with the Black Panther Party. After being implicated in a courtroom shooting in 1970, she went underground but eventually was arrested. However, she was acquitted on all charges in 1972. She later became cochair of the National Alliance Against Racism and Political Repression. Her books include *If They Come in the Morning* (1971), *Women, Race, and Class* (1983), and *Women, Culture, and Politics* (1989).

**Davis, Benjamin O., Jr.** (1912-2002): Career military officer. The son of Brigadier General Benjamin Davis, Sr., the younger Davis became the second African American general in the U.S. military and the first in the U.S. Air Force in 1954. During World War II, he was a decorated pilot and squadron commander of the Tuskegee Airmen. In 1965, President Lyndon B. Johnson promoted him to the rank of lieutenant general, in which capacity he served as chief of staff of U.S. forces in Korea.

**Davis, Benjamin O., Sr.** (1877-1970): Career army officer. Davis served in the Spanish-American War and in the all-black Ninth Cavalry. In 1940, he became the first African American to reach the rank of general in the regular army, when President Franklin D. Roosevelt promoted him to brigadier general. Davis retired from military service in 1948.

**Delany, Martin Robison** (1812-1885): Doctor, author, and abolitionist. Born a slave in what later became West Virginia, Delany fled north when his masters discovered that he could read. He edited the abolitionist newspapers *The Mystery* and *The North Star*. Disappointed with the treatment of blacks in the United States, he recommended founding an African American colony in Africa or South America. In 1863, he was commissioned the first black major in the U.S. Army. He later published *Principal of Ethnology: The Origin of Races and Color* (1879).

**Douglass, Frederick** (c. 1817-1895): Abolitionist and journalist. The most prominent African American of his time, Douglass escaped from slavery in 1838 and fled north. A brilliant orator, he became famous as an agent of the Massachusetts Anti-Slavery Society during the 1840's. After publishing *Narrative of the Life of Frederick Douglass* (1845), he lectured in England and Ireland (1845-1847), earning enough money to purchase his freedom, thereby ending status as a fugitive slave. Douglass founded and served as coeditor of *The North Star*, 1847-1860 (*Frederick Douglass's Paper* from 1851) and came to oppose the radical abolitionism of William Lloyd Garrison and John Brown. After the Civil War, he held several federal government positions. He was U.S. marshal for the District of Columbia (1877-1881); recorder of deeds for the District of Columbia (1881-1886), and U.S. minister to Haiti (1889-1891).

**Du Bois, W. E. B.** (1868-1963): Civil rights activist, scholar, and author. The leader of the Niagara Movement (1905-1909), Du Bois helped found the National Association for the Advancement of Colored People (NAACP) in 1909 and acted as the association's director of publications and editor of *The Crisis* (1909-1934). He was also a professor of sociology at Atlanta University (1932-1944) and served as head of the special research department of the NAACP (1944-1948). Dissatisfied with the pace of social change in the United States, he joined the Communist Party and emigrated to Ghana in West Africa in 1961 to become editor in chief of the Pan-Africanist *Encyclopedia Africana*, sponsored by Ghanaian president Kwame Nkrumah. His numerous books include *The Souls of Black Folk* (1903), *The Negro* (1915), *The Gift of Black Folk* (1924), *Color and Democracy* (1945), *The World and Africa* (1947), and the *Black Flame* trilogy (1957-1961).

**Eisenhower, Dwight D.** (1890-1969): Thirty-fourth president of the United States (1953-1961). A moderate Republican, Eisenhower appointed California governor Earl Warren chief justice of the United States during his first year in office. He expected Warren to behave as a political conservative and was consequently surprised by Warren's social activism, especially after Warren guided the Court to a unanimous ruling in the *Brown v. Board of Education* case in 1954. During the Little Rock crisis three years later, Eisenhower reluctantly sent federal troops into Arkansas to enforce school desegregation. During that same year, 1957, he appointed the federal Civil Rights Commission, which was required by the Civil Rights Act of 1957.

**Evers, Medgar** (1925-1963): Civil rights activist. Appointed Mississippi field secretary of the National Association for the Advancement of Colored People in 1954, Evers fought for enforcement of school integration and advocated the right of African Americans to vote and the boycotting of merchants who discriminated against them. His murder in 1963 made him one of the first martyrs of the Civil Rights movement.

**Farmer, James** (1920-1999): Civil rights leader. One of the organizers of the Congress of Racial Equality (CORE), in 1942, Farmer arranged the first successful sit-in demonstration, at a Chicago restaurant the following year. He later also served as program director of the National Association for the Advancement of Colored People (1959-1961), and he introduced the tactic of the Freedom Ride in 1961 to test principles of desegregation. Farmer left CORE in 1966 and was appointed assistant secretary of Health, Education, and Welfare in 1969. In 1976, he became associate director of the Coalition of American Public Employees.

**Farrakhan, Louis** (1933-    ): Muslim cleric. Born Louis Eugene Walcott, Farrakhan joined the Nation of Islam during the 1950's. He denounced Malcolm X after the latter's split with Elijah Muhammad and succeeded Malcolm as leader of New York's Harlem mosque. Farrakhan left the Nation of Islam after it began accepting white members during the mid-1970's and founded a rival organization that was later known by the same name. In 1984, he supported Jesse Jackson in the presidential campaign, marking a turning point in Black Muslim political involvement. In 1995, he and Benjamin Chavis organized the Million Man March.

**Forten, James** (1766-1842): Abolitionist and entrepreneur. Born of free parents in Philadelphia, Forten served aboard a privateer during the American Revolution, during which he was captured and held prisoner for seven months. While he was in England, he became acquainted with abolitionist philosophy. By 1798, he owned a prosperous maritime company. He became active in the abolitionist movement during the 1830's and joined the American Anti-Slavery Society. He also helped raise funds for William Lloyd Garrison's newspaper *The Liberator* and founded the American Moral Reform Society.

**Fortune, T. Thomas** (1856-1928): Journalist and editor. Fortune worked in various positions for the *New York Sun* during the late 1870's and early 1880's. In 1883, he founded the *New York Age*, which became the leading black journal of opinion in the United States. Fortune crusaded against school segregation and joined Booker T. Washington in organizing the National Negro Business League in 1900. Fortune coined the term "Afro-American" as a substitute for "Negro" in the New York press.

**Gandhi, Mohandas K.** (1869-1948): Indian nationalist leader who had an indirect but strong influence on the American Civil Rights movement. After going to South Africa to practice law, Gandhi became a leader of the Indian civil rights struggle in Natal. While there, he developed the philosophy of nonviolent direct action to force political change that he later introduced to the independence struggle in his native India. Gandhi's philosophy was a powerful influence on the nonviolent strategies of the American Civil Rights movement, and it particularly influenced the philosophy of Martin Luther King, Jr.

**Garrison, William Lloyd** (1805-1879): Abolitionist who published *The Liberator* from 1831 to 1865. He founded the American Anti-Slavery Society in 1833 and was its president from 1843 to 1865. Garrison opposed the Compromise of 1850 and encouraged the separation of the northern and southern states. After the Civil War, he campaigned against mistreatment of Native Americans and in favor of women's suffrage.

**Garvey, Marcus** (1887-1940): Jamaican-born black nationalist leader. Two years after founding the Universal Negro Improvement Association (UNIA) in 1914, Garvey came to the United States, where he founded UNIA branches in cities throughout the northern states. At UNIA's first convention in New York City in 1920, he outlined a plan for the establishment of an African nation-state for American blacks. He preached racial pride through civil rights and economic self-sufficiency. After being convicted of fraud in 1925, he was sent to a federal prison, but his sentence was commuted by President Calvin Coolidge, and he was deported back to Jamaica in

1927. He continued to be active in progressive politics but his influence on developments in the United States waned greatly.

**Gordy, Berry, Jr.** (1929-    ): Songwriter and music producer. Gordy served with the U.S. Army in the Korean War. After a number of failed or unsatisfying jobs in Detroit, Michigan, he began writing hit songs with the help of his sister Gwen Gordy and Billy Davis. In 1959, he formed Motown Record Corporation and a number of related businesses. By the mid-1960's, Gordy had brought black soul music to mainstream American audiences with highly polished performances by artists such as the Supremes, Smokey Robinson, the Four Tops, the Marvelettes, Marvin Gaye, the Jackson Five, Lionel Richie, and Stevie Wonder. He was inducted into the Rock and Roll Hall of Fame in 1988.

**Grace, Charles Emmanuel "Sweet Daddy"** (1881-1960): Religious leader. Born Marcelino Manoel de Graca in the Cape Verde Islands, Grace established the United House of Prayer for All People during the early 1920's. His ministerial style was rooted in faith healing and speaking in tongues. Products such as "Daddy Grace" coffee, tea, and creams were believed to have healing powers. By 1960, Grace's church claimed 25,000 adherents in 375 congregations.

**Graves, Earl** (1935-    ): Publisher and editor. Graves served in the U.S. Army as an officer in the Green Berets (1957-1960) and was an administrative assistant to Robert F. Kennedy (1964-1968). In 1970, he launched *Black Enterprise* to provide African Americans with practical help for succeeding in business. By the late 1990's, the magazine had a subscription base of more than 300,000. Graves also wrote *How to Succeed in Business Without Being White* (1997).

**Haley, Alex** (1921-1992): Journalist and author. Haley got into journalism while serving in the U.S. Coast Guard (1952-1959). He later interviewed Malcolm X for *Playboy* magazine—an assignment that led to his first book, *The Autobiography of Malcolm X* (1965). He then spent a dozen years researching his family history, leading to publication of the novel *Roots* (1976), based on the life of a West African man named Kunta Kinte who was sent to North America in slavery. Haley's book led to a twelve-hour television series, hundreds of interviews and articles, instruc-

tional packets and tapes, and sparked intense interest in genealogy and history among both black and white Americans.

**Hamer, Fannie Lou** (1917-1977): Civil rights activist. After forty
years of working on the same plantation, Hamer lost her job
when she tried to vote. She then began working with the Student Nonviolent Coordinating Committee. She helped register black voters and helped form the Mississippi Freedom
Democratic Party, for which she spoke eloquently in favor of
seating black delegates to the Democratic National Convention in 1964. Hamer herself became one of the first delegates to
the Democratic convention in 1968. She founded Freedom
Farms Corporation in 1969 and toured and spoke widely on
behalf of civil rights legislation.

**Hayes, Rutherford B.** (1822-1893): Nineteenth president of the
United States (1877-1881). Though an ardent Radical Republican early in the Reconstruction era, Hayes moderated his views
and as president ended that era by withdrawing military support for Republican state governments in the South. The end
of Reconstruction left African Americans in the South at the
mercy of resentful white politicians, who enacted discriminatory legislation and effectively disfranchised black voters.

**Hill, Anita** (1956-    ): Professor of law. Hill was a relatively unknown instructor at the University of Oklahoma when she
gained national attention during Senate confirmation hearings for U.S. Supreme Court justice nominee Clarence Thomas
in 1991. At that time, she charged that she had been sexually
harassed when working for Thomas at the Equal Employment
Opportunities Commission in the early 1980's. Afterward, she
withstood attempts by some lawmakers to have the University of Oklahoma Law School fire her and spoke widely
around the country throughout the 1990's in favor of civil
rights and women's rights.

**Hooks, Benjamin** (1925-    ): Lawyer, preacher, and civil rights
leader. Hooks was the first African American to serve as a
judge in a criminal court in Tennessee's Shelby County. He
also served as executive director of the National Association
for the Advancement of Colored People (1977-1992). In that capacity, he vigorously promoted integration, pro-African foreign policy, and progressive employment legislation.

**Howard, Oliver Otis** (1830-1909): U.S. Army officer. Howard entered the Army in 1854 and fought in the Civil War, during which he was promoted to brigadier general in 1861. After the war, he served as a commissioner for the Bureau of Refugees, Freedmen, and Abandoned Lands (1865-1874) and as founder and first president of Howard University (1869-1874). After returning to the Army, he commanded the federal campaign against Chief Joseph of the Nez Perce Indians in the Northwest in 1877 and was superintendent at West Point (1881-1882). Howard was considered one of the few "humanitarian" generals who campaigned on behalf of Indian rights.

**Hughes, Langston** (1902-1967): Writer and poet. After dropping out of Columbia University, Hughes wrote poetry and worked as a cabin boy on a freighter, on which he sailed to Africa. He was later a major figure in the 1920's Harlem Renaissance. His essay "The Negro Writer and the Racial Mountain" (1926) established an early ethic of black pride. He wrote in many fields, including poetry (*The Weary Blues*, 1926; *Fine Clothes to the Jew*, 1927; *Shakespeare in Harlem*, 1942; *Montage of a Dream Deferred*, 1951); librettos (*Street Scene*, 1947); plays (*Mulatto*, 1935); and autobiography (*The Big Sea*, 1940; *I Wonder as I Wander*, 1956).

**Innis, Roy** (1934-    ): Civil rights leader. Innis joined the Congress of Racial Equality (CORE) in 1963 and became its national director in 1968. He also founded the Harlem Commonwealth Council, which was designed to promote black businesses. Controversy over his involvement in recruiting black Vietnam War veterans to fight in Angola's civil war and charges that he misappropriated funds led to important defections from CORE, which became largely inactive in the 1980's.

**Jackson, Jesse** (1941-    ): Civil rights activist, Baptist minister, and politician. Jackson joined the Southern Christian Leadership Conference (SCLC) in 1965 and served as the executive director of its Operation Breadbasket program (1967-1971). He also founded Operation PUSH (People United to Save Humanity) in 1971. His PUSH-EXCEL program for encouraging young students to improve academically received funding from the administration of U.S. president Jimmy Carter. Jackson campaigned for the Democratic nomination for president of the United States in 1984 and 1988. In the latter campaign, he finished a strong second to Michael Dukakis, who lost to George Bush in the November election. His candidacy demonstrated the possibility of an African American eventually being elected president. Afterward, he continued to press for child care, health care reform, housing reform, and statehood for the predominantly African American District of Columbia.

**Johnson, Andrew** (1808-1875): Seventeenth president of the United States. A Tennessee politician, Johnson became one of the rare southerners in the Union government when he was elected vice president in 1864. Abraham Lincoln's assassination shortly after the conclusion of the Civil War suddenly elevated Johnson to the presidency and gave him responsibility for overseeing the postwar reconstruction of the South. However, his inclination to be lenient toward the South pitted him against the Congress, which was dominated by Radical Republicans who subjected him to impeachment and wrested away control of Reconstruction policy. Johnson narrowly survived his impeachment trial and eventually left office under a cloud. However, he later enjoyed some vindication when he was reelected to the Senate.

**Johnson, Jack** (1878-1946): Boxer. The first black heavyweight boxing champion of the world (1908-1915), Jackson became the center of racial controversy as the public called for Jim Jeffries, the white former champion, to come out of retirement to defeat him. Johnson beat Jeffries in 1910 but remained a target of racist attacks through the rest of his life, which Howard Sackler later dramatized in a play, *The Great White Hope* (1967).

**Johnson, James Weldon** (1871-1938): Poet, diplomat, and civil rights leader. As a young man, Johnson was known principally as a lyricist for popular songs, including "Lift Every Voice and Sing" (1899). He later served as U.S. consul in Puerto Cabello, Venezuela (1906-1909), and in Corinto, Nicaragua (1909-1912). From 1920 to 1930, he was executive secretary of the National Association for the Advancement of Colored People (1920-1930). Johnson's many books include *The Autobiography of an Ex-Colored Man* (1912), *The Book of American Negro Poetry* (1922), *God's Trombones* (1927), and *Negro Americans, What Now* (1934).

**Johnson, John H.** (1918-    ): Publisher who addressed the need for mainstream black publications with the establishment of *The Negro Digest* (1942) and *Ebony* (1945). Johnson was also a member of the advisory council of the Harvard Graduate School of Business and a director of the Chamber of Commerce of the United States.

**Johnson, Lyndon B.** (1908-1973): Thirty-sixth president of the United States (1963-1969). A native Texan, Johnson began his political career as state administrator and served in the National Youth Administration (1935-1937). In 1936, he was elected to the House of Representatives as a Democrat. In 1949, he moved from the House to the Senate, in which he became majority leader in 1955-1961. After attempting to win the Democratic nomination for president in 1960, he joined the Democratic ticket under John F. Kennedy and was elected vice president. On Kennedy's assassination in 1963, Johnson became president. Despite his conservative southern background, he became a champion of progressive social programs and articulated what he called the "Great Society." Under his leadership, Congress passed the Civil Rights Act of 1964 and the Voting Rights Act of 1965, which were designed to ensure that African Americans received their full civil rights. Johnson also established the Department of Housing and Urban Development and made Thurgood Marshall the first black Supreme Court justice in 1967.

**Jones, Absalom** (1746-1818): Protestant cleric. In 1794, Jones became the first leader of St. Thomas African Episcopal Church. One year later, he was ordained the first African American Protestant Episcopal priest in the United States.

**Jordan, Vernon** (1935-    ): Lawyer and civil rights leader. Jordan was field secretary for the Georgia branch of the National Association for the Advancement of Colored People (1962-1964). He also served as director of the Voter Education Project of the Southern Regional Council (1964-1968), was executive director of the United Negro College Fund (1970-1972), and executive director of the National Urban League (1972-1981). In 1992, Jordan became a political confidante of President Bill Clinton.

**Kennedy, John F.** (1917-1963): Thirty-fifth president of the United States (1961-1963). After graduating from Harvard in 1940,

Kennedy served as a naval officer during World War II. A Democrat, he was elected a Massachusetts representative to Congress in 1947. After three terms in the House of Representatives (1947-1953), he was elected to the Senate (1953-1960). In 1960, he became the first Roman Catholic elected president of the United States. As president, he established the Peace Corps and the Alliance for Progress in Latin America. An outspoken advocate of civil rights for African Americans, he federalized the Alabama national guard to ensure integration of the state's schools in 1963. His efforts to persuade Congress to pass major civil rights legislation were interrupted by his assassination in late 1963, but his goal was realized by his successor, Lyndon B. Johnson.

**Kennedy, Robert F.** (1925-1968): Politician and lawyer. In 1960, Kennedy managed the presidential campaign of his brother, John F. Kennedy, who made him attorney general of the United States (1961-1964). In that capacity, he was an ardent supporter of civil rights. In 1964, he was elected to the U.S. Senate from his adopted state of New York. He continued to champion civil rights and was mounting a serious challenge for the Democratic nomination for the presidency in 1968 until he was assassinated the same night that he won the California primary. Kennedy's books include *The Enemy Within* (1960), *Just Friends and Brave Enemies* (1962), and *To Seek a Newer World* (1967).

**King, Martin Luther, Jr.** (1929-1968): Civil rights activist and Baptist minister. King earned a doctoral degree from Crozer Theological Seminary in Rochester, New York, in 1955. Afterward, he accepted the pastorate of the Dexter Avenue Baptist Church in Montgomery, Alabama. In 1956, he helped organize the Montgomery bus boycott, which led to the founding of the Southern Christian Leadership Conference, of which he served as first president. Meanwhile, he was also a copastor of Ebenezer Baptist Church in Atlanta (1960-1968). Through the remainder of his life, he was acknowledged as the primary leader of the Civil Rights movement and personally directed many of its campaigns. Some of these led to his arrest. While serving a jail sentence in Birmingham, Alabama, where he was arrested while protesting segregation and unfair hiring practices in 1963, he wrote his classic "Letter from Birmingham

Jail." That same year, he delivered his "I Have a Dream" speech during the historic March on Washington. *Time* magazine named him "Man of the Year" in 1963; the following year, he was awarded the Nobel Peace Prize. Around that same time, he began to speak out forcefully against the Vietnam War and urban poverty, causing many black leaders to question his tactics in the civil rights struggle. He was assassinated in Memphis, Tennessee, in 1968. His January birthday was later made a federal holiday.

**King, Rodney** (1966-     ): California motorist who was severely beaten by Los Angeles police officers in 1991. Caught on a videotape made by a bystander and broadcast nationwide, his beating became a *cause célèbre* and the focus of a criminal trial of the four officers charged with beating him. After a predominantly white jury acquitted the officers in April, 1992, Los Angeles erupted in riots that killed fifty-eight people and caused $1 billion in property damage.

**Lee, Spike** (1957-     ): Filmmaker. While attending New York University's Institute of Film and Television, Lee won the Student Award presented by the Academy of Motion Picture Arts and Sciences for *Joe's Bed-Sty Barbershop: We Cut Heads* (1982). His controversial films, highlighting past and present struggles of African Americans in a land of alien values, include *She's Gotta Have It* (1986), *Do the Right Thing* (1989), *Mo' Better Blues* (1990), *Malcolm X* (1992), and *He Got Game* (1998).

**Lincoln, Abraham** (1809-1865): Sixteenth president of the United States (1861-1865). After a boyhood on pioneer farms in the Midwest, Lincoln was elected to the Illinois state legislature in 1834. While representing Illinois in the House of Representatives (1847-1849), he spoke out against the Mexican War. In 1858, he was defeated in his bid for a seat in the U.S. Senate but established his position against slavery during his famous debates with Stephen A. Douglas during the campaign. In 1860, his election as president of the United States accelerated the movement toward secession by southern states that led to the Civil War, which dominated his presidency. Because of his dedication to preserving the Union, his attitude toward abolishing slavery was equivocal. Nevertheless, he is remembered as the "Great Emancipator" because of his issuance of the

Emancipation Proclamation in early 1863. Aimed only at U.S. states and territories then in rebellion against the United States, that declaration freed no slaves but did make abolition a northern goal in the Civil War. At the conclusion of the war, Lincoln was about to face the challenge of developing a Reconstruction policy for the defeated Confederacy but was assassinated by a disgruntled southerner, John Wilkes Booth.

**Locke, Alain** (1886-1954): Philosopher and writer. After studying at Harvard University, Oxford University, and the University of Berlin, Locke served on the faculty at Howard University (1912-1953). He celebrated black cultural contributions in works such as *The New Negro: An Interpretation* (1925) and a special issue of the journal *Survey Graphic*, which announced the arrival of a "Harlem Renaissance" and published work by Langston Hughes, Zora Neale Hurston, and W. E. B. Du Bois. Locke also wrote or edited *Race Contacts and Inter-Racial Relations* (1916), *Opportunity* (an annual review of the state of black writing), *Negro Art: Past and Present* (1936), and *The Negro and His Music* (1940).

**Lowery, Joseph E.** (1924-    ): Cleric and civil rights leader. The pastor of the Warren Street Church in Birmingham, Alabama (1952-1961), Lowery was one of the cofounders of the Southern Negro Leaders Conference, which evolved into the Southern Christian Leadership Conference (SCLC) in 1957, and served as its first vice president under Martin Luther King, Jr. He became president of the SCLC in 1977 and pastor of Cascade United Methodist Church in Atlanta, Georgia, in 1986.

**McKay, Claude** (1889-1948): Jamaican-born poet, novelist, and essayist. A key figure in the Harlem Renaissance, McKay is noted for his poetry about his experiences with American racism. His poetry volumes include *Constab Ballads* (1912), *Songs of Jamaica* (1912), and *Harlem Shadows* (1922)—which established his reputation as a major Harlem Renaissance figure. McKay's fiction includes the short stories of *Gingertown* (1932) and the novels *Home to Harlem* (1928), *Banjo: A Story Without a Plot* (1929), and *Banana Bottom* (1933). He also published an autobiography, *A Long Way from Home* (1937), and the nonfiction *Harlem: Negro Metropolis* (1940).

**McKissick, Floyd** (1922-1991): Lawyer and civil rights leader. After suing the University of North Carolina at Chapel Hill for admission to its law school, he became the first African American to earn a degree there. He was later the head of the Congress of Racial Equality (1966-1968). From 1968 to 1980, he worked unsuccessfully to establish a new and self-sufficient community in Warren County, North Carolina, known as Soul City.

**Malcolm X** (1925-1965): Black nationalist leader. Malcolm was born Malcolm Little in a Nebraska family that was committed to Marcus Garvey's United Negro Improvement Association. After his father's murder by white racists, he left school and went to New York, where he was convicted of burglary. While in prison, he converted to the Nation of Islam. A brilliant speaker, he began making provocative, antiwhite statements, for which he was expelled from the Nation of Islam by Elijah Muhammad. He then formed the Organization of Afro-American Unity and Muslim Mosque Inc. in 1964. After undertaking a pilgrimage to Mecca, he converted to orthodox Islam, changed his name to El-Hajj Malik El-Shabazz, and moderated his political and social views. In 1965, he was shot to death by Black Muslims. He was the author, with Alex Haley, of *The Autobiography of Malcolm X* (1965).

**Marshall, Thurgood** (1908-1993): Lawyer, civil rights activist, and jurist. Marshall served as chief legal counsel for the National Association for the Advancement of Colored People (1938-1961) and played a key role in the landmark *Brown v. Board of Education* case (1954), in which the U.S. Supreme Court overturned the "separate but equal" doctrine in public education. Marshall won twenty-nine of the thirty-two cases that he argued before the Supreme Court. He later became a federal circuit court judge (1961-1967) and was appointed the first African American justice on the U.S. Supreme Court (1967-1991).

**Meredith, James** (1933-    ): Civil rights activist. Meredith became the first African American to attend the University of Mississippi in 1962. His admission to the university generated riots and the stationing of federal troops on the campus. In 1966, while leading a march to encourage black voter registration, he was shot by a sniper but recovered. That same year, he wrote *Three Years in Mississippi* (1966).

**Morrison, Toni** (1931-    ): Writer. Born Chloe Anthony Wofford, Morrison has incorporated African and African American folklore, legend, and mythology into her novels. Her works also contain many autobiographical references. Her novel *Beloved* (1987), which examines the brutality of American slavery, won the Pulitzer Prize in fiction in 1988 and was made into a motion picture in 1998. In 1993, Morrison became the first African American to win the Nobel Prize in Literature. Her books include *The Bluest Eye* (1970), *Sula* (1974), *Song of Solomon* (1977), *Tar Baby* (1981), and *Jazz* (1992).

**Muhammad, Elijah** (1897-1975): Religious and black nationalist leader. Born Elijah Poole to a former slave, Muhammad became chief assistant to W. D. Fard, the founder of the Lost-Found Nation of Islam, in 1930. Upon Fard's mysterious disappearance in 1934, he succeeded to leadership of the Nation of Islam. In that capacity, he preached racial segregation, black integrity, and the need for economic independence from whites. His support for Japan in World War II and the conviction of three members of the Nation of Islam for the assassination of Malcolm X in 1965 led to unfavorable press coverage, but his movement continued to grow, especially among the underemployed of the major cities.

**Newton, Huey P.** (1942-1989): Black activist. In 1966, Newton was the cofounder, with Bobby Seale, of the Black Panther Party for Self-Defense, which became a major force in California politics. The following year, he was convicted of manslaughter in the killing of an Oakland police officer, but his conviction was later overturned. In 1977, he helped elect Lionel Wilson as the first black mayor of Oakland. After frequently being in legal trouble throughout the 1970's and 1980's, he was killed by a drug dealer in 1989.

**Owens, Jesse** (1913-1980): Track and field athlete. One of the first great all-around track and field athletes, Owens earned four gold medals at the 1936 Berlin Olympics (100- and 200-meter races, 400-meter relay, broad jump). He became internationally famous in that Olympiad when German leader Adolf Hitler refused to present Owens his gold medals. Owens later traveled and spoke widely on the value of sports in breaking down racial barriers.

**Parks, Rosa** (1913-    ): Civil rights activist. While serving as secretary of the Montgomery, Alabama, chapter of the National Association for the Advancement of Colored People during the 1950's, Parks was arrested and fined for refusing to give up her seat to a white passenger on a Montgomery, Alabama, bus. Her arrest sparked a 382-day citywide bus boycott aimed at desegregating public transportation. White harassment eventually led Parks and her family to move to Detroit, Michigan, where she worked in the office of Congressman John Conyers and continued to campaign for civil rights.

**Patterson, Frederick D.** (1901-1988): Educator. A faculty member and later president of Tuskegee Institute, Patterson was also chairman of the R. R. Moton Memorial Institute. In 1944, he organized the United Negro College Fund to aid historically black colleges and universities.

**Payne, Daniel Alexander** (1811-1893): Educator, abolitionist, and cleric. Born in South Carolina to free black parents, Patterson opened a school for black students in Charleston in 1829. After his school was closed by an act of the South Carolina legislature, he traveled north to study and delivered powerful abolitionist speeches throughout the 1840's and 1850's. In 1852, he was elected a bishop of the African Methodist Episcopal Church. In 1863, he bought Wilberforce University from the Methodist Episcopal Church and devoted the rest of his life to developing the university and overseeing missionary endeavors. His writings include *Recollections of Seventy Years* (1888) and *History of the African Methodist Episcopal Church* (1891).

**Powell, Adam Clayton, Jr.** (1908-1972): New York City politician. Instrumental in securing better treatment for African Americans in Harlem during the Depression of the 1930's, Powell succeeded his father as pastor of the Abyssinian Baptist Church in 1936. He also served in various New York government posts until 1944, when he was elected to the U.S. House of Representatives (1945-1967, 1969-1971). While a congressman, he sponsored more than fifty pieces of social legislation, many aimed at ending discrimination against minorities. In 1960, he became chairman of the House Committee on Education and Labor. In 1967, he was censured in the House and unseated for misuse of public funds but was readmitted the following year.

**Powell, Colin** (1937-      ): Military leader and government official. Born in New York City to Jamaican immigrants, Powell joined the U.S. Army and served two tours of duty in the Vietnam War. He later served as a military assistant to the secretary of defense (1983) and as national security adviser to President Ronald Reagan (1987-1989). Under President George Bush, he served as chairman of the joint chiefs of staff (1989-1993)—a position that made him the highest-ranking African American officer in military history, as well as the highest-ranking officer in the United States at the time. In that position, he gained international recognition for his role in conducting the Persian Gulf War (1991). His popularity and vocal support for personal responsibility made him an attractive political candidate after he left the military. He addressed the 1996 Republican National Convention in San Diego, heightening rumors that he might one day run for high office, but he declined to seek office. After George W. Bush was elected president in 2000, Powell became U.S. secretary of state. He distinguished himself as a voice of moderation through the new military conflicts in which the United States became involved but resigned his cabinet post after Bush's reelection in 2004. He was succeeded as secretary of state by Condoleezza Rice.

**Randolph, A. Philip** (1889-1979): Labor leader and civil rights activist. Randolph is remembered as a key figure in the racial integration of American labor. In 1925, he began a successful fight to have the Brotherhood of Sleeping Car Porters recognized as an agent in negotiation with the Pullman Company. His actions led to Pullman's signing a contract with the porters in 1937. In 1941, Randolph was instrumental in persuading President Franklin D. Roosevelt to sign Executive Order 8802, which banned discrimination in employment by companies with defense contracts. Randolph's threat to organize a black boycott of the military draft in 1948 helped persuade President Harry S. Truman to sign Executive Order 9981, which ended racial segregation in the armed forces. Randolph was a symbolic and unifying force when he acted as chairman and provided opening remarks for the 1963 March on Washington. In 1968, he retired as president of the Brotherhood of Sleeping Car Porters.

**Rice, Condoleezza** (1954-    ): Educator and foreign policy expert. From 1989 to 1991, Rice served as a director of Soviet and East European Affairs with the National Security Council. She also served as a strategic adviser to the Joint Chiefs of Staff. In 1990, President George Bush appointed her his assistant for national security affairs, and during that same year, Rice sat at the bargaining table when Bush met Soviet premier Mikhail Gorbachev in Malta. After the Bush administration left office in 1993, Rice became provost at Stanford University; she was the first African American chief academic officer and budget officer at the university and one of the highest-ranking black college administrators in the entire nation. In 2001, newly elected President George W. Bush appointed Rice his national security adviser. During her four years in that office, Rice was considered to be one of the most influential members of the Bush administration. In 2005, after Bush was reelected, he appointed Rice to succeed Colin Powell as secretary of state.

**Robeson, Paul** (1898-1976): Singer and actor. The son of a runaway slave, Robeson earned a law degree at Columbia University and became a successful stage actor after being discovered by playwright Eugene O'Neill during the 1920's. His performance in O'Neill's *The Emperor Jones* (1923) led to a successful singing career. Active in national and international civil and human rights campaigns, Robeson spoke out vigorously for the independence of Europe's African colonies. His trips to the Soviet Union and other associations with communists led to the revocation of his passport in 1950 and a decline in his career. He regained his passport after an eight-year legal battle in 1958 and then moved to London, where he lived until 1963. His published autobiography is *Here I Stand* (1958).

**Robinson, Jackie** (1919-1972): Baseball player; after a stellar career at the University of California at Los Angeles (UCLA), Robinson left in his junior year to play professional football for the Los Angeles Bulldogs. After serving as a lieutenant in the U.S. Army during World War II, he played professional baseball with the Kansas City Monarchs of the Negro American League. In 1947, he became the first black player in modern Major League Baseball history. During his ten-year career with the Brooklyn Dodgers, he won many honors on the field, while responding to hostility from other players and fans with grace. His success paved the way for the expansion of opportunities for black athletes in all professional sports. He was inducted into the Baseball Hall of Fame in 1962.

**Roosevelt, Franklin D.** (1882-1945): Thirty-second president of the United States (1933-1945). During his three-plus terms in office, Roosevelt led the nation through the Great Depression and most of World War II and was seen as a supporter of civil rights for African Americans. He appointed more than two dozen African Americans to federal offices, and those appointees formed an unofficial Black Cabinet. In 1941, Roosevelt signed Executive Order 8802, which prohibited discrimination on the basis of race or color in the defense industry and armed forces. Roosevelt eased restrictions on opportunities for African Americans in the government and the military services but left the decision to order full desegregation of the military to his successor, Harry S. Truman.

**Rustin, Bayard** (1910-1987): Civil rights leader. During the Depression, Rustin organized the Young Communist League (1936-1941). Afterward, he worked with James Farmer on the Chicago Committee of Racial Equality, which developed into the Congress of Racial Equality. He was later a founding member of the Southern Christian Leadership Conference. In 1963, he served as organizational coordinator of the March on Washington, after which he became executive director of the A. Philip Randolph Institute (1964-1979). In 1975, he founded the Organization for Black Americans to Support Israel.

**Scott, Dred** (1795-1858): Missouri slave whose struggle to win his freedom led to one of the most infamous rulings in U.S. Supreme Court history. During the 1850's, he sued for his freedom on the grounds that because he had accompanied his master into the free state of Illinois he should no longer be considered a slave. After going through Missouri's courts, his case reached the U.S. Supreme Court in 1857. In its *Scott v. Sandford* decision, the Court ruled that Scott, as a slave, was not a legal citizen and therefore had no standing before the courts. Scott himself was eventually freed by his owner shortly before his death the following year, but the Supreme Court's ruling in the case defined slaves as noncitizens. It would not be until ratification of the Fourteenth Amendment to the U.S. Constitution in 1868 that African Americans were legally considered citizens.

**Seale, Bobby** (1936-    ): Black activist. Seale was cofounder, with Huey P. Newton, of the Black Panther Party for Self-Defense in 1966. In 1971, he was tried for the kidnapping and killing of a suspected police informant, but his case ended in a mistrial. Disenchanted with revolutionary politics, Seale left the Panthers in 1974. His writings include *Seize the Time: The Story of the Black Panther Party* (1970) and *A Lonely Rage: The Autobiography of Bobby Seale* (1978).

**Sharpton, Al** (1954-    ): Christian cleric and social activist. After gaining prominence for his Pentecostal preaching in Brooklyn, Sharpton became active in the Civil Rights movement. He served as youth director of Jesse Jackson's Operation Breadbasket. He also briefly served as a bodyguard for singer James Brown and worked with fight promoter Don King. In 1971, Sharpton founded the National Youth Movement (later renamed the United African Movement). A politically controversial figure whose motives have often been questioned, Sharpton has been involved in many high-profile racial incidents in New York City, including the Bernhard Goetz murder trial in 1984, the Howard Beach killing in 1986, the Tawana Brawley affair in 1987, and the Bensonhurst killing in 1989. In 2004, he campaigned for the Democratic nomination for the presidency and earned some credibility as a mainstream politician.

**Stevens, Thaddeus** (1792-1868): Radical Republican politician, abolitionist, and advocate of African American civil rights. As a Pennsylvania congressman (1849-1853, 1859-1868), Stevens opposed fugitive slave laws; led the Radical Republican plan for Reconstruction after the Civil War, and was instrumental in framing the Fourteenth Amendment to the U.S. Constitution (1868). He was also one of the leaders in Congress's impeachment of President Andrew Johnson.

**Thomas, Clarence** (1948-    ): Second African American associate justice on the U.S. Supreme Court (1992-    ). After being appointed to the Court by President George Bush in 1991, Thomas had to endure a difficult confirmation battle in the Senate that was highlighted by the testimony of his former aide Anita F. Hill, who accused him of sexual harassment.

Thomas remained a controversial justice because of his refusal to support positions many believed were essential to African American well-being.

**Till, Emmett** (1941-1955): Lynching victim. A Chicago teenager, Till was killed by white racists while visiting relatives in Mississippi. His murder helped call national attention to the virulence of racism in the South, and the speedy acquittal, by an all-white jury, of his accused murderers revealed the failings of the justice system. In 2004, the U.S. Justice Department announced that it was reopening its investigation into Till's murder.

**Truman, Harry S.** (1884-1972): Thirty-third president of the United States (1945-1953). After rising from the vice presidency to the presidency on the death of Franklin D. Roosevelt early in the latter's fourth term, Truman became the first U.S. president to call openly for civil rights legislation to improve the social and political condition of African Americans. In 1946, he appointed the President's Committee on Civil Rights, which the following year issued a report titled *To Secure These Rights*. In 1948, Truman completed the work begun by his predecessor by banning racial segregation in the armed forces with Executive Order 9981.

**Truth, Sojourner** (c. 1797-1883): Abolitionist. Born into slavery as Isabella Baumfree, Truth was freed by the New York State Emancipation Act in 1827. Afterward, she preached and lectured widely to abolitionist audiences, adopting the symbolic name Sojourner Truth in 1843. During the Civil War, she raised money for soldiers and runaway slaves and served as councilor with the National Freedmen's Relief Association. She dictated her autobiography, *The Narrative of Sojourner Truth* (1850).

**Tubman, Harriet** (c. 1820-1913): Abolitionist. Born Araminta Ross in Maryland, Tubman escaped from slavery in 1848. Afterward, she helped rescue more than three hundred slaves in nineteen forays along the Underground Railroad. She also helped John Brown recruit men for his raid on Harpers Ferry in 1858. After 1860, she spoke widely on emancipation and women's rights. During the Civil War, she served as nurse and spy for the Union army and was later buried with military honors.

**Turner, Henry McNeal** (1834-1915): Religious leader. Born to free parents in South Carolina, Turner was tutored by lawyers for whom he worked as a janitor. In 1853, he became a preacher in the Methodist Episcopal Church South. Five years later, he switched his affiliation and preached for African Methodist Episcopal churches in Baltimore and Washington, D.C. (1858-1863). During the Civil War, he served as chaplain to the First U.S. Colored Troops. After the war, he was elected a Georgia State representative (1868-1869, 1870). In 1880, he was elected a bishop of the African Methodist Episcopal Church. After campaigning for full voting rights for African Americans, he advocated a return to Africa when the federal civil rights laws were overturned by the U.S. Supreme Court in 1883. His proclamation that "God is a Negro" anticipated modern black theology.

**Turner, Nat** (1800-1831): Slave rebellion leader. A Virginia slave, Turner planned and led the bloodiest slave revolt in U.S. history in Virginia's Southampton County in 1831. More than sixty slaves and free blacks rose up against white landowners and killed at least fifty-five people, including women and children. All the rebels were eventually killed or executed. Turner himself was caught and tried and hanged. Although his revolt was an isolated event in a remote part of Virginia, it had a profound impact on white southerners, who responded with more repressive laws and a wave of lynchings.

**Walker, Alice** (1944-    ): Writer and poet. Walker's works deal principally with the experiences of black women living in a racist and sexist society. Her early books were critically acclaimed, but she did not become widely popular until publishing her third novel, *The Color Purple* (1982), which won a Pulitzer Prize in fiction and was adapted to film in 1985. Walker has also been a champion of the works of Zora Neale Hurston. Walker has published in several genres, including poetry: *Once* (1968) and *Revolutionary Petunias and Other Poems* (1973); novels: *The Third Life of Grange Copeland* (1970), *Meridian* (1976), and *Possessing the Secret of Joy* (1992); short stories: "In Love and Trouble" (1973) and "You Can't Keep a Good Woman Down" (1976); and criticism: *A Zora Neale Hurston Reader* (1980).

**Warren, Earl** (1891-1974): Former governor of California whom President Dwight D. Eisenhower appointed chief justice of the

United States in 1953. Warren took office at a moment when the Court was facing new challenges to lower court rulings on school segregation. Under Warren's strong leadership, the Court reached a unanimous decision in the landmark *Brown v. Board of Education* (1954) case that outlawed desegregation in public schools and paved the way for new civil rights legislation and additional progressive Supreme Court rulings. Warren himself is remembered for destroying the "separate but equal" doctrine by declaring that "in the field of public education the doctrine of 'separate but equal' has no place. Separate educational facilities are inherently unequal."

**Washington, Booker T.** (1856-1915): Educator. Born a slave in Virginia, Washington became committed to the idea that education would raise African Americans to equality. After teaching Native Americans at the Hampton Institute (1879-1881), he founded the Tuskegee Normal and Industrial Institute in 1881 and served as its president through the rest of his life. He also cofounded the National Negro Business League in 1900. He advised Presidents William Howard Taft and Theodore Roosevelt on racial issues and promoted what has been called the "Atlanta Compromise,"—the doctrine of African Americans accepting segregation in return for greater economic opportunities. His conservative racial views appealed to many white Americans who feared more radical change but were opposed by other African American leaders, including W. E. B. Du Bois. Washington's autobiography, *Up from Slavery* (1901), became one of the most widely read books by African Americans during the early twentieth century.

**Wells-Barnett, Ida B.** (1862-1931): Journalist. Wells-Barnett was editor and part owner of the black newspaper *Memphis Free Speech*. Her vigorous campaigns against lynching led to a mob attack on her newspaper's offices. With Frederick Douglass and Ferdinand L. Barnett, Wells-Barnett wrote "The Reason Why the Colored American Is Not in the World's Columbian Exposition" (1893). She also published the antilynching pamphlet "Red Record" (1895) and defended W. E. B. Du Bois's criticisms of Booker T. Washington in the former's *The Souls of Black Folk* (1903). In 1909, she helped Du Bois found the National Association for the Advancement of Colored People.

**White, Walter** (1893-1955): Civil rights leader. The executive secretary of the National Association for the Advancement of Colored People from 1931 to 1955, White was an energetic and outspoken advocate of African American rights. He was also a fervent campaigner against lynching and fought a long and fruitless campaign for passage of a federal antilynching law. His writings include two fictional accounts of lynchings and a report on African American service in World War II.

**Wilder, L. Douglas** (1931-     ): Virginia politician. A decorated Korean War veteran, Wilder became a successful Virginia trial lawyer and was an officer in the National Urban League during the Civil Rights movement. In 1969, he became the first African American elected to the Virginia senate since Reconstruction. In 1985 he was elected lieutenant governor; four years later, he was elected governor—the first African American elected governor of any U.S. state.

**Wilkins, Roy** (1901-1981): Journalist and civil rights leader. Wilkins was on the staff of the Kansas City *Call* (1923-1931). He served as assistant executive secretary of the National Association for the Advancement of Colored People (NAACP) from 1931 to 1955, when he became the organization's executive secretary. He remained in the latter position until 1964 and then became the NAACP's executive director (1965-1977). He was also chairman of the Leadership Conference on Civil Rights. Wilkins was the editor of *The Crisis* from 1934 to 1949.

**Woodson, Carter** (1875-1950): Scholar. Often known as the "Father of Modern Black History," Woodson formed the Association for the Study of Negro Life and History (later the Association for the Study of Afro-American Life and History) in 1915. A year later, that body established the *Journal of Negro History*. Woodson also founded Associated Publishers in 1920 and the *Negro History Bulletin* in 1921. Woodson is credited with creating Negro History Week, which later expanded into Black History Month. His many books include *The Education of the Negro Prior to 1861* (1915); *The Negro in Our History* (1922), *The Miseducation of the Negro* (1933), and *African Heroes and Heroines* (1939).

**Wright, Richard** (1908-1960): Novelist. Wright used personal experiences from his Mississippi youth to dramatize the brutal effects of racism in such books as *Uncle Tom's Children*, which won the Best Work of Fiction by a Works Progress Administration writer in 1938; *Native Son* (1940); and the largely autobiographical *Black Boy* (1945). A member of the Communist Party from 1933 to 1944, he moved to Paris in 1946. There he continued writing. His later books include *The Outsider* (1953), *Black Power* (1954), *White Man Listen* (1957), and *Eight Men* (1961). *American Hunger* (1977) is a continuation of his autobiography.

**Young, Andrew** (1932-     ): Civil rights activist, politician, and diplomat. An aide and confidant of Martin Luther King, Jr., during the early 1960's, Young was executive vice president of the Southern Christian Leadership Conference in 1967. During the 1970's, he entered Georgia state politics. He served as a Georgia state representative (1973-1977) and was mayor of Atlanta (1981-1989). In between, he was made U.S. ambassador to the United Nations (1977-1979) by President Jimmy Carter, a former governor of Georgia. Young also chaired the Atlanta Committee for the 1996 Olympic Games.

**Young, Whitney** (1921-1971): Educator and civil rights leader. Young was executive director of the St. Paul chapter of the Minnesota Urban League (1950-1954); dean of Atlanta University School of Social Work (1954-1961); and executive director of the National Urban League (1961-1971). During the 1960's, he called for a "domestic Marshall Plan" to end black poverty and helped President Lyndon B. Johnson craft his War on Poverty. In 1969, he received the Medal of Freedom. His writings include *To Be Equal* (1964) and *Beyond Racism* (1969).

*John Powell and the Editors*

# Category Index

## List of Contents

Abolition . . . . . . . . . . . . 1127
Affirmative Action. . . . . . . 1128
Agriculture . . . . . . . . . . . 1128
Arts, Literature, and
　　Music . . . . . . . . . . . . 1128
Black Nationalism . . . . . . . 1128
Civil Rights and Liberties. . . . 1128
Civil Rights Movement . . . . . 1129
Court Cases. . . . . . . . . . . 1129
Crime . . . . . . . . . . . . . . 1131
Demographics . . . . . . . . . 1131
Desegregation . . . . . . . . . 1131
Discrimination . . . . . . . . . 1132
Economics . . . . . . . . . . . 1132
Education. . . . . . . . . . . . 1133
Events. . . . . . . . . . . . . . 1133
Family Issues. . . . . . . . . . 1134
Justice System . . . . . . . . . 1135
Labor and Employment. . . . . 1135
Law Enforcement . . . . . . . 1135
Laws. . . . . . . . . . . . . . . 1136

Media . . . . . . . . . . . . . . 1136
Military . . . . . . . . . . . . . 1136
Mob Violence. . . . . . . . . . 1137
Organizations . . . . . . . . . 1137
Pan-Africanism . . . . . . . . 1138
Peoples . . . . . . . . . . . . . 1138
Politics and Government . . . . 1138
Popular Culture . . . . . . . . 1139
Race Relations . . . . . . . . . 1139
Racism . . . . . . . . . . . . . 1140
Reconstruction . . . . . . . . . 1140
Religion. . . . . . . . . . . . . 1140
Science and Technology. . . . . 1140
Segregation. . . . . . . . . . . 1140
Slave Revolts . . . . . . . . . . 1141
Slave Trade . . . . . . . . . . . 1141
Slavery . . . . . . . . . . . . . 1141
Sports . . . . . . . . . . . . . . 1141
Urbanization . . . . . . . . . . 1141
Voting Rights. . . . . . . . . . 1142
Women's Issues . . . . . . . . . 1142

ABOLITION

Abolition, 1
Abolitionist movement and
　　women, 5
African Methodist Episcopal
　　Church, 26
African Methodist Episcopal Zion
　　Churches, 30
American Anti-Slavery Society,
　　42
American Colonization Society,
　　46
*Amistad* slave revolt, 47
Antislavery laws of 1777 and
　　1807, 58
Bleeding Kansas, 134

Civil War, 226
*Clotilde* capture, 234
Compromise of 1850, 243
Confiscation Acts of 1861 and
　　1862, 249
Emancipation Proclamation, 323
Free blacks, 366
Freedmen's Bureau, 367
Fugitive Slave Law of 1793, 382
Fugitive Slave Law of 1850, 387
Harpers Ferry raid, 436
*Liberator, The*, 532
National Council of Colored
　　People, 654
Negro Conventions, 667
*North Star, The*, 689

Pennsylvania Society for the
Abolition of Slavery, 703
Proslavery argument, 731
Slavery, 826
Slavery and the justice system,
850
Thirteenth Amendment, 922
Turner's slave insurrection, 933
Underground Railroad, 947

AFFIRMATIVE ACTION
*Adarand Constructors v. Peña*, 13
Affirmative action, 15
*Bakke* case, 71
Civil Rights Act of 1991, 198
Employment, 327
Equal Employment Opportunity
Act of 1972, 331
Equal Employment Opportunity
Commission, 338
*Fullilove v. Klutznick*, 391
*United Steelworkers of America v.
Weber*, 962

AGRICULTURE
Agriculture, 32
Atlanta Compromise, 67
Demographic trends, 283
Economic trends, 304
Employment, 327
Great Migration, 399
Sharecropping, 806

ARTS, LITERATURE, AND MUSIC
Anderson's Lincoln Memorial
concert, 51
Black Is Beautiful movement, 114
Film history, 352
Harlem Renaissance, 426
Literature, 537
Media, the, 569
Music, 624
Stereotypes, 898

BLACK NATIONALISM
African Liberation Day, 25
Black Christian Nationalist
Movement, 95
Black Is Beautiful movement, 114
Black nationalism, 118
Black Panther Party, 123
Black Power movement, 129
Black United Students, 132
Combahee River Collective, 241
Congressional Black Caucus, 256
Hampton-Clark deaths, 424
League of Revolutionary Black
Workers, 530
Malcolm X assassination, 559
Million Man March, 593
Million Woman March, 597
Nation of Islam, 631
National Coalition of Blacks for
Reparations in America, 653
Pan-Africanism, 701
Republic of New Africa, 765
Universal Negro Improvement
Association, 969

CIVIL RIGHTS AND LIBERTIES
*Brown v. Mississippi*, 144
Civil Rights Act of 1866, 177
Civil Rights Act of 1957, 182
Civil Rights Act of 1960, 183
Civil Rights Act of 1964, 188
Civil Rights Act of 1968, 195
Civil Rights Act of 1991, 198
Civil Rights Acts of 1866-1875,
199
*Civil Rights* cases, 202
Civil Rights movement, 204
Civil Rights Restoration Act, 215
Colored Women's League, 240
*Edmonson v. Leesville Concrete
Company*, 314
*Edwards v. South Carolina*, 322
Fourteenth Amendment, 357
*Griffin v. Breckenridge*, 413
Integration, 454

King beating case, 515
Marshall's appointment to the
   Supreme Court, 564
National Association for the
   Advancement of Colored
   People, 636
National Association for the
   Advancement of Colored
   People Legal Defense and
   Educational Fund, 643
*National Association for the*
   *Advancement of Colored People*
   *v. Alabama*, 650
National Council of Negro
   Women, 658
Negro Conventions, 667
Niagara Movement, 681
Politics and government, 713
Poll taxes, 723
President's Committee on Civil
   Rights, 729
*R.A.V. v. City of St. Paul*, 735
Rainbow Coalition, 753
*Scott v. Sandford*, 783
Segregation, 790
Separate but equal doctrine, 805
Sit-ins, 818
*Smith v. Allwright*, 875
Thirteenth Amendment, 922
Twenty-fourth Amendment, 941
United States Commission on
   Civil Rights, 954
*United States v. Cruikshank*, 959
Voting Rights Act of 1965, 983
Voting Rights Act of 1975, 990
*Wisconsin v. Mitchell*, 1018

CIVIL RIGHTS MOVEMENT
Birmingham March, 91
Chicago sit-ins, 154
Civil Rights movement, 204
Civil Rights movement and
   children, 214
Civil rights worker murders, 219
Congress of Racial Equality, 250

Council of Federated
   Organizations, 260
*Edwards v. South Carolina*, 322
Freedom Rides, 372
Freedom Summer, 374
Greensboro sit-ins, 406
"I Have a Dream" speech, 449
Integration, 454
Jews and African Americans, 470
Journey of Reconciliation, 481
King assassination, 507
Mississippi Freedom Democratic
   Party, 603
Montgomery bus boycott, 614
National Association for the
   Advancement of Colored
   People, 636
National Association for the
   Advancement of Colored
   People Legal Defense and
   Educational Fund, 643
National Urban League, 659
New York riots, 674
Poor People's March on
   Washington, 725
President's Committee on Civil
   Rights, 729
School desegregation, 770
Segregation, 790
Selma-Montgomery march, 797
Sit-ins, 818
Southern Christian Leadership
   Conference, 879
Student Nonviolent Coordinating
   Committee, 908
Summit Meeting of National
   Negro Leaders, 912
University of Mississippi
   desegregation, 974
Vietnam War, 979

COURT CASES
*Adarand Constructors v. Peña*, 13
*Albemarle Paper Company v.*
   *Moody*, 39

Alexander v. Holmes County Board of Education, 40

Bakke case, 71

Batson v. Kentucky, 90

Bolling v. Sharpe, 137

Brown v. Board of Education, 140

Brown v. Mississippi, 144

Buchanan v. Warley, 147

Burton v. Wilmington Parking Authority, 150

Civil Rights cases, 202

Cooper v. Aaron, 258

Cumming v. Richmond County Board of Education, 276

Edmonson v. Leesville Concrete Company, 314

Edwards v. South Carolina, 322

Evans v. Abney, 340

Fullilove v. Klutznick, 391

Gomillion v. Lightfoot, 397

Green v. County School Board of New Kent County, 404

Griffin v. Breckenridge, 413

Griggs v. Duke Power Company, 415

Groves v. Slaughter, 417

Grovey v. Townsend, 418

Guinn v. United States, 419

Harper v. Virginia Board of Elections, 435

Heart of Atlanta Motel v. United States, 442

Jones v. Alfred H. Mayer Company, 479

Katzenbach v. McClung, 496

Keyes v. Denver School District No. 1, 506

Lassiter v. Northampton County Board of Elections, 530

Louisville, New Orleans, and Texas Railway Company v. Mississippi, 552

McCleskey v. Kemp, 557

McLaurin v. Oklahoma State Regents for Higher Education, 558

Martin v. Wilks, 568

Milliken v. Bradley, 592

Missouri ex rel. Gaines v. Canada, 612

Mobile v. Bolden, 613

Moore v. Dempsey, 619

Moose Lodge v. Irvis, 620

National Association for the Advancement of Colored People v. Alabama, 650

Newberry v. United States, 679

Nixon v. Condon, 685

Nixon v. Herndon, 686

Norris v. Alabama, 687

Palmer v. Thompson, 700

Patterson v. McLean Credit Union, 702

Plessy v. Ferguson, 708

Powell v. Alabama, 727

Powers v. Ohio, 728

R.A.V. v. City of St. Paul, 735

Reitman v. Mulkey, 763

Runyon v. McCrary, 768

Scott v. Sandford, 783

Scottsboro trials, 786

Shaw v. Hunt, 808

Shaw v. Reno, 810

Shelley v. Kraemer, 812

Slaughterhouse Cases, 819

Smith v. Allwright, 875

Strauder v. West Virginia, 907

Swann v. Charlotte-Mecklenberg Board of Education, 913

Sweatt v. Painter, 917

Terry v. Adams, 921

United States v. Classic, 958

United States v. Cruikshank, 959

United States v. Reese, 961

United Steelworkers of America v. Weber, 962

Washington v. Davis, 996

Williams v. Mississippi, 1017

Wisconsin v. Mitchell, 1018

Yarbrough, Ex parte, 1025

CRIME
Brown v. Mississippi, 144
Church bombings, 169
Church burnings, 174
Civil rights worker murders, 219
Clinton massacre, 233
Dyer antilynching bill, 302
Fugitive Slave Law of 1793, 382
Fugitive Slave Law of 1850, 387
Hampton-Clark deaths, 424
Harlins murder, 434
Harpers Ferry raid, 436
Hawkins murder, 441
King assassination, 507
King beating case, 515
Lynching, 553
McCleskey v. Kemp, 557
Malcolm X assassination, 559
Moynihan Report, 623
Newberry v. United States, 679
Orangeburg massacre, 699
Powell v. Alabama, 727
R.A.V. v. City of St. Paul, 735
Scottsboro trials, 786
Simpson murder trial, 813
Till lynching, 931
Tuskegee experiment, 939

DEMOGRAPHICS
Agriculture, 32
Black colleges and universities, 107
Black flight, 112
Black Jews, 115
Cubans and African Americans, 270
Demographic trends, 283
Economic trends, 304
Free blacks, 366
Great Migration, 399
Haitians, 421
Jamaicans, 466
Jews and African Americans, 470
Koreans and African Americans, 520

Native Americans and African Americans, 661
One-drop rule, 698
Segregation on the frontier, 793
Slavery and women, 858
Slavery in Massachusetts, 865
Slavery in Virginia, 870
West Indians, 1002

DESEGREGATION
Alexander v. Holmes County Board of Education, 40
Bolling v. Sharpe, 137
Brown v. Board of Education, 140
Civil Rights Acts of 1866-1875, 199
Civil Rights movement, 204
Cooper v. Aaron, 258
Cumming v. Richmond County Board of Education, 276
Defense industry desegregation, 277
Fair Housing Act, 342
Green v. County School Board of New Kent County, 404
Greensboro sit-ins, 406
Heart of Atlanta Motel v. United States, 442
Integration, 454
Jones v. Alfred H. Mayer Company, 479
Katzenbach v. McClung, 496
Keyes v. Denver School District No. 1, 506
Little Rock school desegregation crisis, 544
McLaurin v. Oklahoma State Regents for Higher Education, 558
Military, 579
Military desegregation, 583
Milliken v. Bradley, 592
Reitman v. Mulkey, 763
Runyon v. McCrary, 768
School desegregation, 770

Segregation, 790
Sit-ins, 818
Southern Manifesto, 887
*Swann v. Charlotte-Mecklenburg
    Board of Education*, 913
*Sweatt v. Painter*, 917
University of Mississippi
    desegregation, 974

DISCRIMINATION
*Adarand Constructors v. Peña*, 13
Affirmative action, 15
*Albemarle Paper Company v.
    Moody*, 39
*Batson v. Kentucky*, 90
Black codes, 103
*Buchanan v. Warley*, 147
*Burton v. Wilmington Parking
    Authority*, 150
Civil Rights Act of 1968, 195
Civil Rights Act of 1991, 198
Civil Rights Acts of 1866-1875,
    199
*Civil Rights* cases, 202
Cowboys, 267
Disfranchisement laws in
    Mississippi, 294
Employment, 327
Equal Employment Opportunity
    Commission, 338
*Evans v. Abney*, 340
Fair Employment Practices
    Committee, 340
Fair Housing Act, 342
Fifteenth Amendment, 347
*Fullilove v. Klutznick*, 391
Gerrymandering, 393
Grandfather clauses, 398
Greensboro sit-ins, 406
*Griggs v. Duke Power Company*,
    415
*Grovey v. Townsend*, 418
*Guinn v. United States*, 419
*Heart of Atlanta Motel v. United
    States*, 442

Jim Crow laws, 476
*Jones v. Alfred H. Mayer Company*,
    479
*Katzenbach v. McClung*, 496
*Louisville, New Orleans, and Texas
    Railway Company v. Mississippi*,
    552
*McCleskey v. Kemp*, 557
*Martin v. Wilks*, 568
*Missouri ex rel. Gaines v. Canada*,
    612
Montgomery bus boycott, 614
*Moose Lodge v. Irvis*, 620
*Nixon v. Condon*, 685
*Nixon v. Herndon*, 686
*Palmer v. Thompson*, 700
*Patterson v. McLean Credit Union*,
    702
*Plessy v. Ferguson*, 708
Poll taxes, 723
*Powers v. Ohio*, 728
*Reitman v. Mulkey*, 763
Restrictive covenants, 766
*Runyon v. McCrary*, 768
Segregation, 790
Separate but equal doctrine, 805
*Shelley v. Kraemer*, 812
Slave codes, 821
Understanding tests, 952
*Washington v. Davis*, 996
White primaries, 1009

ECONOMICS
Agriculture, 32
Brotherhood of Sleeping Car
    Porters, 138
Defense industry desegregation,
    277
Economic trends, 304
Employment, 327
Equal Employment Opportunity
    Act of 1972, 331
Equal Employment Opportunity
    Commission, 338
*Fullilove v. Klutznick*, 391

Great Migration, 399
League of Revolutionary Black
  Workers, 530
Million Man March, 593
Montgomery bus boycott, 614
*Moose Lodge v. Irvis*, 620
Moynihan Report, 623
National Coalition of Blacks for
  Reparations in America, 653
Negro Conventions, 667
*Patterson v. McLean Credit Union*,
  702
Poor People's March on
  Washington, 725
Restrictive covenants, 766
Sharecropping, 806
*Slaughterhouse Cases*, 819
Talented Tenth, 919
United Negro College Fund, 953
*United Steelworkers of America v.
  Weber*, 962
Universal Negro Improvement
  Association, 969

EDUCATION
Affirmative action, 15
Afrocentrism, 31
*Alexander v. Holmes County Board
  of Education*, 40
Ashmun Institute, 62
Atlanta Compromise, 67
*Bakke* case, 71
Black colleges and universities, 107
Black United Students, 132
*Bolling v. Sharpe*, 137
*Brown v. Board of Education*, 140
Civil Rights Restoration Act, 215
*Cooper v. Aaron*, 258
*Cumming v. Richmond County
  Board of Education*, 276
Education, 315
Equal Employment Opportunity
  Act of 1972, 331
*Green v. County School Board of
  New Kent County*, 404

*Keyes v. Denver School District
  No. 1*, 506
Little Rock school desegregation
  crisis, 544
*McLaurin v. Oklahoma State
  Regents for Higher Education*,
  558
*Milliken v. Bradley*, 592
*Missouri ex rel. Gaines v. Canada*,
  612
National Association for the
  Advancement of Colored
  People Legal Defense and
  Educational Fund, 643
Orangeburg massacre, 699
*Runyon v. McCrary*, 768
School desegregation, 770
Science and technology, 776
Student Nonviolent Coordinating
  Committee, 908
*Swann v. Charlotte-Mecklenburg
  Board of Education*, 913
Talented Tenth, 919
United Negro College Fund, 953
University of Mississippi
  desegregation, 974
White Citizens' Councils, 1007

EMPLOYMENT. *See* LABOR AND
EMPLOYMENT

EVENTS
African Liberation Day, 25
*Amistad* slave revolt, 47
Anderson's Lincoln Memorial
  concert, 51
Atlanta Compromise, 67
Baseball's racial integration, 82
Birmingham March, 91
"Black Manifesto," 117
Bleeding Kansas, 134
Brownsville incident, 145
Charleston race riots, 151
Chicago riots, 152
Chicago sit-ins, 154

Chisholm's election to Congress, 161
Church bombings, 169
Civil Rights movement, 204
Civil rights worker murders, 219
Civil War, 226
Clinton massacre, 233
*Clotilde* capture, 234
Colfax massacre, 239
Compromise of 1877, 248
Crown Heights conflicts, 268
Defense industry desegregation, 277
Draft riots, 298
Emancipation Proclamation, 323
Freedom Rides, 372
Freedom Summer, 374
Great Migration, 399
Greensboro sit-ins, 406
Hampton-Clark deaths, 424
Harlem Renaissance, 426
Harlins murder, 434
Harpers Ferry raid, 436
Hawkins murder, 441
"I Have a Dream" speech, 449
Jackson's run for the presidency, 461
Journey of Reconciliation, 481
King assassination, 507
King beating case, 515
Little Rock school desegregation crisis, 544
Los Angeles riots, 548
Malcolm X assassination, 559
Marshall's appointment to the Supreme Court, 564
Miami riots, 576
Military desegregation, 583
Million Man March, 593
Million Woman March, 597
Missouri Compromise, 606
Montgomery bus boycott, 614
MOVE bombing, 621
New York City slave revolt, 669
New York riots, 674

Newark riot, 677
Orangeburg massacre, 699
Poor People's March on Washington, 725
Race riots of 1866, 737
Race riots of 1943, 741
Race riots of 1967, 745
Race riots of the twentieth century, 750
Reconstruction, 755
Scottsboro trials, 786
Selma-Montgomery march, 797
Simpson murder trial, 813
Slavery in Massachusetts, 865
Slavery in Virginia, 870
Stono Rebellion, 902
Summit Meeting of National Negro Leaders, 912
Thomas-Hill hearings, 928
Till lynching, 931
Turner's slave insurrection, 933
Tuskegee experiment, 939
University of Mississippi desegregation, 974
Vietnam War, 979
Washington, D.C., riots, 997
Watts riot, 999
Wilder's election to Virginia governorship, 1010
World War II, 1020

FAMILY ISSUES
Agriculture, 32
Civil Rights movement and children, 214
Demographic trends, 283
Education, 315
Employment, 327
Equal Employment Opportunity Act of 1972, 331
Fair Housing Act, 342
Freedmen's Bureau, 367
Million Woman March, 597
Miscegenation laws, 600
Moynihan Report, 623

National Black Women's Political
Leadership Caucus, 652
*Roots*, 767
School desegregation, 770
Segregation on the frontier, 793
Sharecropping, 806
Slavery, 826
Slavery and families, 835
Slavery and women, 858
Tuskegee experiment, 939
Underground Railroad, 947

JUSTICE SYSTEM
*Batson v. Kentucky*, 90
*Bolling v. Sharpe*, 137
*Brown v. Mississippi*, 144
*Edmonson v. Leesville Concrete
Company*, 314
Hampton-Clark deaths, 424
King beating case, 515
Los Angeles riots, 548
*McCleskey v. Kemp*, 557
*Moore v. Dempsey*, 619
MOVE bombing, 621
National Association for the
Advancement of Colored
People Legal Defense and
Educational Fund, 643
*Norris v. Alabama*, 687
*Powell v. Alabama*, 727
*Powers v. Ohio*, 728
Scottsboro trials, 786
Simpson murder trial, 813
Slavery and the justice system,
850
*Strauder v. West Virginia*, 907
Till lynching, 931
*United States v. Cruikshank*, 959
*Williams v. Mississippi*, 1017
*Wisconsin v. Mitchell*, 1018

LABOR AND EMPLOYMENT
*Adarand Constructors v. Peña*, 13
Affirmative action, 15
Agriculture, 32

*Albemarle Paper Company v.
Moody*, 39
Brotherhood of Sleeping Car
Porters, 138
Civil Rights Act of 1964, 188
Civil Rights Act of 1991, 198
Cowboys, 267
Defense industry desegregation,
277
Economic trends, 304
Employment, 327
Equal Employment Opportunity
Act of 1972, 331
Equal Employment Opportunity
Commission, 338
Fair Employment Practices
Committee, 340
Freedmen's Bureau, 367
*Fullilove v. Klutznick*, 391
Great Migration, 399
*Griggs v. Duke Power Company*,
415
League of Revolutionary Black
Workers, 530
*Martin v. Wilks*, 568
National Urban League, 659
*Patterson v. McLean Credit Union*,
702
Race riots of 1943, 741
Sharecropping, 806
Slavery, 826
Talented Tenth, 919
*United Steelworkers of America v.
Weber*, 962
Universal Negro Improvement
Association, 969
*Washington v. Davis*, 996

LAW ENFORCEMENT
Charleston race riots, 151
Chicago riots, 152
Kerner Commission, 499
Ku Klux Klan Acts, 529
Los Angeles riots, 548
Lynching, 553

Miami riots, 576
MOVE bombing, 621
New York riots, 674
Newark riot, 677
Orangeburg massacre, 699
Race riots of 1866, 737
Race riots of 1943, 741
Race riots of 1967, 745
Race riots of the twentieth
   century, 750
Simpson murder trial, 813
Slavery and the justice system,
   850
Washington, D.C., riots, 997
Watts riot, 999

LAWS
Antislavery laws of 1777 and
   1807, 58
Black codes, 103
Civil Rights Act of 1866, 177
Civil Rights Act of 1957, 182
Civil Rights Act of 1960, 183
Civil Rights Act of 1964, 188
Civil Rights Act of 1968, 195
Civil Rights Act of 1991, 198
Civil Rights Acts of 1866-1875,
   199
Civil Rights Restoration Act, 215
Compromise of 1850, 243
Confiscation Acts of 1861 and
   1862, 249
Disfranchisement laws in
   Mississippi, 294
Dyer antilynching bill, 302
Equal Employment Opportunity
   Act of 1972, 331
Fair Housing Act, 342
Fifteenth Amendment, 347
Fourteenth Amendment, 357
Fugitive Slave Law of 1793, 382
Fugitive Slave Law of 1850, 387
Jim Crow laws, 476
Kansas-Nebraska Act, 490
Ku Klux Klan Acts, 529

Miscegenation laws, 600
Northwest Ordinance, 694
Slave codes, 821
Thirteenth Amendment, 922
Three-fifths compromise, 930
Twenty-fourth Amendment, 941
Voting Rights Act of 1965, 983
Voting Rights Act of 1975, 990

MEDIA
Black Power movement, 129
Church bombings, 169
Cowboys, 267
Film history, 352
Harlem Renaissance, 426
Jackson's run for the presidency,
   461
King beating case, 515
*Liberator, The*, 532
Literature, 537
Little Rock school desegregation
   crisis, 544
Los Angeles riots, 548
Media, the, 569
Million Man March, 593
Million Woman March, 597
Music, 624
*North Star, The*, 689
*Roots*, 767
Simpson murder trial, 813
Stereotypes, 898
Thomas-Hill hearings, 928

MILITARY
Brownsville incident, 145
Buffalo soldiers, 147
Civil War, 226
Confiscation Acts of 1861 and
   1862, 249
Defense industry desegregation,
   277
Draft riots, 298
Emancipation Proclamation, 323
Little Rock school desegregation
   crisis, 544

Military, 579
Military desegregation, 583
Native Americans and African
    Americans, 661
Reconstruction, 755
Tuskegee Airmen, 937
Vietnam War, 979
Watts riot, 999
World War II, 1020

MOB VIOLENCE
Charleston race riots, 151
Chicago riots, 152
Church bombings, 169
Church burnings, 174
Civil Rights movement and
    children, 214
Civil rights worker murders, 219
Clinton massacre, 233
Colfax massacre, 239
Crown Heights conflicts, 268
Draft riots, 298
Dyer antilynching bill, 302
Freedom Rides, 372
Hawkins murder, 441
Kerner Commission, 499
King assassination, 507
King beating case, 515
Ku Klux Klan, 523
Ku Klux Klan Acts, 529
Los Angeles riots, 548
Lynching, 553
Miami riots, 576
MOVE bombing, 621
National Advisory Commission
    on Civil Disorders, 635
New York riots, 674
Newark riot, 677
Orangeburg massacre, 699
*R.A.V. v. City of St. Paul*, 735
Race riots of 1866, 737
Race riots of 1943, 741
Race riots of 1967, 745
Race riots of the twentieth
    century, 750

Till lynching, 931
*United States v. Cruikshank*, 959
University of Mississippi
    desegregation, 974
Washington, D.C., riots, 997
Watts riot, 999

ORGANIZATIONS
African Methodist Episcopal
    Church, 26
African Methodist Episcopal Zion
    Churches, 30
American Anti-Slavery Society,
    42
American Colonization Society,
    46
Ashmun Institute, 62
Baptist Church, 78
Black cabinet, 94
Black Christian Nationalist
    Movement, 95
Black Panther Party, 123
Black United Students, 132
Brotherhood of Sleeping Car
    Porters, 138
Colored Women's League, 240
Combahee River Collective, 241
Congress of Racial Equality, 250
Congressional Black Caucus, 256
Council of Federated
    Organizations, 260
Equal Employment Opportunity
    Commission, 338
Fair Employment Practices
    Committee, 340
Free African Society, 362
Freedmen's Bureau, 367
Freemasons in Boston, 377
Kerner Commission, 499
Ku Klux Klan, 523
League of Revolutionary Black
    Workers, 530
Mississippi Freedom Democratic
    Party, 603
Nation of Islam, 631

National Advisory Commission
on Civil Disorders, 635
National Association for the
Advancement of Colored
People, 636
National Association for the
Advancement of Colored
People Legal Defense and
Educational Fund, 643
National Association of Colored
Women, 651
National Black Women's Political
Leadership Caucus, 652
National Coalition of Blacks for
Reparations in America, 653
National Council of Colored
People, 654
National Council of Negro
Women, 658
National Urban League, 659
Negro Conventions, 667
Niagara Movement, 681
Pennsylvania Society for the
Abolition of Slavery, 703
President's Committee on Civil
Rights, 729
Rainbow Coalition, 753
Republic of New Africa, 765
Southern Christian Leadership
Conference, 879
Student Nonviolent Coordinating
Committee, 908
United Negro College Fund, 953
United States Commission on
Civil Rights, 954
Universal Negro Improvement
Association, 969
White Citizens' Councils, 1007

PAN-AFRICANISM
African Liberation Day, 25
Afrocentrism, 31
Black nationalism, 118
Music, 624
Nation of Islam, 631

Pan-Africanism, 701
Republic of New Africa, 765
Universal Negro Improvement
Association, 969
West Indians, 1002

PEOPLES
Black Jews, 115
Cubans and African Americans,
270
Demographic trends, 283
Free blacks, 366
Haitians, 421
Irish-African American relations,
460
Jamaicans, 466
Jews and African Americans, 470
Koreans and African Americans,
520
Native Americans and African
Americans, 661
One-drop rule, 698
West Indians, 1002

POLITICS AND GOVERNMENT
Black cabinet, 94
Black codes, 103
Black Panther Party, 123
Chisholm's election to Congress,
161
Civil War, 226
Compromise of 1850, 243
Compromise of 1877, 248
Congressional Black Caucus, 256
Disfranchisement laws in
Mississippi, 294
Emancipation Proclamation, 323
Fourteenth Amendment, 357
Gerrymandering, 393
*Gomillion v. Lightfoot*, 397
*Grovey v. Townsend*, 418
*Harper v. Virginia Board of
Elections*, 435
Jackson's run for the presidency,
461

Kansas-Nebraska Act, 490
*Lassiter v. Northampton County Board of Elections*, 530
Marshall's appointment to the Supreme Court, 564
Mississippi Freedom Democratic Party, 603
Missouri Compromise, 606
*Mobile v. Bolden*, 613
MOVE bombing, 621
National Black Women's Political Leadership Caucus, 652
*Newberry v. United States*, 679
*Nixon v. Condon*, 685
*Nixon v. Herndon*, 686
Northwest Ordinance, 694
Politics and government, 713
Poll taxes, 723
President's Committee on Civil Rights, 729
Rainbow Coalition, 753
Reconstruction, 755
Republic of New Africa, 765
*Shaw v. Hunt*, 808
*Shaw v. Reno*, 810
*Smith v. Allwright*, 875
Southern Manifesto, 887
Summit Meeting of National Negro Leaders, 912
Thirteenth Amendment, 922
Thomas-Hill hearings, 928
Three-fifths compromise, 930
Twenty-fourth Amendment, 941
Understanding tests, 952
United States Commission on Civil Rights, 954
*United States v. Classic*, 958
*United States v. Reese*, 961
Voting Rights Act of 1965, 983
Voting Rights Act of 1975, 990
White primaries, 1009
Wilder's election to Virginia governorship, 1010
*Yarbrough, Ex parte*, 1025

POPULAR CULTURE
Anderson's Lincoln Memorial concert, 51
Baseball's racial integration, 82
Black Is Beautiful movement, 114
Black nationalism, 118
Cowboys, 267
Film history, 352
Harlem Renaissance, 426
Literature, 537
Media, the, 569
Music, 624
*Roots*, 767
Sports, 889
Stereotypes, 898

RACE RELATIONS
Atlanta Compromise, 67
Black Jews, 115
Charleston race riots, 151
Chicago riots, 152
Congress of Racial Equality, 250
Cubans and African Americans, 270
Draft riots, 298
Haitians, 421
Harlins murder, 434
"I Have a Dream" speech, 449
Integration, 454
Irish-African American relations, 460
Jamaicans, 466
Jews and African Americans, 470
Koreans and African Americans, 520
Los Angeles riots, 548
Miami riots, 576
Native Americans and African Americans, 661
New York riots, 674
Newark riot, 677
Poor People's March on Washington, 725
Race riots of 1866, 737
Race riots of 1943, 741

Race riots of 1967, 745
Race riots of the twentieth
century, 750
Rainbow Coalition, 753
Slavery and race relations, 843
United States Commission on
Civil Rights, 954
Washington, D.C., riots, 997
Watts riot, 999
West Indians, 1002

RACISM
Clinton massacre, 233
Colfax massacre, 239
Hawkins murder, 441
Jim Crow laws, 476
Kerner Commission, 499
Ku Klux Klan, 523
Ku Klux Klan Acts, 529
Lynching, 553
One-drop rule, 698
Proslavery argument, 731
Tuskegee experiment, 939
White Citizens' Councils, 1007

RECONSTRUCTION
Charleston race riots, 151
Compromise of 1877, 248
Fifteenth Amendment, 347
Fourteenth Amendment, 357
Freedmen's Bureau, 367
Ku Klux Klan Acts, 529
Poll taxes, 723
Race riots of 1866, 737
Reconstruction, 755
*Slaughterhouse Cases*, 819

RELIGION
Abolition, 1
African Methodist Episcopal
Church, 26
African Methodist Episcopal Zion
Churches, 30
Baptist Church, 78

Black Christian Nationalist
Movement, 95
Black church, 97
Black Jews, 115
"Black Manifesto," 117
Church bombings, 169
Church burnings, 174
Free African Society, 362
Jews and African Americans, 470
Nation of Islam, 631
Southern Christian Leadership
Conference, 879

SCIENCE AND TECHNOLOGY
Ashmun Institute, 62
Atlanta Compromise, 67
Black colleges and universities,
107
One-drop rule, 698
Science and technology, 776
Tuskegee experiment, 939

SEGREGATION
Birmingham March, 91
Black codes, 103
Black Power movement, 129
*Buchanan v. Warley*, 147
*Burton v. Wilmington Parking
Authority*, 150
Civil Rights Act of 1968, 195
*Evans v. Abney*, 340
Gerrymandering, 393
*Heart of Atlanta Motel v. United
States*, 442
Integration, 454
Jim Crow laws, 476
*Katzenbach v. McClung*, 496
*Louisville, New Orleans, and Texas
Railway Company v. Mississippi*,
552
*McLaurin v. Oklahoma State Regents
for Higher Education*, 558
Military, 579
*Missouri ex rel. Gaines v. Canada*,
612

*Palmer v. Thompson*, 700
*Plessy v. Ferguson*, 708
Restrictive covenants, 766
Segregation, 790
Segregation on the frontier, 793
Separate but equal doctrine, 805
*Shelley v. Kraemer*, 812

SLAVE REVOLTS
Amistad slave revolt, 47
Fugitive Slave Law of 1793, 382
Fugitive Slave Law of 1850, 387
New York City slave revolt, 669
Slavery, 826
Stono Rebellion, 902
Turner's slave insurrection, 933
Underground Railroad, 947

SLAVE TRADE
*Amistad* slave revolt, 47
Antislavery laws of 1777 and
  1807, 58
*Clotilde* capture, 234
*Groves v. Slaughter*, 417
Pennsylvania Society for the
  Abolition of Slavery, 703
Slavery, 826

SLAVERY
Abolition, 1
Abolitionist movement and
  women, 5
Agriculture, 32
American Anti-Slavery Society, 42
American Colonization Society,
  46
*Amistad* slave revolt, 47
Antislavery laws of 1777 and
  1807, 58
"Black Manifesto," 117
Bleeding Kansas, 134
Civil War, 226
Compromise of 1850, 243
Confiscation Acts of 1861 and
  1862, 249

Economic trends, 304
Emancipation Proclamation, 323
Fugitive Slave Law of 1793, 382
Fugitive Slave Law of 1850, 387
*Groves v. Slaughter*, 417
Kansas-Nebraska Act, 490
Missouri Compromise, 606
Native Americans and African
  Americans, 661
New York City slave revolt, 669
Northwest Ordinance, 694
Pennsylvania Society for the
  Abolition of Slavery, 703
Proslavery argument, 731
*Roots*, 767
*Scott v. Sandford*, 783
Slave codes, 821
Slavery, 826
Slavery and families, 835
Slavery and race relations, 843
Slavery and the justice system,
  850
Slavery and women, 858
Slavery in Massachusetts, 865
Slavery in Virginia, 870
Stono Rebellion, 902
Thirteenth Amendment, 922
Three-fifths compromise, 930
Turner's slave insurrection, 933
Underground Railroad, 947

SPORTS
Baseball's racial integration, 82
Simpson murder trial, 813
Sports, 889
Stereotypes, 898

URBANIZATION
Black flight, 112
Chicago riots, 152
Chicago sit-ins, 154
Crown Heights conflicts, 268
Cubans and African Americans,
  270
Demographic trends, 283

*Evans v. Abney*, 340
Fair Housing Act, 342
Free blacks, 366
National Urban League, 659
New York riots, 674
Newark riot, 677
Race riots of 1943, 741
Race riots of 1967, 745
Race riots of the twentieth
    century, 750
Universal Negro Improvement
    Association, 969
Washington, D.C., riots, 997
Watts riot, 999

VOTING RIGHTS
Black codes, 103
Civil Rights Act of 1960, 183
Civil Rights Act of 1964, 188
Council of Federated
    Organizations, 260
Disfranchisement laws in
    Mississippi, 294
Fifteenth Amendment, 347
Freedom Summer, 374
Gerrymandering, 393
*Gomillion v. Lightfoot*, 397
Grandfather clauses, 398
*Grovey v. Townsend*, 418
*Guinn v. United States*, 419
*Harper v. Virginia Board of
    Elections*, 435
*Lassiter v. Northampton County
    Board of Elections*, 530
Mississippi Freedom Democratic
    Party, 603
*Mobile v. Bolden*, 613
*Newberry v. United States*, 679
*Nixon v. Condon*, 685
*Nixon v. Herndon*, 686
Politics and government, 713
Poll taxes, 723

Rainbow Coalition, 753
Selma-Montgomery march, 797
*Shaw v. Hunt*, 808
*Shaw v. Reno*, 810
*Smith v. Allwright*, 875
*Terry v. Adams*, 921
Three-fifths compromise, 930
Twenty-fourth Amendment, 941
Understanding tests, 952
United States Commission on
    Civil Rights, 954
*United States v. Classic*, 958
*United States v. Reese*, 961
Voting Rights Act of 1965, 983
Voting Rights Act of 1975, 990
White primaries, 1009
Wilder's election to Virginia
    governorship, 1010
*Yarbrough, Ex parte*, 1025

WOMEN'S ISSUES
Abolitionist movement and
    women, 5
Anderson's Lincoln Memorial
    concert, 51
Chisholm's election to Congress,
    161
Colored Women's League, 240
Combahee River Collective, 241
Million Woman March, 597
Miscegenation laws, 600
National Association of Colored
    Women, 651
National Black Women's Political
    Leadership Caucus, 652
National Council of Negro
    Women, 658
Slavery and families, 835
Slavery and women, 858
Thomas-Hill hearings, 928
Underground Railroad, 947

# Personages Index

Abbott, Benjamin, 363

Abbott, Robert S., 288, 309, 400-401

Abdullah Al-Amin, Jamil (H. Rap Brown), 1100

Abel, I. W., 746

Abernathy, Ralph, 616, 800, 881, 1096; and Poor People's March on Washington, 726

Abrahams, Peter, 430

Africa, John (Vincent Leapheart), 621

Ali, Muhammad, 895, 901, 1096; and military conscription, 982

Allen, Richard, 26-27, 44, 98, 363, 655, 1096

Amos, James Ralston, 64

Anderson, Jack, 254

Anderson, Joe, 777

Anderson, Marian, 51-58, 1096

Angelou, Maya, 595, 1097

Anthony, Susan B., 927

Aristide, Jean-Bertrand, 422

Armstrong, Louis, 429

Asante, Molefi Kete, 31-32, 318, 1097

Ashe, Arthur, 895

Ashmun, Jehudi, 64

Atchison, David R., 492

Attucks, Crispus, 277, 663

Bailey, F. Lee, 815

Baird, Absalom, 740

Baker, Ella Jo, 206, 411, 881, 908

Baker, Josephine, 1097

Bakke, Alan, 18, 71-78

Baldwin, James, 431, 542, 1098

Baliles, Gerald L., 1011

Banneker, Benjamin, 44, 777

Baraka, Amiri, 1098

Bargonetti, Jill, 781

Barnett, Ferdinand L., 1124

Barnett, Ross, 975, 978

Bates, Daisy, 215

Batt, John, 378

Beecher, Catharine, 864

Bell, Alexander Graham, 779

Berry, Mary Francis, 594

Bethune, Mary McLeod, 94, 658, 1098

Biden, Joseph, 929

Bidwell, Barnabas, 61

Black, Hugo L., 700, 921, 975; and Ku Klux Klan, 526

Blackwell, David, 780

Blair, Henry, 778

Blueford, Guion, 781

Bond, Julian, 1099; and King, Martin Luther, Jr., 1099

Booth, John Wilkes, 1114

Booth, Sherman M., 854

Bowlegs, Billy, 665

Bowlegs, Jim, 665

Boxill, Bernard R., 457, 459

Bradley, Ed, 574

Bradley, Joseph P., 203, 820

Bradley, Stephen R., 61

Bradley, Thomas, 517, 1099

Bradstreet, Simon, 868

Brady, Tom, 1007

Braun, Carol Moseley, 1099

Brawley, Tawana, 1121

Breckenridge, Calvin, 414

Brennan, William J., 506

Brewer, David J.; *Louisville, New Orleans, and Texas Railway Company v. Mississippi*, 552

Breyer, Stephen G.; and affirmative action, 23

Brooke, Edward W., 343, 746, 1014, 1100

Brown, H. Rap, 909, 1100

Brown, Henry "Box," 949

Brown, James, 1121

Brown, Jim, 901

Brown, John, 135, 436-441, 924, 1100

Brown, Oliver, 215

Brown, Ron, 754

Brown, Tony, 574

Brown, William Wells, 951

Bruce, Blanche K., 241, 717, 1100

Bruce, Josephine B., 241

Bryan, Andrew, 79
Buchanan, Bessie, 162
Buchanan, James, 134, 136
Bull, William, 904
Bunche, Ralph, 1100
Burger, Warren, 414, 416, 915
Burr, Aaron, 60
Burton, LeVar, 768
Bush, George, 1119; and affirmative
    action, 22; and civil rights, 199;
    and Equal Employment
    Opportunity Commission, 339;
    and Haitians, 423; and Supreme
    Court, 928; and Thomas,
    Clarence, 1121
Bush, George W., 722, 1119
Butler, Pierce, 728
Byrd, Harry, 773

Calhoun, John C., 246
Callahan, William W., 788
Caplan, Lincoln, 22
Cardozo, Benjamin N.; *Nixon v.
    Condon*, 685
Carmichael, Stokely, 124, 127, 129-
    130, 212, 375, 473, 501, 909, 1004,
    1101; and Vietnam War, 981
Carter, Jimmy, 257, 965, 1109, 1126
Carter, John Pym, 64
Cary, Mary Ann Shadd, 10
Cato, Gavin, 269
Cavanagh, Jerome, 746
Champion, James, 26
Chaney, James Earl, 219-225, 254,
    263, 375, 472, 908
Charleston, Oscar, 891
Chase, Salmon, 494
Chavis, Benjamin, 593-597, 639, 1101
Chesnut, Mary Boykin, 861
Chionesu, Philé, 597-600
Chisholm, Shirley, 161-168, 465, 721,
    1004, 1101
Clark, Marcia, 814
Clark, Mark, 424-426
Clay, Henry, 46, 244, 246
Cleage, Albert, 96
Cleaver, Eldridge, 127-128, 1102; and
    Vietnam War, 981

Cleveland, Grover, 69
Clinton, Bill, 23, 1097; and church
    burnings, 176; and Haitians, 423;
    and Jackson, Jesse, 754; and
    Jordan, Vernon, 1111
Cochran, Johnnie, 815
Coffin, Levi, 950
Coleman, Marshall, 1014
Colmer, William, 186
Condon, James, 876
Cone, James, 1102
Coney, Asia, 597-600
Connell, Pat, 574
Conner, Eugene "Bull," 92
Conyers, John, 1117
Cook, Coralie Franklin, 241
Cook, John T., 240
Coolidge, Calvin, 1106
Cooper, Jack, 572
Corman, James C., 746
Cornish, Samuel, 571
Coronado, Francisco Vásquez de, 662
Cosby, Bill, 1102
Court, Gus, 261
Craft, William and Ellen, 949
Crandall, Prudence, 5
Cresson, Sarah Emlen, 63
Crummell, Alexander, 1102
Cuffe, Paul, 118, 663
Cuffee, 671
Cullen, Countée, 427, 432
Curry, John Stuart, 438

Danforth, John C., 218
Darden, Christopher, 814
Davis, Angela, 1103
Davis, Benjamin O., Jr., 938, 1022,
    1103
Davis, Benjamin O., Sr., 581, 1020,
    1103
Davis, Billy, 1107
Davis, Jefferson, 228, 246, 301
Davis, Ossie, 573
Day, William R.; *Buchanan v. Warley*,
    147
Dees, Morris, 528
Delany, Martin Robison, 1103
Dellums, Ronald, 167

Dennis, David, 261
Denny, Reginald, 550
DePriest, Oscar, 718
Dew, Thomas R., 732
Dickey, John Miller, 63
Dickinson, Jonathan, 706
Diop, Cheikh Anta, 32
Dirksen, Everett M., 186, 190, 196, 344
Dixon, Thomas, 900
Douglas, Stephen A., 134, 247, 491, 1113
Douglas, William O.; *Lassiter v. Northampton County Board of Elections*, 530
Douglass, Frederick, 3, 44, 367, 538, 656, 663, 689, 832, 924, 951, 1103, 1124; and Garrison, William Lloyd, 690; and *The North Star*, 689-693; and Thirteenth Amendment, 925; and Truth, Sojourner, 11
D'Souza, Dinesh, 1002
Du Bois, W. E. B., 70, 108, 119, 317, 400, 570, 637, 1104; and Niagara Movement, 501, 682; and Pan-Africanism, 701-702; and "Talented Tenth," 919-921; and United Nations, 587; and Washington, Booker T., 1124; writings of, 539
Dukakis, Michael, 1110
Duke, David, 527
Dunbar, Paul Laurence, 540
Dyer, L. C., 303

Eastland, James O., 186, 942, 993
Edmundson, William, 705
Eisenhower, Dwight D., 588, 912, 1104; and Anderson, Marian, 55, 57; and civil rights, 882; and Civil Rights Act of 1960, 184; and Little Rock school desegregation crisis, 259, 544-548, 774; and military segregation, 589; and Summit Meeting of National Negro Leaders, 912-913; and Warren, Earl, 1123; and World War II, 1023
Eisenstein, Zillah, 242

Elder, Lee, 896
Ellington, Duke, 428, 572
Ellison, Ralph, 431, 542
Ervin, Sam, 197, 962
Evers, Medgar, 170, 450, 1105

Fard, W. D., 631-632, 1116
Farmer, James, 163, 372, 481, 1105, 1120
Farrakhan, Louis, 121, 257, 634, 1105; and Jackson, Jesse, 464, 1105; and Jews, 474; and Malcolm X, 1105; and the media, 594; and Million Man March, 593-597
Faubus, Orval, 258-259, 544-548, 774
Fernando, 870
Ferraro, Geraldine, 465
Field, Stephen J., 820
Fillmore, Millard, 246
Fitzgerald, Ella, 428
Fitzhugh, George, 734, 830
Foraker, Joseph B., 146
Forman, James, 911
Forten, James, 26, 534, 1105
Forten, James, Jr., 778
Fortune, T. Thomas, 306, 1106; and Washington, Booker T., 1106
Foster, Bill, 236
Foster, Stephen, 626
Fox, George, 704
Frankfurter, Felix, 397, 921
Franklin, Benjamin, 378, 704, 922
Franklin, Raymond S., 845
Frazier, Demita, 242
Frederickson, George, 844
Frémont, John C., 247

Gandhi, Mohandas K., 154, 251, 407, 481, 508, 1106; and King, Martin Luther, Jr., 1106
Garnet, Henry Highland, 951
Garrettson, Freeborn, 363
Garrison, William Lloyd, 2, 5, 9, 42, 832, 853, 863, 935, 1106; and Douglass, Frederick, 690; and *The Liberator*, 532-537; opponents of, 732; and Thirteenth Amendment, 925
Garvey, Marcus, 115, 120, 403, 467,

632, 640, 969-974, 1004, 1106; and
    Malcolm X, 1115; and Pan-
    Africanism, 701; and Washington,
    Booker T., 970
Gates, Daryl, 517, 548
Geary, John W., 135
George, David, 79
George, Walter, 888
Geronimo, 148
Gerry, Elbridge, 394
Gibson, Josh, 891
Giddings, Doras, 364
Ginsburg, Ruth Bader; and
    affirmative action, 23
Glazer, Nathan, 455, 458
Goetz, Bernhard, 1121
Goldman, Ronald, 814
Goldwater, Barry, 223
Gonzales, Pancho, 895
Goode, Mal, 574
Goode, Wilson, 622
Goodell, William, 853
Goodman, Andrew, 219-225, 263,
    375, 472, 908
Gorbachev, Mikhail, 1119
Gordy, Berry, Jr., 1107
Gordy, Gwen, 1107
Gore, Al, 722
Gourdine, Meredith, 781
Grace, Charles Emmanuel "Sweet
    Daddy," 1107
Granger, Lester B., 660, 912
Grant, Ulysses S., 240, 529, 759; and
    civil rights, 201
Graves, Earl, 1005, 1107
Green, Charles, 240
Greenberg, Jack, 645, 648
Griffith, D. W., 900
Grimké, Angelina, 8, 861
Grimké, Charlotte Forten, 240
Grimké, Sarah, 8, 861
Grovey, Richard Randolph, 876
Gumbel, Bryant, 574

Hale, John P., 491
Haley, Alex, 539, 767-768, 1107
Hall, Prince, 377-381
Hamer, Fannie Lou, 101, 1108

Hamilton, Alexander, 60, 707
Hammond, James Henry, 733
Hampton, Fred, 424-426
Hampton, Wade, 151, 717
Hannah, Marc, 780
Harding, Warren, 302
Harlan, John M., 271, 480, 764, 791
Harlins, Latasha, 434, 522
Harper, Frances Ellen Watkins, 10
Harris, Bernard, 781
Harris, Fred R., 500
Harrison, Pat, 303
Harrison, Thomas, 704
Hart, Gary, 462
Hastie, William, 94, 1020
Hawkins, Yusuf, 441-442
Hayden, Lewis, 951
Hayes, George E. C., 645
Hayes, Rutherford B., 248-249, 717,
    755, 1108
Henderson, Fletcher, 428
Henry, Aaron, 260
Higginson, Thomas Wentworth, 437
Hill, Anita, 928-930, 1108, 1121
Hill, Larry, 176
Hilliard, Asa, 32
Hitler, Adolf, 1116
Holder, Eric, 1004
Holland, Spessard L., 942-943
Holmes, Oliver Wendell; *Moore v.*
    *Dempsey*, 619
Holmes, Oliver Wendell, Jr., 875
Hooker, John Lee, 628
Hooks, Benjamin, 574, 639, 1108
Hoover, Herbert, 1098
Hoover, J. Edgar, 127; and civil
    rights worker murders, 222; and
    urban rioting, 998
Hopkins, Pauline E., 541
Houser, George M., 481
Houston, Charles, 812
Howard, Oliver Otis, 1109
Howe, Julia Ward, 862, 927
Howe, Samuel Gridley, 437
Hughes, Charles Evans; *Brown v.*
    *Mississippi*, 144; *Missouri ex rel.*
    *Gaines v. Canada*, 612; *Norris v.*
    *Alabama*, 688

Hughes, Henry, 734, 844
Hughes, Langston, 65, 403, 427, 431, 541, 1109
Hughes, Richard J., 678
Humphrey, Hubert H., 189, 965
Hunter, Robert, 671-672
Hurston, Zora Neale, 430, 543, 1114, 1123

Imes, Elmer Samuel, 780
Innis, Roy, 251, 1109
Ito, Judge Lance, 814

Jackson, Andrew; and Seminole Wars, 665
Jackson, Jesse, 474, 1109; and Chicago riots, 153; and Clinton, Bill, 754; and Democratic Party, 754; and Farrakhan, Louis, 464, 1105; and Korean Americans, 521; presidential candidacy, 461-466; and Rainbow Coalition, 753-754; and Reagan, Ronald, 462-463
Jackson, Jimmie Lee, 799
Jackson, Mahalia, 628
Jacob, John, 661
Jay, John, 60, 707
Jefferson, Thomas; and Northwest Ordinance, 694; and slavery, 61
Jeffries, Edward J., 744
Jemison, T. J., 881
Jenkins, Herbert, 746
Jenkins, Howard, 645
Jennings, Thomas L., 778
Johnson, Andrew, 103, 178, 218, 361, 1110; and civil rights, 200-201, 756; impeachment of, 180, 926; and Reconstruction, 103, 106, 179-180, 357, 371, 714, 738, 755, 926; and Stevens, Thaddeus, 1121
Johnson, Andrew (student), 484
Johnson, Frank M., 801
Johnson, Jack, 894, 1110
Johnson, James Weldon, 1110
Johnson, John H., 571, 1111
Johnson, Lyndon B., 182, 1111; and affirmative action, 15, 71, 962; and civil rights, 189, 195, 343, 888;

and Civil Rights Act of 1964, 191; and Kerner Commission, 499-506; and King, Martin Luther, Jr., 189; and Ku Klux Klan, 527; and Marshall, Thurgood, 567; and riots, 211, 676, 678, 751; and Selma-Montgomery march, 800-802; and Vietnam War, 981; and voting rights, 799, 985, 990
Johnston, Samuel, 383
Jones, Absalom, 26, 98, 363, 366, 1111
Jones, Elaine, 648
Jones, Jane Elizabeth, 10
Jones, LeRoi (Amiri Baraka), 1098
Jones, Quincy, 629
Joplin, Scott, 627
Jordan, Vernon E., Jr., 661, 1111
Joseph, Chief, 1109
Julian, Percy, 780
Just, Ernest, 780

Karenga, Ron, 114
Katzenbach, Nicholas, 985
Keith, George, 705
Kelly, Harry F., 744
Kennedy, Anthony M., 315, 728
Kennedy, John F., 1111; assassination of, 189, 562; and Birmingham March, 92-93; and civil rights, 183, 189, 332, 343, 444, 451, 499, 720, 910; and Malcolm X, 634; and Marshall, Thurgood, 648; and Meredith, James, 976
Kennedy, Robert F., 222, 1107, 1112; and civil rights, 499; and Meredith, James, 975
Kennedy, Ted, 217
Kenyatta, Jomo, 701
Kerner, Otto, 153, 500, 635, 746, 998
Key, Elizabeth, 870
King, Don, 1121
King, Martin Luther, Jr., 101, 209, 473, 616, 908, 912, 1112; assassination of, 196; and Birmingham March, 91-94; and Bond, Julian, 1099; and Gandhi, Mohandas K., 1106; "I Have a Dream" speech, 449-454, 509; and

Johnson, Lyndon B., 189; "Letter from Birmingham Jail," 92, 209, 450, 978; and Malcolm X, 799; and the media, 251; and Poor People's March on Washington, 726; and Student Nonviolent Coordinating Committee, 411; and Vietnam War, 212, 981; and Watts riot, 1001; and Young, Andrew, 1126

King, Rodney, 515-519, 522, 548, 752, 816, 1113

King, Rufus, 608

Koon, Stacey, 516, 549

Kozol, Jonathan, 457

Kunta Kinte, 767-768, 1107

Latimer, Lewis Henry, 779

Lawrence, Robert, 781

Leaphart, Vincent, 621

Lee, George, 261

Lee, Robert E., 301

Lee, Spike, 355, 1113

LeFlore, John, 742

Leibowitz, Samuel, 789

L'Enfant, Pierre, 777

Levison, Stanley, 881, 883

Lewis, John, 253

Lewis, Monroe, 240

Liele, George, 79

Lincoln, Abraham, 247, 862, 1113; assassination of, 926; and Civil War, 227, 298-302; Emancipation Proclamation, 323-326; and Reconstruction, 177; and slavery, 250, 323-326

Lincoln, C. Eric, 98

Lindsay, John V., 500

Liuzzo, Viola Lee, 527

Locke, Alain, 1114

Logan, James, 706

Lopez, Narcisco, 490

Louis, Joe, 894-895, 901

Lowery, Joseph E., 881, 1114

Lowry, Robert, 295

McCormick, Cyrus, 777

McCoy, Elijah, 778

McCullough, William M., 746

McDuffie, Arthur, 752

McKay, Claude, 427, 432, 467, 1004, 1114

McKissick, Floyd, 1115

McNair, Ronald, 781

McReynolds, James C., 728

Maddox, Alton, 270

Madikizela-Mandela, Winnie, 1094

Malcolm X, 121, 124, 129, 539, 559, 633, 1115; assassination of, 559-564, 1116; and civil rights, 190; and Farrakhan, Louis, 1105; and Haley, Alex, 1107; and Kennedy, John F., 634; and King, Martin Luther, Jr., 799; and the media, 562

Malone, Annie Turnbo, 779

Mamiya, Lawrence H., 98

Mandela, Nelson, 275

Manley, Norman, 701

Mann, Woodrow, 546, 774

Mansfield, Michael H., 942

Margold, Nathan, 771

Marrant, John, 379

Marshall, Thurgood, 13, 65, 641, 644, 771, 792, 812, 918, 1115; appointed to Supreme Court, 564-568; and Johnson, Lyndon B., 1111; retirement of, 928

Martinet, Louis, 709

Mary, Alexander A., 709

Mason, James, 388

Matney, William C., Jr., 574

Matthew, Wentworth Arthur, 115

May, Samuel, 42

Mays, Benjamin, 508

Mays, Willie, 901

Meagher, Timothy, 236

Meredith, James H., 129, 375, 646, 974-979, 1115

Mfume, Kweisi, 1093, 1095

Micheaux, Oscar, 353

Miller, Samuel F., 819

Mitchell, Arthur W., 718-719

Mitchell, Clarence, 195

Mitchell, Parren, 167

Mitchell, William H., 951

Monagas, Lionel, 573

Mondale, Walter F., 343, 462-465
Monroe, James, 610
Morley, Burton R., 742
Morrison, Toni. 542-543, 1116
Moses, Robert, 261
Motley, Constance Baker, 646, 1004
Mott, Lucretia, 8
Moynihan, Daniel Patrick, 468, 623, 845
Muhammad, Elijah, 120, 539, 631-635, 1116; and Malcolm X, 559-564, 1115
Muhammad, Warith "Wallace," 634
Murray, Anna, 689
Murray, Anna E., 241
Murrow, Edward R., 573

Nabrit, James M., Jr., 645
Nasser, Gamal Abdel, 701
Neville, Dinah, 704
Newton, Huey P., 121, 124, 132, 1116
Nixon, L. A., 875
Nixon, Richard M.; and Chisholm, Shirley, 165-166; and Congressional Black Caucus, 256, 721; and school desegregation, 40
Nkrumah, Kwame, 701, 1101, 1104
Norris, Isaac, 706
Nott, Josiah, 734, 829

Oglethorpe, James, 904
O'Neill, Eugene, 139, 1119
Owen, Robert Dale, 924
Owens, Jesse, 1116

Padmore, George, 701
Paige, Satchel, 891
Paine, Thomas, 707
Pánfilo de Narváez, 662
Parker, Theodore, 437
Parks, Rosa, 101, 209, 615-616, 1117
Patterson, Frederick D., 953, 1117
Patterson, Mary Jane, 241
Patterson, Orlando, 826, 845
Patterson, Robert B., 1007
Payne, Daniel Alexander, 1117
Payton, Philip A., Jr., 402
Peden, Katherine Graham, 746

Pemberton, Israel, 704
Pemberton, James, 704
Pennington, James, 655
Person, Waverly, 781
Peters, Brock, 354
Phillips, Wendell, 535, 832, 924
Pickering, William, 608
Picket, Bill, 268
Pierce, Franklin, 134, 490, 494
Pilmore, Joseph, 366
Pinchback, P. B. S., 716, 1014
Plessy, Homer Adolph, 709
Poitier, Sidney, 354, 1004
Powell, Adam Clayton, 130
Powell, Adam Clayton, Jr., 1117
Powell, Colin, 582, 1003, 1118; and Vietnam War, 982
Powell, Isaac, 781
Powell, James, 674
Powell, Laurence, 516
Powell, Lewis F., Jr., 19; *Batson v. Kentucky*, 90; *McCleskey v. Kemp*, 557
Price, Hugh, 661
Purvis, Robert, 951
Purvis, W. B., 779

Rainey, Ma, 431
Randolph, A. Philip, 139, 279-280, 341, 450, 587, 719, 912, 1118; and March on Washington movement, 1020
Rayburn, Sam, 888
Read, George, 383
Reagan, Ronald; and affirmative action, 22; and civil rights, 218, 957; and Equal Employment Opportunity Commission, 339; and Haitians, 423; and Jackson, Jesse, 462-463; and Powell, Colin, 1118
Redding, Louis, 645
Reed, Ishmael, 543
Rehnquist, William H., 1019; *Martin v. Wilks*, 568; *Moose Lodge v. Irvis*, 620; *Shaw v. Hunt*, 809
Revels, Hiram R., 717, 926
Reynolds, Grant, 279

Reynolds, Humphrey, 779
Rice, Condoleezza, 1118-1119
Rice, Thomas D. "Big Daddy," 476
Rickey, Branch, 82-90
Rillieux, Norbert, 778
Robb, Charles S., 1011
Roberts, Owen J., 876
Robeson, Paul, 572, 892, 1119
Robinson, Elizabeth, 8
Robinson, Jackie, 82-90, 892, 1024, 1119
Robinson, Spotswood W., III, 645
Rodgers, Jonathan, 574
Romney, George, 747
Roosevelt, Eleanor, 94
Roosevelt, Franklin D., 278, 341, 746,
    1120; and Bethune, Mary
    McLeod, 1099; and black cabinet,
    94; and Davis, Benjamin O., Sr.,
    1103; and the Depression, 35;
    desegregation of defense
    industries, 277-283; election of,
    719; and military segregation,
    585; and World War II, 1020
Roosevelt, Theodore, 1124; and
    Brownsville incident, 145-146; in
    Spanish-American War, 149
Rush, Benjamin, 365, 704, 922
Russell, Richard B., 186, 942-944
Russwurm, John B., 571
Rustin, Bayard, 155, 450, 481-490,
    881-882, 1120

Sacagawea, 664
Sackler, Howard, 1110
Sanborn, Franklin B., 437
Schwerner, Michael Henry, 219-225,
    254, 263, 375, 472, 908
Scott, Dred, 783-786, 1120
Scott, Winfield, 490
Screvane, Paul, 676
Seale, Bobby, 121, 124, 1116, 1121
Sedgwick, Theodore, 383
Seymour, Horatio, 301
Shabazz, El-Hajj Malik El- (Malcolm
    X), 1115
Sharpe, John, 671
Sharpton, Al, 270, 1121
Shelton, Robert, 527

Shores family, 796
Shuttlesworth, Fred, 881
Simmons, William J., 525
Simpson, Nicole Brown, 814
Simpson, O. J., 768, 813-818
Smith, Barbara, 242
Smith, Bessie, 428, 431
Smith, Beverly, 242
Smith, Gerrit, 437, 692, 853
Smith, James McCune, 655
Smith, Lamar, 261
Soto, Hernando de, 662
Sowell, Thomas, 456, 468, 1002
Sparks, Chauncey, 742
Spingarn, Joel E., 638, 640
Stanton, Edwin McMasters, 300
Stanton, Elizabeth Cady, 927
Stanton, Frederick P., 135
Stearns, George Luther, 437
Steele, Charles Kenzie, 881
Steele, Shelby, 848
Steinberg, Stephen, 468
Stephens, Alexander, 494
Stevens, Thaddeus, 1121
Stewart, Potter, 414, 480; *Mobile v.
    Bolden*, 613
Stokes, Carl B., 721
Stone, John M., 295
Stone, Lucy, 8, 10, 927
Stoneman, George, 739
Stowe, Harriet Beecher, 862
Stringfellow, Thornton, 733
Sumner, Charles, 201, 494
Sutherland, George; *Powell v.
    Alabama*, 728

Taft, William Howard, 1124
Taney, Roger Brooke, 417
Tapisco, Jacob, 26
Tappan, Arthur, 42, 535
Taylor, Zachary, 246
Temple, Lewis, 778
Terrell, Mary Church, 241
Thomas, Clarence, 14, 928-930, 1121;
    and affirmative action, 22, 929;
    and Equal Employment
    Opportunity Commission, 339;
    and Hill, Anita, 1108

Thomas, Franklin, 1004
Thomas, J. B., 608
Thompson, William C., 163
Thornton, Charles B. (Tex), 746
Thurmond, Strom, 445, 720, 888
Tilden, Samuel J., 248
Till, Emmett, 554, 931-932, 1122
Toomer, Jean, 541
Toure, Kwame (Stokely Carmichael), 1101
Touré, Sékou, 1101
Townsend, Robert, 355
Trotter, William Monroe, 501, 637, 919
Truman, Harry S., 281, 1122; and civil rights, 455, 556, 585, 719, 729-731, 812, 1024, 1122; desegregation of military, 579, 587, 590
Trumbull, Lyman, 106
Truth, Sojourner, 11, 44, 862-863, 1122; and Douglass, Frederick, 11
Tubman, Harriet, 11, 44, 538, 863, 924, 950, 1122
Turner, Henry McNeal, 1123
Turner, Nat, 1123
Tustennuggee Emartha (Jim Boy), 664

Underwood, Oscar, 303

Van Buren, Martin, 49
Vassa, Gustavas, 537
Venable, James, 527
Villa, Pancho, 148
Vinson, Fred M., 142, 918

Wade, Wyn, 1008
Waite, Morrison R., 759
Walcott, Derek, 1004
Walker, Alice, 543, 1123
Walker, Madame C. J., 779
Wallace, George, 172, 800-801, 945, 991
Wallace, Henry, 588
Walthall, Edward C., 295
Ward, Samuel Ringgold, 367
Warmoth, Henry Clay, 717

Warren, Earl, 137, 208, 772, 1123; *Brown v. Board of Education*, 142
Washington, Booker T., 108, 316, 538, 639, 681, 919, 970, 1124; accommodationist program, 501; Atlanta Compromise, 67-70; and Du Bois, W. E. B., 1124; and Fortune, T. Thomas, 1106; and Garvey, Marcus, 970; and National Negro Business League, 306
Washington, George, 277, 377, 777; and slavery, 383-384, 950
Waters, Muddy, 628
Weaver, John D., 146
Weaver, Robert, 94
Webster, Daniel, 389
Wells, Benjamin, 26
Wells, James Madison, 739
Wells-Barnett, Ida B., 1124
West, Cornel, 471
Whatcoat, Richard, 363
Wheatley, Phillis, 540
Whipper, William, 951
White, Byron R.; *Washington v. Davis*, 996
White, Walter, 341, 585, 639, 744, 1022, 1125
White, William, 364
Whitfield, James H., 538
Whittier, John Greenleaf, 42
Wilder, L. Douglas, 1010-1017, 1125
Wilkins, Roy, 500, 639, 912, 1125
Williams, Eric, 701
Wilson, Lionel, 1116
Winfrey, Oprah, 574
Winthrop, John, 866
Wise, Henry A., 439-440
Woods, Granville, 779
Woods, Tiger, 896
Woodson, Carter G., 32, 1125
Wright, Fielding, 720
Wright, Richard, 430, 542, 1125

York, 663
Young, Andrew, 1015, 1126
Young, Whitney M., Jr., 661, 1126

# Subject Index

Abbott, Benjamin, 363
Abbott, Robert S., 288, 309, 400, 401
Abdullah Al-Amin, Jamil (H. Rap Brown), 1100
Abel, I. W., 746
*Abelman v. Booth*, 854
Abernathy, Ralph, 616, 800, 881, 1096; and Poor People's March on Washington, 726
Abolition, 1-4, 59, 832, 853, 923; American Anti-Slavery Society, 42-46; and Brown, John, 1100; and Emancipation Proclamation, 323-326; and National Council of Colored People, 654-657; Newspapers, 2, 5, 10, 532-537, 689-693; and proslavery argument, 731-735; and Underground Railroad, 947-952; and women, 5-13
Abrahams, Peter, 430
*Abrams v. Johnson*, 810
Accommodationism, 316, 501, 919; and Atlanta Compromise, 67-70
*Adarand Constructors v. Peña*, 13-14, 22
Affirmative action, 13, 15-24, 210, 334, 455; and National Urban League, 661; and quotas, 71-78, 211, 339, 961; and Thomas, Clarence, 929
Africa, John (Vincent Leapheart), 621
African American music, 901
African Communities League, 971
*African Intelligencer, The*, 64
African Liberation Day, 25
African Methodist Episcopal Church, 26-30, 98, 366; book publishing, 570; and Payne, Daniel Alexander, 1117; and Turner, Henry McNeal, 1123
African Methodist Episcopal Zion Churches, 30-31; book publishing, 570
"Afro-American," 1106

Afrocentrism, 31-32, 131, 318
Agricultural Adjustment Act of 1933, 36
Agriculture, 32-39, 304, 306; and demographics, 289; research, 779; sharecropping, 308, 806-808
AIDS conspiracy theory, 940
Alabama; affirmative action, 21; Birmingham March, 91-94; bombings, 169-171, 174, 526; Children's Crusade, 214; *Clotilde* capture, 234-239; demographics, 399; elections, 984; and Freedom Rides, 372; gerrymandering, 348, 395, 397-398; Jim Crow laws, 477; Lowndes County Freedom Organization, 124; Mobile riot, 741-745; Montgomery bus boycott, 209, 614-619; and National Association for the Advancement of Colored People, 650-651; poll taxes, 435, 724; Scottsboro cases, 687-688, 727-728, 786-790; Selma-Montgomery march, 209, 797-804; Tuskegee experiment, 939-940; Tuskegee Institute, 67, 108
Alabama Dry Dock and Shipbuilding Company, 742
Albany, Georgia, 910
*Albemarle Paper Company v. Moody*, 39-40
*Alexander v. Holmes County Board of Education*, 40-42, 143
Ali, Muhammad, 895, 901, 1096; and military conscription, 982
All African People's Revolutionary Party, 25
*All-Negro Hour, The* (radio program), 572
All-volunteer force, 580
Allen, Richard, 26-27, 44, 98, 363, 655, 1096

*Allen v. Board of Elections*, 987
American and Foreign Anti-Slavery Society, 535
American Anti-Slavery Society, 2, 42-46, 534, 922, 1105-1106
American Civil Liberties Union, 789
American Colonization Society, 1, 28, 43, 46, 64, 533
American Indian Movement, 665
American Indians, 197
American Moral Reform Society, 1106
American Negro Academy, 1103
*Amistad*, 47-51
Amos, James Ralston, 64
*Amos and Andy* (radio program), 571
Anderson, Jack, 254
Anderson, Joe, 777
Anderson, Marian, 51-58, 1096
Angelou, Maya, 595, 1097
Anthony, Susan B., 927
Anti-Defamation League, 595
Anti-Semitism, 525, 594
Antislavery laws of 1777 and 1807, 58-62
Antislavery societies, 7-8, 533, 667, 703, 832, 922
Aristide, Jean-Bertrand, 422
Arkansas; bombings, 169; elections, 718; Jim Crow laws, 477; poll taxes, 435
Armstrong, Louis, 429
Arson and black churches, 174
Asante, Molefi Kete, 31-32, 318, 1097
Ashe, Arthur, 895
Ashmun, Jehudi, 64
Ashmun Institute, 62-66
Association for the Protection of Colored Women, 659
Astronauts, 781
At-large elections, 987
Atchison, David R., 492
Atlanta Compromise, 67-70, 316, 1124
Atlanta University, 108, 570, 682, 919
Attucks, Crispus, 277, 663
Autobiographies, 538; Anderson, Marian, 57; Douglass, Frederick, 538, 689; Powell, Colin, 1005; Washington, Booker T., 538, 970
*Autobiography of Malcolm X, The*, 539
Aviators, 937-939

Back Panthers (military), 1022
Back-to-Africa movements, 28, 42, 64, 81, 380, 533, 701; American Colonization Society, 46
Bailey, F. Lee, 815
Baird, Absalom, 740
Baker, Ella Jo, 206, 411, 881, 908
Baker, Josephine, 1097
*Baker v. Carr*, 397
Bakke, Alan, 18, 71-78
*Bakke* case, 18, 71-78, 339, 962
Baldwin, James, 431, 542, 1098
Baliles, Gerald L., 1011
Banking practices, 197
Banneker, Benjamin, 44, 777
Baptist Church, 78-82, 98; and King, Martin Luther, Jr., 1112
Baraka, Amiri, 1098
Bargonetti, Jill, 781
Barnett, Ferdinand L., 1124
Barnett, Ross, 975, 978
Baseball, 889, 1119; integration of, 82-90
Basketball, 893
Bates, Daisy, 215
*Batson v. Kentucky*, 90-91, 314
Batt, John, 378
"Battle Hymn of the Republic, The" (Howe), 862
Beaumont, Texas, riots, 743
Beecher, Catharine, 864
Bell, Alexander Graham, 779
*Beloved* (Morrison), 543
*Berea College v. Kentucky*, 771
Berry, Mary Francis, 594
Bethel African Methodist Episcopal Church, 365
Bethune, Mary McLeod, 94, 658, 1098
Bethune-Cookman College, 1098
*Beulah* (radio program), 571
Biden, Joseph, 929
Bidwell, Barnabas, 61

Bigotry, 788
Bill of Rights, U.S., 179
Birmingham, Alabama; church bombings, 171; demographics, 291
Birmingham March, 91-94
*Birth of a Nation* (film), 352-354, 525, 844, 900
"Black Belt," 765
Black "brute" and "buck" stereotypes, 899
Black Cabinet, 94-95, 1120
Black Christian Nationalist Movement, 95-97
Black church, 97-103, 119; and Turner, Henry McNeal, 1123
Black codes, 103-107, 179, 200, 368, 715, 738, 790, 834; and Jim Crow laws, 476
Black colleges and universities, 132-133, 369, 954; sports, 893
*Black Enterprise*, 571, 1005, 1107
Black flight, 112-114
Black History Month, 1125
Black Is Beautiful movement, 114-115
Black Jews, 115-117
*Black Journal* (television), 574
"Black Manifesto," 117-118
Black middle class/black underclass relations, 596
*Black Monday*, 1007
Black nationalism, 96, 101, 118-123, 129, 242, 631; and Black Panther Party, 123-129; and Garvey, Marcus, 1106; and Malcolm X, 1115; and Pan-Africanism, 702; and Universal Negro Improvement Association, 969-974
Black Panther Party, 121, 123-129, 132, 424; and Carmichael, Stokely, 1101; and Cleaver, Eldridge, 1102; and Davis, Angela, 1103; and Newton, Huey P., 1116; and Seale, Bobby, 1121
Black Power movement, 97, 101, 114, 129-132, 210, 212, 473, 748, 909;

and Baraka, Amiri, 1098; and Carmichael, Stokely, 1101; and Cleaver, Eldridge, 1102; and National Urban League, 661
Black Star Line, 972
*Black Stars*, 571
Black studies, 133
Black United Students, 132-133
*Black Woman's Voice*, 659
Black, Hugo L., 700, 921, 975; and Ku Klux Klan, 526
Blackwell, David, 780
Blair, Henry, 778
Blaxploitation films, 355
Bleeding Kansas, 134-137, 437
Blueford, Guion, 781
Blues, 431, 627
Body of Liberties, 866
Boll weevil, 35
*Bolling v. Sharpe*, 137-138
Bond, Julian, 1099; and King, Martin Luther, Jr., 1099
Book publishing, 570
Booth, John Wilkes, 1114
Booth, Sherman M., 854
Border Ruffians, 135, 436
Boston; Freemasons, 377-381; *Liberator, The*, 532-537
Boston massacre, 277
Bowlegs, Billy, 665
Bowlegs, Jim, 665
Boxill, Bernard R., 457, 459
*Boynton v. Virginia*, 253
Bradley, Ed, 574
Bradley, Joseph P., 203, 820
Bradley, Stephen R., 61
Bradley, Thomas, 517, 1099
Bradstreet, Simon, 868
*Bradwell v. Illinois*, 761
Brady, Tom, 1007
Braun, Carol Moseley, 1099
Brawley, Tawana, 1121
Breckenridge, Calvin, 414
*Breedlove v. Suttles*, 435, 987
Brennan, William J., 506
Brewer, David J.; *Louisville, New Orleans, and Texas Railway Company v. Mississippi*, 552

Breyer, Stephen G.; and affirmative action, 23
Brooke, Edward W., 343, 746, 1014, 1100
Brooklyn Dodgers, 82-90
Brotherhood of Sleeping Car Porters, 138-140, 279, 309, 341, 450, 1118
*Browder v. Gayle*, 617
Brown, H. Rap, 909, 1100
Brown, Henry "Box," 949
Brown, James, 1121
Brown, Jim, 901
Brown, John, 135, 436-441, 924, 1100; and Tubman, Harriet, 1122
Brown, Oliver, 215
Brown, Ron, 754
Brown, Tony, 574
Brown, William Wells, 951
*Brown II*, 142, 955
*Brown v. Board of Education* (1954), 140-144, 180, 192, 208, 258, 318, 404, 456, 506, 544, 566, 614, 641, 645-646, 712, 792, 914, 955, 975; and Marshall, Thurgood, 1115; and Southern Manifesto, 773, 887-889; and Warren, Earl, 1124; and White Citizens' Councils, 1007
*Brown v. Mississippi*, 144-145
Brownsville incident, 145-146
Bruce, Blanche K., 241, 717, 1100
Bruce, Josephine B., 241
Bryan, Andrew, 79
Buchanan, Bessie, 162
Buchanan, James, 134, 136
*Buchanan v. Warley*, 137, 147, 640, 812
Buffalo soldiers, 147-150
Bull, William, 904
Bunche, Ralph, 1100
Burger, Warren, 414, 416, 915
Burr, Aaron, 60
Burton, LeVar, 768
*Burton v. Wilmington Parking Authority*, 150-151, 620
Bush, George, 1119; and affirmative action, 22; and civil rights, 199; and Equal Employment Opportunity Commission, 339; and Haitians, 423; and Supreme Court, 928; and Thomas, Clarence, 1121
Bush, George W., 722, 1119
*Bush v. Vera*, 810
Busing. *See* School busing
Busing and integration, 456
Butler, Pierce, 728
Byrd, Harry, 773

Calhoun, John C., 246
Callahan, William W., 788
Capital punishment, 557-558
Capitalism, 226
Caplan, Lincoln, 22
Cardozo, Benjamin N.; *Nixon v. Condon*, 685
Carmichael, Stokely, 124, 127, 129-130, 212, 375, 473, 501, 909, 1004, 1101; and Vietnam War, 981
Carter, Jimmy, 257, 965, 1109, 1126
Carter, John Pym, 64
Carver, George Washington, 779
Cary, Mary Ann Shadd, 10
Catholic Conference of Bishops, 218
Cato, Gavin, 269
Cavanagh, Jerome, 746
Censuses, 285, 287, 305
Champion, James, 26
Chaney, James Earl, 219-225, 254, 263, 375, 472, 908
Charleston, Oscar, 891
Charleston race riots, 151-152
Chase, Salmon, 494
Chavis, Benjamin, 593-597, 639, 1101
Chesnut, Mary Boykin, 861
Chicago; demographics, 399; elected officials, 718; and Great Migration, 288, 309; Ku Klux Klan, 526; radio programs, 572; riots, 152-154; sit-ins, 154-160, 406-413, 818-819; television stations, 574
Chicago Committee of Racial Equality, 1120
*Chicago Defender*, 288, 309, 401
Children in the Civil Rights movement, 214-215
Children's Crusade, 214

Chionesu, Philé, 597-600
Chisholm, Shirley, 161-168, 465, 721, 1004, 1101
Christianity, 78, 97, 363, 533, 821
Christopher Commission, 517
Church bombings, 169-174
Church burnings, 174-177
Citizens' Councils of America, 1008
Citizenship, 347, 357; and slavery, 783-786, 1120
Civil liberties, 228
Civil Rights Act of 1866, 177-182, 332, 703, 756, 925
Civil Rights Act of 1871, 180
Civil Rights Act of 1875, 332, 759
Civil Rights Act of 1957, 182-183, 185, 720, 954-958
Civil Rights Act of 1960, 183-188, 955
Civil Rights Act of 1964, 93, 188-195, 210, 332, 343, 375, 451, 455, 496, 720, 775, 798, 956; and Johnson, Lyndon B., 1111
Civil Rights Act of 1968, 195-198; and restrictive covenants, 767
Civil Rights Act of 1991, 198-199, 416; and employment discrimination, 568
Civil Rights Acts of 1866-1875, 199-202, 343, 370, 834
Civil rights and liberties, 347
*Civil Rights* cases, 201, 202-204, 478-479, 710, 759
Civil Rights Commission, 183
Civil Rights movement, 100, 131, 182, 204-214, 318, 472, 559, 614, 642, 674, 985, 997, 1001; Birmingham March, 91-94; and Congress of Racial Equality, 253; Freedom Rides, 372-374; Freedom Summer, 374-377; and King, Martin Luther, Jr., 1112; and Little Rock school desegregation crisis, 544-548, 774; and the media, 374, 488, 573, 727, 799, 910; and National Urban League, 661; and politics, 721; and Poor People's March on Washington, 725-727; and school desegregation, 770-

776; Selma-Montgomery march, 797-804; sit-ins, 406-413, 818-819; Student Nonviolent Coordinating Committee, 908-912; and television, 573; and Vietnam War, 981-982; and voting rights, 720; and World War II, 584
Civil Rights Restoration Act of 1988, 215-219
Civil rights worker murders, 219-225, 254, 263, 375, 472, 908
Civil Service Commission, 334
Civil War, 226-233, 924; draft riots, 298-302; and Emancipation Proclamation, 323-326; Fifty-fourth Massachusetts Colored Regiment, 230; and Harpers Ferry raid, 436-441; and Native Americans, 665; sectional issues, 851; and slavery, 323-326, 851
Civil War Amendments, 202, 819-820, 925
Clark, Marcia, 814
Clark, Mark, 424-426
*Classic, United States v. See United States v. Classic*
Clay, Henry, 46, 244, 246
Cleage, Albert, 96
Cleaver, Eldridge, 127-128, 1102; and Vietnam War, 981
Cleveland, Grover, 69
Clinton, Bill, 23, 1097; and church burnings, 176; and Haitians, 423; and Jackson, Jesse, 754; and Jordan, Vernon, 1111
Clinton massacre, 233-234
*Clotilde* (ship), 234-239
Cochran, Johnnie, 815
Coffin, Levi, 950
COFO. *See* Council of Federated Organizations
*Colegrove v. Green*, 397
Coleman, Marshall, 1014
Colfax massacre, 239-240
College entrance examinations, 319
Colleges and universities, 107-112; book publishing, 570; United Negro College Fund, 953-954

Collins v. Hardyman, 414
Colmer, William, 186
Color Purple, The (Walker), 543, 1123
Colored Farmers' Alliance, 33
Colored Women's League, 240-241
Combahee River Collective, 241-243
Combahee River Collective Statement, 242
Commandment Keepers Ethiopian Hebrew Congregation, 115
Commission for Racial Justice, 1101
Commission on Civil Rights, 185. See United States Commission on Civil Rights
Committee Against Jim Crow in Military Service, 587
Committee for Improving the Industrial Conditions of Negroes in New York, 659
Commonwealth, 862
Communist Party, 786; and Davis, Angela, 1103; and Du Bois, W. E. B., 1104; and farmworkers, 35; and Rustin, Bayard, 1120; and Wright, Richard, 1126
Compromise of 1850, 243-247, 385, 387, 490, 851, 923, 1106
Compromise of 1877, 248-249
Condon, James, 876
Cone, James, 1102
Coney, Asia, 597-600
Confiscation Acts of 1861 and 1862, 249-250
Congress, U.S.; antilynching bill, 556; Black Caucus, 256-258; Black representatives, 161-168, 718; and Chisholm, Shirley, 161-168; and gerrymandering, 393-398, 808-811; Missouri Compromise, 606-611; and Reconstruction, 716; and redistricting, 393-397, 808-811; Southern Manifesto, 887-889. See also individual laws
Congress of Racial Equality, 210, 250-255, 375, 675, 910; and Council of Federated Organizations, 260; and Farmer, James, 1105; and Freedom Rides,

372-374; and Greensboro sit-ins, 408; and Innis, Roy, 1109; and Journey of Reconciliation, 481-490; and McKissick, Floyd, 1115; and Rustin, Bayard, 1120
Congressional Black Caucus, 256-258, 422, 721; and Nixon, Richard M., 721
Connecticut; and fugitive slave laws, 385
Connell, Pat, 574
Conner, Eugene "Bull," 92
Conscientious objectors, 251
Conscription. See Military conscription
Conscription Act of 1863, 298-302
Conspiracy Act of 1708 (New York), 671
Constitution, U.S.; color-blindness of, 791; enumeration clause, 607, 697, 714, 930-931; and fugitive slaves, 387; and gerrymandering, 394; King, Martin Luther, Jr., on, 453; and slavery, 382, 608, 852; and understanding tests, 952-953. See also individual amendments
Constitutional Convention, 606, 697; and slavery, 713-714, 852, 930-931
Conyers, John, 1117
Cook, Coralie Franklin, 241
Cook, Helen A., 240
Cook, John T., 240
Coolidge, Calvin, 1106
Cooper, Anna J., 241
Cooper, Jack, 572
Cooper v. Aaron, 258-259
CORE. See Congress of Racial Equality
Corman, James C., 746
Cornish, Samuel, 571
Coronado, Francisco Vásquez de, 662
Corrigan v. Buckley, 641, 812
Cosby, Bill, 1102
Cotton farming, 32-34, 286, 304
Council of Federated Organizations, 214, 220, 260-267, 374-377, 604
Court, Gus, 261

Cowboys, 267-268
Craft, William and Ellen, 949
Crandall, Prudence, 5
Cresson, Sarah Emlen, 63
Crime and race/ethnicity, 786
Crime Control Act of 1934, 526
*Crisis, The*, 501, 571, 637, 660, 1125
Crop-lien farming, 33
Crown Heights conflicts, 268-270, 474
*Cruikshank, United States v. See
    United States v. Cruikshank*
Cruikshank, William, 959-960
Crummell, Alexander, 1102
Crusade for Citizenship, 883
Cuba, 490; and slave trade, 50;
    slavery in, 47
Cuban Americans, 273, 577
Cubans, 270-276
Cuffe, Paul, 118, 663
Cuffee, 671
Cullen, Countée, 427, 432
Culture of poverty, 624
*Cumming v. Richmond County Board
    of Education*, 140, 276-277
Curry, John Stuart, 438

Danforth, John C., 218
Darden, Christopher, 814
Davis, Angela, 1103
Davis, Benjamin O., Jr., 938, 1022,
    1103
Davis, Benjamin O., Sr., 581, 1020,
    1103
Davis, Billy, 1107
Davis, Jefferson, 228, 246, 301
Davis, Ossie, 573
*Davis v. Bandemer*, 395
Dawson, William L., 718
Day, William R.; *Buchanan v. Warley*,
    147
Daytona Educational and Industrial
    School for Negro Girls, 1098
Declaration of Independence; and
    Million Woman March, 598
Declaration of Sentiments, 42, 535
Dees, Morris, 528
Defense industry desegregation,
    277-283

*DeFunis v. Odegaard*, 17
Delany, Martin Robison, 1103
Dellums, Ronald, 167
Democratic Party, 281, 490, 604, 718,
    722; and Jackson, Jesse, 461-466,
    754; and Reconstruction, 717
Demographics, 283-294; Black flight,
    112-114; and economic trends,
    304-314; farmworkers, 37
Dennis, David, 261
Denny, Reginald, 550
DePriest, Oscar, 718
Desegregation; defense industries,
    277-283; public schools, 40, 137,
    192, 207, 215, 258, 456, 506, 614,
    912-913
Detroit riots, 743, 745-746, 751, 1001,
    1021
Dew, Thomas R., 732
Dickey, John Miller, 63
Dickinson, Jonathan, 706
Diop, Cheikh Anta, 32
Dirksen, Everett M., 186, 190, 196, 344
Discrimination, 674; employment,
    327; housing, 458; by private
    parties, 203; racial and ethnic, 600
Disfranchisement laws, 184; in
    Mississippi, 294-298
"Dixiecrats," 282, 719-720
Dixon, Thomas, 900
*Do the Right Thing*, 356
Dodge Revolutionary Union
    Movement, 530-532
Douglas, Stephen A., 134, 247, 491,
    1113
Douglas, William O.; *Lassiter v.
    Northampton County Board of
    Elections*, 530
Douglass, Frederick, 3, 44, 367, 538,
    656, 663, 689, 832, 924, 951, 1103,
    1124; and Garrison, William
    Lloyd, 690; and *North Star, The*,
    689-693; and Thirteenth
    Amendment, 925; and Truth,
    Sojourner, 11
Draft, military. *See* Military
    conscription
Draft riots, 298-302, 460

Dred Scott case. See *Scott v. Sandford*

D'Souza, Dinesh, 1002

Dual federalism, 758

Du Bois, W. E. B., 70, 108, 119, 317, 400, 570, 637, 1104; and Niagara Movement, 501, 682; and Pan-Africanism, 701-702; and "Talented Tenth," 919-921; and United Nations, 587; and Washington, Booker T., 1124; writings of, 539

Dukakis, Michael, 1110

Duke, David, 527

Dunbar, Paul Laurence, 540

Dyer, L. C., 303

Dyer antilynching bill, 302-304

East St. Louis riot of 1917, 751

Eastern European Jews, 470

Eastland, James O., 186, 942, 993

*Ebony*, 571, 1111

Eclipse, 237

Economic trends, 304-314

*Edmonson v. Leesville Concrete Company*, 314-315

Edmundson, William, 705

Education, 68, 292, 315-321, 328, 369, 457, 655; colleges and universities, 107-112, 132-133, 369, 893; integration of University of Mississippi, 974-979; and school desegregation, 770-776; and separate but equal doctrine, 917-918; United Negro College Fund, 953-954; and Washington, Booker T., 1124

*Edwards v. South Carolina*, 322

Eisenhower, Dwight D., 588, 912, 1104; and Anderson, Marian, 55, 57; and civil rights, 185, 187, 882; and Civil Rights Act of 1960, 184; and Little Rock school desegregation crisis, 259, 544-548, 774; and military segregation, 589; and Summit Meeting of National Negro Leaders, 912-913; and Warren, Earl, 1123; and World War II, 1023

Eisenstein, Zillah, 242

Elder, Lee, 896

Elementary and Secondary Education Act of 1965, 775

Ellington, Duke, 428, 572

Ellison, Ralph, 431, 542

Emancipation, compensated, 42, 361

Emancipation Day, 926

Emancipation Proclamation, 2, 228, 250, 323-326, 452, 692, 738, 1114

*Emperor Jones, The* (O'Neill), 139, 1119

Employment, 327-331, 368, 401; broadcasting, 574. See also Labor

Employment Act of 1946, 333

Employment discrimination, 192, 198-199, 415-417, 568, 702-703, 962-968, 996-997; and National Urban League, 661

*Encyclopedia Africana*, 1104

Enforcement Act of 1870, 347, 716, 961

English Bill, 136

Equal Employment Opportunity Act of 1972, 331-338, 962

Equal Employment Opportunity Commission, 193, 210, 332, 338-339, 416, 956; and Thomas, Clarence, 929

Equal Pay Act of 1963, 332

Equal Rights Party, 692

Ervin, Sam, 197, 962

Estevanico Dorantes, 662

Ethnic identity, 118

Ethnocentrism, 844

Evangelicalism, 43

*Evans v. Abney*, 340

Evers, Medgar, 170, 450, 1105

Executive Order 8802, 277-283, 341, 585, 719, 1020, 1120; and Randolph, A. Philip, 1118

Executive Order 9008, 729-731

Executive Order 9980, 730

Executive Order 9981, 282, 583-591, 719, 730, 1122; and Randolph, A. Philip, 1118

Executive Order 10925, 332

Executive Order 11063, 343

Executive Order 11246, 962

Fair Employment Practices Committee, 280, 340-342, 1020
Fair Housing Act of 1968, 342-346, 480
Fair Housing Amendments Act of 1988, 345
Family and socialization, 320, 623
Family demographics, 291-293
Fard, W. D., 631-632, 1116
Farmer, James, 163, 372, 481, 1105, 1120
Farrakhan, Louis, 121, 257, 634, 1105; and Jackson, Jesse, 464, 1105; and Jews, 474; and Malcolm X, 1105; and the media, 594; and Million Man March, 593-597
Faubus, Orval, 258-259, 544-548, 774
FBI. *See* Federal Bureau of Investigation
Federal Bureau of Investigation, 127, 131; and church burnings, 175; and Civil Rights movement, 452; and civil rights murders, 222; and Clark-Hampton deaths, 424; and Freedom Summer, 376; and King, Martin Luther, Jr., assassination, 512; and Ku Klux Klan, 526
Federal Communications Commission, 22, 574
Federal Corrupt Practices Act of 1910, 680
Federal Council on Negro Affairs, 94-95
Fellowship of Reconciliation, 481-490
Fernando, 870
Ferraro, Geraldine, 465
Field, Stephen J., 820
Fifteenth Amendment, 184, 201, 205, 294, 332, 347-352, 398, 419, 756, 875, 988; and voting rights, 961
Fifth Amendment, 137-138, 180, 784
Fifty-fourth Massachusetts Colored Regiment, 230
Fillmore, Millard, 246
Films, 352-357, 376, 844; and stereotypes, 901
First Amendment, 180, 1019

Fisk Jubilee Chorus, 626
Fisk University, 539, 570, 1021
Fitzgerald, Ella, 428
Fitzhugh, George, 734, 830
Florida; bombings, 169; Cuban community, 270-276, 422; Haitian community, 422; Hispanic communities, 110; Jamaican community, 467; Jim Crow laws, 477; poll taxes, 724; presidential election of 2000, 722; riots, 576-578; Seminole Wars, 662; slave trade, 235; slavery, 285
Football, 462, 814, 892, 901, 997
Foraker, Joseph B., 146
Forman, James, 911
Forten, James, 26, 534, 1105
Forten, James, Jr., 778
Fortune, T. Thomas, 306, 1106; and Washington, Booker T., 1106
Foster, Bill, 236
Foster, Stephen, 626
Fourteenth Amendment, 137-138, 142, 179, 201, 332, 343, 357-362, 710, 756, 764, 834, 875, 925, 960; and *Civil Rights* cases, 202-204; and gerrymandering, 395; and Stevens, Thaddeus, 1121; and White primaries, 1009-1010
Fourth Amendment, 180
Fox, George, 704
*Frank v. Mangum*, 619
Frankfurter, Felix, 397, 921
Franklin, Benjamin, 378, 704, 922
Franklin, Raymond S., 845
Frazier, Demita, 242
Frederickson, George, 844
Free African Society, 27, 44, 98, 362-366
Free blacks, 1, 366-367; demographics of, 286-287
Free Produce Society, 29, 365
Free-soil movement, 45, 134, 245
Free-Soil Party, 135, 437, 491
Free State Party, 134, 436
Freedmen's Bureau, 178, 201, 306, 316, 367-371, 716, 738
Freedom Farms Corporation, 1108

Freedom Rides, 210, 252-253, 372-374, 910; and Farmer, James, 1105
Freedom Summer, 220, 262, 264, 374-377, 910
*Freedom's Journal*, 571
Freemasons, 377-381
Frémont, John C., 247
Fugitive Slave Law of 1793, 382-386
Fugitive Slave Law of 1850, 387-391, 490, 923
Fugitive slave laws, 853, 948
Fugitive slaves; and Underground Railroad, 947-952
*Fullilove v. Klutznick*, 20, 391-393

Gallup polls, 772
Gandhi, Mohandas K., 154, 251, 407, 481, 508, 1106; and King, Martin Luther, Jr., 1106
Garnet, Henry Highland, 951
Garrettson, Freeborn, 363
Garrison, William Lloyd, 2, 5, 9, 42, 832, 853, 863, 935, 1106; and Douglass, Frederick, 690; and *Liberator, The*, 532-537; opponents of, 732; and Thirteenth Amendment, 925
Garvey, Marcus, 115, 120, 403, 467, 632, 640, 969-974, 1004, 1106; and Malcolm X, 1115; and Pan-Africanism, 701; and Washington, Booker T., 970
*Garvey's Watchman*, 970
Gates, Daryl, 517, 548
Geary, John W., 135
George, David, 79
George, Walter, 888
Georgia; Atlanta Compromise, 67-70; Baptist Church, 79; bombings, 169; capital punishment, 557; demographics, 291, 399; elections, 613, 718, 984; and Freedom Rides, 372; gerrymandering, 396; Jim Crow laws, 477; Ku Klux Klan, 353, 525; lynching, 554; schools, 271, 770; slave trade, 61, 285
*Georgia v. McCollum*, 91
Geronimo, 148

Gerry, Elbridge, 394
Gerrymandering, 348, 393-398, 944, 956; and schools, 506; *Shaw v. Hunt*, 808-811
Gibson, Josh, 891
Giddings, Doras, 364
Gillem Board, 586
Ginsburg, Ruth Bader; and affirmative action, 23
Glazer, Nathan, 455, 458
*Go Tell It on the Mountain* (Baldwin), 543
Goetz, Bernhard, 1121
Gold rush; California, 245
Goldman, Ronald, 814
Goldwater, Barry, 223
Golf, 895
*Gomillion v. Lightfoot*, 348, 395, 397-398
*Gone with the Wind* (film), 844, 899
*Gong Lum v. Rice*, 140
Gonzales, Pancho, 895
Goode, Mal, 574
Goode, Wilson, 622
Goodell, William, 853
Goodman, Andrew, 219-225, 263, 375, 472, 908
Gorbachev, Mikhail, 1119
Gordy, Berry, Jr., 1107
Gordy, Gwen, 1107
Gore, Al, 722
Gourdine, Meredith, 781
Grace, Charles Emmanuel "Sweet Daddy," 1107
Grandfather clauses, 205, 348, 398-399, 419-420, 640
Granger, Lester B., 660, 912
Grant, Ulysses S., 240, 529, 759; and civil rights, 201
Graves, Earl, 1005, 1107
*Gray v. Sanders*, 162
Great Depression, 278, 399, 632, 640, 789
Great Migration, 288, 308, 310, 399-404; and sharecropping, 808
Green, Charles, 240
*Green v. County School Board of New Kent County*, 41, 143, 404-405, 914
Greenberg, Jack, 645, 648

Greensboro, North Carolina, 818
Greensboro sit-ins, 209
*Gregg v. Georgia*, 557
*Griffin v. Breckenridge*, 413-415, 480
Griffith, D. W., 900
*Griggs v. Duke Power Company*, 15, 334, 415-417, 996
Grimké, Angelina, 8, 861
Grimké, Charlotte Forten, 240
Grimké, Sarah, 8, 861
*Grove City College v. Bell*, 217
*Groves v. Slaughter*, 417
Grovey, Richard Randolph, 876
*Grovey v. Townsend*, 206, 418-419, 687, 876, 958, 1010
*Guest, United States v. See United States v. Guest*
*Guinn v. United States*, 205, 348, 398, 419-420, 640
Gulf War, 1118
Gumbel, Bryant, 574

Haiti, 379
Haitians, 421-423; refugees, 273
Hale, John P., 491
Haley, Alex, 539, 767-768, 1107
Hall, Prince, 377-381
Hamer, Fannie Lou, 101, 1108
Hamilton, Alexander, 60, 707
Hammond, James Henry, 733
Hampton, Fred, 424-426
Hampton, Wade, 151, 717
Hampton Institute, 67, 570, 1124
Hannah, Marc, 780
Harding, Warren, 302
Harlan, John M., 271, 480, 764, 791
Harlem, New York, 972; riots, 744, 750
Harlem Commonwealth Council, 1109
Harlem Renaissance, 403, 426-433, 540, 628, 1114; and Hughes, Langston, 1109; and Locke, Alain, 1114
Harlins, Latasha, 434, 522
Harper, Frances Ellen Watkins, 10
*Harper v. Virginia Board of Elections*, 207, 435-436, 725, 945, 987
Harpers Ferry raid, 436-441, 1122

Harris, Bernard, 781
Harris, Fred R., 500, 746
*Harris, United States v. See United States v. Harris*
Harrison, Pat, 303
Harrison, Thomas, 704
Hart, Gary, 462
Hastie, William, 94, 1020
Hate crimes, 441, 735-736, 1018; church bombings, 169-174; Clinton massacre, 233-234
*Havens v. Coleman*, 345
Hawkins, Yusuf, 441-442
Hayden, Lewis, 951
Hayes, George E. C., 645
Hayes, Rutherford B., 248-249, 717, 755, 1108
Head Start, 165
*Heart of Atlanta Motel v. United States*, 442-449, 497
Henderson, Fletcher, 428
*Henderson v. United States*, 712
Henry, Aaron, 260
Higginson, Thomas Wentworth, 437
Hill, Anita, 928-930, 1108, 1121
Hill, Larry, 176
Hilliard, Asa, 32
Hip-hop, 630
Hitler, Adolf, 1116
*Hodges v. United States*, 480
Holder, Eric, 1004
Holland, Spessard L., 942-943
*Hollywood Shuffle*, 355
Holmes, Oliver Wendell; *Moore v. Dempsey*, 619
Holmes, Oliver Wendell, Jr., 875
Homestead Act of 1862, 794
Hooker, John Lee, 628
Hooks, Benjamin, 574, 639, 1108
Hoover, Herbert, 1098
Hoover, J. Edgar, 127; and civil rights worker murders, 222; and urban rioting, 998
Hopkins, Pauline E., 541
*Hopwood v. Texas*, 1094
Houser, George M., 481
Housing; restrictive covenants, 766-767

Housing and Community Development Act of 1974, 346
Housing and Urban Development Act of 1968, 346
Housing and Urban Development, U.S. Department of, 196
Housing discrimination, 195-198, 342-346, 479-480, 763-767; *Buchanan v. Warley*, 147
Houston, Charles, 812
Howard, Oliver Otis, 1109
Howard Beach, 1121
Howard University, 54, 252, 565, 570, 780, 1013, 1109; and Locke, Alain, 1114
Howe, Julia Ward, 862, 927
Howe, Samuel Gridley, 437
Hughes, Charles Evans; *Brown v. Mississippi*, 144; *Missouri ex rel. Gaines v. Canada*, 612; *Norris v. Alabama*, 688
Hughes, Henry, 734, 844
Hughes, Langston, 65, 403, 427, 431, 541, 1109
Hughes, Richard J., 678
Humphrey, Hubert H., 189, 965
Hunter, Robert, 671-672
Hurston, Zora Neale, 430, 543, 1114, 1123

"I Have a Dream" speech, 449-454, 509, 1113
Illinois, 696
Illiteracy; and slavery, 569, 855
Imes, Elmer Samuel, 780
Immigration Act of 1921, 525
Immigration and Nationality Act of 1952, 467
Immigration and Nationality Act of 1965, 467
Income levels, 292
Indentured servants, 327, 382, 384, 854, 858, 865, 873
Indiana; and fugitive slave laws, 385
Indiana Territory, 696
Innis, Roy, 251, 1109
Integration, 454-459
Intelligence testing, 319

International Labor Defense, 786
Interracial and interethnic marriage, 600
Interstate Commerce Commission, 254
*Invisible Man* (Ellison), 542
Irish Americans, 300, 460-461, 739
Italian Americans, 441
Ito, Judge Lance, 814

*J. E. B. v. Alabama*, 91
Jackson, Andrew; and Seminole Wars, 665
Jackson, Jesse, 474, 1109; and Chicago riots, 153; and Clinton, Bill, 754; and Democratic Party, 754; and Farrakhan, Louis, 464, 1105; and Korean Americans, 521; presidential candidacy, 461-466; and Rainbow Coalition, 753-754; and Reagan, Ronald, 462-463
Jackson, Jimmie Lee, 799
Jackson, Mahalia, 628
Jacob, John, 661
Jamaican Americans, 466-469
Jamaicans; Universal Negro Improvement Association, 969-974
*James v. Bowman*, 1026
Jay, John, 60, 707
Jazz, 428, 627
Jefferson, Thomas; and Northwest Ordinance, 694; and slavery, 61
Jeffries, Edward J., 744
Jemison, T. J., 881
Jenkins, Herbert, 746
Jenkins, Howard, 645
Jennings, Thomas L., 778
*Jet*, 571, 932
Jews, 17, 115-117, 470-475, 766; and Civil Rights movement, 883; Crown Heights conflicts, 268-270; and Farrakhan, Louis, 594; and Jackson, Jesse, 464, 474; and quotas, 966; and reparations, 117
Jim Crow laws, 190, 195, 207, 279, 401, 476-479; education, 141; and military, 587, 1024; and *Plessy v. Ferguson*, 711

Johnson, Andrew, 103, 178, 218, 361, 1110; and civil rights, 200-201, 756; impeachment of, 180, 926; and Reconstruction, 103, 106, 179-180, 357, 371, 714, 738, 755, 926; and Stevens, Thaddeus, 1121
Johnson, Andrew (student), 484
Johnson, Frank M., 801
Johnson, Jack, 894, 1110
Johnson, James Weldon, 1110
Johnson, John H., 571, 1111
Johnson, Lyndon B., 182, 1111; and affirmative action, 15, 71, 962; and civil rights, 189, 195, 343, 888; and Civil Rights Act of 1964, 191; and civil rights worker murders, 222; and Kerner Commission, 499-506; and King, Martin Luther, Jr., 189; and Ku Klux Klan, 527; and Marshall, Thurgood, 567; and riots, 211, 676, 678, 751; and Selma-Montgomery march, 800-802; and Vietnam War, 981; and voting rights, 799, 985, 990
Johnston, Samuel, 383
Jones, Absalom, 26, 98, 363, 366, 1111
Jones, Elaine, 648
Jones, Jane Elizabeth, 10
Jones, LeRoi (Amiri Baraka), 1098
Jones, Quincy, 629
*Jones v. Alfred H. Mayer Company,* 196, 479-480, 703, 766, 769
Joplin, Scott, 627
Jordan, Vernon E., Jr., 661, 1111
Joseph, Chief, 1109
Journey of Reconciliation, 252, 481-490
Julian, Percy, 780
Juries, 90-91, 314-315, 619-620, 687-688, 728-729, 760, 907, 1017-1018; and fugitive slaves, 382, 388-390; and slaves, 872
Just, Ernest, 780
Just So Publishers, 570

Kansas-Nebraska Act of 1854, 134, 490-496, 851
Karenga, Ron, 114

Katzenbach, Nicholas, 985
*Katzenbach v. McClung,* 496-498
Keith, George, 705
Kelly, Harry F., 744
Kennedy, Anthony M., 315, 728
Kennedy, John F., 1111; assassination of, 189, 562; and Birmingham March, 92-93; and civil rights, 183, 189, 332, 343, 444, 451, 499, 720, 910; and Malcolm X, 634; and Marshall, Thurgood, 648; and Meredith, James, 976
Kennedy, Robert F., 222, 1107, 1112; and civil rights, 499; and Meredith, James, 975
Kennedy, Ted, 217
Kent State University, 133; shooting, 700
Kentucky; Jim Crow laws, 477
Kenyatta, Jomo, 701
Kerner, Otto, 153, 500, 635, 746, 998
Kerner Commission, 153, 499-506, 635, 679, 746-747, 749, 751, 998
Key, Elizabeth, 870
*Keyes v. Denver School District No. 1,* 506-507
King, Don, 1121
King, Martin Luther, Jr., 101, 209, 473, 616, 908, 912, 1112; assassination of, 196, 507-515; and Birmingham March, 91-94; and Bond, Julian, 1099; and Gandhi, Mohandas K., 1106; "I Have a Dream" speech, 449-454, 509; and Johnson, Lyndon B., 189; "Letter from Birmingham Jail," 92, 209, 450, 978; and Malcolm X, 799; and the media, 251; and Poor People's March on Washington, 726; and Student Nonviolent Coordinating Committee, 411; and Vietnam War, 212, 981; and Watts riot, 1001; and Young, Andrew, 1126
King, Rodney, 515-519, 522, 548, 752, 816, 1113
King, Rufus, 608
Klanwatch Project, 527
Knights of the White Camelia, 524

Koon, Stacey, 516, 549
Korean Americans, 434, 518, 520-523
Korean War, 579, 589, 1013
Kozol, Jonathan, 457
Ku Klux Klan, 178, 201, 375, 478, 523-529, 1025-1026; and Reconstruction, 717; and Snapple, 940; and White Citizens' Councils, 1007
Ku Klux Klan Acts, 524, 529
Kunta Kinte, 767-768, 1107

Labor, 327-331; and affirmative action, 15-24; agriculture, 32-39, 806-808; and Civil War, 226; competition with Irish Americans, 460; defense industries, 277-283; and Equal Employment Opportunity Act, 331-338; and Equal Employment Opportunity Commission, 338-339; and Fair Employment Practices Committee, 340-342; and Freedmen's Bureau, 368; and Great Migration, 400; and Jim Crow laws, 476; League of Revolutionary Black Workers, 530-532; and National Urban League, 659-661; and Native Americans, 662; occupations, 108, 305, 309; railroads, 138-140; and Randolph, A. Philip, 1118; sharecropping, 806-808; and urbanization, 311; and Washington, Booker T., 317; and World War II, 467, 1021. *See also* Slavery
Labor movement, 131, 139, 279, 530-532
*Lance v. Wilson*, 398
*Lassiter v. Northampton County Board of Elections*, 530, 953
Latimer, Lewis Henry, 779
Lawrence, Robert, 781
LDF. *See* National Association for the Advancement of Colored People Legal Defense and Educational Fund

League of Revolutionary Black Workers, 131, 530-532
Leaphart, Vincent, 621
Lecompton Constitution, 135
Lee, George, 261
Lee, Robert E., 301
Lee, Spike, 355, 1113
LeFlore, John, 742
Legal Defense Fund. *See* National Association for the Advancement of Colored People Legal Defense and Educational Fund
Leibowitz, Samuel, 789
L'Enfant, Pierre, 777
"Letter from Birmingham Jail" (King), 92, 209, 450, 978, 1113
Levison, Stanley, 881, 883
Lewis, John, 253
Lewis, Monroe, 240
Lewis and Clark expedition, 663
*Liberator, The*, 2, 5, 44, 532-537, 690, 732, 1106
Liberty Party, 45, 535, 692
Liele, George, 79
Lincoln, Abraham, 247, 862, 1113; assassination of, 926; and Civil War, 227, 298-302; Emancipation Proclamation, 323-326; and Reconstruction, 177; and slavery, 250, 323-326
Lincoln, C. Eric, 98
Lincoln-Douglas debates, 134, 924
Lincoln University, 62-66
Lindbergh law, 526
Lindsay, John V., 500
*Listen Chicago* (radio program), 572
Literacy tests, 190, 205, 207, 296, 348, 419, 530, 718, 961; and grandfather clauses, 398-399; Mississippi, 294-298; outlawing of, 530, 990-996; and understanding tests, 952-953; and Voting Rights Act of 1965, 985
Literature, 537-544; and Harlem Renaissance, 426-433; *Roots*, 767-768
Little Rock school desegregation crisis, 208, 215, 258, 544-548, 646, 774; and the media, 572

Liuzzo, Viola Lee, 527
Local Public Works Capital
    Development and Investment Act
    of 1976, 391
Locke, Alain, 1114
Logan, James, 706
Lopez, Narcisco, 490
Los Angeles; Harlins murder, 434;
    King beating case, 515-519, 1113;
    police, 515-519, 548, 814-816, 1000;
    Simpson murder trial, 813-818;
    Watts riot, 999-1002
Los Angeles riots of 1992, 518, 522,
    548-552, 752
Lost-Found Nation of Islam, 1116
Louis, Joe, 894-895, 901
Louisiana; bombings, 169;
    demographics, 291; elections, 718,
    984; Jim Crow laws, 477; New
    Orleans riot, 737-741; *Plessy v.*
    *Ferguson*, 708-713; slavery, 285
Louisiana Purchase, 244, 606, 851
*Louisiana v. United States*, 953
*Louisville, New Orleans, and Texas*
    *Railway Company v. Mississippi*,
    552
*Loving v. Virginia*, 601, 712
Lowery, Joseph E., 881, 1114
Lowndes County Freedom
    Organization, 124
Lowry, Robert, 295
Lynching, 302, 524, 553-557, 960,
    1021; Dyer antilynching bill, 302-
    304; and rape, 900; Till, Emmett,
    931-932, 1122

McCarthyism, 253
*McCleskey v. Kemp*, 557-558, 997
McCormick, Cyrus, 777
McCoy, Elijah, 778
McCullough, William M., 746
*McDonald v. Santa Fe Transportation*
    *Company*, 962
McDuffie, Arthur, 752
McKay, Claude, 427, 432, 467, 1004,
    1114
McKissick, Floyd, 1115
*McLaurin v. Oklahoma State Regents*

*for Higher Education*, 141, 558-559,
    772
McNair, Ronald, 781
McReynolds, James C., 728
Maddox, Alton, 270
Madikizela-Mandela, Winnie, 1094
Magazines, 571; *African Intelligencer,*
    *The*, 64; *Black Enterprise*, 571, 1005,
    1107; *Black Woman's Voice*, 659;
    *Crisis, The*, 501, 571, 637, 660, 1125;
    *Ebony*, 571, 1111; *Jet*, 571, 932; and
    Johnson, John H., 1111; *Negro*
    *Digest, The*, 571, 1111; *Opportunity*,
    660; *Sister's Magazine*, 659;
    *Southern Workman, The*, 570
Magnet schools, 458
Maine; abolitionism, 10; and
    Missouri Compromise, 244, 606-
    611; slavery, 607
"Majority-minority" districts, 808-
    811
Malcolm X, 121, 124, 129, 539, 559,
    633, 1115; assassination of, 559-
    564, 1116; and civil rights, 190;
    and Farrakhan, Louis, 1105; and
    Haley, Alex, 1107; and Kennedy,
    John F., 634; and King, Martin
    Luther, Jr., 799; and the media,
    562; and Vietnam War, 981
Malone, Annie Turnbo, 779
Mamiya, Lawrence H., 98
Mandela, Nelson, 275
Manley, Norman, 701
Mann, Woodrow, 546, 774
Mansfield, Michael H., 942
March on Selma, 911
March on Washington, 209, 211, 911;
    and "I Have a Dream" speech,
    449-454; and National Urban
    League, 661; and Randolph, A.
    Philip, 1118; and Rustin, Bayard,
    1120
March on Washington movement,
    341, 719, 1020
Margold, Nathan, 771
Mariel boatlift, 272
Marrant, John, 379
Marshall, Thurgood, 13, 65, 641, 644,

771, 792, 812, 918, 1115; appointed to Supreme Court, 564-568; and Johnson, Lyndon B., 1111; retirement of, 928
*Martin v. Wilks*, 568
Martinet, Louis, 709
Mary, Alexander A., 709
Maryland; demographics, 291
Mason, James, 388
Massachusetts; abolitionism, 7; Freemasons, 377-381; and fugitive slave laws, 385; and slave trade, 868; slavery, 59, 865-869
Matney, William C., Jr., 574
Matthew, Wentworth Arthur, 115
May, Samuel, 42
Mays, Benjamin, 508
Mays, Willie, 901
Meagher, Timothy, 236
Media, 569-576; and Black Panther Party, 124; and Civil Rights movement, 92-93, 374, 488, 573, 727, 799, 910; and Congressional Black Caucus, 256; and Farrakhan, Louis, 594; and King, Martin Luther, Jr., 251; and lynching, 556; and Malcolm X, 562; and Million Man March, 594; and music, 624-631; and Simpson murder trial, 813-818; and stereotypes, 900-901; and Thomas-Hill hearings, 928-930; and University of Mississippi, 976; and Wilder, L. Douglas, 1011
Medical sciences, 781
Memphis; radio stations, 573; riots, 737-741
*Memphis Free Speech*, 1124
Mennonites, 705
Men's liberation, 335
Meredith, James H., 129, 375, 646, 974-979, 1115
*Meredith v. Fair*, 646
*Metro Broadcasting v. Federal Communications Commission*, 22
Mexican War, 244, 387, 851
Mfume, Kweisi, 1093, 1095
Miami riots of 1980, 272, 576-579, 752

Micheaux, Oscar, 353
Michigan, 696
Military conscription, 580, 587, 980, 1023; and Ali, Muhammad, 982; Civil War, 228, 298-302; World War II, 1020
Military desegregation, 278, 455, 579, 583-591; and Randolph, A. Philip, 1118
Military history, 579-583; Brownsville incident, 145-146; buffalo soldiers, 147-150; desegregation of defense industries, 277-283; Vietnam War, 979-983; World War II, 1020-1025
Military Reconstruction Acts of 1867, 716
Militia Act of 1862, 298
Miller, Samuel F., 819
*Miller v. Johnson*, 396
*Milliken v. Bradley*, 592-593
Million Man March, 593-597, 634; and Chavis, Benjamin, 1101
Million Woman March, 597-600
Minimum wage laws, 36, 289; and agricultural workers, 310
*Minor v. Happersett*, 761
Minority business enterprises, 391
Minority "set asides," 392
Minstrel shows, 476, 626-627; and basketball, 893
Miscegenation laws, 600-603, 699; banning of, 712
Mississippi, 374, 603, 910; bombings, 169; and Council of Federated Organizations, 260-267; demographics, 291, 399; elected officials, 722; elections, 718, 984; Freedom Summer, 374-377; Jim Crow laws, 477; lynching, 554; poll taxes, 435; and slave trade, 417; University of Mississippi, 974-979
*Mississippi Burning* (film), 376, 527, 1018
Mississippi Freedom Democratic Party, 375, 603-606, 911, 1098, 1108

*Mississippi University for Women v. Hogan*, 21

Missouri Compromise, 61, 244, 492, 606-611, 783, 851; and Kansas-Nebraska Act, 490

*Missouri ex rel. Gaines v. Canada*, 141, 612

Mitchell, Arthur W., 718-719

Mitchell, Clarence, 195

Mitchell, Parren, 167

Mitchell, William H., 951

Mobile, Alabama, 236, 742; curfew, 477; elections, 613; riot, 741-745

*Mobile v. Bolden*, 613, 988

"Model" minorities, 1003

Monagas, Lionel, 573

Mondale, Walter F., 343, 462-465

Monroe, James, 610

Montgomery bus boycott, 204, 209, 614-619, 1096, 1117

*Moore v. Dempsey*, 619-620, 640

*Moose Lodge v. Irvis*, 151, 620-621, 813

*Morgan v. Virginia*, 481

Morley, Burton R., 742

Morrison, Toni, 542-543, 1116

Moses, Robert, 261

Motley, Constance Baker, 646, 1004

Motown Records, 629, 1107

Mott, Lucretia, 8

MOVE, Philadelphia police bombing of, 621-623

Movies. *See* Films

Moynihan, Daniel Patrick, 468, 623, 845

Moynihan Report, 623-624

Muhammad, Elijah, 120, 539, 631-635, 1116; and Malcolm X, 559-564, 1115

Muhammad, Warith "Wallace," 634

*Muhammad Speaks*, 562

Murray, Anna, 689

Murray, Anna E., 241

Murrow, Edward R., 573

Music, 624-631; and Harlem Renaissance, 426-433; and radio, 572, 628-629; and slavery, 840

Muslim Mosque, Inc., 563

Mutual Black Network, 573

NAACP. *See* National Association for the Advancement of Colored People

Nabrit, James M., Jr., 645

*Narrative of the Life of Frederick Douglass*, 689

Nasser, Gamal Abdel, 701

Nation of Islam, 120, 474, 539, 559, 631-635; book publishing, 570; and Farrakhan, Louis, 1105; and Malcolm X, 1115; and Muhammad, Elijah, 1116

National Advisory Commission on Civil Disorders, 153, 635-636, 678, 746, 751, 998

*National Anti-Slavery Standard*, 10, 691

National Association for the Advancement of Colored People, 70, 147, 302, 317, 341, 375, 556, 614, 636-643, 742, 746, 786, 792, 875, 912, 921, 1104; book publishing, 570; and Chavis, Benjamin, 1101; and Council of Federated Organizations, 260; and Evers, Medgar, 1105; and Farmer, James, 1105; and Hooks, Benjamin, 1108; and Johnson, James Weldon, 1110; and Jordan, Vernon, 1111; and lynching, 900; and Marshall, Thurgood, 1115; membership, 585; and Niagara Movement, 684; and Parks, Rosa, 1117; and restrictive covenants, 812; and school desegregation, 771; and Wells-Barnett, Ida B., 1124; and White, Walter, 1125; and Wilkins, Roy, 1125; and World War II, 1022

National Association for the Advancement of Colored People Legal Defense and Educational Fund, 140, 405, 592, 641, 643-649, 771

*National Association for the Advancement of Colored People v. Alabama*, 650-651

National Association of Colored Women, 241, 651-652

National Black Caucus of State Legislators, 721
National Black Feminist Organization, 242
National Black Network, 573
National Black Women's Political Leadership Caucus, 652-653
National Coalition of Blacks for Reparations in America, 653-654
National Conference of Black Mayors, 721
National Council of Black Mayors, 721
National Council of Colored People, 654-657
National Council of Negro Women, 658-659, 1099
National Council of Women, 241
National League of Colored Women, 240-241
National League on Urban Conditions Among Negroes, 659
National Negro Business League, 306, 1106, 1124
National Organization for Women, 218
National Urban League, 659-661, 912; and Jordan, Vernon, 1111; and Wilder, L. Douglas, 1125; and Young, Whitney, 1126
Native Americans, 661-666; and buffalo soldiers, 147-150; and fugitive slaves, 947
*Native Son* (Wright), 542
N'COBRA. *See* National Coalition of Blacks for Reparations in America
Negro Act of 1740, 905
Negro Conventions, 28, 655, 667-669, 1096
Negro Declaration of Independence, 682
*Negro Digest, The,* 571, 1111
Negro Factories Corporation, 972
Negro Leagues, 891
*Negro World, The,* 972
*Negro Yearbook, The,* 570
Neville, Dinah, 704

New England Anti-Slavery Society, 44, 922
*New National Era,* 692
"New Negro," 429
New Orleans; Jim Crow laws, 477; riots, 737-741
New York; and fugitive slave laws, 385
*New York Age,* 1106
New York City; demographics, 399; Hawkins murder, 441-442; slave revolt, 669-674
New York Manumission Society, 60
New York riots, 674-676
Newark riots, 677-679, 751, 1001
*Newberry v. United States,* 418, 679-681, 686, 958, 1009
Newspapers, 571; *Black Panther, The,* 127; *Chicago Defender,* 288, 309, 401; *Commonwealth,* 862; *Freedom's Journal,* 571; *Garvey's Watchman,* 970; *Liberator, The,* 2, 5, 532-537; *Memphis Free Speech,* 1124; *Muhammad Speaks,* 562; *Mystery, The,* 1103; *National Anti-Slavery Standard,* 10; *Negro World, The,* 972; *New York Age,* 1106; *North Star, The,* 571, 689-693; *Provincial Freeman, The,* 10
Newton, Huey P., 121, 124, 132, 1116
Niagara Movement, 317, 501, 637, 681-685, 920, 1104
Nicodemus, Kansas, 795
Nixon, L. A., 875
Nixon, Richard M.; and Chisholm, Shirley, 165-166; and Congressional Black Caucus, 256, 721; and school desegregation, 40; and Supreme Court, 915
*Nixon v. Condon,* 206, 418, 641, 685-687, 876, 1009
*Nixon v. Herndon,* 205, 348, 418, 685-687, 875, 1009
Nkrumah, Kwame, 701, 1101, 1104
NOI. *See* Nation of Islam
Nonviolence, philosophy of, 908
Nonviolent direct action, 618
Nonviolent resistance, 618

Norris, Isaac, 706
*Norris v. Alabama*, 687-688
North Carolina; elections, 718; Jim Crow laws, 477
*North Star, The*, 571, 689-693, 1104
Northwest Ordinance of 1787, 244, 382, 608, 694-698, 824, 851
Nott, Josiah, 734, 829

Oberlin College, 950
Oberlin Rescuers, 2
Office for Civil Rights, 216
Oglethorpe, James, 904
Ohio, 696
One-drop rule, 698-699
One person, one vote concept, 613
O'Neill, Eugene, 139, 1119
Operation Breadbasket, 462, 1109, 1121
Operation PUSH, 463, 1109
*Opportunity*, 660
Orangeburg massacre, 699-700
Ordinance of 1784, 694
*Oregon v. Mitchell*, 350
Organization for Black Americans to Support Israel, 1120
Organization of Afro-American Unity, 563, 1115
Owen, Robert Dale, 924
Owens, Jesse, 1116

Pacifism, 535
Padmore, George, 701
Paige, Satchel, 891
Paine, Thomas, 707
*Palmer v. Thompson*, 700-701
Pan-Africanism, 701-702; and Carmichael, Stokely, 1101
Pánfilo de Narváez, 662
Panic of 1837, 44
*Paradise, United States v.* See *United States v. Paradise*
Parker, Theodore, 437
Parks, Rosa, 101, 209, 615-616, 1117
Patents, 777
Patterson, Frederick D., 953, 1117
Patterson, Mary Jane, 241
Patterson, Orlando, 826, 845
Patterson, Robert B., 1007

*Patterson v. McLean Credit Union*, 198, 702-703
Payne, Daniel Alexander, 1117
Payton, Philip A., Jr., 402
Peden, Katherine Graham, 746
Pemberton, Israel, 704
Pemberton, James, 704
Pennington, James, 655
Pennsylvania; and fugitive slave laws, 385; slavery in, 703
Pennsylvania Society for the Abolition of Slavery, 703-708
Peremptory challenge, 314
Persian Gulf War, 582
Person, Waverly, 781
Peters, Brock, 354
Phillips, Wendell, 535, 832, 924
Pickering, William, 608
Picket, Bill, 268
Pierce, Franklin, 134, 490, 494
Pilmore, Joseph, 366
Pilots, 937-939
Pinchback, P. B. S., 716, 1014
Plessy, Homer Adolph, 709
*Plessy v. Ferguson* (1896), 140, 180, 207, 258, 478, 641, 708-713, 791, 917; and schools, 770; and separate but equal doctrine, 805
Poets, 540; and abolitionist movement, 10; and Harlem Renaissance, 427, 431
Poitier, Sidney, 354, 1004
Police brutality, 93, 126, 153, 274, 450, 509, 516, 548; and King, Rodney, 515-519; and riots, 272, 548-552, 576-579, 677, 739, 745-749, 751-752, 1000; and Scottsboro case, 788
Politics and government, 713-723
Poll taxes, 205-206, 296, 347, 718, 723-725, 961, 1018; banning of, 435-436, 941-947, 990; and grandfather clauses, 398-399; Mississippi, 294-298; and Twenty-fourth Amendment, 941-947; and Voting Rights Act of 1965, 983, 986
Poor People's Campaign, 1001

Poor People's March, 725-727
Port Chicago incident, 1023
Porters, 138-140, 279, 309, 401
Poverty, 675, 725-727; and race, 320, 330, 623
Powell, Adam Clayton, 130
Powell, Adam Clayton, Jr., 1117
Powell, Colin, 582, 1003, 1118; and Vietnam War, 982
Powell, Isaac, 781
Powell, James, 674
Powell, Laurence, 516
Powell, Lewis F., Jr., 19; *Batson v. Kentucky*, 90; *McCleskey v. Kemp*, 557
*Powell v. Alabama*, 688, 727-728
*Powers v. Ohio*, 91, 728-729
President's Committee on Civil Rights, 556, 719, 729-731, 1024, 1122
Price, Hugh, 661
*Prigg v. Commonwealth of Pennsylvania*, 385, 388
Private discrimination; *Moose Lodge v. Irvis*, 620
Project C, 92
Proposition 14, 343
Proslavery argument, 1, 437, 731-735, 936
*Provincial Freeman, The*, 10
Public accommodations, desegregation of, 252
Public Health Service, U.S., 939-940
Public schools; desegregation of, 192, 913
Public Works Employment Act of 1977, 392
Puritans, 537, 866, 869
Purvis, Robert, 951
Purvis, W. B., 779

Quakers; and Underground Railroad, 950
Queen Anne's War, 672
Quotas. *See* Affirmative action

Race; one-drop rule, 698-699
"Race music," 572

Race relations; and slavery, 843-850
Race riots, 745-749
Race riots of 1866, 737-741
Race riots of 1943, 281
Race riots of the twentieth century, 635, 750-753
Racial discrimination; and White Citizens' Councils, 1007-1009
Racism; and proslavery argument, 731-735
Radical Reconstructionism, 524
Radical Republicans, 524, 714
Radio broadcasting, 571; and music, 572, 628-629
Ragtime, 626
Rainbow Coalition, 462, 753-754
Rainey, Ma, 431
Randolph, A. Philip, 139, 279-280, 341, 450, 587, 719, 912, 1118; and March on Washington movement, 1020
Rap music, 630
*R.A.V. v. City of St. Paul*, 735-736
Rayburn, Sam, 888
Read, George, 383
Reagan, Ronald; and affirmative action, 22; and civil rights, 218, 957; and Equal Employment Opportunity Commission, 339; and Haitians, 423; and Jackson, Jesse, 462-463; and Powell, Colin, 1118
Reapportionment, 397
Reconstruction, 248, 359, 524, 529, 714, 755-763, 790; Colfax massacre, 239-240; Compromise of 1877, 248-249; and Hayes, Rutherford B., 1108; Jim Crow laws, 476-479; race riots, 737-741; and sharecropping, 806-808; *Slaughterhouse Cases*, 819-820; and Stevens, Thaddeus, 1121
Reconstruction Acts, 201
Red Scare, 525
Redding, Louis, 645
Redistricting, 808-811; and gerrymandering, 393-397
Redlining, 344

Reed, Ishmael, 543

*Reese, United States v. See United States v. Reese*

Refugees; Cuban, 421; U.S. policy, 273, 421

*Regents of the University of California v. Bakke. See Bakke* case

Rehnquist, William H., 1019; *Martin v. Wilks*, 568; *Moose Lodge v. Irvis*, 620; *Shaw v. Hunt*, 809

*Reitman v. Mulkey*, 343, 763-765

Reparations; and National Coalition of Blacks for Reparations in America, 653-654; and Republic of New Africa, 765

Republic of New Africa, 765-766

Republican Party, 247, 357, 420, 494, 536; and Reconstruction, 714

Restrictive covenants, 340, 766-767, 812-813

Restrictive or racial covenants, 480

Resurrection City, 725

Revels, Hiram R., 717, 926

Revivalism, 78

Reynolds, Grant, 279

Reynolds, Humphrey, 779

Rhode Island; and fugitive slave laws, 385

Rhythm and blues, 628

Rice, Condoleezza, 1118-1119

Rice, Thomas D. "Big Daddy," 476

*Richmond v. J. A. Croson Company*, 21, 198

Rickey, Branch, 82-90

Rillieux, Norbert, 778

Riots, 211, 741-745; Los Angeles, 999-1001; Memphis, 737-741; New Orleans, 737-741

Robb, Charles S., 1011

Roberts, Owen J., 876

Robeson, Paul, 572, 892, 1119

Robinson, Elizabeth, 8

Robinson, Jackie, 82-90, 892, 1024, 1119

Robinson, Spotswood W., III, 645

Rock and roll, 628

Rodgers, Jonathan, 574

*Rogers v. Lodge*, 613

*Rome v. United States*, 350

Romney, George, 747

Roosevelt, Eleanor, 94

Roosevelt, Franklin D., 278, 341, 746, 1120; and Bethune, Mary McLeod, 1099; and Black cabinet, 94; and Davis, Benjamin O., Sr., 1103; and the Depression, 35; desegregation of defense industries, 277-283; election of, 719; and military segregation, 585; and World War II, 1020

Roosevelt, Theodore, 1124; and Brownsville incident, 145-146; in Spanish-American War, 149

*Roots* (Haley), 767-768, 1097, 1107

*Runyon v. McCrary*, 480, 703, 768-770

Rush, Benjamin, 365, 704, 922

Russell, Richard B., 186, 942-944

Russwurm, John B., 571

Rustin, Bayard, 155, 450, 481-490, 881-882, 1120

Sacagawea, 664

Sackler, Howard, 1110

St. George's Methodist Episcopal Church, 26, 98, 363

Sanborn, Franklin B., 437

Savoy Ballroom, 428

*Schnell v. Davis*, 348

School busing, 167, 404-405, 456, 506-507, 592-593, 913-917; and Ku Klux Klan, 527; and Nixon, Richard M., 915

School desegregation, 768-776; Little Rock crisis, 544-548, 774; and White Citizens' Councils, 1007-1009

Schwerner, Michael Henry, 219-225, 254, 263, 375, 472, 908

Science and technology, 776-782

SCLC. *See* Southern Christian Leadership Conference

Scott, Dred, 783-786, 1120

Scott, Winfield, 490

*Scott v. Sandford*, 200, 396, 783-786, 923, 1120

Scottsboro cases, 687-688, 727-728, 786-790

Screvane, Paul, 676
Seale, Bobby, 121, 124, 1116, 1121
Second Amendment, 180
Secret Six, 437
Sectionalism, 244
Security Act of 1739, 903
Sedgwick, Theodore, 383
Segregation, 150, 372, 674, 790-793, 848, 890; de facto and de jure, 790; Jim Crow laws, 476-479; and *Plessy v. Ferguson*, 708-713; restrictive covenants, 766-767
Segregation on the frontier, 793-797
Self-incrimination, immunity against, 144
Selma-Montgomery march, 209, 797-804
Seminole Wars, 662, 664
Separate but equal doctrine, 192, 208, 552, 612, 614, 641, 791, 805-806; *Cumming v. Richmond County Board of Education*, 276-277; and education, 917-918; *McLaurin v. Oklahoma State Regents for Higher Education*, 558; and *Plessy v. Ferguson*, 708-713
Separate spheres, 6
Set-asides, 14
Seventy, The, 44
Seymour, Horatio, 301
Shabazz, El-Hajj Malik El- (Malcolm X), 1115
Sharecropping, 33, 35-36, 308, 327, 806-808, 834, 846; demise of, 310; and demographics, 289
Sharpe, John, 671
Sharpton, Al, 270, 1121
*Shaw v. Hunt*, 808-810
*Shaw v. Reno*, 396, 809-811
*Shelley v. Kraemer*, 147, 480, 766, 812-813
Shelton, Robert, 527
Sheridan Broadcasting, 573
Shores family, 796
Shuttlesworth, Fred, 881
Simmons, William J., 525
Simpson, Nicole Brown, 814
Simpson, O. J., 768, 813-818

*Sister's Magazine*, 659
Sixteenth Street Baptist Church, bombing of, 215
*Slaughterhouse Cases*, 710, 758, 819-820
Slave codes, 821-826, 855; Massachusetts, 866; Ohio, 824; South Carolina, 905; Virginia, 821, 854, 870
Slave narratives, 537, 839
Slave rebellions, 48, 669, 750
Slave trade, 235, 828, 831; *Clotilde* capture, 234-239; demographics of, 283, 286; and economy, 304; internal, 246, 304, 417; outlawing of, 922
Slavery, 202, 226, 249, 327, 826-835, 850; and agriculture, 32, 304; of American Indians, 662; "badges and incidents," 202, 480; and citizenship, 783-786; and Civil War, 323-326, 851; in Connecticut, 60; cotton gin and, 60; demographics of, 283, 285-286; and Emancipation Proclamation, 323-326; and families, 835-843; in Georgia, 61; Great Awakening and, 78; and illiteracy, 569, 855; and justice system, 850-857; legalization of, 821, 870; in Massachusetts, 59, 865-869; and national politics, 713; and Native Americans, 664; in New Hampshire, 59; in New Jersey, 60; in New York, 60, 669; and Northwest Ordinance, 694-698; in Northwest Territory, 823; in Pennsylvania, 59; proslavery argument, 731-735; and race relations, 828, 843-850; and reparations, 653-654; in Rhode Island, 59; in South Carolina, 61; and Thirteenth Amendment, 922-927; and U.S. Constitution, 382, 852; and Underground Railroad, 947-952; in Vermont, 59; in Virginia, 870-875; and women, 858-865

Smith, Barbara, 242

Smith, Bessie, 428, 431

Smith, Beverly, 242

Smith, Gerrit, 437, 692, 853

Smith, James McCune, 655

Smith, Lamar, 261

*Smith v. Allwright*, 206, 348, 641, 686-687, 875-879, 1010

SNCC. *See* Student Nonviolent Coordinating Committee

Social reform movements and women, 6

Society of Free People of Color, 28, 365

Society of Friends (Quakers), 5-6, 59, 704, 922, 950

Sons of Liberty, 229

Soto, Hernando de, 662

Soul City, 1115

*Soul on Ice* (Cleaver), 1102

*Souls of Black Folk, The* (Du Bois), 70, 539

South Carolina; bombings, 169; demographics, 399; elections, 718, 984; Jim Crow laws, 477; slave trade, 61, 285; Stono Rebellion, 902-907

*South Carolina v. Katzenbach*, 350, 530, 987

Southern Christian Leadership Conference, 209, 375, 450, 618, 879-887, 908, 1096; Birmingham March, 91-94; and Chavis, Benjamin, 1101; and Council of Federated Organizations, 260; and Jackson, Jesse, 1109; and King, Martin Luther, Jr., 1112; and Lowery, Joseph E., 1114; and Poor People's March on Washington, 725-727; and Rustin, Bayard, 1120; and Selma-Montgomery march, 798; and Young, Andrew, 1126

Southern Conference of Black Mayors, 721

Southern Manifesto, 773, 887-889

Southern Poverty Law Center, 1099

Southern Tenant Farmers Union, 36

*Southern Workman, The*, 570

Sowell, Thomas, 456, 468, 1002

Spanish-American War, 149, 277, 583

Sparks, Chauncey, 742

Spingarn, Joel E., 638, 640

Spirituals, 625

Spoils system, 492

Sports, 889-898; Ali, Muhammad, 1096; Johnson, Jack, 1110; Owens, Jesse, 1116; Robinson, Jackie, 1119

Springfield, Illinois; race riot, 683

Stanton, Edwin McMasters, 300

Stanton, Elizabeth Cady, 927

Stanton, Frederick P., 135

States' rights, 208, 246, 389, 610

States' Rights Party (Dixiecrats), 720

Stearns, George Luther, 437

Steele, Charles Kenzie, 881

Steele, Shelby, 848

Steinberg, Stephen, 468

Stephens, Alexander, 494

Stereotypes, 353, 898-902

Stevens, Thaddeus, 1121

Stewart, Potter, 414, 480; *Mobile v. Bolden*, 613

Stokes, Carl B., 721

Stone, John M., 295

Stone, Lucy, 8, 10, 927

Stoneman, George, 739

Stono Rebellion, 902-907

Stowe, Harriet Beecher, 862

*Strauder v. West Virginia*, 760, 907

Stringfellow, Thornton, 733

Student Nonviolent Coordinating Committee, 117, 129, 210, 375, 908-912, 1100; and Carmichael, Stokely, 1101; and Council of Federated Organizations, 260; founding of, 411; and Hamer, Fannie Lou, 1108; and Selma-Montgomery march, 798

Student rights movement, 132

Students for a Democratic Society, 133

Summit Meeting of National Negro Leaders, 912-913

Sumner, Charles, 201, 494

Supreme Court, U.S.; and Marshall, Thurgood, 564-568; on

redistricting, 395; and Thomas, Clarence, 1121
Sutherland, George; *Powell v. Alabama*, 728
*Swain v. Alabama*, 90
*Swann v. Charlotte-Mecklenberg Board of Education*, 456, 592, 913-917
*Sweatt v. Painter*, 141, 559, 612, 771, 792, 917-918
Syphilis, 939-940

Taft, William Howard, 1124
Talented Tenth, 318, 639, 919-921
*Talton v. Mayes*, 197
*Tan*, 571
Taney, Roger Brooke, 417
Tapisco, Jacob, 26
Tappan, Arthur, 42, 535
Taylor, Zachary, 246
Television broadcasting, 573; and Civil Rights movement, 573; impact of, 92, 130; *Roots*, 767-768
Temple, Lewis, 778
Tenant farming, 33
Tennessee; demographics, 291; Jim Crow laws, 477; Memphis riot, 737-741
Tennis, 895
Tenth Amendment, 925
Terrell, Mary Church, 241
*Terry v. Adams*, 348, 878, 921-922, 1010
Texas; Jim Crow laws, 477; lynching, 554-555; poll taxes, 435; riots, 743
Third Amendment, 180
Thirteenth Amendment, 2, 200, 203, 231, 358, 710, 755, 922-928; and *Civil Rights* cases, 202-204
Thomas, Clarence, 14, 928-930, 1121; and affirmative action, 22, 929; and Equal Employment Opportunity Commission, 339; and Hill, Anita, 1108
Thomas, Franklin, 1004
Thomas, J. B., 608
*Thomas, United States v.* See *United States v. Thomas*
Thomas-Hill hearings, 928-930
Thompson, William C., 163

*Thornburg v. Gingles*, 988
Thornton, Charles B. (Tex), 746
Three-fifths compromise, 357, 360, 607, 697, 714, 852, 930-931
Thurmond, Strom, 445, 720, 888
Tilden, Samuel J., 248
Till, Emmett, 554, 931-932, 1122
*To Kill a Mockingbird* (film), 354
*To Secure These Rights*, 281, 587, 730-731
Tobacco farming, 32, 286, 304
Toomer, Jean, 541
Toure, Kwame (Stokely Carmichael), 1101
Touré, Sékou, 1101
Townsend, Robert, 355
Trotter, William Monroe, 501, 637, 919
Truman, Harry S., 281, 1122; and civil rights, 455, 556, 585, 719, 729-731, 812, 1024, 1122; desegregation of military, 579, 587, 590
Trumbull, Lyman, 106
Truth, Sojourner, 11, 44, 862-863, 1122; and Douglass, Frederick, 11
Tubman, Harriet, 11, 44, 538, 863, 924, 950, 1122
Turner, Henry McNeal, 1123
Turner, Nat, 1123
Turner's slave insurrection, 732, 933-937
Tuskegee Airmen, 937-939, 1022; and Davis, Benjamin O., Jr., 1103
Tuskegee experiment, 939-940
Tuskegee Institute, 67, 108, 316, 570, 639, 953, 970; and Carver, George Washington, 779; and Patterson, Frederick D., 1117; and Washington, Booker T., 1124
Tustennuggee Emartha (Jim Boy), 664
Twenty-fourth Amendment, 941-947, 990

UNCF. *See* United Negro College Fund
*Uncle Tom's Cabin* (Stowe), 390, 490, 862

Underground Railroad, 44, 825, 863, 924, 947-952; and Tubman, Harriet, 1122; and women, 10-11

Understanding tests, 952-953

Underwood, Oscar, 303

UNIA. *See* Universal Negro Improvement Association

Union League, 524, 716

United African Movement, 1121

United Auto Workers, 530-532, 746, 1021

United House of Prayer for All People, 1107

United Negro College Fund, 109, 953-954, 1111; and Patterson, Frederick D., 1117

United Negro Improvement Association; and Malcolm X, 1115

United States Colored Infantry Regiments, 147-150

United States Commission on Civil Rights, 954-958

*United States v. Classic*, 419, 876, 958-959, 1010

*United States v. Cruikshank*, 201, 759, 959-960

*United States v. Harris*, 759

*United States v. Paradise*, 21

*United States v. Reese*, 759, 961

*United States v. Thomas*, 348

*United Steelworkers of America v. Weber*, 17, 962-968

Universal Negro Improvement Association, 120, 403, 560, 969-974, 1106

University of Alabama, 978

*University of California v. Bakke*. See *Bakke* case

University of Georgia, 978

University of Mississippi, 974-979, 1115

*Up from Slavery* (Washington), 538, 970, 1124

Urban unrest, 674, 677, 997

Urbanization, 112, 288-291; and labor, 311; and National Urban League, 659-661

Van Buren, Martin, 49

Vassa, Gustavas, 537

Venable, James, 527

Vermont; and fugitive slave laws, 385

Vietnam War, 212, 979-983; and Civil Rights movement, 981-982; and King, Martin Luther, Jr., 1113; and women, 980

Vietnamese Americans, 527

Villa, Pancho, 148

Vinson, Fred M., 142, 918

Virginia; bombings, 169; demographics, 291, 399; election of L. Douglas Wilder, 1010-1017; elections, 718; Jim Crow laws, 477; poll taxes, 435; slavery, 870-875; Turner's slave insurrection, 933-937

*Virginia v. Rives*, 761

Vote, right to, 347, 398

Voting rights, 183, 204, 294, 360, 419-420, 529, 603, 716, 961, 1025-1026; and at-large elections, 613; and Civil Rights movement, 720; and disfranchisement, 717; and gerrymandering, 393-397; and grandfather clauses, 398-399; *Lassiter v. Northampton County Board of Elections*, 530; and poll taxes, 723-725; and understanding tests, 952-953; and White primaries, 418-419, 685-687, 1009-1010

Voting Rights Act of 1965, 207, 212, 349, 435, 455, 720, 878, 956, 983-989, 999; and Johnson, Lyndon B., 1111; and redistricting, 395; and Selma-Montgomery march, 797-804; and understanding tests, 952-953

Voting Rights Act of 1975, 990-996

Wade, Wyn, 1008

Waite, Morrison R., 759

Walcott, Derek, 1004

Walker, Alice, 543, 1123

Walker, Madame C. J., 779

*Walker v. City of Birmingham*, 646

Wallace, George, 172, 800-801, 945, 991

Wallace, Henry, 588

Walthall, Edward C., 295

War Manpower Commission, 742

*War Without Violence* (Shridharani), 251

Ward, Samuel Ringgold, 367

*Wards Cove Packing Company v. Atonio*, 198, 416

Warmoth, Henry Clay, 717

Warren, Earl, 137, 208, 772, 1123; *Brown v. Board of Education*, 142

Washington, Booker T., 108, 316, 538, 639, 681, 919, 970, 1124; accommodationist program, 501; Atlanta Compromise, 67-70; and Du Bois, W. E. B., 1124; and Fortune, T. Thomas, 1106; and Garvey, Marcus, 970; and National Negro Business League, 306

Washington, D.C., riots, 997-999

Washington, George, 277, 377, 777; and slavery, 383-384, 950

Washington Colored Woman's League, 240-241

*Washington v. Davis*, 996-997

Waters, Muddy, 628

Watts riot, 212, 751, 999-1002

Weaver, John D., 146

Weaver, Robert, 94

Webster, Daniel, 389

Wells, Benjamin, 26

Wells, James Madison, 739

Wells-Barnett, Ida B., 1124

*Wesberry v. Sanders*, 395

West, Cornel, 471

West Indians, 268-270, 1002-1006; Jamaicans, 466-469

Whatcoat, Richard, 363

Wheatley, Phillis, 540

Whig Party, 245, 490

Whipper, William, 951

White, Byron R.; *Washington v. Davis*, 996

White, Walter, 341, 585, 639, 744, 1022, 1125

White, William, 364

White Citizens' Councils, 641, 1007-1009

White flight, 113

White League, 239

White primaries, 205, 348, 418-419, 641, 645, 680-681, 685-687, 958, 1009-1010; *Smith v. Allwright*, 875; *Terry v. Adams*, 921-922

White supremacist groups, 523

White supremacy, 171, 529

*White v. Regester*, 988

Whitfield, James H., 538

Whittier, John Greenleaf, 42

Wilberforce University, 1117

Wilder, L. Douglas, 1010-1017, 1125

Wilkins, Roy, 500, 639, 912, 1125

Williams, Eric, 701

*Williams v. Mississippi*, 1017-1018

Wilmington Ten, 1101

Wilmot Proviso, 244, 851

Wilson, Lionel, 1116

Winfrey, Oprah, 574

Winthrop, John, 866

Wisconsin, 696

*Wisconsin v. Mitchell*, 737, 1018-1019

Wise, Henry A., 439-440

Woman suffrage, 927

Women; in literature, 1123; Million Woman March, 597-600; National Association of Colored Women, 651-652; National Black Women's Political Leadership Caucus, 652-653; National Council of Negro Women, 658-659; and slavery, 858-865; and Underground Railroad, 950; and Vietnam War, 980; Women's movement, 242

Women's Center for Education and Career Advancement, 658

Woods, Granville, 779

Woods, Tiger, 896

Woodson, Carter G., 32, 1125

Woodward, Isaac, 1024

World War I, 277; and Great Migration, 308

World War II, 281, 1020-1025; and
    Civil Rights movement, 584; and
    labor, 467, 1021; and Louis, Joe,
    894; and Muhammad, Elijah,
    1116; and race riots, 741-745;
    Tuskegee Airmen, 937-939
Wright, Fielding, 720
Wright, Richard, 430, 542, 1125
Wyandotte Constitution, 136

Yama Craw Church, 80
*Yarbrough, Ex parte*, 760, 1025-1026
*Yick Wo v. Hopkins*, 1017
York, 663
Young, Andrew, 1015, 1126
Young, Whitney M., Jr., 661, 1126
Young Communist League, 1120

Zoning, 344
Zoot-suit riots, 743